Mark —   5/28/98

    Thanks for all your help,
in more ways then I yet know.

Sexual Addiction

Sexual Addiction

An Integrated Approach

AVIEL GOODMAN, M.D.

INTERNATIONAL UNIVERSITIES PRESS, INC.
MADISON   CONNECTICUT

Library of Congress Cataloging-in-Publication Data
Goodman, Aviel.
    Sexual addiction : an integrated approach / Aviel Goodman.
        p.   cm.
    Includes bibliographical references and index.
    ISBN 0-8236-6063-X
    1. Sex addiction.   I. Title.
    RC560.S43G66   1997
    616.85'83—dc21   97-27415
                                                                              CIP

Grateful acknowledgment is made to the following:
    Ouote on page 11 from O. Fenichel, Neurotic Acting Out, *Psychoanal. Rev.,* Volume 32, page 197, 1945 is reprinted by permission of Guilford Press.
    Quote on page 13 from O. Fenichel, *The Psychoanalytic Theory of Neurosis,* 1945, page 324 is reprinted by permission of W.W. Norton, New York. Copyright, 1945, by W.W. Norton & Company, Inc., New York, NY.
    Quote on pages 13 and 14 from *Diagnostic and Statistical Manual of Mental Disorders,* 3rd edition, revised (DSM-III-R), page 246, Washington, DC: American Psychiatric Association, 1987 is reprinted with permission from the *Diagnostic and Statistical Manual of Mental Disorders, Third Edition, Revised.* Copyright 1987 American Psychiatric Association.
    Quote on pages 15 and 16 from *Diagnostic and Statistical Manual of Mental Disorders, Fourth Edition,* page 609, Washington, DC: American Psychiatric Association, 1994 is reprinted with permission from the *Diagnostic and Statistical Manual of Mental Disorders, Fourth Edition,* Copyright 1994 American Psychiatric Association.
    Quote on page 54 from *Chemical Dependency and Intimacy Dysfunction,* edited by E. Coleman, pages 196–197 is reprinted by permission of The Haworth Press, Inc., Binghamton, New York.
    Quote on page 62 from S. Freud, The Psychogenesis of a Case of Homosexuality in a Woman, 1920, *Standard Edition,* Volume 18, pages 167–168, London: Hogarth Press, copyright 1955 is reprinted by permission of HarperCollins, New York.
    Quote on page 235 from *Diagnostic and Statistical Manual of Mental Disorders, Fourth Edition,* pages 522–523, Washington, DC: American Psychiatric Association, 1994 is reprinted with permission from the *Diagnostic and Statistical Manual of Mental Disorders, Fourth Edition,* copyright 1994 American Psychiatric Association.

Table of Contents

Preface

This book presents an approach to sexual addiction that is integrated, in the sense that it brings together psychoanalytic, biological, behavioral, and social–interpersonal aspects of sexual addiction within a coherent theoretical framework. Readers may notice that many more pages are devoted to psychoanalytic material than to material from the other disciplines. The reasons for this imbalance are twofold: First of all, much more theoretical material on sexual addiction and on related subjects (perversions, paraphilias, pathological hypersexuality) has been produced by psychoanalytic investigators than by the writers and researchers of all of the other disciplines combined. Consequently, more psychoanalytic material is available to review, and more is available for assimilation into an integrated theory. Second, the psychoanalytic material on sexual addiction and on related subjects is closer to subjective experience, more rich in detail, and more directly relevant to the clinician–patient relationship than is the biological, behavioral, or social–interpersonal material. Thus, in my opinion, the psychoanalytic material can contribute more to our understanding and treatment of individuals who suffer from sexual addiction, whatever treatment modality we may choose to emphasize.

Before I proceed, I would like to address a few potential concerns. The descriptions in this book of individual patients' histories and psychopathology have been disguised sufficiently to make sure that no one with whom I have worked could be recognized from my descriptions. The descriptions are intended to be illustrative examples, not case reports.

Second, the psychoanalytic theories that I review in this book and the theory that I propose are all subject to the criticisms that socioculturally sensitive thinkers have directed at psychoanalytic theories for their emphasis on the role of the mother in the development of psychopathology. First of all, critics have argued, many children are not raised in intact families, and the child's primary caregiver is not necessarily his or her mother, but can also be an aunt, or an older sister, or a grandmother, or even a father. This argument is valid, and in many theoretical discussions "primary caregiver" could be substituted for "mother" without significant change in the theory's meaning. Nonetheless, throughout most of this book, I refer to the child's primary and secondary caregivers as the child's mother and father, respectively. I do so partly to remain consistent with the investigators whose theories I review, but even more so because some of the material that I discuss would be too difficult to convey clearly in terms of primary and secondary caregivers, without further specification. Unless the caregivers' genders and relationship to one another were specified, some of the meaning in the material would be lost. Critics have argued also that psychoanalytic theories overstate the etiological significance in psychopathology of the individual's mother, and that such overstatement in effect amounts to "mother-bashing." I both disagree and agree with this argument. My disagreement derives from my belief that the mother (or, perhaps more accurately, the primary caregiver) does, in fact, have a much more deep and pervasive influence on a child's development than does any other person or environmental factor. I believe that this pattern is not an artifact of our culture, but is more fundamentally a property of our biology. In all mammalian species, the mother (or another lactating female) is the individual who is most closely involved in caring for the young during their earliest, most developmentally sensitive periods. My agreement with this argument derives from my sense that, while psychoanalytic theory discusses in detail the role of the mother in the development of her child's psychopathology, it typically devotes considerably less attention to the mother's role in healthy development and to how she fosters the development of her child's character strengths and inner resources. Some might justify this imbalance on the grounds that psychoanalysis originated as a clinical science, and that it consequently is more interested in understanding the development and treatment of pathological conditions than in understanding healthy development. I, however, am not convinced that we can thoroughly understand the one without a good understanding of the other.

Third, I would like to explain my gender choice for third person pronoun references to an indefinite patient or subject. Since the majority of individuals who suffer from sexual addiction, the majority who suffer from psychoactive substance addictions, and the majority who suffer from pathological gambling are male, I use the male gender when my discussions of these conditions requires a singular pronoun. For the same reason, I use the female gender when my discussion of bulimia requires a singular pronoun. In so doing, I do not intend to imply that female sex addicts, female substance addicts, female gamblers, or male bulimics are any less worthy of consideration than are their other-gender counterparts. When I discuss addiction and addictive disorders in general, I occasionally use a male pronoun to refer to an indefinite subject or patient. Typically, I do so when the discussion concerns aspects of the subject's childhood relationship with his or her mother. Clarity about the referents of pronouns is easier to maintain when the subject is male, since the subject's mother is always female.

Finally, while I intend this book to function as a fundamental reference resource, I do not consider it to be a finished product but a work in progress. From another perspective, I experience the book less as an inert thing than as a living creature, which will continue to grow and to change through interaction with its environment. I anticipate that the findings of further research may require modification of some theoretical points that are presented here; and I would not be shocked to learn of relevant research or theory, already published, that my net had failed to snare. I look forward to receiving whatever input or feedback can facilitate this book's continuing growth.

Acknowledgments

I would like to express my grateful appreciation to Keith Horton, Peg Keenan, Mike Moore, and Dave Stagner, for reviewing the manuscript and providing me with valuable feedback; to Jeff Siegel, for actualizing my graphics; to John Nemiah, for encouraging and supporting my development as a writer; to Mark Leffert, for facilitating transformations of narcissism; and to Diane Grace Goodman, for coparenting this entire project. I would like also to thank my patients, who have inspired me to write this book and to whom it is rightfully dedicated.

Part I.

Frame of Reference

Before we can talk meaningfully about theories of or treatments for a clinical condition, we need a frame of reference that helps us to organize our thoughts about what the condition is. Such a frame of reference can be provided by clinical case narratives, or by verbal definitions that identify the condition's location in our conceptual network. We begin with a series of clinical vignettes, which serve to ground our subsequent theoretical explorations in the real human suffering that our theories are intended to enable us more effectively to relieve.

Introduction

Harold was a fast-track executive in his middle thirties. Handsome, athletic, bright, and likeable, he seemed destined for a
highly successful career. His Achilles' heel was, as he would say,
his "weakness for the fair sex." Women often found Harold to
be attractive; and when an attractive woman indicated to him that
she was interested in him sexually, he found himself unable to
resist—or, more accurately, he found himself unable to want to
resist. He experienced himself almost as a victim, sexually drawn
by women against his will. He was unaware that his banter with
women was flirtatious, and that his general manner was seductive
in a way that invited women to approach him sexually. Harold's
college sweetheart had ended their engagement after he repeatedly broke promises to her that he would stop fooling around with
other women. The company that employed Harold had leased an
apartment in the city so he could stay over when he was working
late. He began to use the apartment for midday sexual liaisons,
and his lunch breaks stretched longer and longer. His formerly
superior work performance began to slacken, and he did not
receive an expected promotion. Harold was convinced that he
was passed over because his immediate boss, whom he believed

3

to be jealous of him for his successes with women, had bad-mouthed him to the higher-ups. Harold's senior boss, who was also a mentor to him, warned him that he could lose his job if he was unable to keep his business and pleasure separate. Harold resolved that he would turn over a new leaf, and for six weeks he engaged in sexual activity with no one other than his girl friend. Then, he was out of town on business and had just finished dinner with his work team after a difficult but successful negotiation. He commented that he was feeling mellow from the wine, but that his neck and back were still tight. When his secretary offered to give him a back rub, he accepted the offer without a moment's thought, and they wound up in bed together. After his return, Harold continued to engage in sexual activity with his secretary. She noticed that he was also meeting with another woman who worked in the office, and she began to pressure Harold for an exclusive relationship. When he then rebuffed her, she filed a suit against him for sexual harassment. He was fired immediately.

Joe was an electrician in his midtwenties who had used alcohol and other drugs heavily in high school. He dropped out of college in his freshman year and went to work in his uncle's electrical contracting business. After a serious accident on the job while he was intoxicated, Joe quit using alcohol and other drugs. Over the next several months, he found that his sexual fantasies and urges to masturbate were becoming more frequent and more intense than they previously had been. Since his middle teens, Joe had masturbated nearly every night before going to sleep, unless he was having sex with a girl friend or a woman he had picked up. Some mornings during his first year of being drug-free, Joe would get strong urges to masturbate. He found that if he did not act on these urges, he would remain "horny" all day, which would make him restless, distracted, and irritable. Consequently, he started to masturbate in the mornings also, even though he would sometimes be late for work as a result. Some months later, Joe began to get urges to masturbate when he was at work, particularly if he saw a woman at the job site. Again, he found that if he did not masturbate, he would become very uncomfortable and would be unable to focus on his work. No longer sufficiently excited by his fantasies, Joe began to purchase pornography. He also discovered "channel cruising": compulsively flipping through the television channels in search of images by which to masturbate. Before long, Joe was masturbating five or six times a day, even more when he felt under stress. He was chronically tired from lack of sleep, he had received a second warning about tardiness and inattentiveness at work, and he felt disgusted with himself; but each time he tried to stop masturbating, he would fail. Sexual fantasies accompanied by arousal would intrude into his consciousness throughout the day, and he would feel as though he were going to explode. When he began a new sexual relationship, he would throw away his collection of pornography and he would resolve to quit masturbating, or at least cut down to once a day. Within a few months, though, he would lose control of his masturbation, his sexual interest in his girl friend would fade, and the relationship would fall apart. Frustrated by channel cruising, Joe acquired a VCR and began to buy pornographic videos. He also started using telephone sex services. When he had "maxed out" his credit cards, he applied for new ones and then ran them also up to their limits. He got behind on his rent, and the power company threatened to cut him off unless he paid his bill. Socially isolated, deeply in debt, and about to lose his job, Joe realized that his preoccupation with masturbation and pornography was ruining his life, but he felt powerless. Meanwhile, he also was beginning to sense that pornography and phone sex no longer excited him as much as they used to. He started going to shopping malls specifically for the purposes of looking at women and girls, whom he would later fantasize about raping while he masturbated. When he then began to feel compelled to study the patterns of the women who worked in the malls and to compile schedules of their comings and goings, he became scared that he was in danger of acting on his fantasies. At that point, he sought help.

Walter was a cardiologist in his early forties who first began to use cocaine regularly and to frequent prostitutes when he was in medical school. Since his early teens, he had masturbated nearly every night before going to sleep, and sometimes once or twice during the day as well. He dated little, partly from feelings of inadequacy, and partly from a fear of commitment and of having to respond to another person's demands. Walter found that sex with a prostitute could relieve his loneliness without requiring any commitment. Being with a prostitute also gave him a sense of power and of being in control, which mixed well with the feelings that he got from cocaine. Drugs and prostitutes consumed much of the money that he had intended to use for books and living expenses, and his schoolwork began to suffer from his long nights and weekends of drugs and sex. He tried several times to stop or cut back, but was unable to do so. Under threat of expulsion from medical school, Walter went through chemical dependency treatment. He remained drug-free for about five months. One night, about four months after leaving treatment, the prostitute for whom he had just bought a drink teasingly asked him if he was scared to have a drink with her, and he ordered one for himself too. When she later offered him a line of cocaine, his resistance had been lowered by the alcohol and the familiar scenario, and he saw no compelling reason to pass it up. Three years later, he was in treatment again. This time, he was instructed to stay away from prostitutes as part of his sobriety plan. For ten years, Walter avoided prostitutes and remained abstinent from alcohol and other drugs of abuse. He married, completed his residency and cardiology fellowship, had a child, and joined an active practice. During this time, he rarely had urges to use alcohol or other drugs, and the urges that arose were easy for him to resist. Urges to get a prostitute, however, were a daily struggle. Occasionally, on his way home from work, he would find himself driving through the sleazy part of town where prostitutes waited on street corners, without knowing how he got there. Sometimes, he was able to resist the urge for a prostitute only by masturbating several times a day, and he was becoming increasingly dependent on sadomasochistic pornography. One night, his wife told him that she was disappointed that he did not have more sexual interest in her. He left the house in a rage, started driving, and wound up in the sleazy part of town. When a prostitute came up to his car, he was about to drive off, but reasoned that he deserved a treat. One "harmless" sip of the prostitute's beer led to a beer for himself, and then another, and then a quest for cocaine. By the time he got to treatment again, he had lost his family and his medical license.

Andrea was a maritime lawyer in her late thirties whose expertise in one area of the law led her to do a lot of traveling. She had been treated for depression and bulimia in her twenties, and she was no longer bingeing or purging. However, she still exercised every day, and she was preoccupied with her body. Her chronic depression had shifted to an irregular alteration between a restless, irritable dysphoria and a driven vivacity that verged on hypomania. After being in a string of abusive relationships from her late teens to her early thirties, Andrea decided to stay single, a decision that was reinforced by her itinerant life-style. When she traveled for business, Andrea's typical pattern was to work intensively during the day and into the evening, and then to go out to a bar and pick up a man. She enjoyed the attention, the feeling of power, and the freedom of never having to see the man again. She had intercourse without any form of contraception, which led to four pregnancies that were terminated by abortion (the first when she was in her teens), and she managed to avoid ever being tested for HIV. After once being robbed by a man whom she had picked up, Andrea resolved to stop taking such chances. For the next four business trips, she did not engage in any sexual adventures, though she felt so tense and restless in the evenings that she thought she would explode. On the fifth trip, she could no longer stand the tension, and she resumed her pattern. Another time she was robbed and then raped. She did not go to the police, expecting that they would just blame her for having invited the man to her room. This time, her resolution to quit lasted for just two trips. Only after the next adverse incident, in which she was beaten so badly that she required several days of hospitalization and consequently was unable to fulfill her work commitments, did Andrea finally seek help.

Phil, a college dropout in his late twenties, had difficulty holding a job, though he was a capable computer programmer and a gifted musician. He had no close friends and spent much of his free time by himself, either working on his computer or playing his electric piano through headphones. Sometimes he would go to a casino, which he said that he did in order to be

around other people. Phil had been involved in two brief relationships with women, both of whom he drove away by his demanding
possessiveness and paranoid jealousy. He tended to develop obsessive crushes on women whom he hardly knew, and he would
then feel driven to watch and follow them. Complaints of harassment by female coworkers had led to his being fired from three
jobs, and he was once arrested for stalking. Phil masturbated several times a day, even at work. At night, he sometimes called
random telephone numbers until he found a woman who would
answer his questions about her sex life while he masturbated.
When he had an urge to masturbate and did not act on it, he
experienced a disorganizing panic that would intensify until he
felt that he was about to die. He found that he could not resist
these urges, even when his job or legal trouble was at stake. The
strongest urge that Phil experienced was to expose his penis to a
woman and masturbate while she looked on in shock and fear.
For this reason, he particularly liked to expose himself in elevators, when he and a woman were the only passengers. Even after
two arrests, one conviction, and one occasion on which a woman's
boyfriend beat him severely, Phil felt driven to continue riding
elevators and hunting for unaccompanied women. One time, Phil
targeted a woman who had once been raped, after which she
vowed that she would never be victimized like that again. She
carried a handgun, and when Phil turned toward her with his
penis exposed, she panicked and shot him. He survived, thanks
in part to the woman's immediate 911 call. Six months after being
discharged from the hospital, he was arrested again for exposing
his penis to a woman in an elevator.

These five individuals were different in many important ways,
but they had one trait in common. All of them engaged in some
form of sexual behavior in a pattern that was characterized by
recurrent failure to control the behavior and continuation of
the behavior despite significant harmful consequences. These two
characteristics of the behavioral pattern, recurrent failure to control the behavior and continuation of the behavior despite significant harmful consequences, represent the key features of
addictive disorders. A condition in which some form of sexual

behavior is employed in a pattern that fits the definition of an addictive disorder merits the designation *sexual addiction.*

Sexual addiction is not a new concept. The term *sexual addiction* was used more than half a century ago by Fenichel (1945a, p. 385); and a half century earlier, in 1897, Freud (1892–1899) had referred to masturbation as "the primal addiction" from which all other addictive disorders derive. Sexual addiction is, however, a controversial concept. The intensity of this controversy is unfortunate, since it tends to divert attention away from scientific discourse about the understanding and treatment of the condition to which the term refers. Nonetheless, such a degree of controversy is understandable. Few other subjects so directly touch our most conflicted wishes and fears; and few other subjects have such potential for sensationalistic exploitation. Moreover, the term *addiction* has acquired semantic, emotional, and ideological baggage of its own, which would have constituted sufficient justification to replace it with another term, had another, equally suitable term been available. While the controversial nature of a term would be a poor reason for choosing it over other terms that are otherwise equally suitable, it would be no less a poor reason for abandoning the term in favor of other terms that are otherwise less suitable.

This book proceeds from the premise that a condition exists in which the subject engages in some form of sexual behavior in a pattern that is characterized by two key features: recurrent failure to control the behavior, and continuation of the behavior despite significant harmful consequences. Part I of the book frames our approach to this condition. Rather than beginning with terminology, definitions, and diagnostic criteria, this Introduction has introduced the condition with stories. In the process, it also has introduced our cast of characters, whom we shall get to know more intimately in the clinical vignettes of chapter 9. Chapter 1 launches directly into issues of terminology, beginning with the question of how this condition should be designated and classified. A review of the three main contenders—sexual compulsivity (classified as a form of obsessive–compulsive disorder), sexual impulsivity (classified as an impulse-control disorder), and sexual addiction (classified as an addictive disorder)—reveals that sexual addiction is the most suitable of the three, and arguments against the concept of sexual addiction are thoroughly addressed. Part II focuses on the theoretical understanding of this condition. Chapters 2, 3, and 4 review biological theories, sociocultural and cognitive–behavioral theories, and psychoanalytic theories of paraphilias, sexual addiction, sexual compulsivity, and perversion. The psychoanalytic theories are both more numerous and richer than the others, so their review requires a larger number of pages. Chapter 5 presents my integrated theory of sexual addiction, according to which this disorder is an expression in sexual behavior of the addictive process, the psychobiological process that I hypothesize underlies all addictive disorders. My integrated understanding of addiction and the addictive process forms the nucleus of this theory, and it is discussed in detail. Part III is devoted to the diagnosis and treatment of sexual addiction. Chapter 6 begins with a definition of and diagnostic criteria for sexual addiction, which are followed by the differential diagnosis of sexual addiction and epidemiological data. In chapter 7, a range of approaches to treating sexual addiction are reviewed, including medication, behavior modification, cognitive–behavioral therapy, therapeutic groups, couples and family therapy, psychodynamic psychotherapy, and integrated treatment. In chapter 8, a version of integrated treatment is suggested as a general guideline for formulating individualized treatment plans. Part III concludes with a series of illustrative clinical vignettes.

1

Terminology: Compulsion, Impulsivity, or Addiction?

> *In most cases it is not very purposeful to start an analytic investigation with an exact definition of the phenomenon to be investigated. The exact definition should rather be the result of the research, not its starting point. But an inexact definition, as an approximate description, is necessary to make clear what one is going to talk about [Fenichel, 1945a, p. 197].*

Over one hundred years ago, Krafft-Ebbing (1886) described a condition in which a person's

> [S]exual appetite is abnormally increased to such an extent that it permeates all his thoughts and feelings, allowing of no other aims in life, tumultuously, and in a rut-like fashion demanding gratification without granting the possibility of moral and righteous counter-presentations, and resolving itself into an impulsive, insatiable succession of sexual enjoyments. . . . This pathological sexuality is a dreadful scourge for its victim, for he is in constant danger of violating the laws of the state and of morality, of losing his honor, his freedom and even his life [pp. 70–71].

11

Most clinicians agree that what Krafft-Ebbing described as pathological sexuality does exist, in the form of paraphilias and syndromes of similarly driven nonparaphilic sexual behavior. Questions remain, however, about how this condition should be classified and designated: as an obsessive–compulsive disorder (sexual compulsivity or compulsive sexual behavior), as an impulse-control disorder (sexual impulsivity or impulsive sexual behavior), or as an addictive disorder (sexual addiction). Since the issue of classification and designation not only is controversial but also has far-reaching implications for both theory and treatment, I consider it in detail.

OBSESSIVE–COMPULSIVE DISORDER

Arguments in favor of classifying this syndrome of sexual behavior as a form of obsessive–compulsive disorder (OCD) emphasize the defensive function of the sexual activity, how it operates to reduce anxiety and other painful affects. Proponents of these arguments further note that when sexual activity is blocked, individuals who suffer from this condition experience discomfort (Quadland, 1985; Weissberg and Levay, 1986). Hollander (1993) included paraphilias and "nonparaphilic sexual compulsions" among the conditions that he labeled as obsessive–compulsive spectrum disorders, because some symptoms, comorbidity, possible causes, familial transmission, and response to specific pharmacologic and behavioral treatments partially overlap with OCD.

Compulsions, however, are defined in DSM-IV (the standard diagnostic manual in psychiatry, psychology, social work, and other related fields) as "repetitive behaviors (e.g., hand washing, ordering, checking) or mental acts (e.g., praying, counting, repeating words silently) the goal of which is to reduce anxiety or distress, not to provide pleasure or gratification" (APA, 1994, p. 418). Typical compulsive behaviors, such as washing or checking, are simple and stereotyped. In most cases, they are intended to prevent a dreaded event or to reduce distress, rather than to achieve a desired goal or state. Compulsions are "either not connected in a realistic way with what they are designed to neutralize or prevent or are clearly excessive" (APA, 1994, p. 423); and even when patients lack insight that a compulsive behavior is irrational, they do not experience it as providing pleasure.[1] The sexual behavior in this syndrome, meanwhile, is rarely intended consciously to prevent a dreaded event; and, while reduction of distress contributes to motivation to engage in the sexual behavior, pleasure or gratification also contributes significantly, particularly in the early stages of the syndrome. Moreover, most of the symptomatic behaviors in the sexual syndrome are more complex and less stereotyped in their observable features than are typical compulsive behaviors. The sexual behaviors may be repeated often, but they are not themselves repetitive. Finally, during their enactment, symptomatic sexual behaviors are more often egosyntonic (i.e., accepted by the subject as consistent with his or her sense of self) than are compulsive behaviors. This difference in how the urge to engage in the behavior feels to the subject was emphasized by Fenichel (1945a):

> The compulsion neurotic feels forced to do something that he does not *like* to do, that is, compelled to use his volition against his own desires; the pervert feels forced to "like" something, even against his will. Guilt feelings may oppose his impulses; nevertheless at the moment of his excitement he feels the impulse as ego syntonic, as a something [sic] he wants to do in the hope of achieving positive pleasure [p. 324].

More recently, DSM-III-R (APA, 1987) explicitly clarified the relationship between compulsion and the sexual behavior syndrome that we are considering:

> Some activities, such as eating (e.g., Eating Disorders), sexual behavior (e.g., Paraphilias), gambling (e.g., Pathological Gambling),

---

[1]Psychoanalytically oriented readers might correctly object that all symptoms, including compulsions, are compromise formations that express drive as well as defense. DSM-IV, however, addresses only conscious experience (e.g., of pleasure), and does not consider drives or gratifications that may be unconscious. I wish here neither to endorse nor to condemn this practice in DSM-IV, only to point out the basis for divergent interpretations. The formulation that I propose later, which presents the distinction between compulsion and addic-

or drinking (e.g., Alcohol Dependence or Abuse), when engaged in excessively may be referred to as 'compulsive.' However, the activities are not true compulsions because the person derives pleasure from the particular activity, and may wish to resist it only because of its secondary deleterious consequences [p. 246].

"Compulsion," as it is defined in DSM-IV, thus does not seem to be an appropriate designation for the sexual behavior that characterizes this syndrome.

Additional evidence against classifying this syndrome as a compulsive disorder emerged from studies that assessed response to treatment with antidepressant medications. A study by Kafka (1991) found no significant difference between the response of paraphilic symptoms to imipramine and their response to fluoxetine, while another study by Kruesi and his colleagues (Kruesi, Fine, Valladares, Phillips, and Rapoport, 1992) found no significant difference between the response of paraphilic symptoms to desipramine and their response to clomipramine. This pattern of similar response to serotonergic and noradrenergic antidepressants resembles the response pattern that is typically observed in depression, but differs from the response pattern that is typically observed in OCD. The symptoms of OCD typically respond significantly more strongly to fluoxetine or clomipramine than they do to tricyclic antidepressants; and they respond particularly poorly to desipramine, which has relatively little serotonergic activity. The study by Kruesi's group (1992) also noted a placebo response rate of 17 percent, which is worthy of note because placebo response in adults with OCD is rare. Meanwhile, Stein and his colleagues (1992) observed that serotonin reuptake blockers were helpful in treating paraphilias and "sexual addictions," but in a less robust and specific way than they were helpful in treating sexual obsessions or compulsions that occurred in OCD. Stein's group found moreover that the sexual symptoms of patients with these conditions and comorbid depression improved when their mood improved, while those of patients with

_____

tion to be more dimensional than categorical, is compatible with both psychoanalytic and empirical descriptive approaches.

these conditions and comorbid OCD often did not improve when their OCD improved. These findings suggest that, while this sexual syndrome could be related to OCD, it is unlikely to be a form of OCD.

We pause for one final thought about whether to classify this syndrome of sexual behavior as a compulsion: a thought that would constitute a weak argument in a debate, but nonetheless deserves consideration. Dodes (1995) distinguished between compulsions and addictions on the basis of the predominant affect that arises when the behavior is prevented. He observed that, when a compulsive behavior is prevented (at the time of the urge to engage in it), the predominant affect that arises is anxiety. Meanwhile, he noted, when an addictive behavior is prevented (at the time of the urge to engage in it), anxiety may emerge, but the predominant affect that arises is rage. When an individual who engages in some form of sexual behavior, in a pattern that is characterized by recurrent failure to control and continuation despite harmful consequences, is prevented from engaging in that sexual behavior (at the time of the urge to engage in it), the predominant affect that typically arises is rage. (As I implied above, this point would be unlikely to sway anyone who remained convinced that the syndrome should be classified as a compulsion, but it is worth thinking about.)

IMPULSE–CONTROL DISORDER

Barth and Kinder (1987) argued that this sexual syndrome should be designated "sexual impulsivity," since it met the diagnostic criteria for atypical impulse control disorder in the then-current DSM-III. DSM-IV includes the following description of impulse-control disorders:

> The essential feature of Impulse-Control Disorders is the failure to resist an impulse, drive, or temptation to perform an act that is harmful to the person or to others. For most of the disorders in this section, the individual feels an increasing sense of tension or arousal before committing the act and then experiences pleasure,

gratification, or relief at the time of committing the act. Following the act there may or may not be regret, self-reproach, or guilt [p. 609].

The DSM description of impulse-control disorder does indeed seem to accurately characterize this sexual syndrome.

Objections to classifying this syndrome as an impulse-control disorder generally depend on arguments that the sexual behavior is in fact not impulsive but planned, and that considerable time may separate a sexual act from the affect-evoking incident that instigated it. Pithers (1990), writing about sex offenders, noted that, while victims may be selected opportunistically, the act itself has usually been nurtured for a considerable time in the offender's fantasies. He described the sex offender's deviant sexual fantasies as planning sessions for future behavior. The validity of Pithers' argument seems to rest on how "impulsive" is defined. The DSM definition of impulse-control disorder does not require that impulsive acts be entirely unplanned. If it did, and if fantasy were considered to be a form of plan, then few clinical examples would qualify as impulse-control disorders.

At the same time, the description of impulse-control disorders not only fits this sexual syndrome; it seems to characterize substance dependence equally well. If substance dependence, which is readily acknowledged to be an addictive disorder, is also an impulse-control disorder, then a condition that meets the diagnostic criteria for impulse-control disorder is not thereby precluded from classification also as an addictive disorder.

ADDICTIVE DISORDER

What, then, is the difference between impulse-control disorder and addictive disorder? This question can be answered only if a behaviorally nonspecific definition of addictive disorder is available. More to the point, the term *nonparaphilic sexual addiction,* which was listed in DSM-III-R as an example of a Sexual Disorder Not Otherwise Specified, was excluded from DSM-IV because there were "no scientific data to support a concept of sexual behavior that can be considered addictive" (Schmidt, 1992, p. 254). However, no definition of "addictive" or "addiction" was specified, which left unclear what kinds of scientific data could have constituted support for the concept of sexual addiction. Discussion of whether a syndrome should be classified as an addiction is difficult in the absence of a clear and meaningful definition of addiction.

The definition of addiction is itself a matter of controversy, and DSM-IV does not employ the term at all. A provisional set of diagnostic criteria for addictive disorder can, however, be derived from the DSM-IV criteria for substance dependence, the prototypal addictive disorder, by replacing the specific terms *substance* and *substance use* with the nonspecific term *behavior*, and by replacing "characteristic withdrawal syndrome for the substance" with a general definition of withdrawal that applies to all categories of behavior. Employing this method, I (Goodman, 1990, 1995a, p. 44) proposed the following set of behaviorally nonspecific diagnostic criteria for addictive disorder:

Addictive Disorder (or Addiction)
A maladaptive pattern of behavior, *leading to clinically significant impairment or distress*, as manifested by three (or more) of the following, occurring at any time in the same 12-month period:
(1) tolerance, as defined by either of the following:
　(a) a need for markedly increased amount or intensity of the behavior to achieve the desired effect
　(b) markedly diminished effect with continued involvement in the behavior at the same level of intensity
(2) withdrawal, as manifested by either of the following:
　(a) characteristic psychophysiological withdrawal syndrome of physiologically described changes and/or psychologically described changes upon discontinuation of the behavior
　(b) the same (or a closely related) behavior is engaged in to relieve or avoid withdrawal symptoms
(3) the behavior is often engaged in over a longer period, in greater quantity, or at a higher level of intensity than was intended
(4) there is a persistent desire or unsuccessful efforts to cut down or control the behavior

(5) a great deal of time is spent in activities necessary to prepare for the behavior, to engage in the behavior, or to recover from its effects

(6) important social, occupational, or recreational activities are given up or reduced because of the behavior

(7) the behavior continues despite knowledge of having a persistent or recurrent physical or psychological problem that is likely to have been caused or exacerbated by the behavior [1995a, p. 44].

This set of diagnostic criteria for addictive disorder is provisional and, like the sets of diagnostic criteria in the DSM series, it may need to be revised in the light of further developments in scientific research or theory. We might find, for example, that the number of criteria required (3) is too low, or that the required time frame (12 months) is unnecessarily long. Or we might determine that adding (or substituting) items from the DSM-IV diagnostic criteria for pathological gambling—such as preoccupation, engaging in the behavior to escape from problems or to relieve dysphoric moods, or lying to conceal the extent of the behavior—enhances the discriminative utility of the criteria set. The important point is that behaviorally nonspecific diagnostic criteria for addictive disorder can be formulated that are consistent with the form and content of DSM-IV, that are expressed in the same descriptive language, and that are no less reliable and valid than are the DSM-IV diagnostic criteria for substance dependence.

Along with the diagnostic criteria, I proposed a simple definition of addiction, which facilitates preliminary diagnosis of an addictive disorder. Addiction was defined as a condition in which a behavior that can function both to produce pleasure and to relieve painful affects is employed in a pattern that is characterized by two key features: (1) recurrent failure to control the behavior, and (2) continuation of the behavior despite significant harmful consequences. "Recurrent failure to control" was noted to mean not that addicted individuals invariably lose control when they engage in the behavior, but that their predictions that they would remain in control of the behavior have repeatedly proved

they noted that "sexual compulsions" share features of both OCD and substance addictions. The preceding discussion indicated that a syndrome of behavior that provides immediate pleasure, respite from painful affects, and harmful consequences shares significantly more features with substance addictions than it does with OCD. Such a syndrome is therefore more appropriately classified as an addictive disorder than as an obsessive-compulsive disorder.

The foregoing discussion leads us to conclude that "sexual addiction" is the most appropriate designation for the syndrome of sexual behavior that we are considering. Grouping this syndrome with the substance addictions is further supported by their phenomenological similarities. Orford (1978) observed that patients' descriptions of their subjective experience of the sexual behavior syndrome are qualitatively similar to patients' descriptions of their experience of drug addiction. Goodman (1995a) expanded on Orford's observation and noted a number of other characteristic features that are shared by sexual addiction and substance addiction. These characteristic features include: (1) characteristic course—the disorder typically begins in adolescence or early adulthood and follows a chronic course with remissions and exacerbations; (2) behavioral features—narrowing of behavioral repertoire, continuation of the behavior despite harmful consequences; (3) individuals' subjective experience of the condition—sense of craving, preoccupation, excitement during preparatory activity, mood-altering effects of the behavior, sense of loss of control; (4) progressive development of the condition—craving, loss of control, narrowing of behavioral repertoire, and harmfulness of consequences all tending to increase as the duration of the condition increases; (5) experience of tolerance—as the behavior is repeated, its potency to produce reinforcing effects tends to diminish; (6) experience of withdrawal phenomena—psychological and/or physical discomfort when the behavior is discontinued; (7) tendency to relapse—that is, to return to harmful patterns of behavior after a period of abstinence or control has been achieved; (8) relationship between the condition and other aspects of affected individuals' lives—for example, neglect of other areas of life as the behavior assumes priority; and (9) recurrent themes in the ways individuals with these conditions relate to others and to themselves—including low self-esteem, self-centeredness, denial, rationalization, and conflicts over dependency and control. Significantly, the recognized hallmarks of addiction—experiences of craving, loss of control, tolerance, and withdrawal—characterize sexual addiction as well as substance addiction.

REVIEW OF ARGUMENTS AGAINST THE CONCEPT OF SEXUAL ADDICTION

Arguments against the concept of sexual addiction can be organized into four groups: conventional, scientific, sociological, and moral. Each group will be reviewed in turn.

Conventional

A number of arguments against the concept of sexual addiction have emerged from conventional assumptions about addiction: that addiction means physical dependence and withdrawal, that addiction necessarily entails a 12-step approach, and that addiction necessarily implies abstinence as the only reasonable treatment goal. Levine and Troiden (1988) stated, "sex is not a form of addiction. Strictly speaking, addiction is 'a state of physiological dependence on a specific substance arising from habitual use of that substance'" (pp. 356–357). They further objected that a pattern of sexual behavior could not be called an addiction because "abrupt withdrawal from sexual behavior does not lead to forms of physiological distress" (p. 357). Similarly, Barth and Kinder (1987) argued that the syndrome of sexual behavior that we are considering "involves no foreign substances or withdrawal states, and as such should not be labeled as an addiction" (p. 21). Current psychobiological theories of addiction to alcohol and other drugs, however, tend to emphasize the emotional effects that addicts wish to achieve (W. M. Cox and Klinger, 1988) and the activation of centrally coded affect systems (Baker, Morse, and Sherman, 1987), rather than unmediated chemical effects or physical withdrawal symptoms. Many investigators of the neurobiology of drug addiction, including Miller, Dackis, and Gold (1987), Goldstein (1989), and Jaffe (1992), agree that tolerance and neuroadaptation can contribute to maintaining or increasing drug use, but are neither necessary nor sufficient for the development of addiction. In agreement with these investigators, the description of substance dependence in DSM-IV includes the sentence, "Neither tolerance nor withdrawal is necessary or sufficient for a diagnosis of Substance Dependence" (p. 178). Furthermore, psychological research has demonstrated that withdrawal in drug addiction is not simply an automatic physiological response to decreased levels of exogenous chemicals, but is a complex process that is significantly shaped by learning (Wikler, 1971, 1973, 1980a,b; Ludwig and Wikler, 1974; O'Brien, 1975; Leventhal and Cleary, 1980; Sideroff and Jarvik, 1980; Childress, McLellan, and O'Brien, 1986; Sherman, Jorenby, and Baker, 1988; Childress, Ehrman, Rohsenow, Robbins, and O'Brien, 1992). The objection to the concept of sexual addiction on the grounds that addiction is a physiological condition can be answered also at a philosophical level. According to this objection, the sexual behavior syndrome cannot be an addictive disorder because it is a psychological condition, while addictions are physiological conditions. This argument presupposes a dichotomy between psychological states and physiological states. Meanwhile, contemporary psychiatric and philosophical theory affirms an essential unity of the psychological and the physiological, in which every event that is described in psychological terms is identical with an event that is described in some set of physiological terms (Rado, 1946, 1949; Feigl, 1967, 1981; Globus, 1973; Booth, 1978; Maxwell, 1978; Reiser, 1984; Macdonald, 1989; Goodman, 1991, 1994a, in press a, in press b). Thus, to speak of dependence or distress that is psychological but not physiological is not meaningful.

Satel (1993) gave voice to a concern that is shared by many mental health professionals when she objected to the term *sexual addiction* on the grounds that many believe that the term *addiction* necessarily implies a 12-step approach to both understanding and treating the condition. Satel argued that the 12-step approach typically conceptualizes addiction in terms of the "disease model," treats addiction in 12-step groups, and tends to exclude other perspectives that might be helpful. First of all, we can note that use of the term *addiction* in the context of behaviors other than psychoactive substance use did not originate with the 12-step approach. In 1897, Freud (1892–1899) identified masturbation as an addiction when Bill W, the founder of Alcoholics Anonymous, was only 2 years old (he was born on November 26, 1895), and he discussed "Addiction to gambling" (1928, p. 193, p. 194) seven years before AA was founded (1935) and 29 years before Gamblers Anonymous was founded (1957). Fenichel's (1945a) classic text, *The Psychoanalytic Theory of Neurosis,* discussed "sexual addiction" (p. 385), "food addiction" (p. 381), and "love addicts" (p. 382) years before the founding of Sex Addicts Anonymous (1978), Overeaters Anonymous (1960), or Sex and Love Addicts Anonymous (1976).

Satel's concerns about what the 12-step approach implies can also be addressed directly, beginning with the "disease model." Arguments both for and against the disease model of addiction are often hampered by insufficient clarification of the meaning of the term *disease.* A comprehensive review of the definition of disease in medicine (Wakefield, 1992) concluded that disease is most usefully defined as "harmful dysfunction," wherein *dysfunction* is a scientific term that refers to the failure of an organismic process to perform a natural function, and *harmful* is a value term that refers to consequences that occur to the person because of the dysfunction and are deemed negative by sociocultural standards. The concept of disease does not necessarily imply the presence of an observable lesion or tissue damage. Otherwise, it would exclude such conditions as migraine, trigeminal neuralgia, and idiopathic epilepsy. Neither does the concept of disease necessarily imply that discrete dichotomous categories separate those who suffer from a condition from those who do not. Most disease conditions in medicine either are defined by some quantitative point on a continuum (such as occurs with hypertension and anemia) or are constituted by processes that are at extreme ends

of continua (such as occurs in coronary atherosclerosis and cancer [i.e., neoplastic cells develop also in healthy individuals, but
at a low enough rate that the healthy immune system can keep
them under control]). The concept of disease does not necessarily imply a clearly defined exogenous pathogen that makes individuals sick simply through exposure, regardless of their previous
states of health; nor does it necessarily imply that treatment consists of the exogenous application of technological products in
order to defeat the pathogen and cure the condition. Most diseases in medicine are chronic conditions that develop gradually
through a process that involves complex interactions over time
between genetic and environmental factors; and many of these
diseases do not get cured, but become stabilized or go into a
remission that may depend, in part, on maintaining a healthy life-
style. In short, the typical disease in medicine is not an acute
infectious disease but a chronic disease, which also represents
the most appropriate disease model for understanding addiction
(and most other psychiatric conditions). Finally, the concept of
disease does not necessarily imply that the afflicted person who
assumes a "sick role" thereby adopts a passive attitude, while
other people take responsibility for their lives. Parsons, the sociol-
ogist who coined the phrase *sick role,* specified that an element
of the sick role is the expectation that afflicted individuals want
to get well, seek competent help, and do whatever they can to
promote their recovery (Parsons, 1951). More recently, the no-
tion that the disease concept implies passivity in recovery was
specifically rebutted in a report of the Joint Committee of the
National Council on Alcoholism and Drug Dependence and the
American Society of Addiction Medicine to Study the Definition
and Criteria for the diagnosis of Alcoholism (Morse and Flavin,
1992). Satel was thus mistaken when she indicated that the disease
concept entails that sufferers are "victims of constitutional disturbance" (Satel, 1993, p. 237), that the condition is caused by a
demonstrable organic lesion, and that all other life problems are
necessarily secondary to the condition. The description of sexual
addiction as a "disease," therefore, is not inappropriate; nor
would such a description be inappropriate for any other psychiatric disorder.

Turning our attention now to treatment, Alcoholics Anonymous and other 12-step groups have long been recognized as being helpful to many individuals who have addictively used alcohol or other drugs. However, no evidence exists that involvement in such groups is necessary for an individual to discontinue addictive use of psychoactive substances. Moreover, even those alcoholics and drug addicts who believe in the 12-step system have increasingly been discovering that attendance at 12-step groups is not sufficient treatment for their disorders, and many 12-step group attendees either seek individual psychotherapy or take psychiatric medication (or do both). For example, S. Brown (1985) reported that 64 percent of recovering alcoholics in AA would like an additional form of therapy, though many did not seek it for fear that it would challenge their belief in AA. In her survey, Brown found that 45 percent of the recovering alcoholics in AA did seek psychotherapy, and that more than 90 percent found it to be helpful. In short, the valuable role that 12-step groups can play in supporting an individual's recovery from addiction does not entail that they are either necessary or sufficient for recovery. At the same time, the value of 12-step groups is not necessarily limited to addictive disorders. Emotions Anonymous and Emotional Health Anonymous function for individuals who are struggling with emotional problems in much the same way as Alcoholics Anonymous functions for individuals who are struggling with addictive use of alcohol. In theory, at least, many individuals who suffer from a broad range of psychiatric disorders could conceivably benefit from the supportive, ego-enhancing functions of 12-step groups. The assumption of an exclusive association between addiction and the 12-step model thus does an injustice to both addiction and the 12-step model. Satel's third concern about the 12-step approach was that it tends to exclude other perspectives that might be helpful. Indeed, Alcoholics Anonymous for many years embodied an antiprofessional bias and encouraged its members to mistrust medication and psychotherapy. For a variety of reasons, this attitude has evolved, and 12-step groups on the whole are more likely now to recognize the value of other approaches to treatment than they formerly were. Nonetheless, each individual group has its own character, and some groups are more inclined than are others to cling to belief systems that exclude other perspectives. In sum, the 12-step approach is less dogmatic and monolithic, and its association with addiction less exclusive, than may initially appear. Satel's objection to "sexual addiction" on the grounds that many believe that the term *addiction* necessarily implies a 12-step approach can be answered also at another level. If many believe that a term necessarily implies a certain approach, and that approach turns out in many cases to be either unnecessary or insufficient for a condition to which that term is more suitable than are other terms, then the appropriate resolution is not to dump the term but to educate those individuals whose beliefs are inconsistent with scientific and clinical reality. The term *addiction* is not "owned" by the 12-step approach. It belongs no less to relapse prevention, and to psychoanalysis, and to psychopharmacology. The term deserves to be evaluated independently of the approach, as the approach deserves to be evaluated independently of the term, for its suitability to the syndrome of sexual behavior that we have been considering.

Other assumptions about what is implied by the term *addiction* have also fueled arguments against the concept of sexual addiction. Coleman (1986) stated, "The danger of describing sex as an addiction is that it presupposes that the individual is addicted to all forms of sexual behavior rather than a specific sexual object or set of sexual behaviors, and following this model, suggests abstinence as a treatment goal" (p. 7). The first assumption, that sexual addiction presupposes addiction to all forms of sexual behavior, is comparable to the statement that drug addiction presupposes addiction to all types of drugs. These statements are valid only to the extent that addiction is understood as a process that involves a propensity to addictively engage in a behavior, and not as the actual manifestation of addictive behavior patterns. An individual who engages addictively in sexual behavior will tend to "specialize" in only one or a few types of sexual behavior, much as an individual who uses drugs addictively will tend to specialize in only one or a few types of drugs. And, similar to drug addiction, in which drugs other than the drug of choice still retain the potential to be used addictively, forms of sexual behavior that are not the sex addict's act of choice remain in the addictive domain. However, it is not the case that a sex addict by definition addictively engages in all types of sexual behavior, any more than a drug addict by definition addictively uses all types of drugs.

The assumption that treatment of an addictive disorder necessitates lifelong abstinence also merits a closer look. Even in the field of alcoholism treatment, this assumption is not universally accepted. A number of research studies have been published that indicate that at least some individuals who once used alcohol addictively can learn to use alcohol in moderation (Sobell and Sobell, 1973, 1976, 1984; Armor, Polich, and Stambul, 1978; Foy, Nunn, and Rychtarik, 1984; Sanchez-Craig, Annis, Bornet, and MacDonald, 1984; Nordstrom and Berglund, 1987; Rychtarik, Foy, Scott, Lokey, and Prue, 1987; C. G. Watson, 1987; also reviews by Heather and Robertson, 1983; Marlatt, 1983; W. R. Miller, 1983; Chase, Salzberg, and Palotai, 1984; Roizen, 1987). This research is mentioned without endorsement of a position on either side of the question, only to illustrate that the necessity of lifelong abstinence is an issue of science to be evaluated empirically, not an issue of dogma to be affirmed without question. We can also observe that what constitutes abstinence for an alcoholic or a drug addict may be subject to different interpretations. Few would now endorse the position that abstinence for a psychoactive substance addict applies only to the substance that was his or her drug of choice; for example, that a cocaine addict must remain abstinent from cocaine but can use alcohol ad lib. Many would say that once an individual has addictively used one mood-altering drug, proper abstinence would mean abstinence from all mood-altering drugs. This definition of abstinence, however, is impractical, because the category of mood-altering drugs is excessively broad. It includes caffeine, a psychostimulant the use of which is not usually described as a violation of abstinence. Moreover, it includes all psychiatric medications, many of which have no association with addictive use and may be therapeutically necessary. At the furthest extreme, any medication that is taken to relieve a condition that affects mood (such as hypothyroidism or allergy symptoms) can be considered a mood-altering drug. These distinctions between acceptable and unacceptable mood-altering drugs seem arbitrary, until we shift away from a categorical definition of unacceptability that specifies what kinds of drug are unacceptable, and toward a functional definition that specifies what functional qualities of unacceptable drugs make them unacceptable. We can then see that what would make a drug unacceptable for a particular individual would be a high likelihood that the individual would use it addictively; that is, in a manner that is characterized by recurrent failure to control the drug use and by continuation of the drug use despite significant harmful consequences. Abstinence in psychoactive substance addiction, then, could be defined functionally as abstaining from (not using) any drug that would be likely to be engaged in addictively. When abstinence is understood in this functional way—the only way that it can remain a coherent concept in practice—then abstinence in sexual addiction would be defined as abstaining from (not engaging in) any sexual behavior that would be likely to be engaged in addictively; that is, in a manner that is characterized by recurrent failure to control the sexual behavior and by continuation of the sexual behavior despite significant harmful consequences. When abstinence from addictive behavior is understood in the way that makes most sense, the applicability of lifelong abstinence to sexual addiction is no longer problematic.

Scientific

What are here termed the scientific arguments against the concept of sexual addiction have been enumerated by Coleman (1986). The first, a philosophical or semantic argument, is that free use of the word *addiction* has rendered the term meaningless, so all-inclusive that it lacks pragmatic value. Satel (1993) also argued that "inclusion of any compulsive self-destructive behavior under the term *addiction* creates several problems," among which are dilution of the meaning of the term. This potential problem with the term *addiction* is what prompted me to propose the definition and diagnostic criteria for addiction that were cited in the preceding section of this chapter. The definition is scientifically meaningful, and the diagnostic criteria are as specific, reliable, and valid as are comparable criteria in DSM-IV. The proposed definition and diagnostic criteria for addiction clearly do not include all compulsive self-destructive behaviors, and the significance of the distinction between addictive and compulsive was discussed in the preceding section.

Coleman also argued that many of the clinicians who treat individuals who engage addictively in sexual behavior have not been properly trained. To whatever extent this claim may be valid, it is not an argument against the concept of sexual addiction but an argument in favor of better training. Effective treatment of sexual addiction requires understanding not only of addictions, but also of psychodynamics, family systems theory, group dynamics, and cognitive–behavioral therapy. The ability to recognize major mood disorders and psychotic disorders is also necessary, as is a high level of self-awareness and an ability to manage one's own issues and feelings. If this combination of qualities is scarce, then education in the mental health fields may need to be reassessed; but such scarcity would have no bearing on the validity of the sexual addiction concept.

Coleman's final scientific argument against the concept of sexual addiction concerns the lack of research "which documents the existence of such a conceptualization" (p. 8), and the lack of research that documents the effectiveness of treatment methods that have been derived from this concept. Part I of this book addresses the first concern, and indicates not only the concept's existence but also its value. The second concern represents not an argument against sexual addiction but a call for treatment effectiveness research. While the need for such research does not distinguish sexual addiction from many other psychiatric disorders, sexual addiction has a much shorter history as a legitimate area of study. Approaches to treating sexual addiction are still in the process of being developed, and whether a specific treatment method can be said to have been derived from the addiction concept or from some other theoretical concept is not clear—and, perhaps, not particularly important.

Sociological

Sociological arguments against the concept of sexual addiction revolve around the idea that "addiction" is no more than a label for behavior that deviates from social norms. This viewpoint is represented by statements of Levine and Troiden (1988): "sexual addiction and sexual compulsion represent pseudoscientific codifications of prevailing erotic values rather than bona fide clinical entities" (p. 349); and "psychosexual disorders are social constructions: that is, stigmatizing labels attached to sexual patterns that diverge from culturally dominant sexual standards" (p. 355). As Coleman (1986) observed, sociological theorists are concerned (1) that "this concept can potentially be used to oppress sexual minorities . . . because they do not conform to the moral values of the prevailing culture (or therapist)" (p. 8); and (2) that "mental health professionals using such conceptualizations have become simply instruments of such conservative political views and have made people who do not fit into a narrow, traditional sexual life-style feel bad, immoral, and, now mentally ill" (p. 8).

These are cogent and powerful criticisms, but they are not applicable to sexual addiction, as it is defined in this book (an explicit definition of and a set of diagnostic criteria for sexual addiction, which are based on those for addiction that I discussed in the present section, are presented in chapter 6). The present definition of sexual addiction is quite consistent with Levine and Troiden's (1988) statement that "there is nothing inherently pathological in the conduct that is labeled sexually compulsive or addictive" (pp. 355–356). Contrary to Levine and Troiden's assumption, the concept of sexual addiction does not entail that any form or pattern of sexual behavior is in itself defined as an addiction. According to the definition and diagnostic criteria that have been presented here, a pattern of sexual behavior is designated sexual addiction, not on the basis of what the behavior is, but on the basis of how the behavior relates to and affects a person's life. Any sexual behavior has the potential to be engaged in addictively, but constitutes an addictive disorder only to the extent that it occurs in a pattern that meets the diagnostic criteria or accords with the definition. Whether a pattern of sexual behavior qualifies as sexual addiction is determined not by the type of behavior, its object, its frequency, or its social acceptability, but by how this behavior pattern relates to and affects an individual's life, as indicated in the definition and specified in the diagnostic criteria.

Other sociological arguments are less readily dismissed. Coleman (1986) noted that "no matter how one defines sexual compulsivity or addiction, there seems to be an implicit comparison to normalcy" (p. 8), and that global assessment concepts such as *preoccupation, out of control, unmanageability,* and *negative consequences* are potentially subjective and value-laden assessments. Orford (1978) observed that control-uncontrol is not a dichotomy but a continuum with arbitrary cut-off points, and he reiterated Kinsey's argument that "it is impossible to separate normal and abnormal in other than an arbitrary way" (p. 302). Levine and Troiden (1988) emphasized that these distinctions depend on the therapist's value orientation and purposes, as well as on culturally induced perceptions of what constitutes sexual impulse control. One study by Hecker and her colleagues (Hecker, Trepper, Wetchler, and Fontaine, 1995) found that therapists' values did influence their patterns of diagnosing sexual addiction. The relevance of this study to present concerns is, however, difficult to assess, since the therapists were not provided with a definition of or diagnostic criteria for sexual addiction. This deficiency is particularly significant, since none of the clinical vignettes that the investigators presented to their therapist subjects indicated loss of control or continuation of the behavior despite harmful consequences. Thus, according to the definition of sexual addiction that was presented here, none of the vignette cases in Hecker et al.'s study would have been diagnosed (even equivocally) as sexual addiction. The limitations of this study notwithstanding, there is no question that all of the assessments that are specified or implied in the diagnostic criteria for sexual addiction represent continua rather than dichotomies, and that the distinctions between "pathological" and "healthy" are ultimately arbitrary and reflect the values of the culture and the therapist. These points are, however, no more applicable to sexual addiction than they are to addictive disorders that involve other behaviors, and indeed to virtually all psychiatric diagnoses. In fact, a number of theorists (e.g., King, 1954; Agich, 1983; Wakefield, 1992) have stated that the distinctions between disease and health in all of medicine are sociohistorically relative (not absolute) points on continua, and that they reflect the underlying assumptions and values of the culture and the physician.

Moral

Moral arguments against the concept of sexual addiction are based on a concern that the designation of this pattern of sexual behavior as an addiction undermines individuals' responsibility for their behavior. This concern is shared by groups at opposite ends of the political spectrum. Those at the conservative end fear that the concept of sexual addiction may be employed to absolve individuals of responsibility, that individuals who use sexual behavior addictively can hide behind the diagnosis of "sex addict" and thereby can evade accountability for the consequences of their behavior. Meanwhile, those at the liberal end fear that the concept of addiction may be used to deprive individuals of personal responsibility and freedom of choice, defining sex addicts as victims who must be saved, even if they do not want to be (e.g., Szasz, 1974).

These concerns constitute a context in which the approach that has been developed in other addictive disorders can be particularly helpful. Alcoholics Anonymous often utilizes aphorisms to condense key aspects of its philosophy into packages that can be easily carried by oral tradition. One such aphorism is, "The alcoholic is not responsible for his disease, but is responsible for his recovery." Like alcoholics and drug addicts, individuals who use sexual behavior addictively are not responsible for having their addictive disorder, nor for the feelings, fantasies, and impulses that it entails; but they are responsible for what they do about their addictive disorder and for how they act in response to their feelings, fantasies, and impulses. This distinction—between responsibility for the disease and responsibility for recovery—applies also to other medical conditions, and failure to appreciate it has characterized many critiques of the medical model. Blume (1987) observed that the supposition that the disease concept entails avoidance of responsibility conflates the medical concept of disease with the legal concept of insanity, and added that recognizing addiction as a disease does not absolve addicts from the consequences of their behavior but indicates that rehabilitation is most likely if treatment is built into the consequences.

Part II.

Theories of Sexual Addiction

Theories of sexual addiction can be grouped into five general categories: biological, sociocultural, cognitive-behavioral, psychoanalytic, and integrated. While we review these theories, let us keep two considerations in mind.

First, most of the theories that we review here were not developed specifically to account for sexual addiction, but rather for the related category of paraphilias or perversions. Until recently, sexual addiction was not clearly defined in a way that made it suitable for scientific study. Moreover, as our discussion in chapter 1 indicated, the concept of sexual addiction continues to be surrounded by considerable controversy. Paraphilias or perversions, on the other hand, have an established history as psychiatric diagnoses. They also include a number of conditions that constitute serious law enforcement problems, and they thus attract the interest and resources that serious law enforcement problems attract. I am including theories of paraphilias or perversions in this discussion of theories of sexual addiction, partly because at least some components of these theories may be applicable also to sexual addiction, and partly because limiting the discussion to theories that were

37

developed specifically to account for sexual addiction would result in an unsatisfyingly brief and narrow discussion. By lumping theories of paraphilias or perversions and theories of sexual addictions together in this way, however, I do not mean to imply an equivalence between paraphilias and sexual addictions. The term *paraphilias* designates the category of disorders in the current diagnostic classification system that is most similar to the category of disorders that is designated by the term *sexual addictions,* and the two categories share a large area of overlap. Nonetheless, as I discuss in detail in chapter 6, the two categories are not identical. They are defined differently, and each category includes a significant number of disorders that are not included in the other (i.e., nonparaphilic sexual addictions and paraphilias that do not meet the diagnostic criteria for an addictive disorder). Consequently, some components of the theories that have been formulated for paraphilias may be less applicable than others are to nonparaphilic sexual addictions, and the distinctions between those components that are more and those that are less applicable remain to be clarified. Moreover, theories of paraphilias typically do not discriminate between (1) those components that apply to all paraphilic syndromes, and (2) those components that apply only to paraphilic syndromes that do not meet the diagnostic criteria for sexual addiction. (The difference between perversions and sexual addictions is considered at the beginning of chapter 4.)

Second, sexual addiction, like substance dependence, is not a unitary disorder but a heterogeneous class of disorders. Thus, a variety of different theories could be useful in explaining and understanding sexual addiction, each within its own realm of applicability; and the usefulness of a particular theory could vary from one case of sexual addiction to another.

2

Biological Theories

Biological theories of sexual addiction include those that attribute the disorder to an endocrine abnormality, those that attribute it to brain pathology, and those that consider it to be a "spectrum disorder," a member of a family of psychiatric disorders that share significant features.

ANDROGEN ABNORMALITY

Recent reviews of endocrinologic studies indicated little support for theories that attribute paraphilias or sexually aggressive behavior to abnormalities of androgen metabolism (Langevin, Ben-Aron, Coulthard, Heasman, Purins, Handy, Hucker, Russon, Day, Roper, Bain, Wortzman, and Webster, 1985; Hucker and Bain, 1990; Marshall and Barbaree, 1990a). In 1985, Langevin and his colleagues reviewed a large number of studies and formed an "overall impression" that the serum level of testosterone may be positively related to aggressiveness and to sexual arousability, but they noted that the studies' results were inconsistent and that their methodologies were open to question. Langevin's group (1985) also assessed serum levels of LH (luteinizing hormone, a pituitary hormone that stimulates secretion of testosterone), FSH (follicle-stimulating hormone, a pituitary hormone that stimulates spermatogenesis), and DHAS (dehydroandrosterone, the primary product of hepatic metabolism of testosterone) in sexually aggressive men. They found that levels of LH and FSH were elevated in some sadists, and that DHAS was elevated in all of the sexually aggressive men that they studied, more so in the nonsadistic than in the sadistic subjects. (Elevated DHAS typically indicates an elevated level of testosterone. Testosterone inhibits secretion of LH and FSH by a feedback process, so elevated testosterone that results from autonomous endocrine pathology is usually associated with decreased levels of LH and FSH. Increased levels of LH and FSH, in the context of elevated testosterone, suggests that the origin of the elevated testosterone is above the neck: either in the pituitary gland, which secretes LH and FSH; or in the hypothalamus, which secretes the gonadotropin-regulating hormone that stimulates pituitary synthesis and release of LH and FSH.) Five years later, Hucker and Bain (1990) concluded that the suggestion that there may be an abnormality of androgen metabolism in individuals who display aberrant sexual behavior is not well supported by experimental evidence. They noted that the studies that they reviewed were characterized by small groups of subjects and yielded conflicting results, and that positive results often either were not replicable or had marginal clinical meaning. Also in 1990, Marshall and Barbaree reviewed studies that assessed hormone levels in rapists, and concluded that, while there may be a few whose aggressive sexual behavior is driven by chronically high androgen levels, the primary problem for the majority appears to be impaired inhibitory control over sex and aggression. Thus, even in the small proportion of cases of sexual addiction that are characterized by aggressive sexual behavior, androgen abnormalities do not seem to play an etiologically significant role.

BRAIN PATHOLOGY

Most studies of the relationship between paraphilic or hypersexual behavior and brain pathology have focused on the temporal lobes. Temporal lobe epilepsy may be associated with changes in sexual behavior. Most often the results are loss of libido and impotence. However, in other cases libido increases and, in some epileptic individuals, paraphilic or hypersexual behavior appears. The sexual behaviors that have been most frequently associated with epilepsy are fetishism and transvestism, although a wide range of sexual behavior anomalies have been reported (Epstein, 1960, 1961; Kolarsky, Freund, Machek, and Polak, 1967; Blumer, 1970; Mohan, Salo, and Nagaswami, 1975; Hoenig and Kenna, 1979; Purins and Langevin, 1985).

In a pilot study, Langevin's group (Langevin et al., 1985) found significant anatomical temporal lobe abnormalities (by CT scan), most often on the right side, in 56 percent of sexual sadists. Another study by Langevin (1990) replicated the pilot study and further found right temporal horn dilatation and atrophy (by CT scan) to be more common in sadists than in controls.

Scott's group (Scott, Cole, McKay, Golden, and Liggett, 1984) and Hucker's group (Hucker, Langevin, Wortzman, Dickey, Bain, Handy, Chambers, and Wright, 1988) examined brain function in sex offenders with the Luria-Nebraska Neuropsychological Test Battery. Scott's group found that 55 percent of the offenders who had forcibly assaulted an adult scored in the brain-damaged range, that an additional 32 percent showed "borderline performance," and that 18 percent performed within normal limits. Of the pedophiles, 36 percent met the criteria for diagnosing brain dysfunction, 29 percent performed in the borderline range, and 36 percent were neuropsychologically normal. Hucker's group found that 31 sexually aggressive offenders were more impaired on the LN test than were 12 nonviolent, non-sex-offender controls. While these studies could not localize the brain impairment because the LN test lacks anatomical specificity, another study by Hucker's group (Hucker, Langevin, Wortzman, Bain, Handy, Chambers, and Wright, 1986) that utilized the Halsted-Reitan test battery and CT scans, as well as the LN test, yielded results that indicated the left hemisphere as a problem area in heterosexual, homosexual, and bisexual pedophiles. On the CT, left anterior and left temporal horns were dilated.

Flor-Henry and his coinvestigators (Flor-Henry, Koles, Reddon, and Baker, 1986; Flor-Henry and Lang, 1988) recorded EEGs on 50 exhibitionists and 50 controls, at rest and during verbal and nonverbal tasks. They concluded that exhibitionists showed altered left hemisphere function and disruption of interhemispheric EEG relationships.

Hendricks and his coinvestigators (Hendricks, Fitzpatrick, Hartman, Quaife, Stratbucker, and Graber, 1988) and Langevin's group (Langevin, Bain, Wortzman, Hucker, Dickey, and Wright, 1988) described cerebral blood flow alterations, skull densities, and right temporal lobe pathologies in sexually aggressive patients, and they described left temporal lobe abnormalities in pedophiles. Employing a more selective methodology, Langevin (1990) was able to discern a link between temporal lobe impairment and sexually anomalous behavior that was independent of criminality in general, was distinct from general learning disabilities, was not a function of alcohol abuse, and seemed to be unrelated to general violence. Results of this study also suggested that sadists and pedophiles show differential temporal lobe pathology, with sadists showing structural abnormalities in the right lobe, while pedophiles appear to have abnormalities in the left lobe.

The studies that were reviewed are consistent in their findings of right temporal lobe abnormalities in sexual sadists and left temporal lobe abnormalities in pedophiles. Such lateralization of functional disorder in association with temporal lobe pathology is not unique to paraphilia, and has been described also in personality characteristics that are associated with epilepsy. In a National Institutes of Health compilation (Bear, 1979), patients who had right temporal lobe epilepsy displayed excessive emotional tendencies, while patients who had left temporal lobe epilepsy manifested ideational traits such as a sense of personal destiny, moral self-scrutinizing, and a tendency toward philosophical explanation.

Interestingly, in none of the paraphilia studies did the authors speculate about etiologic relationships between the brain abnormalities and the sexual behavior abnormalities with which they were associated. Perhaps they appreciated the distinction between correlation and cause, and were reluctant to attribute to one set of abnormalities a causal role in the development of another set of abnormalities that were observed at the same time. To the extent that temporal lobe abnormalities are correlated with some forms of paraphilia, further correlation could be hypothesized to exist between the development of the temporal lobe abnormalities and the development of the paraphilic disorders. The etiology of these paraphilic disorders could then be approached by understanding the development of the temporal lobe abnormalities with which the paraphilic disorders are associated. Such understanding extends beyond the realm that currently available empirical data can support. Consequently, no viable theory has been proposed that links brain pathology with the etiology of (one or more forms of) paraphilia. We might also note that the temporal lobes are large structures that are critically involved in a variety of complex psychobiological functions, including emotion, memory, audition, and language comprehension. The association of temporal lobe abnormalities with paraphilic or hypersexual behavior is a valuable starting point for understanding the neurobiology of these behavior patterns, but research findings will need to be more specific before they can be of much help in elucidating the etiology of paraphilias.

Meanwhile, a demonstration of etiologic relationships between brain abnormalities and paraphilias would not necessarily indicate what we could infer about the etiology of sexual addiction. Paraphilic or hypersexual behavior that results from demonstrable brain pathology is only rarely associated with tolerance (diminution of reinforcing effects as the behavior is repeated), with psychophysiological withdrawal symptoms on discontinuation of the behavior, or with a persistent desire to cut down or control the behavior. Our understanding of the relationship between sexual addiction and brain pathology could be enhanced by neurobiological and neuropsychological research with subjects who meet the diagnostic criteria for sexual addiction.

"SPECTRUM DISORDER" THEORIES

Hollander and his colleagues (Stein, Hollander, Anthony, Schneier, Fallon, Liebowitz, and Klein 1992; Anthony and Hollander, 1993; Hollander, 1993) identified sexual addiction as an obsessive–compulsive spectrum disorder, a member of a family of disorders that share with OCD some symptoms, comorbidity, possible causes, familial transmission, and response to specific pharmacological and behavioral treatments. These investigators conceptualized OCD spectrum disorders as being distributed along a phenomenological and neurobiological spectrum of harm avoidance, from a compulsive, risk-aversive pole to an impulsive, risk-seeking pole, and they proposed that compulsivity and impulsivity lie on a phenomenological and neurobiological spectrum. In the terms of this theory, the sexual obsessions and compulsions of OCD are at the more compulsive end of the spectrum, whereas paraphilias and nonparaphilic sexual addictions are at the more impulsive end. Hollander and his colleagues hypothesized that the central component of the neurobiological abnormalities that are associated with OCD spectrum disorders is a disturbance in serotonergic function.

In 1992, both Kafka and Prentky (1992) and McElroy and her colleagues (McElroy, Hudson, Pope, Keck, and Aizley, 1992) proposed that sexual addiction (paraphilias plus either nonparaphilic sexual addictions [Kafka and Prentky, 1992] or compulsive sexual behaviors [McElroy et al., 1992]) is an affective spectrum disorder, a member of a family of disorders that share with affective disorders a number of clinically significant features. In an earlier paper, Kafka (1991) had hypothesized that "hypersexuality" be considered an atypical or reversed neurovegetative symptom of a depressive disorder. He suggested that the syndrome could be conceptualized as a sexual dysregulation disorder in comorbid association with a primary mood disorder, analogous to the relationship of bulimia to mood disorders. Sexual dysregulation could be observed in two dimensions: an increase in or intensification of nonconventional sexual interest and an increase in sexual desire. One year later, Kafka and Prentky (1992), after reviewing the comorbidity of sexual addictions with mood disorders and the apparent response of sexual addiction symptoms to several classes of antidepressants, proposed that sexual addictions may be affective spectrum disorders. They also speculated that impulse disorders, among which they included sexual addictions, share a diathesis for mood disorder and a common perturbation of central serotonin pathophysiology. The shift from considering sexual dysregulation as a symptom of a mood disorder to considering it as a variant expression of a mood disorder diathesis may have been the next step in developing the analogy with bulimia, which had recently been characterized as an affective spectrum disorder (Hudson and Pope, 1990); or it may have reflected a general evolution in psychiatry toward a more integrated and developmental understanding of psychiatric pathology.

McElroy and her colleagues (1992) hypothesized that impulse-control disorders, in which category they included paraphilias and compulsive sexual behavior, as well as substance abuse disorders, bulimia, and obsessive–compulsive disorder, represent forms of "affective spectrum disorder." This hypothesis was based on findings that these disorders share a number of clinically significant features with affective disorders, including demographic and clinical characteristics, phenomenology, family history, biology, and response to treatment. A review of relevant literature indicated (1) high rates of comorbid mood disorder, anxiety disorder, substance abuse disorder, and eating disorders in patients with impulse control disorders; (2) high rates of mood and substance use disorders in first-degree relatives of patients with impulse control disorders; and (3) a positive response of impulse control disorder symptoms to affect-regulating agents. The authors then proposed that impulse control disorders not elsewhere specified are forms of affective spectrum disorder, on the grounds of (a) the phenomenologic similarities between these disorders and both obsessive–compulsive disorder and bulimia, which they identified as forms of affective spectrum disorder; and (b) evidence that links these disorders with several other disorders that they identified as forms of affective spectrum disorder (including panic disorder, obsessive–compulsive disorder, attention deficit disorder, and major depression). The authors emphasized that they were not arguing that impulse control disorders are caused by affective spectrum disorder, but rather, that these disorders may share the same postulated underlying physiological abnormality as the other forms of affective spectrum disorder. Studies were then reviewed that provided evidence that impulse control disorders, like other forms of affective spectrum disorder, may share an abnormality in serotonergic transmission.

These two theories, obsessive–compulsive spectrum disorder theory and affective spectrum disorder theory, have much in common, from the manner in which the theories were presented to their emphasis on abnormalities in serotonergic function. In fact, obsessive–compulsive spectrum disorders could be understood to represent a subset of affective spectrum disorders, a relationship that was implied in the paper by McElroy's group (1992) and that does not seem to be contradicted in the reviewed papers by Hollander and his colleagues (Stein et al., 1992; Anthony and Hollander, 1993; Hollander, 1993). If this relationship between the spectra is provisionally accepted as valid, the next step would be to clarify the distinction—at first descriptively, and then neurobiologically—between obsessive–compulsive spectrum disorders and those affective spectrum disorders that are not obsessive–compulsive disorders. Issues of terminology also would have to be addressed. If "obsessive–compulsive spectrum" refers to a continuum that is compulsive at one end and impulsive at the other end, does it make sense that the name of the spectrum includes the word *compulsive* but not the word *impulsive?* Also, McElroy and her colleagues (1992), noting the phenomenologic similarities among impulsive disorders, paraphilias, substance abuse disorders, and bulimia, and the high rates of other impulsive disorders in individuals with these disorders, alluded to a suggestion that all of these conditions should be classified as *impulse-control* disorders. The same argument could be adduced also in favor of classifying all of these conditions as *addictive disorders,* a term that the earlier discussion indicated was more suitable.

The spectrum disorder theories considerably enhance our understanding of sexual addiction and its relationship to other psychiatric disorders. At the present point in the development of biological psychiatry, though, these theories are more theories of classification and pathophysiology than theories of etiology. The spectrum disorder theories hypothesize that sexual addiction, along with a large number of other psychiatric disorders, is associated with abnormalities in serotonergic function. They also suggest that a genetically transmitted diathesis predisposes an individual to develop one or more of these disorders. We could speculate further that this diathesis involves a predisposition to develop an abnormality in serotonergic function. In order to proceed beyond this speculation, biological theories of sexual addiction would need to address (1) how sexual addiction (or addiction in general) differs neurobiologically from other affective spectrum and obsessive–compulsive spectrum disorders, and (2) how the neurobiological abnormalities that are associated with sexual addiction (or addiction in general) develop.

3

Sociocultural and Cognitive–Behavioral Theories

SOCIOCULTURAL THEORIES

No sociocultural theories have been developed specifically to account for the etiology of sexual addiction. Most of the sociocultural theories have been concerned primarily with sexual aggression, while the sociocultural components of psychoanalytic theories have addressed either perversion or addiction in general.

In recent years, a number of publications have addressed the sociocultural contribution to the etiology of sexual aggression from a feminist perspective (reviewed in Herman, 1990; Stermac, Segal, and Gillis, 1990). They describe the androcentric, power-oriented structure of our society, they identify relationships between sexual aggression and social attitudes toward women, and they criticize the social acceptance and the prevalence of sexual aggression in various forms. While these characteristics of our society are likely to be correlated with a significant prevalence of sexual aggression against women, such correlations do not necessarily indicate the nature of the relevant causal relationships. For example: Do these destructive characteristics of our society generate and shape sexual aggression against women? Does sexual aggression against women, in various forms, generate and shape these destructive characteristics of our society? Or does some third factor generate and shape both sexual aggression against women and these destructive characteristics of our society? The answer is likely to involve all of the above, in a nonlinear, dialectical process. Moreover, while almost all males in our society are exposed to much the same array of sociocultural messages, images, and attitudes, only a limited number of men engage in sexually aggressive behaviors. Sociocultural factors undoubtedly foster and shape the expression of sexually aggressive behavior. However, an adequate understanding of the development of sexual aggression in some but not all men in our sociocultural milieu requires that other, more specific factors be considered. Thus, as Marshall (1989) concluded, theories that attribute sexually aggressive behavior to sociocultural messages, images, and attitudes are inadequate to account for the etiology of sexual aggression.

Psychoanalysis, in general, has been interested primarily in the meaning-providing functions of the sociocultural milieu, rather than in its possible causal functions. A number of psychoanalysts have emphasized the importance of the sociocultural context in determining what constitutes a perversion or paraphilia, and what such behavior might mean to the individual who engages in it. Khan (1969) stated that "perversion-formations are much nearer to cultural artifacts than disease syndromes as such" (p. 555), and Goldberg (1995) observed that the sociocultural environment is relevant to the definition of perversion, "not so much as a standard but rather as playing a particular role in the psyche of the individual" (p. 22).

Other psychoanalytically oriented theorists (Wurmser, 1978; Goodman, 1996b) discussed the relationship between addiction in general and the technological orientation of our society, which idealizes control and promotes a reliance on external, material things that we can control as a means of solving our inner emotional and spiritual problems. These sociocultural hypotheses, isolated from the psychoanalytic formulations that constitute the bulk of these authors' theories, do not address why some individuals in our society develop clinically significant addictive disorders but most do not, even though virtually all are exposed to the same set of sociocultural influences.

In short, while sociocultural factors are critical determinants of how sexuality is expressed and of how normal sexual behavior is defined, they are of limited utility in explaining sexual aggression, perversion, or addiction in general. Their utility in explaining sexual addiction is unlikely to be significantly greater. Nonetheless, sociocultural factors are worthy of attention and study. In addition to their defining and meaning-providing functions, they shape the etiologic pathway of sexual addiction (and of other psychiatric disorders as well), and they can function as a steady pressure toward relapse. Moreover, those who treat sexual addiction are exposed to the same sociocultural influences as are those who suffer from it. As Carnes (1989) observed, "all helping professionals struggle with two levels of pathology: the illness of the people who need help and the cultural pathology" (p. 49). We clinicians are no more capable than is anyone else of transcending our sociocultural context. But the more aware we are of how our sociocultural context influences our perceptions, our beliefs, and our feelings, the less likely are such contextual influences to undermine our therapeutic effectiveness.

COGNITIVE–BEHAVIORAL THEORIES

Blair and Lanyon (1981) broadly divided the psychological theories of exhibitionism (a paraphilic disorder that often but not always meets the diagnostic criteria for sexual addiction) into two categories, "behavioral" and "psychodynamic." They observed that, since the behavioral view is concerned more with altering behavior in the present than with explaining how a behavior pattern developed, behavioral explanations for sexual deviation have been few and of little value. Meanwhile, they noted, while psychodynamic theories offer more plausible explanations of the nature of sexual deviation, they have not been tested and indeed are very difficult to test in any way that satisfies the requirements of empirical science.

One notable behavioral theory of sexual deviation was proposed by McGuire, Carlisle, and Young (1965). McGuire et al. did not define "sexual deviation," which seems to be approximately synonymous with "paraphilia" and "perversion." (We can note, again, that this theory was not developed specifically to account for sexual addiction. Its intended range of applicability thus probably would have included many but not all conditions that meet the diagnostic criteria for sexual addiction, and it would also have included a number of conditions that do not meet the diagnostic criteria for sexual addiction.) On the basis of their study of 45 sexual deviants, they hypothesized that deviant patterns of sexual arousal develop gradually by conditioning processes when the subject repeatedly masturbates to deviant fantasies. The authors speculated that most individuals who use deviant fantasies when they masturbate do so because their first real sexual experience was of that deviant type, as was the case for three-quarters of the patients in their study. In effect, their etiologic theory is that individuals whose first "real sexual experience" (presumably, the first sexual experience that involves orgasm) is of a deviant nature are thereafter inclined to employ fantasies of that kind of deviant sexual behavior when they masturbate; and that, subsequently, the frequent pairing of these fantasies with orgasm further amplifies the sexual arousal stimulus value of the fantasies and of the behaviors that they depict. The authors' thesis, that repeated masturbation to deviant fantasies increases the sexual arousal stimulus value of the fantasies, makes sense, and entails implications for treatment of sexual addiction that are worth pursuing. Their theory of the etiology of sexual deviation, however, does not seem to fare well under scrutiny. First of all, not all individuals whose first real sexual experience was deviant become sexual deviants (particularly women, who are more likely than men to have been sexually abused in childhood or adolescence but much less likely than men to become sexual deviants), and not all sexual deviants had their first orgasm in a deviant sexual experience. Other factors besides the first real sexual experience must also be etiologically significant. Moreover, this theory implies a correspondence between the specific type of sexual deviance that was involved in an individual's first real sexual experience and the specific type of deviance that he later enacts. The evidence for such specificity is sparse, and the theory would have difficulty accounting for the high frequency of sexual deviants who engage in more than one type of sexual deviance, or who switch their preference from one type of deviance to another.

Since the publication of Blair and Lanyon's paper in 1981, a number of investigators (M. F. Schwartz and Brasted, 1985; Coleman, 1986, 1987; Carnes, 1989) have proposed psychological theories of sexual addiction, which the investigators identified as cognitive–behavioral theories. These theories are neither clearly behavioral nor clearly psychodynamic, but incorporate elements of both approaches, along with elements of cognitive, social learning, and family systems theories.

Schwartz and Brasted (1985) attributed the origin of "sexual impulsivity" to an irrational belief system that consists of poor self-image, unrealistic expectations of what life has to offer, anticipation of personal failure, and a general feeling of helplessness. They added that religious beliefs and social expectations also play roles in the development of the disorder, by burdening the individual with shame, guilt, and low self-esteem. Finally, they proposed that marital difficulties can lead to or exacerbate addictive sexual behavior.

The theory that was presented by Coleman (1986, 1987) attributed the development of "compulsive sexual behavior" to two dynamics, one that predisposes an individual to compulsively use substances or behaviors as a means of alleviating emotional pain, and a second that leads individuals who are thus predisposed to select certain sexual behaviors as their preferred mode of pain alleviation. According to Coleman's theory, the basis of the predisposition is some type of intimacy dysfunction in an individual's family of origin, such as child abuse or neglect. In response to this trauma, the child develops a sense of shame, perceiving himself or herself to have been the cause of the abuse or neglect, and as a result experiencing feelings of unworthiness and inadequacy. Shame and low self-esteem interfere with healthy interpersonal functioning, intimate relationships are dysfunctional or nonexistent, and loneliness compounds the individual's low self-esteem. Coleman identified these events and feelings as the origin of the compulsive predisposition:

> All of these events and feelings cause psychological pain for the client, and in order to alleviate this pain, the client begins to search for a "fix," or an agent which has analgesic qualities to it. For some, this agent is alcohol. For others, it could be drugs, certain sexual behaviors, particular foods, working patterns, gambling behaviors, etc. All seem to cause physical and psychological changes which alleviate the pain and provide a temporary relief [1986, p. 9; 1987, pp. 196–197].

Coleman hypothesized that the specific dynamic that then leads predisposed individuals to use sexual behavior for their "fix" is a background of restrictive and conservative attitudes regarding sexuality. Coleman mentioned sexual abuse as one of the forms of child abuse or neglect that contribute to the general predisposition to compulsively depend on an external substance or behavior as a means of alleviating emotional pain, but he did not identify sexual abuse as a factor in the selection of sexual behavior as the specific means of alleviating pain.

Carnes (1989) also distinguished between an individual's general addictive tendencies and the catalytic events and/or environments that interact with the addictive tendencies to precipitate a specific addictive problem. He represented the general addictive tendencies as a set of three core beliefs: (1) I am a bad, unworthy person; (2) no one would love me as I am; and (3) my needs will not be met if I have to depend on others. The faulty belief system that develops around these core beliefs then promotes the impaired thinking—denial, rationalization, self-righteousness, and blame of others—that enables addictive behavior to flourish. Carnes attributed the development of addictive core beliefs to addicts' families of origin. He characterized these families as unbalanced along the dimensions of structure and intimacy, with structure being either chaotic or rigid and intimacy being either enmeshed or disengaged. As a result of this family pathology, many of the child's basic human needs remain unmet. The child, consequently, not only fails to develop healthy self-esteem, but also learns that other people are unreliable, that one can count only on oneself, and that to survive one must remain in control. What has been discussed so far applies to all forms of addiction. Sex addicts then develop a fourth core belief that distinguishes them from other addicts: (4) sex is my most important need. Carnes ascribed the development of this core belief to childhood experiences of being sexually abused, either overtly or covertly. He noted that "covert incest," in which parents are flirtatious, suggestive, or sexually titillating with their children, may be even more pathogenic than is overt incest. In addition to the distress and shame that are experienced by victims of overt incest, covert incest children are likely also to feel crazy, doubting that their sense of reality is reliable.

The theories that were presented by Schwartz and Brasted, Coleman, and Carnes are quite compatible with each other. While they vary in breadth and depth, none of the theories seems to be saying anything with which any of the others would seriously disagree. The most purely cognitive-behavioral of the three, Schwartz and Brasted's theory focuses on a system of irrational beliefs that resemble those that Beck and others (Beck, 1967; Beck, Rush, Shaw, and Emery, 1979) described in cognitive theories of depression. Schwartz and Brasted offered no etiologic hypothesis about how the irrational belief system develops. Moreover, they did not consider what distinguishes those individuals with low self-esteem and depressing thoughts who become sexually impulsive from those who become depressed (and not sexually impulsive). These shortcomings do not, however, invalidate Schwartz and Brasted's theory, but rather suggest that it is a cognitive–behavioral analogue of the biological theory according to which sexual addiction is an affective spectrum disorder. Coleman identified two dynamics in the development of compulsive sexual behavior, one that predisposes an individual to compulsively use pleasure-producing substances or behaviors as means of alleviating emotional pain, and a second that leads predisposed individuals to select certain sexual behaviors as their preferred "fix." I consider this point to have been Coleman's

most significant theoretical contribution, not only to our understanding of sexual addiction, but to our understanding of all addictive disorders. I believe that it represents the most important
concept in the entire body of theories of addiction. Coleman's
description of the development of the first dynamic was clear,
intuitively sound, and consistent with the more detailed psychoanalytic theories. His account of the second dynamic as being the
result of restrictive and conservative attitudes regarding sexuality,
however, seems to be insufficient. Sexually compulsive individuals
come from a broad range of cultural backgrounds, and not every
compulsively predisposed individual who grows up in a sexually
restrictive or conservative subculture becomes sexually compulsive. Selection of sexual behavior by compulsively predisposed
individuals, therefore, must be guided by factors that are more
specific than are cultural attitudes about sexuality (as we noted
in our earlier consideration of sociocultural theories of etiology).
Carnes' account of sexual addiction synthesized cognitive–behavioral and family systems approaches to yield a theory that was
both far-reaching and experience-near. His thoughts on the development of general addictive tendencies probably deserved
more attention in the substance addiction field than they received. Interestingly, Carnes focused on the use of sexual behavior as a substitute means of gratifying unmet needs. As we
considered earlier, gratification represents the primary function
of impulsive behavior. Coleman, meanwhile, focused on the use
of sexual behavior as a means of alleviating emotional pain, which
represents the primary function of compulsive behavior. Addiction, we recall, involves both gratification and alleviation of emotional pain. Carnes and Coleman thus seemed to be emphasizing
complementary aspects of addiction.

SEXUAL ADDICTION AND CHILDHOOD SEXUAL ABUSE

The relationship between sexual addiction and childhood sexual
abuse has been the focus of considerable attention (McGuire,
Carlisle, and Young, 1965; Hammer, 1968; Coleman, 1987;
Carnes, 1989; Anderson and Coleman, 1990; M. F. Schwartz,

1992). In a study by Kafka and Prentky (1994), 12 percent of 34 men with paraphilias and 19 percent of 26 men with "paraphilia-related disorders" (nonparaphilic sexual addictions) reported that they had been sexually abused. Carnes (1989) asked a group of men and women who used sexual behavior addictively, and a comparison group of men and women who did not, whether they had been sexually abused as children. He found that 39 percent of the 160 male sex addicts and 63 percent of the 24 female sex addicts reported having been sexually abused, as compared to 8 percent of 78 nonaddicted men and 20 percent of 98 nonaddicted women. The study did not consider whether sexual addiction treatment, sexual addiction support groups, self-help books, or other collateral factors might have differentially influenced the sex addict group to report sexual abuse at a higher rate than did the nonaddicted group: for example, by educating them about what constitutes sexual abuse, by facilitating their recall of dissociated memories, or by suggesting a means by which they could justify their harmful sexual behavior.

More serious questions about the specificity of these findings are suggested by Hanson and Slater's (1988) review of empirical literature on the proportion of child sexual abusers who were themselves sexually victimized as children. The review revealed that, while individual studies ranged between 0 and 67 percent, an average of about 28 percent of the offenders reported having been sexually victimized as children. This rate was higher than the base rate for community samples of nonoffending males (about 10%), but was similar to the rates that were found in populations of offenders whose offenses were nonsexual. The authors concluded, "The relationship between childhood sexual victimization and sexually abusing children as an adult does not appear to be specific; rather, it is probable that many forms of childhood maltreatment can lead to many forms of behavioral and psychological problems in adulthood" (p. 486). The methodology of this review itself, however, is subject to question. When the conclusions of a review are to so great an extent dependent on averages of numbers, all relevant studies should be included. A study by Hammer (1968) of sex offenders at Sing Sing, which was not included in this review, found that 74 percent had experienced an overt seduction in childhood by some incestual figure, compared to 18 percent of nonsex offenders. The omission of this study raises concerns about how studies were selected for inclusion in the review. Moreover, when reported findings of different studies on a particular variable range from 0 to 67 percent, the chance is good that methodological differences among the studies contributed significantly to the outcome variability. Under such circumstances, the information that a simple average of the numbers provides might not be particularly meaningful. We can also keep in mind that the applicability to sexual addiction of Hanson and Slater's conclusions may be limited by the significant differences between sexual addiction and sexual offense, as were noted earlier.

Meanwhile, questions about the specificity of childhood sexual victimization, similar to those that were raised by Hanson and Slater (1988) in regard to nonsexual criminal behavior, could be raised also with respect to other psychiatric disorders. A large number of studies have documented the association between childhood sexual abuse and adult psychopathology, most notably borderline personality disorder (Herman, Perry, and van der Kolk, 1989; Zanarini, Gunderson, Marino, Schwartz, and Frankenburg, 1989; Ogata, Silk, Goodrich, Lohr, Westen, and Hill, 1990; Swett, Surrey, and Cohen, 1990; Margo and McLees, 1991; Links and van Reekum, 1993; J. B. Murray, 1993; Salzman, Salzman, Wolfson, Albanese, Looper, Ostacher, Schwartz, Chinman, Land, and Miyawaki, 1993; Weaver and Clum, 1993). While most of the patients who were the subjects of these studies were female, one study of 125 consecutive male psychiatric outpatients (Swett, Surrey, and Cohen, 1990) found that 48 percent reported histories of sexual abuse and/or physical abuse, and that a reported history of childhood abuse was correlated with more severe psychiatric symptoms and significantly higher mean scores on the global severity index of the SCL-90-R. The higher incidence of childhood sexual victimization in sex addicts than in the general population could thus reflect a high degree of comorbidity between sexual addiction and borderline personality disorder, or a correlation between sexual addiction and other serious psychopathology. Finally, a high correlation between childhood sexual abuse and sexual addiction, even if specific to sexual addiction, would not necessarily mean that sexual abuse was the critical factor in that disorder's etiology. Sexual abuse of children is highly correlated with a disturbed family environment, and it could be a marker for other pathogenic factors with the family environment (a point that Paris and Zweig-Frank [1992] made when they discussed the high incidence of childhood sexual abuse in patients with borderline personality disorder).

An association between childhood sexual abuse and sexual addiction makes intuitive sense, and the personal significance of sexual abuse in the histories of the sex addicts who report it is difficult to deny. A hypothesis that childhood sexual abuse is etiologically significant in the development of sexual addiction is credible and worthy of empirical study. Caution is advised, however, in interpreting the results of such studies. The etiology of psychiatric disorders is typically more complex, multifactorial, and nonlinear than our models can accommodate.

4

Psychoanalytic Theories

More material on the etiology of sexual addiction is available in the psychoanalytic literature than in the literature of all other areas of psychiatry and psychology combined. Before proceeding, however, three points are worth mentioning. First of all, comparison of psychoanalytic theories with biological or behavioral theories is difficult, since psychoanalysis operates within a hermeneutic as well as an empirical scientific paradigm (Strenger, 1991; Goodman, 1994b, in press a, in press b). The two paradigms differ in their languages of discourse and their ways of knowing. While biological psychiatry and behavioral psychology define their subjects in physical terms of observational description and employ methods of objective observation and predictive generalization, psychoanalysis focuses more (though not exclusively) on subjects associated with mental terms that relate to subjective experience, and it employs methods of understanding and interpretation of meanings (Goodman, 1994a, in press a, in press c). In general, psychoanalysis is oriented more toward enhancing our understanding of a person's experience than toward enhancing the completeness of our causal explanations; and, within the realm of causal explanation, psychoanalytic theory is more suitable for narrative, after-the-fact explanation that can enhance our understanding of a developmental process, than it is for predictive explanation that can enhance our ability to predict observable events. Freud articulated this distinction in his paper, "The Psychogenesis of a Case of Homosexuality in a Woman" (1920):

> So long as we trace the development from its final outcome backwards, the chain of events appears continuous, and we feel we have gained an insight which is completely satisfactory or even exhaustive. But if we proceed the reverse way, if we start from the premises inferred from the analysis and try to follow these up to the final result, then we no longer get the impression of an inevitable sequence of events which could not have been otherwise determined. We notice at once that there might have been another result, and that we might have been just as well able to understand and explain the latter. The synthesis is thus not so satisfactory as the analysis; in other words, from a knowledge of the premises we could not have foretold the nature of the result.
>
> It is very easy to account for this disturbing state of affairs. Even supposing that we have a complete knowledge of the aetiological factors that decide a given result, nevertheless what we know about them is only their quality, and not their relative strength. Some of them are suppressed by others because they are too weak, and they therefore do not affect the final result. But we never know beforehand which of the determining factors will prove the weaker or the stronger. We only say at the end that those which succeeded must have been stronger [pp. 167–168].

Thus, as Person (1986) noted, psychoanalytic theory can shed light on the meaning of a perversion without necessarily establishing a definitive etiology.

Second, while *perversion* is the term in the psychoanalytic literature, the meaning of which is most similar to the definition of *sexual addiction,* the meanings of the two terms are not identical. Laplanche and Pontalis (1967) defined perversion as "deviation from the 'normal' sexual act when this is defined as coitus with a person of the opposite sex directed towards the achievement of orgasm by means of genital penetration" (p. 306). They continued that perversion is present where orgasm is reached with sexual objects other than an opposite sex adult or through regions of the body other than the genitals; or where orgasm is subordinated absolutely to certain extrinsic conditions, which may even be sufficient in themselves to bring about sexual pleasure. Moore and Fine (1968) similarly defined perversions as "A variety of sexual practices that deviate in aim or object choice from the accepted norm of heterosexual genital union" (p. 72). They further distinguished true perversion from occasional sexual variations in which normal people may engage, usually during foreplay: "A true perversion implies an habitual (although not necessarily exclusive) type of behavior. . . . In a true perversion the deviant behavior is persistent, and is more important to the individual than is heterosexual genital intercourse" (p. 72). More contemporary psychoanalytic attempts to define perversion take into account that the inclusion criteria for " 'normal' sexual act" have expanded, and they recognize that psychoanalytic theorists disagree about whether homosexuality is a perversion. However, they typically do not include impaired control or harmful consequences among their criteria. We can infer that the group of all individuals with paraphilic sexual addictions and the group of all individuals with perversions overlap considerably, but are not identical. The relationship between nonparaphilic sexual addictions and perversion is a separate matter, and is considered below.

Finally, psychoanalytic theory does not consider perversions to be diagnostically specific, but recognizes that a wide variety of psychiatric diagnoses and levels of personality organization may be present in perverse individuals. Consequently, the psychoanalytic understanding of a perversion in the individual case is inseparable from the psychoanalytic understanding of the person and of how perverse behavior interacts with his or her underlying psychodynamics and character.

This chapter presents the psychoanalytic theories of perversion and pathological hypersexuality in two forms: a detailed chronological review of individual investigators' contributions and an integrative recap. While the integrative recap covers the theoretical territory as a whole, the chronological review (1) reveals the historical development of the theoretical themes, and

(2) presents the specific contexts from which the material in the recap was drawn.

PERVERSION

Freud

Freud's understanding of perversion was most extensively presented in *Three Essays on the Theory of Sexuality* (1905). In this paper, Freud proposed that perversion originates in a failure to successfully negotiate the developmental watershed that is represented by the oedipal crisis. As a result of some combination of constitutional and situational factors, the child's ego is unable to manage in a progressive manner the castration anxiety that the oedipal situation evokes. Identification with the same-gender parent is not realized, and the child fails to resolve the oedipal crisis. As a defense against overwhelming castration anxiety, according to Freud, the child then elaborates the fantasy that the mother possesses a phallus. This fantasy, according to Freud, becomes the "nuclear illusion" of perversion. Freud understood perversion to be the libidinal cathexis of a developmentally inappropriate object that emerges as a regressive attempt to cope with castration anxiety that the ego is unable to manage in healthier, more adaptive ways. Freud also noted, in this early paper, the prevalence of perverse elements in healthy sexuality and the continuity between perversion and health in the sexual realm: "No healthy person, it appears, can fail to make some addition that might be called perverse to the normal sexual aim; and the universality of this finding is in itself enough to show how inappropriate it is to use the word perversion as a term of reproach" (p. 160).

In a later paper, "Fetishism" (1927), Freud theorized that the child is able to preserve the fantasy of the maternal phallus, and thereby to deny the threat of castration, by disavowing his perception that a woman does not possess a penis. (Fetishism, a condition in which the affected individual requires the presence of a particular inanimate object in order to experience sexual excitement or orgasm, is often considered to be the prototype of perversion.) As Freud then described in "Splitting of the Ego in

the Process of Defence'' (1940), the child is able to simultaneously (''side by side'') affirm and disavow perception of the woman's penislessness by initiating a process of ''splitting of the ego,''
a defensive disruption of the ego's synthetic function.

The fantasy that the mother possesses a phallus can be understood at two levels. At one level, that a female also has a phallus
disarms the threat of castration that the absence of a penis on
females may seem to imply. At another level, that females as well
as males can possess this sign of maleness suggests either that
male and female genders are not differentiated, or that an individual can be both male and female. The three papers to which
the preceding paragraphs referred focused on the first level,
which highlights the fantasy's function of defense against castration anxiety, while the second level was emphasized in Freud's
paper, ''On the Sexual Theories of Children'' (1908). According
to the theory that Freud presented in ''On the Sexual Theories
of Children,'' the fantasy that everyone, females as well as males,
possesses a penis emerges at first as a natural process of the (male)
child's mind. This original fantasy develops early in childhood,
before the threat of castration enters consciousness. In fact, the
subsequent awareness of the genital difference, which marks the
dissolution of the original fantasy, is the spark that ignites castration anxiety. When these four papers are considered together,
Freud seems to have been saying that the fantasy of the maternal
phallus does not arise de novo as a defensive response to castration anxiety, but represents an aspect of the original fantasy of
gender nondifferentiation or bipotentiality that emerges initially
as a natural process before the advent of castration consciousness,
and then later is reactivated as a means of warding off castration
anxiety. A question remains whether a fixation at the original
fantasy of gender nondifferentiation or bipotentiality may predispose the child to regress to it in response to the castration complex. The significance of this discussion becomes more apparent
when we consider later psychoanalytic theories that focus on the
relationships among perversion, identity, and the fantasy of gender nondifferentiation or bipotentiality.

In ''Splitting of the Ego in the Process of Defence'' (1940),
which was unfinished at the time of its posthumous publication,

Freud briefly mentioned two points that foreshadowed major developments in our understanding of perversion. First, he observed that the "rift in the ego" or disruption of ego-synthetic function, which begins as a focal split that is limited to the perception of female penislessness, not only does not heal but "increases as time goes on" (p. 276). This seemingly localized defensive operation thus can function as a developmental nidus for a broad range of ego weaknesses and impairments in character integration. Second, Freud identified a counterphobic, hypermasculine characerological theme that both is potentiated by the splitting of the ego and at the same time deepens the split. Freud noted that this characerological theme functions to "overcompensate" (p. 277) for the child's castration anxiety. Literally, castration anxiety refers to the oedipal phase boy's intense fear that his father will punish him for oedipal masturbatory fantasies by depriving him of his phallus. The psychodynamic implications of castration indicate that castration anxiety can be more comprehensively understood to represent the anxieties that are associated with feelings of being small, inadequate, helpless, and vulnerable to being brutally deprived of one's bodily integrity, of one's identity as a male, and of one's ability to connect libidinally with females. This understanding of castration anxiety enables a richer appreciation of its significance, in both narcissistic and object-relational terms. Similarly, the counterphobic, hypermasculine characerological theme that develops to compensate for and to ward off castration anxiety can be appreciated as (1) a compensatory fantasy to counter feelings of being small, inadequate, helpless, and vulnerable (i.e., a narcissistic process); (2) a survival operation to prevent the destruction of one's identity and sense of self (i.e., a narcissistic process); and (3) a desperate attempt to preserve one's ability to connect libidinally with females, which has both oedipal and preoedipal implications (i.e., an object-related process).

In sum, the crucial precipitant of the process that eventuates in perversion, according to Freud, is castration anxiety that exceeds the regulatory capacity of the child's ego. While such a mismatch could result from either impaired ego function or unusually intense castration anxiety (or some combination of the two), Freud favored ego weakness as an explanation. He noted that ego weakness results from some combination of constitutional and situational factors, which I interpret to mean some combination of genetic predisposition and pathogenic experiences during the preoedipal period. I believe that no theoretical or clinical work since the publication of these papers has undermined the validity of Freud's basic theory. However, I do not believe that Freud's theory is an adequate theory of perversion. While ego weakness and overwhelming castration anxiety may contribute to the genesis of perversion, they are nonspecific factors that contribute to the genesis of a large variety of neurotic conditions. Defensive splitting of the ego also is not specific to perversion; and neither, I suspect, is the illusion of a maternal phallus, which can be understood as the fantasy of gender nondifferentiation or gender bipotentiality (for a discussion of the ubiquity of this fantasy, see Kubie [1974]). Moreover, if the illusion of a maternal phallus were specific to perversion, it would not provide an etiologic explanation so much as require one.

Payne

Early psychoanalytic literature tended to focus narrowly on neurotic symptoms and to underappreciate the character pathology from which the symptoms emerge. Writing about fetishism, Payne (1939) was one of the first investigators to observe that a perversion "is only one manifestation of a pathological mental state, which includes attacks of depression and anxiety, the presence of fears and phantasies of a paranoid type, suicidal tendencies . . . and serious inhibitions" (p. 161).

Payne identified two primary factors in the development of fetishism, weakness of the ego and weakness of genitality. According to her formulation, the core of the fetishist's pathology is a fusion of sexuality with sadism, which derives from his childhood sadistic fantasies about his parents' sexual relationship, his introjection of a sadistic primal scene, and his sadistic impulses toward his parents. Payne stated that the fetishist's weakness of ego is an aspect of his weakness of genitality, and reflects "interference with the libidinization, formation and integration of the body ego, especially of the penis imago" (p. 165). Unfortunately, this paper did not further clarify the nature of this interference or the origins of the weaknesses of ego and genitality. Payne observed that the weakness of ego development leads to an exaggeration of early defensive processes, particularly projection and introjection, and an exaggerated dependence on introjected objects, which is associated with an impaired ability for sustained identification. She suggested that the primary function of fetishism is to control sadistic impulses.

Fenichel

Fenichel (1945a) authored the first publication in which the term *sexual addiction* appeared (p. 384). Fenichel also was the first investigator to focus on the function of perversion as a means of defending against intolerable affects. He stated that the perverse sexual act "is carried out not only to obtain pleasure or to achieve punishment but also to get rid of an unbearable painful tension and to be relieved of a state of depression" (p. 384). Elsewhere, he observed that the primary purpose of perversion was to enable the individual to master, escape from, deny, or be reassured against depression and anxiety. Like Freud, Fenichel noted the counterphobic aspect of perverse actions. Also like Freud, he identified castration anxiety as the form of anxiety that is most relevant to the etiology of perversion, and regression to pregenital sexuality as a critical step in the developmental path from castration anxiety to perversion. On this subject, though, Fenichel differed from Freud in that, in addition to noting the alternate means of libidinal gratification that regression could enable, he emphasized the feeling of security that could be provided by regression to the component of infantile sexuality that had originally given the child a feeling of security. Fenichel saw the regressive drive in perversion as a condensation of instinctual urge and defensive striving for security.

Elsewhere, Fenichel observed that perversion represents a fixation at the oral phase of development, "in which striving for sexual satisfaction and striving for security were not yet differentiated from each other" (p. 368). He continued that, typical of those who function at the oral level, individuals with perversions demonstrate a desperate need for love, approval, affection, and prestige, which are experienced as necessary for survival, and they tend to react with violence to frustration of their needs. They experience other human beings in their world, not as persons or whole objects, but as deliverers of needed supplies. What Fenichel described under the name of perversion was not simply a disorder of perverse sexual behavior but a disorder of character or personality, which we would now identify as a narcissistic disorder. The main conflict that these individuals face, according to Fenichel, is between a tendency toward violence (in response to frustration) and a tendency to repress all aggressiveness through fear over loss of love; that is, fear of being more deprived of love in the future than they already are. He added that individuals with perversions are exquisitely intolerant of tensions, noting that they "act as if any tension were a dangerous trauma . . . any tension is felt as hunger was felt by the infant, that is, as a threat to their very existence" (p. 368). Fenichel attributed this abnormal sensitivity to constitutional factors, to experiences that foster fixation on oral and skin erotism, and to early experiences of trauma. Perversion, in Fenichel's schema, develops when the striving for sexual satisfaction, which is already poorly differentiated from the need for security, is condensed with the striving for narcissistic supplies.

Gillespie

Like Fenichel, Gillespie (1952) attributed perversion to a (partial) regression to the oral phase that is motivated primarily by castration anxiety. He added, however, that the castration anxiety that perverts experience is not an ordinary castration anxiety but one that has been modified by pregenital, especially oral, developments and also by the regression that occurs to defend against it. This regression, Gillespie observed, activates latent oral and anal sadism, which is then projected. The paranoid anxieties that result from this projection interact with or merge with castration anxiety, which consequently becomes more primitive and more intense. Gillespie did not speculate on what might make perverts more vulnerable initially to regress in response to castration anxiety, but his theory suggests how, once initiated, the process of defensive regression followed by intensification of anxiety could be self-perpetuating. Gillespie also offered an explanation for the splitting that characterizes perversion, which differs from the explanation that was proposed by Freud. For Freud, splitting develops initially as a target-specific defense, in order to preserve the fantasy of a maternal phallus. In Gillespie's formulation, meanwhile, splitting results from regression to the oral–sadistic stage, a stage in the development of ego function and object relations in which, Gillespie noted, splitting is a developmentally normal process. These different explanations for splitting in perversion are, of course, not mutually exclusive.

Bak

Bak's contributions to the psychoanalytic understanding of perversion include a paper (1953) and a book chapter (1965). In these theoretical works, Bak stayed quite close to Freud, closer than did Fenichel. But the minor changes that were conveyed in his understanding of ego weakness, and in his description of the phallic phase conflict between separation anxiety and castration anxiety, clarified Freud's concepts and provided an important bridge to later theories that were more informed by object relations theory.

While Bak's paper (1953) focused on fetishism, his theory appears to be applicable to other perversions as well. Bak observed that ego weakness could be constitutional, or it could develop secondarily through physiological dysfunctions or through disturbances in the mother–child relationship. He then suggested that ego weakness could account for inordinate separation anxiety, which results in clinging to the mother or to a substitute part of her. First, to Freud's principle that ego weakness results from some combination of constitutional and situational factors, Bak added the idea that situational factors could be physiological as well as psychological. Then, to Freud's statement that ego weakness leaves the child unable to manage castration anxiety in a progressive manner, Bak added the suggestion that ego weakness interferes also with the child's ability to tolerate separation anxiety. Bak then discussed the crisis that occurs in the phallic phase when the male child becomes aware of the genital difference between himself and his mother. Acceptance of his genital difference means giving up his pregenital identification with the phallic (or undifferentiated) mother and, in so doing, proceeding to separate from her. At the same time, the small boy's wish to give up his penis in order to maintain his pregenital identification with his mother threatens him with castration. The boy is thus caught between two desperate anxieties, separation anxiety and castration anxiety, both of which are unusually intense and intolerable when he also suffers from ego weakness. Bak then presented the denial of maternal penislessness, which forms the nucleus of fetishism, as a compromise between the wish to remain identified with the mother and the wish to maintain an intact, uncastrated self. He described the fantasy of a maternal phallus as a defense against the boy's wish to shed his penis, which he would otherwise perceive as an obstacle to maintaining his identification with his mother. Although Bak's paper preceded Mahler's earliest work on separation-individuation (Mahler and Gosliner, 1955), his discussion of the relationship between pregenital identification with the mother, separation, and perversion formed the cornerstone of later theories of perversion that focused on separation-individuation and gender identity (for example, those of Stoller, Socarides, and Ovesey and Person, which are discussed below).

In his later chapter on aggression and perversion, Bak (1965) reiterated his thesis that the dominance of pregenitality in sexual function is common to all perversions and involves a denial of heightened castration anxiety and a marked bisexual identification. Meanwhile, he also shifted his emphasis from separation anxiety to aggression. This shift can be understood more as a narrowing of focus than a change of direction, since, according to Bak, the danger toward which defenses against aggression are primarily directed is destruction of the (maternal) object. Since destruction of the object entails separation from the object (unless the object is devoured by the subject), threats that the object will be destroyed typically evoke separation anxiety. Bak noted constitutional and environmental factors that can contribute to an intensified aggressive drive. He identified overstimulation during the undifferentiated phase of development as the primary environmental factor. Such overstimulation may result both in damage to the neutralization function of the ego, and in the establishment of discharge patterns prior to ego development. When neutralization is impaired, Bak observed, the ego must develop other ways to protect itself and the object against unneutralized aggression. In perversion, several means of defense against aggression are employed: (1) denial of aggression, which is sustained both by projection—generally onto the father, which intensifies castration anxiety—and by libidinized reverence of the substitute or partial object; (2) identification with the maternal object, which reinforces the primary pregenital female identification and sets the stage for a bisexual identity; and (3) splitting and partial projection of the self in establishing narcissistic object relationships. Both the projection of aggression and the intensified female identification contribute to increased castration anxiety and a correspondingly increased need to deny castration. Splitting of the self, meanwhile, enables a narcissistic object relation to be maintained. Denial of castration and splitting of the self are then the foundations on which perversion develops.

Greenacre

Greenacre (1953, 1955, 1968, 1970, 1979) presented a theory of perversion that was more explicitly grounded in object relations theory and preoedipal development than were the theories of her predecessors. Greenacre attributed the origin of perversion to preoedipal disturbances in ego development, which result in (1) a distortion of maturing libidinal functions in order to meet narcissistic needs: (2) an intensification of castration anxiety; and (3) a tendency to rely on denial and splitting. Freud identified overwhelming castration anxiety as the dynamic origin of perversion; but, beyond alluding to ego weakness that results from constitutional and situational factors, he did not address what makes the castration anxiety of future perverts so overwhelming. Greenacre suggested that disturbed ego development intensifies castration anxiety in three ways: (1) the capacity of a defective ego to handle anxiety in general is impaired; (2) castration fear and guilt are amplified when insufficiently metabolized preoedipal aggression is directed toward the oedipal rival (and perhaps also is projected onto him); and (3) the bodily disintegration anxiety of earlier phases persists and fuses with castration anxiety.

While Payne (1939) wrote of ego weakness in perversion and Gillespie (1952) noted the etiologic importance of pregenital factors, Greenacre was the first investigator to consider in depth the relationships among perversion formation, psychic development, and early developmental history. The primary origin of the conditions that lead to perversion, according to Greenacre, is the impairments of object relations, body image, and self-image that result from a disturbed mother–infant relationship. When projected aggression exacerbates castration anxiety during the subsequent phallic and oedipal periods, the maturing sexual drives are distorted in the interest of bolstering the body image. A vicious cycle then emerges in which recurring castration panic triggers ritualized sexual behavior, which "may have more narcissistic than object-related value" (1968, pp. 57–58).

Greenacre identified two chronological periods when the child is particularly sensitive to pathogenic influences: during the first 18 to 24 months of life, and during the fourth year (ages 3 to 4). She emphasized that a pathogenic influence "is probably not in most instances the single traumatic event, but the existence of continuous traumatic conditions or the recurrence of severe traumas" (1953, p. 90). In the first period, the most significant influences are disturbances in the mother–infant relationship, particularly inadequate contact or overstimulation (i.e., activities that provide more sensoriaffective stimulation than the infant's motor discharge system can handle). Greenacre focused on how contact with the mother can function to modulate the infant's physical and emotional distress, and she revived Freud's hydraulic metaphor to convey this central component of her theory. She observed that varying combinations of mistreatment, overstimulation, and maternal deprivation can result in aggressive energy that exceeds the infant's capacity for physiological discharge. This aggressive energy, when it is insufficiently modulated by maternal contact, becomes "body-bound" and/or "overflows." Body-bound aggression manifests as body tension and a predisposition to anxiety reactions. The overflow can find discharge in rages, Greenacre noted, or it can be channeled to the genital zones as premature stimulation of erotized responses for which the infant is not maturationally ready. Greenacre identified four consequences of such precocious genitalization: (1) distortions in body ego development; (2) emergence of autoerotic habits that "blend with or displace the purer form of the transitional object" (1970, p. 448); (3) promotion of sadomasochistic elements in the incipient erotic response; and (4) intensification of problems of the oedipal period, "which is especially burdened by persistent narcissistic elements" (1979, p. 101). We can speculate that a likely fifth consequence would be an enduring tendency to automatically channel aggression and tension into genital excitement. Greenacre mentioned also the potential importance of occurrences during the first two years that disturb the developing body image. Examples include physical conditions that produce either actual changes in body size (such as edema) or subjective sensations of sudden changes in size (as might occur with fever). Such occurrences, she added, affect the infant's sense of his own body and can leave an imprint on the early emerging ego.

During the fourth year, Greenacre stated, a child is particularly sensitive to intensification of castration anxiety by real traumatic events that can be associated with castration, especially injuries that involve bleeding and mutilation, whether to oneself or to someone else. She observed, however, that more generally significant during this second sensitive period are the continuation of chronic or recurrent traumatic conditions from the first era, and the special effects of ordinary phallic phase developments under the impact of body image disturbances that originated during the first era.

Greenacre (1968) alluded to but did not name a disturbance in gender identity that characterizes perversions, which can be described as either bisexual or insufficiently male. She attributed this gender identity disturbance first of all to the persistence of unusually strong primary identifications with the mother, which results, according to Greenacre, from the infant's inadequate contact with the mother during the first eighteen months of life. Another factor that contributes to an insufficiently differentiated male gender identity is impaired postoedipal identification with the father, which, Greenacre observed, is a casualty of the boy's disturbed object relations. An attenuated capacity for object relationship and a corresponding increase in narcissistically driven aggression combine to replace object-related jealousy with envy, spite, and derogation, which in turn interfere with the boy's freedom to identify with his father.

While she initially believed that a syndrome of perversion always reflects a polymorphous perverse organization, usually in the context of an unstable or psychopathic character, Greenacre (1968) later observed that perverse development can occur also in relatively good character structures. She proposed that the degree to which perversion infiltrates the character with polymorphous perverse organization depends partly on the nature of the individual's superego development.

Greenacre noted that fetishism occurs almost exclusively in males. She attributed the gender difference to the greater visibility of the male's genitals, noting that "any failure of genital responsiveness in the male not only interferes with his sexual gratification, but is visible to both himself and his mate. Invoking an increased narcissistic wound, it requires a more drastic remedy" (1979, p. 96). As conditions in the female that correspond to perversion, Greenacre identified kleptomania and certain drug addictions. We could probably add bulimia to her list.

Glover

Glover (1940–1959, 1964) based his understanding of perversions on two features of sexuality by which it can function to enhance self-regulation: (1) the capacity of sexual behavior to relieve mental pain that is associated with guilt, anxiety, or depression; and (2) the capacity of libidinization to neutralize unconscious sadism or to reduce it to a less primitive level. The disposition to develop perversion, according to Glover, depends on three factors: (1) an excess of infantile anxiety; (2) unconscious sadism that is reinforced by a pathological degree of reactive aggression, which is consequent to infantile frustration; and (3) the countering of anxiety and guilt by the exaggeration of infantile components of sexuality, which moreover helps to contain aggressive impulses. While libidinization helps to contain aggression, sadistic impulses at the same time provide channels through which sexual energies are poured back into infantile object relations. These sexualized sadistic impulses, Glover noted, then activate the protective mechanisms of perversion formation. Later in life, when mental pain is intense enough to give rise to regression, primitive sexuality in the form of a manifest perversion can erupt as a means of relieving the pain.

Epstein

While both Freud (1905) and Bak (1953) alluded to constitutional factors, Epstein (1960) was the only psychoanalytic investigator who attempted to integrate biological theory and psychoanalytic theory to account for a form of perversion. Epstein identified the primary disturbance in fetishism as a state of increased organismic excitability or impaired organismic control, which he regarded as the product of cerebral pathophysiology. He suggested that some of the major manifestations of this state appear to be related to seizurelike phenomena that are found in temporal lobe dysfunction. We can infer that the heightened excitability or dyscontrol that Epstein described would amplify the child's sensoriaffective responsiveness, with the result that his or her affects and inner conflicts would be unusually intense.

Epstein characterized the typical mother–child relationship of the fetishist in much the same way as did other psychoanalytic investigators of perversion. He added, though, that increased organismic excitability or dyscontrol intensifies the child's responses to disturbed maternal behavior, and thereby exacerbates its pathogenic potential. According to Epstein's theory, excessive maternal closeness and seductiveness, in the context of heightened excitability, evoke unusually intense sexual feelings in the child. Epstein proposed that an unpredictable alternation between such stimulating maternal closeness and maternal rejection, in the context of heightened excitability, results in unusually strong needs to possess the mother orally. The condensation of oral needs with sexual feelings, he continued, further intensifies the sexual strivings and makes their satisfaction feel necessary for survival. The immature sexual apparatus, however, cannot discharge the sexual excitation, and anxiety may accompany the mounting tension. In this situation of increased excitation coupled with an unusually intense drive to possess (with its connotation of to destroy) the mother, castration fears are greatly magnified, and the anxiety increases. The solution, Epstein stated, is provided by the fetish, the symbolic mother that can be safely possessed. The fetish functions to reduce motor tension and is of particular use during periods of increased fear of abandonment. Fetishistic behavior, according to Epstein's theory, represents a result of both the forces of excitability–dyscontrol and attempts to establish control by providing a focus toward which sexual and aggressive drives are directed.

Cerebral hyperexcitability or dyscontrol, and the affective overresponsiveness with which it is associated in Epstein's theory, could represent the kind of constitutional factor that Freud (1905) and Bak (1953) hypothesized as contributing to the ego's impaired ability to manage castration anxiety, and that Bak (1965) and Kernberg (1967) proposed as a possible source of an excessive intensity of aggression. Epstein's theory also indicates ways in which constitutionally based affective overresponsiveness can interact with experiential factors in the mother–child relationship to intensify the child's responses and thereby also to intensify the pathogenic potential of disturbed maternal behavior. We may wonder to what extent the child's affective overresponsiveness itself contributes to the unusual closeness of the mother–child relationship, and to what extent the child's experience of rejection may reflect biologically based intensification of the child's affective responses to unmet needs, in addition to whatever the mother's actual behavior may contribute. Interestingly, at no point in his paper does Epstein refer to the cerebral hyperexcitability or dyscontrol in his theory as constitutional, innate, or genetically based. He thus leaves open the possibility that these abnormalities of cerebral functioning could result from processes that occur after birth. Although cerebral hyperexcitability or dyscontrol remains a nonspecific concept in Epstein's theory, the associated affective overresponsiveness constitutes an important bridge between neurobiological and psychoanalytic understandings of sexual addiction (and of other psychiatric disorders as well).

Hammer

Hammer (1968) focused primarily on the relationship between childhood seduction and the development of sexual deviation. Unlike the overt and covert preoedipal seductions to which other psychoanalytic investigators referred, the seductions that Hammer described occurred between the oedipal period and puberty. Hammer discussed the harmful effects that such massive premature instinctual stimulation can have on both the ego and the superego.

Concerning the ego, Hammer noted that fulfillment of incestuous wishes that are usually unconscious tends thereafter to make adequate repression impossible. Having experienced gratification of sexual impulses that ordinarily remain unconscious and ungratified, he stated, the ego subsequently does not tolerate frustration. Ego functions are stunted: an adequate ability to integrate and control impulses does not develop, and the capacity for neutralization and sublimation is greatly impaired.

Concerning the superego, Hammer identified the chief consequence of childhood seduction, which typically is initiated by a superego figure (a parent or parent substitute), as massive disillusionment. Such disillusionment tends to be associated with a shattering of ideals and a sense that superego standards no longer apply, that rules have no meaning. Hammer observed that the superego does not vanish but in fact becomes exceedingly rigid, harsh, and punitive, characteristics that he attributed to an intensified reaction of the superego to sexual overstimulation. Hammer did not consider other factors that could contribute to excessively rigid, harsh, and punitive superego functions, such as infiltration of the superego with projected aggression, insufficient superego integration, regression to primitive superego precursors, and splitting of the superego (splitting of the superego is discussed in chapter 5). The outcome of this process, according to Hammer, is a "spotty" superego that "can cause guilt but cannot, in collaboration with the weakened ego, afford controls" (p. 15). Hammer concurred with other psychoanalytic investigators that future perverts suffer from unusually intense castration anxiety during the oedipal phase, against which they defend themselves by regressing to preoedipal levels. Their weakened egos and spotty superegos then allow their preoedipal impulses, which have been energized by the premature sexual overstimulation, to override the remaining internal and external restraints.

Parkin; Zavitzianos

Papers on fetishism by Parkin (1963) and by Zavitzianos (1971) essentially reaffirmed the theoretical ideas that had been presented by Greenacre and others. Zavitzianos extended Greenacre's idea that kleptomania and certain drug addictions in females correspond to perversions in males, by proposing that fetishism implies a specific organization that is found also in kleptomania and in most cases of sexual promiscuity in women.

Khan

Khan (1962, 1964, 1969, 1979) added to earlier theorists a deeper understanding of object relations and of the vicissitudes of ego functioning. His paper, "The Role of Polymorph-Perverse Body-Experiences and Object Relations in Ego-Integration" (1962), explored the relationships among a disturbed mother–child system, distorted ego development, and the genesis of perversion. Khan emphasized that the pathogenic trauma in the etiology of perversion is a long persistence of disturbed interaction with the mother, rather than a single event or series of events. He observed that, as a consequence, an age level at which etiologically significant events typically occur cannot be specified. Nonetheless, his discussion of pathogenic processes in the mother–child relationship focused on the toddler age. According to Khan, the typical mother of the future pervert has a low tolerance for her child's distress and frustration, and moreover has specific difficulty in handling his increasing anal-phase separateness, defiance, and aggression. She disavows the rage and hate that these developments evoke in her, Khan continued, and she oscillates unpredictably between actions that seduce the toddler's ego, by sponsoring precocious ego maturity, and actions that seduce his id, by providing oversolicitous body love. The mother sponsors precocious ego maturity in the child by avidly affirming his nascent ego functions, by encouraging him to channel his pregenital libido into ego processes, functions, and defense mechanisms, and by treating him "as if" he were more mature and more integrated than his current development allows. Meanwhile, a consequence of the mother's affective dissociation is that, while she continues to comply with the child's body needs in a primitive way, she no longer cathects her participation in these activities. Her denial of the deprivation value of her withdrawal of cathexis from the child's body, Khan added, makes it impossible for the child overtly to react with aggression or to experience mourning, loss, and separateness. Instead, he institutes a dissociation in his self-experience, which can manifest clinically as "the ego treating the body (in contrast to the self) as the lost object" (p. 259).

Khan continued that, in response to the mother's sponsorship, the child's ego develops precociously, along with an identification with the mother on a mental level. At the same time, the child clings to a more primitive autoerotic bond with the mother, autoerotic in that the child focuses on getting pleasurable satisfaction from the mother while continuing to disregard her as an object. Perhaps even more etiologically significant than these distortions of ego development and instinctual development, Khan suggested, is the failure of integration between the two processes. Ego and instinct then develop in parallel, rather than in interplay, while each continuously "tries to bring the other under the dominance of its own aims and activity patterns" (p. 256). Khan observed that this developmental dissociation leads to disturbances both of instinctuality-affectivity and of ego function. The dissociated instinctuality-affectivity that develops outside the realm of ego regulation manifests in a formless, tense, inflammable emotionality. Perverts experience this emotionality as a threat to their ego, which they fear will be overridden either by the emotionality or by "crude id cathexes." They consequently cling to their ego functions and try to use them omnipotently to resist affectivity and regression. Meanwhile, Khan noted, they also crave to actualize and share this emotionality through sentient object-contact—a craving that their archaic anxieties and desperate defenses inevitably defeat. From the ego side, the precocious heightening of ego processes facilitates exploitation of the erotic potentiality of the body ego as a means of releasing affective tension. This technique, however, devitalizes object cathexes, with the result that true object cathexes come to be replaced by ego interests. Moreover, the aforementioned dissociation of instinctuality-affectivity and the excessive displacements from pregenital libidinal processes to ego processes leaves the ego out of touch with id cathexes. Khan observed that the subjective state that results is a persistent dread; a fear of alienation, instinctual emptiness, and inner deadness.

Khan identified two levels of functions that polymorph-per-verse body experiences and object relations can serve. On one level, they can function as a regressive form of affect defense: either to discharge tensions that are associated with insufficiently regulated affectivity, or to ward off dread by simulating a contradiction of the feared alienation, emptiness, and deadness. On another level, polymorph-perverse body experiences and object relations can represent a self-engineered attempt to achieve " 'a corrective emotional experience' " (1962, p. 247). Khan noted that these experiences can function as a mode of body empathy: a new means of self-perception that can facilitate the sorting out of confused images, memories, and affects. Even more critical, polymorph-perverse body experiences can express a search for an object (person) with and through whom the splits in the personality and the ego can be healed. They thus can represent reparative attempts to restore missed opportunities for ego integration. Khan described this second level of the functions of polymorph-perverse body experiences as "progressive," and he proposed that this progressive potentiality could be engaged in treatment and channeled to enable perverts to achieve insight and ego integration.

In a brief chapter on female homosexuality, Khan (1964) identified perversion as a magical defensive exploitation of pre-genital instinctuality in the service of fleeing from and denying dependency, inner hate, anxiety, and ego weakness. He attributed its development to distorted ego integration and libidinal development, particularly during the phallic phase. According to Khan's formulation, perverse sexual practices originate in a disturbed early mother–child relationship, which distorts both ego integration and libidinal development. During the phallic phase, the child attempts to express and psychically to articulate the consequent primitive conflicts and archaic affectivity through magical activity, restitutive masturbatory experiences, and submission to socialization. In the future pervert, these attempts fail, and the child falls back to a regressive solution in order to cope with the overwhelming affects and conflicts that this developmental impasse entails.

Khan's later paper, "Role of the 'Collated Internal Object' in Perversion-Formations" (1969), introduced a new element in his theory of the etiology and dynamics of perversion. *Collated internal object* is a term that Khan employed to designate a kind of representational structure that consists of amalgamated but not integrated residues of early self-experiences and partial object experiences. Such partial object experiences may include, in addition to aspects of both parents, the mother's dissociated unconscious processes and her fantasies about the child. In the context of a disturbed mother–child relationship, the precocious development of the pervert's ego enables him to compensate by idealizing those bits of environmental provision that fit his needs, intensifying in fantasy the fragments of maternal care that he receives, and compiling these idealized bits and fantasied fragments into a "collated internal object" (even though it was his own term, Khan usually set quotation marks around "collated internal object"). Khan hypothesized that the collated internal object is the equivalent in the pervert's psychic inner reality of what Winnicott described as the transitional object in normal development. The normal child develops a transitional object to facilitate separation from the good enough mother. The future pervert, on the other hand, receives disturbed infant care from the start, and develops a collated internal object to enable psychological survival in the absence of a good enough mother.

Khan proposed that the strictly intrapsychic nature of the collated internal object generates a continuous inner pressure to externalize it. Perverse sexual events and intimacies are the pervert's attempts to actualize his collated internal object and to experience it as an external reality. They provide a setting for this type of intrapsychic structure to be acted out, actualized, and known. Unfortunately, the hope that another person can embody and actualize this collated internal object is doomed to failure. In the course of the sexual "game," the other person's own needs and characteristics will gradually begin to impinge. The inevitable result is disillusionment. Khan stated that the primary affect in the pervert's inner reality is not so much depression as disillusionment, and that the pervert's basic anxiety is the twofold threat of annihilation and of catastrophic disillusionment. He observed that the pervert attempts to protect himself from traumatic disillusionment by striving after intensity of erotic experience. This intensity functions as the pervert's substitute for object relating.

Khan's three papers in the 1960s presented different components of his theory, which were then reworked and integrated in his book, *Alienation in Perversion* (1979). In this book, Khan described in more detail the pathogenic mother–child relationship that provides the matrix in which perverse tendencies develop. In the typical case, according to Khan, the mother idolizes the child, cathecting something very special in him and yet not cathecting him as a whole person. The child senses his mother's feelings and fantasies about him, internalizes this "idolized self" that his mother has created, and learns to tolerate the resultant dissociation in his experience of his self. Meanwhile, the mother's incapacity to administer doses of life experience that are phase-adequate for the child causes ego distortion. The potentially overwhelming intensity of the child's insufficiently modulated affects necessitates premature ego development and precocious use of defenses. As reliance on the body ego for release of tension devitalizes object cathexes, true object cathexes are replaced by ego interests. In the process, Khan noted, the mother and aspects of the child's self that are related to her through primary identification or through object-instinctual satisfactions become decathected. Associated with this split between ego interests and object cathexes is an analogous split between ego development and instinctual development. Khan reiterated a point that he had introduced in his 1962 paper, that ego and instinct systems then develop in a relationship of antagonistic parallelism, instead of a relationship of interplay, each trying to bring the other under the dominance of its own aims and activity patterns. In his book, though, Khan emphasized that the ego depletion (apathy) and instinctual dissatisfaction that result from this developmental disintegration motivate a search for an object that will enable the individual to unite these two parallel processes. The combination of ego precocity and developmental antagonism between ego and instincts also fosters an inordinate need to control, to "bring everything under the omnipotence of the ego." The stage has now been set, Khan continued, for the developmental moment when the mother becomes self-conscious about her intensive attachment to and investment in the child and abruptly withdraws, usually around the oedipal phase. The mother's withdrawal of cathexis causes the child to experience separation trauma, which is registered unconsciously as abandonment, panic, and threat of annihilation. Moreover, the mother's denial of the deprivation value of her withdrawal of cathexis prevents the child from reacting overtly with aggression or experiencing separateness, loss, and mourning. In response, the child intensifies the cathexis of his internalized idolized self and hides it from the environment. He also institutes a dissociation by which his ego treats his body as the "lost object," which is a composite of (1) good memories and pleasant affects that are associated with the lost good mother; (2) identification with the denial by the mother of her hate and rejection; and (3) repressed rage. Perverse body experiences then emerge as both a regressive attempt to discharge painful affects and a mode of body empathy in the service of differentiation and integration.

Khan observed that, once perverse sexual behavior emerges, it is maintained not only by its gratifying aspects but moreover by the potent reinforcement that is provided by both the general defensive functions of perverse experience and the functions of acting out in perversion. The general defensive functions of perversion include the following: (1) excited sexual states operate as a manic defense against acknowledgment of the disruptive upheavals in the pervert's childhood and of the consequent threats of despair, ego disintegration, and personality dissolution; (2) gratification from sexual discharge is a screen experience that is directed against anxiety states; (3) the cathexis of perverse experience protects against affective surrender to the object; and (4) perverse experience protects against awareness of the impoverishment of the pervert's true self, that it is "a very opaque state of nothingness" (1979, p. 176). The functions of acting out in perversion include the following: (1) passive traumatic intrapsychic states that threaten the pervert's ego are transformed into active, ego-directed mastery of objects in external reality; (2) libidinization of activity binds and partially neutralizes archaic sadistic and aggressive impulses, which otherwise could overwhelm the pervert's intrapsychic systems of regulation; (3) perverse activity mitigates the deadness in the pervert's internal world that results from archaic, excessive defenses against unconscious sadism and aggression; and (4) exteriorization (externalization) of primitive object relations and identifications provides the pervert with a chance to correct pathological processes that threaten to over-power his ego from within.

Finally, Khan proposed that, in perversion, the sexual object plays the part of an "as-if transitional object." He referred to Winnicott's (1953) statement that if the integration of ego functions is disturbed as a result of an inadequate maternal holding environment, then what in normal childhood are transitional objects turn into perverse relationships to objects (human and non-human) in adult life. Khan emphasized that the found object of perverse activity is not a real transitional object, but a target for externalization of a conglomeration of introjected part objects and primitive body states that he termed the *collated internal object*. The illusion that the found object can actualize and heal the collated internal object eventually shatters on the reality of the object. The result is disillusionment, which constitutes the primary affect in the pervert's inner reality. Khan noted that perversion develops out of a fundamental alienation from self, and represents an attempt to find personalization through sexual experiences: an attempt that inevitably fails.

Kernberg

Kernberg (1967) initially addressed the development of perversion in his discussion of borderline personality organization. He observed that individuals with a borderline personality organization develop an excessive degree of pregenital aggression, as a result of some combination of constitutional predisposition and excessive frustration of early needs. In children of both genders, according to Kernberg, excessive pregenital (especially oral) aggression tends to induce a premature development of genital–oedipal strivings, which results in a pathological condensation of pregenital and genital needs under the overriding influence of aggressive aims. In the boy, pregenital fears of the mother reinforce oedipal fears and prohibitions against sexual impulses, and a typical image of a dangerous, castrating mother develops. Projection of pregenital aggression onto the father and displacement of oral–aggressive conflicts from the mother onto the father further reinforces castration anxiety. Possible solutions to this conflictual situation include: (1) homosexuality, (2) perversion, and (3) promiscuity, in which attempts to gratify oral–aggressive needs in a heterosexual relationship reflect a fantasy of revenge against the frustrating oral mother by "robbing" her sexually of what she denied orally. In the girl, premature genital strivings for the father are used as a substitute gratification of oral–dependent needs that have been frustrated by the dangerous mother. This effort tends to be undermined by contamination of the father with pregenital aggression that is deflected from the mother and projected onto him, and by reinforcement of penis envy by oral rage and oral envy. The girl's possible solutions, according to Kernberg, include: (1) a flight into promiscuity, in an attempt to deny penis envy and dependency on men; and (2) a general reinforcement of masochistic trends, to placate the harsh superego that was internalized under the influence of projected aggression.

In his later book, *Aggression in Personality Disorders and Perversions,* Kernberg (1992) discussed the integrative function of sexual excitement as a basic affect that can overcome the primitive splitting of love and hate. He noted that the degree to which perverse tendencies are transformed into action depends on several factors: (1) the predominance of aggressive components over libidinal components in the individual's instinctual equilibrium; (2) the degree of superego regression or of disintegration of the superego; (3) the predominance of splitting processes in the ego; (4) the consolidation of a pathological grandiose self; and (5) the degree of weakening and loss of ego boundaries. One of Kernberg's central points was that polymorphous-perverse trends are part of healthy adult sexuality (as Freud [1905] also had observed). Manifest perversion develops when normal polymorphous-perverse sexuality gets co-opted by an individual's character pathology. Thus, Kernberg wrote, "the task of treating perversion is to free infantile polymorphous perverse sexuality from its entanglement with the surrounding psychopathology" (p. 276). Kernberg observed that the dynamics of perversion in a particular case vary with the individual's underlying character organization. He continued that organized perversions at a neurotic level of character organization present the psychodynamics that were originally proposed by Freud, while cases of stable perversion in the context of a borderline personality organization typically present the dynamics that were described by the British and French schools.

Kohut

Kohut (1971, 1977; Tolpin and Kohut, 1985) considered the perverse sexual drive to be a "disintegration product" that appears with the breakup of the primary merged subject–selfobject unit, and that is then enlisted in an attempt to bring about the lost merger, and thus the repair of the self, by pathological means. He traced the origin of perversion to sexualization that develops during childhood as an attempt to reconstitute a sense of self that is crumbling as a result of insufficient empathic selfobject responses from others. Kohut described three primary functions that are served by the perverse use of sexuality: (1) provision of intense feeling stimulation to reassure the self that it is alive and whole; (2) defense against depressive affect; and (3) expression of incorporative longings to fill in missing narcissistic structure. Via sexualization and perverse activities, the child attempts to soothe, to reassure, or to stimulate himself in order to substitute for the emotionally unavailable selfobject. Since loss of the selfobject's self-regulating function generally leads to more severe regressive states, the use of perverse sexual activity to provide this function stems the tide of regression and preserves the child's self. Kohut observed that the sexualization of pathological narcissistic constellations, particularly the pathological hypercathexis of the grandiose self, is furthermore used to counter the overwhelming affects that accompany the lowering of self-esteem in humiliation. Later in life, he noted, perverse sexual behavior can again be employed as a "counterfeit selfobject" to shore up a fragile or fragmenting sense of self or to protect against fears of abandonment. Tolpin and Kohut identified perversion as a form of addiction and noted, "like all addictions, it is meant to do away with a defect in the self, to cover it, or to fill it via frantic, forever repeated activity" (1985, p. 248). For Kohut, the tendency to rely on genital activity to provide selfobject functions derives from the narcissistic as well as the object-libidinal significance of the genitals, particularly during the phallic phase. At that point in development, Kohut (1972) wrote, the genitals "constitute the *leading zone of the child's* (bodily) narcissism—they are not only the instruments of intense (fantasied) *object-libidinal* interactions, they also carry enormous *narcissistic* cathexes. . . . The genitals are thus the focal point of the child's narcissistic aspirations and sensitivities during the phallic phase" (p. 374).

McDougall

Like many other psychoanalytic investigators whose writings on perversion were separated by many years, McDougall (1972, 1986) presented what amounted to two separate theories of perversion. She began her earlier paper, "Primal Scene and Sexual Perversion" (1972), by stating that sexual behaviors that are commonly regarded as perverse can occur also as part of a healthy sexual relationship. What distinguishes the pervert, she continued, is that he has no choice, that his sexuality is fundamentally compulsive. While McDougall identified a number of psychodynamic functions that perversion serves, she attributed its compulsive character primarily to a quest for the father, for someone who can stand between the child and the omnipotent mother, and whose "ideal phallus" can then be internalized. McDougall observed that the crucial factors that set the stage for perversion arise in the oedipal phase, but that the earlier mother–child relationship establishes the infrastructure of perversion by laying the foundation for how the child will approach the conflicts of the oedipal phase: "Behind the trauma of the mother's missing penis lies the global shadow of the missing mother" (p. 381). McDougall speculated that the mother of the future pervert, in addition to being missing (emotionally), denigrates the father's phallic function and gives the child the sense that he is a phallic substitute. The father, she added, appears also to contribute to his own exclusion, either actively or passively. Along with an idealized image of his mother, then, the child develops a representation of himself as an ideal child, the center of his mother's universe, and a representation of his father as devalued and excluded. The future pervert's inner world, according to McDougall, is populated by split representations of both parents. On the more conscious level, the child experiences the mother as an unattainable phallic ideal and the father as a denigrated object who is unsuitable as a model for identification. Unconsciously, in the split-off counterpart, the mother is experienced as mortally dangerous. The fear and hatred that this experience evokes typically is displaced to other objects. Meanwhile, behind the image of the denigrated father lies an idealized father or fantasy of an idealized phallus—a role that is frequently attributed to the mother's own father, or to a religious figure, or to God.

Once the infrastructure for perversion has been laid by earlier disturbances in the mother–child relationship, McDougall continued, the crucial factor is the "fatal revelation" during the oedipal phase that the child cannot fulfill the mother's desire. He moreover does not know what will satisfy her, nor does he know what his role is. The mother has denigrated the father's manliness, often with his passive collusion, so the child is ill inclined to turn to his father or to identify with him. McDougall proposed that the child who lacks an idealizable father from whom he can internalize phallic qualities is then driven to seek an external, symbolic father-object (1) to protect him from being destroyed by merging into the mother; (2) to provide him scaffolding for his separate male identity; and (3) to offer him a potent object for identification (so he will not be humiliated, as was his father). She noted that a critical motivating force in perversion is thus the drive to maintain one's own sense of identity, to stem the panic that accompanies a threatened loss of identity sense. Lack of a father in the internal representational world is of itself deeply threatening to a male's identity feeling. McDougall observed that the perverse sexual act "permits some illusory recovery of the paternal phallus, albeit in idealized and disguised forms; it thus fulfils an essential function in affirming separate identity and affords some protection against the overwhelming dependence on the maternal imago, and the equally dangerous desire to merge with her" (p. 379).

McDougall agreed with earlier psychoanalytic investigators that a primary function of perverse sexual behavior is to ward off intense castration anxiety. She added that the unusual intensity of castration anxiety in perverts results not only from ego deficits but also from the fragility of the future pervert's male identity. Significantly, McDougall's sentence that identified warding off castration anxiety as a function of perversion ended with the parenthetic clause: "(and in these individuals with their relatively fragile ego structure, any of life's irritations and disappointments is liable to arouse inadequacy feelings which call for immediate solution through the magical sex act)" (p. 378). Her implicit equation of castration anxiety with inadequacy feelings (shame) suggests that the classical understanding of perversion as a defense against castration anxiety and the self psychology understanding of perversion as a compensation for narcissistic injury may not be so far apart as they initially appear. McDougall identified a number of additional functions that perverse sexual behavior can serve: (1) to seek in an external object or situation what is missing in the internal world; (2) to protect the object (presumably, from one's own aggression); (3) to defend against depressive guilt; and (4) to manipulate the other person's sexual response, "actively making the object suffer what one once passively endured" (p. 378).

In her later paper, "Identifications, Neoneeds and Neosexualities" (1986), McDougall again identified the primary factor in the etiology of perversions as pathology in the mother–child relationship. Her focus shifted, however, from the twisted triangle and the quest for the ideal phallus to the disturbed dyad and impaired self-regulation. In the typical case, she observed, the mother consciously or unconsciously regards the infant as "a libidinal or narcissistic extension of herself" (p. 22), who is destined to repair her sense of personal inner damage. Pathology in the mother–child relationship interferes with the process of internalization, through which the child develops an autonomous psychic structure. McDougall proposed that the internalization process seems to break down specifically at the stage of transitional phenomena, and that this breakdown impedes the child's use of transitional objects in his or her efforts to separate from the maternal figure. Among the consequences of impaired internalization is a fragile sense of self, which is accompanied by an excessive fear of losing one's identity or sense of self. McDougall noted that perverse sexuality then develops to serve a number of homeostatic and adaptive functions. It compensates for what is missing or damaged in the individual's internal world that would regulate feelings and self functions. The sex act disperses feelings of violence, thereby preserving both external and internal objects from the subject's hatred and destructiveness. It shores up fragile ego boundaries and preserves the individual's sense of self, which is threatened by disintegration. Perverse sexual excitement functions also to counteract the feeling of inner deadness that is associated with a barren internal object world. The perverse sexual object and scenario become containers for the individual's split-off parts, which are mastered, in illusory fashion, by controlling the object or the scenario. Finally, McDougall suggested that the repetitive perverse scenario often reflects an acting out of an unconscious psychological drama that stemmed from the parents' unconscious erotic desires and conflicts.

Chasseguet-Smirgel

Chasseguet-Smirgel (1974, 1981) characterized perversion as a form of defense against feelings of inadequacy, shame, or narcissistic mortification that follow the oedipal child's recognition of his or her inability to sexually satisfy the parent of the other gender. She identified these feelings as a core component of the castration complex, as McDougall had done: "The reality is not that the mother is castrated, but that the mother has a vagina that the little boy cannot fill" (1974, p. 350). Chasseguet-Smirgel agreed with other psychoanalytic investigators that a central dynamic of perversion concerns denial of the genital difference between the sexes, but she added that what makes awareness of the genital difference so threatening is that it entails recognition of the difference between the generations, "which, for the sexual pervert, is equivalent to being sent to nothingness" (1974, p. 350). This threat of annihilation then mobilizes denial of the difference between the sexes, regression from genital sexuality, and idealization of pregenital sexuality. The idealization of pregenital instincts and part objects serves two narcissistic functions. In addition to compensating for the narcissistic threat of genital inadequacy, this idealization enables the future pervert to idealize his self by fusing with his idealized pregenital objects and instincts. In Chasseguet-Smirgel's words, "He mirrors himself in his exalted instincts, as he mirrored himself once in his mother's eyes, there to find the confirmation of his adorable perfection" (1974, p. 352).

As did most psychoanalytic investigators, Chasseguet-Smirgel identified failure to manage the castration complex as the etiologic fulcrum of perversion, and she attributed this failure to pregenital distortions. Similar to McDougall (1972), Chasseguet-Smirgel proposed that the mother of the future pervert encourages her son to believe that, with his infantile sexuality, he is a perfect partner for her, and therefore that he has no reason to admire or to emulate his father. Consequently, the young boy's ego ideal, instead of directing itself toward the genital father and his penis, remains henceforth attached to a pregenital model. Furthermore, deficient identification with the father and his penis results in deficits in both ego and identity (or sense of self). A primary function of perverse sexual activity is to fill in or to compensate for these functional and narcissistic deficits. Chasseguet-Smirgel noted that some individuals with a perverse character organization turn to creative activity in order to "confer upon themselves their missing identity" (1974, p. 352). This transformation of perversion seems to parallel the process that Kohut (1966, 1971) described as transformation of narcissism.

Rosen

Rosen (1979a,b) addressed perversion from a perspective that was informed primarily by drive theory and ego psychology. He considered perverse symptoms to represent a compromise between instinctual impulses (to discharge sexual tension and to establish a sexual object relationship) and ego defenses (to ward off oedipal anxieties, especially castration anxiety). Rosen discussed the pervert's characteristic pathology in terms of drive, superego, and ego components of psychic function. His initial focus was on increased drive intensity, which he attributed primarily to childhood sexual trauma from seduction, debasement, or deprivation, singly or in combination. Rosen observed that the childhood traumas of seduction or humiliation that seem to form the initial core of the later perversion occur in relation to the mother during preoedipal years. He continued that pregenital sexual seduction is traumatic because the intensity of the experience is beyond the infant's capacity to endure it. The ego anxiety that is aroused by being out of control is, meanwhile, countered by the hyperlibidinization that accompanies the pleasure in the experience. When active separation, deprivation, or rejection then follows the seduction, Rosen added, the sense of loss is doubly traumatic and contributes to a longing to repeat the experience of pleasurable closeness and togetherness. The groundwork has thus been laid for a pattern of compulsively repeating traumatic aspects of pleasure and frustration as a means of gaining ego mastery, and for a defensive process of turning passive into active that is enacted by doing to others what has been done to oneself. Rosen identified other significant consequences that can follow precocious libidinization of early mother–child experience—which, he added, can occur through actual seduction or through more subtle maternal narcissistic excitement. Precocious libidinization fosters both a high capacity for libidinal excitement and an undue sensitivity to frustration or rejection, which together promote the use of libidinal excitement to defend against the threat of rejection or object loss and the accompanying affects of frustration and hostility. Rosen also noted that childhood frustrations and traumas, whether related to precocious libidinization or to the caregiver's failure to meet the child's more basic needs for nurturance and soothing, lead to an intensification of aggressive drives. Intensified aggressive drives then increase the sadism of the oral and anal phases, as well as increasing phallic castration anxiety. Ultimately, Rosen stated, the most important result of childhood seduction is hyperlibidinization or erotization of anxiety, ego defenses, aggressive drives, and the accompanying affects. He added that narcissistic constellations are also libidinized, in order to protect the emerging self from the traumas of being dominated, overwhelmed, and devalued.

Following the developmental trajectory, Rosen observed that the excessive stimulation of precocious libidinization leads to an amplification of oedipal phase phenomena. A heightened awareness of sexual differences increases castration anxiety, which is defended against by regression to pregenital and especially oral defenses. Increased castration anxiety intensifies comparison to and competitiveness with the father, which tend to result in feelings of inadequacy and envy, instead of enhanced identification and masculine pride. Rosen noted that the father plays a crucial role in the development of perversion by failing to protect the child against the mother's anxieties and influences. The father's adequately masculine presence is essential for a boy to develop his own masculinity and to disentangle himself from preoedipal enmeshments and identifications with his mother.

Returning to consider the regressive defenses that are employed to protect against the intensified castration anxiety, Rosen observed that they involve drive regression and a regressive defusion of libidinal and aggressive drives. Aggression is thus deneutralized: it remains commingled with erotic elements, but it is no longer modulated through integration with them. This process leads to an increase in sadism, which gives rise to further anxieties that concern the dangers to object and to self that are inherent in sadism. Further defenses must then be instituted to ensure the safety of both. Rosen referred to a statement by Bak (1965) that perverse symptoms are regressive adaptations of the ego to secure gratification without destroying the object or endangering the part of the self that is identified with the object. Masochistic perversions, meanwhile, involve a conflict between hostile wishes and

placatory expiation of guilt, which is intended to preserve the
loved object. Rosen noted that masochism in perversions derives
less from punitive superego pressures than from an unconscious
fantasy of omnipotent mastery, which gains pleasurable gratification through suffering. The primary superego pathology in perversion, according to Rosen, concerns structural defects or
lacunae, which derive from the parents' superego pathology or
their tolerance of perverse behavior, and from deficient internalization of the ego ideal. The poorly integrated, grandiose ego
ideal embodies standards that are impossible to satisfy or to attain,
which leaves the individual's sense of self-esteem inherently unstable. Rosen noted that superego pathology then results in distorted
ego functioning. Weak, defective, and poorly integrated superego
functions fail to provide sufficient energy and structure for the
ego to contain the surging sexual and aggressive drives of the
oedipal phase. (We can infer that Rosen was referring to weak,
defective, and poorly integrated functions of superego forerun-
ners or precursors, not of the superego proper, which is generally
understood to develop through internalizations that accompany
the resolution of the Oedipus complex.) To keep from being
overwhelmed, the ego adopts as its own the powerful piece of
infantile sexuality that has been intensified by overstimulation,
and uses it to oppose and to manage the oedipal drives. Rosen
observed that the inadequacy of ego functioning in perversion
reflects not only superego pathology, but also defects in the ego
itself, which stem from pathology in the early mother–child relationship. However, he did not discuss ego defects in as much
detail as he discussed drive intensification.

While ego psychology structured the core of Rosen's theory,
object relations theory contributed to its elaboration. The object
relations component of his understanding of perversion was summarized in the sentence, "The perverse act in the adult is a plea
for togetherness and help, and a sexualized attack for the failure
to provide it, symbolically enacted in relation to the whole world,
directed at the primary object once more, still on a part-object
level, and with a disturbed sense of reality as a result" (1979a,
p. 47).

Each of the next four investigators (or pairs of investigators) to be reviewed—Stoller, Ovesey and Person, Socarides, and Glasser—focused on the psychodynamic and etiologic significance of the separation–individuation process and its characteristic conflicts. All of these investigators except Glasser emphasized the importance of separation–individuation factors in the development of gender identity.

Stoller

Stoller (1970, 1975) encapsulated his theory of perversion in the title of his book, *Perversion: The Erotic Form of Hatred* (1975). He understood perverse activity to be motivated primarily by fantasies of revenge for childhood victimization, usually at the hands of the individual's parents or their surrogates. Perversion, he wrote, "takes form in a fantasy of revenge hidden in the actions that make up the perversion and serve to convert childhood trauma to adult triumph" (1975, p. 4). Stoller identified the dynamic forces in perversion as hatred and sadism, and noted that the method of revenge is to dehumanize and humiliate the other during the perverse act or fantasy. He hypothesized that sexual excitement in perversion is most likely to be set off at the moment when adult reality resembles the childhood trauma or frustration.

Stoller stated that the difference between perversions and normal sexual behavior may depend on the frustrations and gratifications that the individual experienced during infancy and childhood, particularly in the mother–child relationship. Although he alluded also to gratification and victimization, Stoller focused on the etiologic importance of frustration by the parents of the child's biological demands. Stoller noted that the child typically experiences his parents' frustration of his urges as sadistic, and that "the tensions of each libidinal stage . . . are struggles in which triumph for the child would consist of being in control while the other person loses control" (1975, p. 128). Stoller observed that the transformation of frustration and hatred into mastery is not unique to perversion, but is an important process in healthy development. He noted that individuals often develop mastery by creating fantasies or modes of activity that symbolize restitution for passively suffered frustration. In perversion, the revenge fantasy represents restitution by a reversal of roles: "One moves from victim to victor, from passive object of others' hostility and power to the director, ruler; one's tormentors in turn will be one's victims. With this mechanism, the child imagines himself parent, the impotent potent" (1975, p. 106). The genesis of perversion, according to Stoller, thus seems to involve a hybrid of two defensive processes that protect an individual from being overwhelmed by trauma: turning passive into active, and identification with the aggressor.

Stoller proposed that the type of childhood trauma that leads to perversion is one that is directed at one's anatomical sexual apparatus or at one's masculinity (or femininity). He identified the affect that such traumas evoke as "castration anxiety," which he interpreted to mean anxiety about not simply the loss of one's genitals but the loss of one's identity as a male (or female) and of the aspects of one's sense of self and sense of belonging that relate to gender identity. Stoller stated that males are more vulnerable than are females to disturbances of gender identity. Early in life, both males and females identify with their mothers and thereby develop a primary female identity. In order to become masculine, then, the boy faces the developmental task of transforming his original identification with femaleness and femininity. Stoller suggested that failure to complete this transformation of gender identity is "the greatest promoter of perversion" (1975, p. 99). This theoretical principle, which probably owes its origin to Bak (1953), forms the cornerstone also of the theories of Ovesey and Person (1973, 1976; Person and Ovesey, 1978) and of Socarides (1973, 1988). Stoller proposed that perversion could originate in a "triad of hostility": (1) rage at losing the bliss of identification with the mother; (2) fear of failing to escape the mother's orbit (which is accompanied by resentment that she continues to pull him in); and (3) rage at being stuck in such a predicament, in which either alternative entails a major loss. We may note that the frustrations and predicaments that Stoller discussed, however important they may be in the etiology of perversion, are not specific to perversion but are characteristic of normal male development. Stoller did not consider what historical or constitutional factors might distinguish an individual who is likely later to develop a perversion from one who is not; for example, what factors might disturb the transformation to a male gender identity.

Ovesey and Person

Ovesey and Person (Ovesey and Person, 1973, 1976; Person and Ovesey, 1978) challenged Freud's (1905) principle that neuroses are the negative of perversions. They stated that neuroses and perversions alike represent compromise solutions to unconscious conflict at both preoedipal and oedipal levels of development; and they proposed that sexual symptoms, whether neurotic or perverse, can be understood primarily as various ways of allaying castration anxiety. They then focused on castration anxiety, which they described not as a basic form of anxiety but as a derivative of two types of component fantasy: (1) castration, homosexual attack, and being killed by the competitive male, originally the father; and (2) entrapment, engulfment, castration, and being killed during intercourse by the "vagina dentata" (vagina with teeth) of the female, originally the mother. Ovesey and Person stated that these fantasies typically are fused together and experienced as total annihilation. In the neurotic sexual disorders, they continued, the pathognomonic symptoms are inhibitors of pleasure. In order to allay castration anxiety, neurotic sexual symptoms impair the individual's sexual capacity, either partially or totally. In the perversions, meanwhile, the pathognomonic symptoms are facilitators of pleasure. They become the precondition—by allaying castration anxiety—for erotic arousal and release of the sexual impulse. Ovesey and Person noted, however, that the difference between inhibition and release of sexual discharge is not the only distinction between sexual neuroses and perversions. They agreed with earlier theorists that perversions differ from neuroses also in that they are characterized by a prevalence of splits in the ego, a predominance of projective and introjective identification in their object relations, and uncertainty about the boundaries of the self image and the body image.

Ovesey and Person's theory of the etiology of perversions (among which they focused on transsexualism, effeminate homosexuality, and transvestism) emphasized disturbances in separation–individuation and in the development of identity, particularly gender identity. Both boys and girls begin life in a subjective state of undifferentiated, primitive identification with the mother, and then later gradually differentiate their self representations from their mother representations. In addition to differentiating self representations that are separate from their representations of their mothers, boys must also disidentify from their mothers, in order to consolidate their gender identity. This pressure to disidentify from their mothers intensifies boys' separation anxiety during the separation–individuation phase of development. According to Ovesey and Person, some boys attempt to allay the intensified separation anxiety by clinging to a regressive fantasy of symbiotic fusion with their mothers, which entails a reversion to or continuation of the primitive female identification. The wish of these boys to maintain a female identification in order to ward off separation anxiety then comes into direct contradiction with their emerging male gender identity. The core of Ovesey and Person's theory is that those boys who will later develop a perversion navigate this contradiction by splitting their egos into incompatible male and female gender identities, which constitutes a fundamental disorder of the sense of self. Moreover, in order to preserve the mother as a good object, these boys typically split the maternal object representation into good and bad, and transfer the attributes of the bad mother to the paternal object representation, a process that was described also by Kernberg (1967). Abhorrence of a masculine identification with the hated father further reinforces the female identification. Ovesey and Person continued that both the unstable self representation with its partial female identification, and the transfer of bad mother attributes to the father image, then serve to potentiate castration anxiety. While the authors did not describe how these dynamics could potentiate castration anxiety, we can see (1) that a partial female identification could threaten a boy's sense of male identity (and all that a male identity entails); and (2) that projection onto the father of primitive aggressive, sadistic, or devouring attributes of the preoedipal mother representation could exacerbate the danger that the oedipal father is perceived to embody.

Ovesey and Person identified disturbed family dynamics as the primary factor that distinguishes the boys who will later develop perversions. In what they described as a typical case, the mother turns toward her son for gratifications that she does not receive from her husband. She is seductive and overpowering in her closeness to the boy. Ovesey and Person hypothesized that the mother uses the son to gratify herself sexually, but represses the sexual nature of her interest by denying his masculinity. The father, meanwhile, maintains his distance and fails to intervene with the mother in behalf of his son.

Ovesey and Person's (1976) description of the relationships among psychostructural vulnerability, painful affects, external reality, and perverse enactment in transvestism seems applicable also to other forms of perversion. They noted that transvestites tend to be anhedonic and to chronically experience feelings of loneliness and emptiness. They find relief from these painful affect states through preoccupation with perverse fantasies and through enactment of such fantasies. Ovesey and Person observed that the fragility of transvestites' reality sense and of their object relations renders them unusually vulnerable to external stress. Transvestites' self-regulatory systems are characteristically unstable and are easily overwhelmed by threats to their masculinity or to their dependent security. When stress overwhelms their self-regulatory systems, then, transvestites are beset by intense urges to enact, to convert their fantasies into reality. Moreover, Ovesey and Person noted, transvestites are typically unable to get what they need from real objects, as a result of impairments in both assertiveness and capacity to receive. They increasingly rely on fantasies and enactments to alleviate their anxiety, and their involvement with real objects diminishes even more. Enactment becomes a way of lending objective validity to their fantasies, and thus of reestablishing contact with substitutive symbolic objects to replace the objects that they have lost.

Socarides

Socarides (1988) distinguished between oedipal and preoedipal
forms of perversion. He considered the oedipal form not to be
true perversion, however, but rather to be perverse behavior that
is secondary to regression in a neurotic character. The central
conflicts in such cases, he observed, are structural conflicts that
concern the relationship between the subject's sexual or aggressive wishes and his own prohibitions and ideals. In the characteristic pattern, Socarides stated, unresolved castration anxiety leads
to the adoption of a negative oedipal position and a partial regression to anal and oral modes of being. Perverse symptoms are not
integrated into the character structure, but remain ego alien and
dreaded. Object relations, defenses, and other ego functions of
oedipal perverts are of the sort that typify neurotic individuals.
(In light of the distinctions that I discussed in chapter 1 between
"compulsion" and "addiction," syndromes of the type that Socarides identified as "perverse behavior" in an oedipal or neurotic character would probably be classified as sexual
compulsions. Meanwhile, syndromes of the type that Socarides
identified as "perversion proper" would be classified as sexual
addiction, if they met the criteria of recurrent loss of control and
continuation despite harmful consequences.)

Socarides (1973, 1988) considered perversion proper to be
a preoedipal disorder that originates in a fixation during the
separation–individuation period of development. The central
conflicts in this condition, according to Socarides, are object relations conflicts that derive from the simultaneous desire for and
dread of merging with the preoedipal mother. The predominant
form of anxiety in perversion proper, Socarides proposed, is not
castration anxiety but a variable mix of separation anxiety and
annihilation anxiety, the latter of which manifests around themes
of engulfment, ego dissolution, self-fragmentation, loss of self or
ego boundaries, and identity diffusion. In such cases, perverse
symptoms are integrated into the character structure and are ego
syntonic. Object relations, defenses, and other ego functions are
at the preoedipal level. Self boundaries fluctuate, splitting pre-
dominates over repression, remembering is often replaced by acting out, and affect regulation may be impaired.

Socarides observed that perverts lack normal self-esteem, suffer from impaired ego boundaries and self-concept, and have disturbed relations to internalized objects. He noted that perverts' ego and superego functions are insufficiently structuralized, which leads them to employ and evoke object representations to perform for them the controlling, guiding, approving, comforting, and punishing functions that individuals with a structuralized ego and superego are able to do automatically.

Perverse sexual behavior in perversion proper, according to Socarides, functions (1) to regulate self-esteem and to secure a narcissistic balance; (2) to ward off traumatic anxieties; (3) to remedy feelings of emptiness, helplessness, inertia, deadness, and grief; (4) to overcome aggression; and (5) to consolidate and stabilize a sense of self. It also facilitates the denial or disavowal of the "nuclear conflict" between the desire to merge with the preoedipal mother and the dread of the loss of self that such merging would entail. Socarides echoed Khan's (1965) statement that, by inducing dependence in their partners and compelling them into instinctual surrender, perverts also augment their sense of power, reduce their sense of isolation, and capture a pseudoempathy for the external world through a primitive mode of communication. Sexual partners, props, and rituals are employed as "sexual selfobjects," the function of which is to substitute for missing structures and for the functions that they perform.

Socarides hypothesized that perversion originates in a failure to traverse the separation–individuation phase and a consequent failure to achieve intrapsychic separation from the mother. In this context, he referred to Greenson's (1968) description of how the development of gender identity—or, as Socarides preferred, "gender-defined self-identity"—is more difficult for the preoedipal boy than it is for the preoedipal girl. The boy must undo the primary female identification with the mother before he can identify with the father, a difficulty from which the girl is exempt. The extent to which a boy can identify with his father depends on his ability first to disidentify from his mother. Socarides suggested that the gender asymmetry of this developmental challenge helps to explain the higher incidence of perversions in men than in women. Failure to traverse the separation–individuation phase, he continued, leads to faulty gender-related self identity, severe ego deficits, and an abnormally intense persistence of the nuclear conflict between the desire for and the dread of merging with the preoedipal mother. Among the difficulties that typically result are (1) disturbances both in the sense of self and in the development of sexual identity; (2) disturbed body self schematization; (3) impaired body ego and early ego development; (4) fluid ego boundaries; (5) a predominance of primitive mental mechanisms; (6) introjective and projective anxieties; (7) fears of invasion and engulfment; (8) an increase in early aggression; and (9) fluctuating states of object relationships.

Socarides stated that the original anxiety from which sexual perversions arise concerns the threat of being engulfed or annihilated as a result of the wished-for merger. During the oedipal phase, this preoedipal anxiety is compounded by castration anxiety, and specific ego and superego problems are similarly superimposed on the preoedipal fixation. Socarides observed that the oedipal phase is crucial for symptom formation because the capacity to develop symptoms in response to inner conflict requires psychic structure that does not crystallize until the oedipal phase. He added that the choice of a specific perversion is multifactorial, noting that it is influenced by traumas and by organizing experiences that provide the needed confluence of sexual stimulation, affective alteration, and narcissistic stabilization at vulnerable periods of libidinal phase progression.

Glasser

Glasser (1978, 1979, 1986) identified the nucleus of perversion as a fixation at what he called the "core conflict": the conflict between a longing for complete merger with the object and a fear of being engulfed and thereby annihilated as a separate identity. A considerable degree of isomorphism can be appreciated between Glasser's "core conflict," Socarides' (1973, 1988) "nuclear conflict," and the conflict that Bak (1953) described between separation anxiety (which, we can infer, is associated with the wish to be united with the mother) and castration anxiety (which, we can infer, is associated with the wish to maintain an intact self). Glasser observed that, as a result of this fixation, the child fears closeness and intimacy as annihilating, while he fears separateness and independence as desperate isolation. The threat of annihilation by merger with the mother, Glasser continued, provokes an aggressive reaction that is aimed at the preservation of the child's self and the destruction of the mother. Aggression is directed not only at the mother but also at anything that is involved in seeking to reestablish contact with the mother, including the child's own ego functions. Destruction of the mother, however, would bring about object loss and abandonment. Glasser noted that the child's ego may deal with this conflictual situation by splitting its affective impulses toward the mother and by denying (disavowing) the aggressive component. Often the aggressive component is projected onto the mother, who is then experienced as engulfing or intrusive. The child's ego can also split the internal representation of the object, in order to retain a loving relationship to one part and direct aggression toward the other part. Later in development, the child will have the opportunity to displace these aggressive feelings onto a third person, such as the father. Now, the child can displace the aggression only onto his self, frequently onto his body. The individual then treats his or her body not only as a vehicle for the expression of affects but also as an object (a theme that was noted also by Khan, 1962).

In perversions, Glasser observed, the ego attempts to resolve the core complex and its attendant conflicts and dangers by sexualization. Sexualization, according to Glasser, converts aggression, the wish to destroy, into sadism, the wish to hurt and to control. Glasser noted that the conversion of aggression into sadism can serve a number of functions. It can preserve the relationship with the mother, who is no longer threatened by total destruction, and thereby can stabilize the system. It can provide a sense of control, since a crucial component of sadistic pleasure is the implication that the object is experiencing what the individual wants her to experience. And, by conveying a sense that both participants are involved in the same affective situation, it can approach the longed-for merger with the object, while safe-guarding against the loss of self in the process. Conversion of aggression into sadism via sexualization can thus bring about a kind of resolution of the core conflict. Glasser observed that, in the perversions, no psychic function is free from being sexualized, including ego functions. Sexualization may be observed most frequently in those ego functions that were employed to make the earliest contact with the object.

Glasser (1978, 1979) located the origin of perversion in a pathological mother–child relationship. In the typical case, he observed, the mother has a markedly narcissistic character and relates to her child in narcissistic terms. She uses the child as a means of gratifying her own emotional needs, and she fails to recognize or tune her attention to the child's emotional needs. In her narcissism, the mother is both overattentive and neglectful. Her overattentiveness in treating the child as a part of herself is experienced by the child as intrusive or engulfing, it reinforces his annihilatory anxieties, and it amplifies his aggression toward her. Her neglect, emotional self-absorption, and insensitivity to her child's needs both frustrate him and arouse his abandonment anxieties, and thus also amplify his aggression toward her. The anxieties and aggression that are aroused in the child by the mother's overattentiveness and neglect intensify the affects and conflicts that are related to the core complex. Moreover, to the extent that the mother is responsive, her positive attentions tend to be inconsistent and undependable, often even teasing. The frustration, disappointment, and bewilderment that the child experiences in response to his mother's inconsistencies can further intensify his core complex anxieties and aggression, and can infuse them with a terrifying sense of unpredictability. Glasser hypothesized that the feelings that have been evoked by inconsistent responsiveness contribute to a subsequent sadistic need to control the object and to determine exactly how she feels and responds. He further noted that the child's coming to deal with his aggression through sexualization may itself be induced by the mother. The sexually stimulating (and frustrating) behavior of the mother may predispose the child to sexualize the conflicts around merging and individuation.

Glasser proposed that, in children who are fixated at the core complex, the oedipal prism is distorted. A central feature of this distortion, he noted, is that emotional relationships have a predominantly sadomasochistic character. Accordingly, the oedipal wish is not so much to destroy or castrate father as to humiliate or denigrate him: it is sadistic, rather than aggressive. Castration may represent humiliation as well as damage, and it is frequently expressed in sadistic or masochistic terms. Moreover, Glasser observed, the mother features more significantly than the father in the child's emotions, so the oedipal situation more closely resembles a dyadic relationship than a triadic one. The mother is often the predominating, castrating figure; and castration anxiety can often be traced to core complex anxieties. The so-called "phallic mother," Glasser noted, is a latter-day version of the powerful mother of the core complex. The father invariably has a lesser status in the future pervert's emotional life than in the case of a normal child, and he often seems to serve the function of a convenient figure for the displacement of various drives, split-off from those that are directed toward the mother.

Glasser observed that, in perversions, superego integration is impaired because identification is feared as invasive and annihilatory. While the individual wishes to comply with the superego, he also fears that submission to the superego would result in total annihilation of the self, so he regards defying the demands of the superego as an act of survival. Under such circumstances, Glasser added, passive resistance to prescriptive demands is more pervasive than active resistance to proscriptive limits.

Glasser continued that, with the increase of sexual drives at puberty, the core complex desire to establish absolute closeness (to merge) with the mother is intensified. When this intensified desire is allied with the increased capability of the ego to achieve its goals and, paradoxically, the weakened defensive strength of the ego, the danger of absorption into the mother and consequent annihilation is most intense and the aggressive response most extreme, which in turn entails the danger of destroying the object. The defensive reaction to this danger exploits the previously learned measure of sexualizing the situation, which can now make use of newly acquired sexual energies and capacities. Thus does perverse activity begin in earnest.

Stolorow

Stolorow (1975a,b, 1979) focused on the narcissistic functions that perversion serves. He characterized perverse sexual activity as a sexualized attempt (1) to restore and maintain the cohesiveness, the stability, and the positive affective coloring of a crumbling self representation; (2) to ward off self-depletion and self-fragmentation; (3) to revive a sense of having a cohesive self; and (4) to restore self-esteem. Stolorow made clear that he was referring to the self representation and the subjective sense of self, not to "self" as a functional or organizational entity. He noted that, in normal development, psychosexual experiences, fantasies, and enactments serve the function of consolidating the structural cohesion and temporal stability of self and object representations. He then proposed that developmentally arrested individuals, in whom self and object representations are insufficiently structuralized, may revive this developmental function of early psychosexual experiences in order to shore up a precarious and imperiled representational world. Stolorow mentioned also that both orgasm and the experience of having an impact on an audience (real or imaginary) have the capacity to increase an individual's sense of having a bounded and cohesive self. He hypothesized that the bidirectional potential of orgasm, which both promises enhancement of self-articulation and threatens self-dissolution, may account for the elaborate ritualization with which structurally deficient individuals typically surround their perverse sexual acts.

Stolorow observed that perversion is subject to the principle of multiple function. In addition to being an attempt to maintain a cohesive, stable, and positively toned self representation, perversion also represents primitive vicissitudes of object-instinctual investments and an effort to defend against dreaded object situations. Stolorow then proposed that the distribution of importance among the various functions in a particular individual depends on the individual's character organization. For neurotically organized individuals, perversion may function principally as a regressive defense against the threat of castration or as a hostile, vindictive triumph over traumatogenic early objects. In these individuals, the narcissistic function of sustaining the self representation occupies a position of low priority in the motivational hierarchy for perverse sexual activity. Meanwhile, for developmentally arrested individuals who have deficits in their ego functions and in their representational worlds, the most urgent function of perverse activity is likely to reflect their need to restore or maintain self and object representations that are threatened with dissolution. In these individuals, the narcissistic function occupies a high priority position in the motivational hierarchy for perverse sexual activity. Thus, Stolorow noted, "the clinical task is to determine the relative motivational priority or urgency of the manifold functions served by perverse fantasies and acts for a particular patient at a particular point in time" (1979, p. 41). The distinction between perversion that is associated with a neurotic personality organization and perversion that is associated with a narcissistic or borderline personality organization was discussed also by Socarides (1988) and by Kernberg (1992).

Goldberg

In his initial paper on the subject, Goldberg (1975) traced the origin of perversion to insufficient availability of the archaic object. The neutralization of drives and the formation of psychic structure through internalization, Goldberg observed, are interdependent developmental processes that both depend on the availability of the object. When the object is not sufficiently available, the consequently deficient drive neutralization and stunted psychic structuralization result in unmodulated drives and defects in the psychic structure. The individual is left with a deficient capacity to master many kinds of affects, which, when aroused, are then experienced as traumatic. Virtually any affect is capable of being experienced as traumatic: not only painful affects, such as shame and disappointment, but also pleasurable affects, such as joy and excitement. According to Goldberg, sexualization and perverse behavior allow for the mastery of overwhelming affects by recreating a situation that the individual, at an earlier time, had experienced as overwhelming. By sexualizing the entire situation, the individual converts a passive experience of being overcome by painful affects into an opportunity for active mastery in a sexual manner. At times, the feelings during the perverse activity are totally sexual; but at other times, a painful affect, such as humiliation or embarrassment, becomes part of the sexual experience. Goldberg proposed that these affects reflect an earlier traumatic situation in which a fragile narcissistic equilibrium was disrupted. He described perversions as "sexual displays of missing structure" (p. 341), which, in effect, function in lieu of the missing structure to stabilize the fragile narcissistic equilibrium.

In his book, *The Problem of Perversion: The View from Self Psychology*, which was published twenty years later, Goldberg (1995) placed greater emphasis on how perversion can function to maintain self-cohesion and to control the selfobject, and less emphasis on how it can promote mastery by converting passive to active. He also paid more attention to the origins of perversion. Goldberg observed that perversion serves three primary functions: (1) to fill in a structural defect, to maintain self-cohesion, to prevent regression, or to heal impending fragmentation; (2) to handle affects; and (3) to maintain or to control the relationship with a selfobject. While Goldberg did not make the connections explicit, we can see that these three functions represent three aspects of a single process. As a result of a structural defect that impairs the capacity of the pervert's self-regulatory system to manage affects, incipient affects threaten to overwhelm the system and thus to trigger either self-fragmentation or a regression that defends against self-fragmentation. This threat of self-fragmentation leads the pervert desperately to hold onto and to control whatever person or thing or activity serves a selfobject function. Goldberg described the process by which sexualization comes to be employed as a means of affect regulation:

> The specific activity of sexualizing is used to handle the feelings associated with narcissistic injury, namely, the failure of a selfobject. That activity soon becomes available for the management of

feelings that cover various situations, and the success of sexualization thereupon becomes the obliteration of feeling itself. In this way, all sorts of intense and potentially distressing feelings can be handled by sexualization [1995, p. 90].

While sexualization in perversion can be used to handle almost any kind of affect, Goldberg focused on two groups of affects that are particularly likely to trigger sexualization: (1) inadequacy, helplessness, or inability to control the other; and (2) empty depression, hollowness, or deadness. Goldberg also described the complex reciprocal relationship that exists between sexualization and narcissistic rage. He observed that both sexualization and narcissistic rage can function to substitute for and to defend against the experience of almost every other affect, and that either can be understood as a substitute for or a defense against the other. He further noted how each process can be activated in an attempt to compensate for the other. When rage threatens a tenuous relation with a selfobject, sexualization can be activated in order to hold onto the selfobject and to forestall further regression or fragmentation. Conversely, when sexualization evokes shame and humiliation, a rage reaction can be activated in order to right the self and to correct the narcissistic balance.

Turning from functions to origins, Goldberg identified three basic ingredients of perversion: (1) a diffuse narcissistic vulnerability, which is due to a structural defect in both idealization and grandiosity; (2) a vertical split of the self, which originates in an active disunification in the self in order to maintain a connection with a self-sustaining other or a selfobject (a process similar to the one that Winnicott [1952] described in the development of a "false self"); and (3) sexualization of the self. Goldberg attributed these developments to a disturbed mother–child relationship, in which the mother fails to respond adequately to the needs of the child during critical periods early in the development of affect regulation. He alluded to the importance of the oedipal period in the development of perversion, but he noted that the future pervert's disavowal, splitting, and sensitivity to castration anxiety derive from structural weaknesses of preoedipal origin.

Goldberg observed that damage to the self can result when parents fail to respond appropriately to their oedipal child's developmental needs. However, he did not say anything further about what distinguishes the oedipal periods of future perverts from the oedipal periods of others who do not develop perversions. In a similar vein, while Goldberg considered in some detail the dynamics and origins of the diffuse narcissistic vulnerability and the vertical split of the self that are associated with perversion, he did not address the third and most specific ingredient, the sexualization of the self. His theory does not indicate why some individuals with narcissistic vulnerabilities and vertical splits become perverts, rather than drug addicts or garden-variety narcissists. Meanwhile, Goldberg was one of the few psychoanalytic investigators of perversion who considered the sociocultural context. He noted that the sociocultural environment is relevant to the definition of perversion, "not so much as a standard but rather as playing a particular role in the psyche of the individual" (p. 22).

S. A. Mitchell

S. A. Mitchell (1988) observed that perversion can function (1) to defend against anxiety-ridden object relations; (2) to repair an inadequate sense of self; (3) to regulate self-esteem; and (4) to ward off dysphoric affects that derive from childhood abandonments, intrusions, and misattunements. He stated that individuals who engage in perverse activity have failed to fully separate and individuate from the intrapsychic representations of their mothers. They consequently feel that their identity as a separate person is constantly being threatened by fusion or engulfment from internal or external objects. They may experience sexual behavior as a domain in which they can assert their independence. Mitchell noted that perverse sexual behavior can therefore function both to defy the overbearing influence of the internal mothering figure and to define one's separate identity and self-boundaries.

PATHOLOGICAL HYPERSEXUALITY

Most of the psychoanalytic literature that addresses the etiology and dynamics of perversions does not extend the analysis to pathological hypersexuality, disorders in which socioculturally normal sexual behavior is practiced in a pattern of unhealthy excess. Two notable exceptions are Kernberg (1967) and Kohut (1971), who discussed both perversion and promiscuity in the context of character pathology and identified the same etiologic and psychodynamic factors in both syndromes.

A number of other psychoanalytic investigators wrote specifically about pathologically excessive heterosexual behavior, variously called "hypersexuality" or "Don Juanism" or "nymphomania." Fenichel (1945a) stated that both Don Juan behavior and nymphomania result from the condensation of the striving for sexual satisfaction with the striving for getting narcissistic supplies in order to maintain self-esteem. Erotic successes are intended to contradict feelings of inferiority and to reassure fears over loss of love. Fenichel noted also that when the urge to engage in this type of sexual behavior is not immediately satisfied, the individual is likely to develop sadistic reactions. Fenichel considered excessive masturbation to be a *forme fruste* of Don Juanism or nymphomania, which is practiced by hypersexual individuals who either lack the capacity for alloplastic action or are too inhibited.

While Fenichel focused on the gratification function of hypersexual behavior, Eisenstein (1956) emphasized its defensive functions. Addressing hypersexuality in males, he observed that it serves (1) to ward off castration anxiety; (2) to support repression or disavowal of passive homosexual wishes; (3) to restore self-esteem; (4) to overcome depressive tendencies; and (5) to counteract guilt and shame feelings by proving that the individual is worthy of being loved and favored. M. Klein (1957) addressed both the gratifying and the defensive functions of pathological hypersexuality. She stated that pathological hypersexuality is motivated (1) by a quest for sexual gratification, to compensate for inadequate oral gratification; and (2) by a need to defend against hatred of and wishes to destroy the oral mother, toward whom

ambivalent feelings operate. Klein focused on the premature intensification of genital desires and trends that can result when
the child's excessive envy of the mother interferes with adequate
oral gratification. The major consequence of such premature genitality, according to Klein, is a mixing up of oral and genital
trends, through which "the oral relation becomes genitalized and
the genital trends become too much coloured by oral grievances
and anxieties" (p. 195). The ultimate incapacity of genital acts
to satisfy oral needs, Klein noted, perpetuates the insatiable driv-
enness of "obsessional" masturbation, promiscuity, and compulsive sexual activity. M. Hoffman (1964) suggested that
hypersexuality functions both as a substitute means of maintaining self-esteem, and as an antidote to feelings of depression.
Eber (1981) emphasized the counterphobic use of hypersexual
behavior as a defense against shame anxiety. Shainess (1983) also
noted the function of sexual conquest as a defense against feelings of inadequacy, and she observed that the misuse of another
person indicates a superego deficit as well. Representing a self
psychology perspective, Trop and Alexander (1992) identified
the compulsive need for multiple sex partners as an attempt by
the individual to bolster a fragile sense of self by securing affirming and mirroring responses. Most recently, W. Myers (1995)
observed that "sexual addiction" serves a self-regulatory purpose
that is geared toward overcoming feelings of anhedonia or depression and toward neutralizing rage that derives from childhood interactions with the parents.

The most comprehensive theory of pathological hypersexuality was presented by Hershey (1989), who identified this pattern
of behavior as a manifestation of a character neurosis that integrates perverse processes into its defensive organization. The
character pathology also involves an incompletely integrated superego and a defense against or denial of superego affects. Hershey stated that pathological hypersexuality is characterized by
the predominance of ego interests over superego and id interests,
much as Khan (1979) had noted in regard to perversion. Sex is
enacted not from desire (id), but from an intent to regulate mood
and to further ego interests of mastery, power, and control. Hershey stated also that pathological hypersexuality involves a process

of regressive deintegration and idealization of deobjectified (de-personalized) drive derivatives. Ego interests thus take precedence over object interests as well as over id interests. The primary functions of pathological hypersexual behavior, according to Hershey, are to regulate mood and to defend against oedipal conflicts and affects, particularly those that relate to inadequacy. Hershey's etiologic theory follows the theory that Khan presented for perversion, which we considered earlier. In brief, pathology in the mother–child relationship results in chronic persistent trauma to the child, in response to which he develops a "collated internal object," Khan's term for an amalgamation of representational residues of early self-experiences and partial object experiences, which functions in place of a normal transitional object. Later in life, in sexualized situations, this collated internal object is activated and externalized onto the object of idealized drive, which is then manipulated and used in the service of soothing the self and avoiding depression. In effect, Hershey presented pathological hypersexuality as a perversion that employs sociocultural normal sexual behavior. This reshaping of the term *perversion* to describe a psychodynamic process, rather than a pattern of overt behavior, is consistent with most of the psychoanalytic work on perversion and echoes a statement that Devereux enunciated thirty-five years earlier: "A sexual relationship in which the behavior is normal but the object relationship defective is essentially perverted" (Panel, 1954, p. 337).

SEXUALIZATION: COEN

Finally, a paper on sexualization by Coen (1981) was an important contribution to the psychoanalytic understanding of both perversion and pathological hypersexuality. Coen (1981) defined sexualization generally as "the ego's defensive uses of sexuality" (p. 907), and more specifically as "the extensively elaborated use of sexual behavior and fantasy, in which defense has greater urgency and significance in the patient's motivational hierarchy than does sexual drive gratification" (p. 917). He identified sexualization as a key process in both perversion and pathological hypersexuality. In sexualization, Coen observed, sexual behavior and the grandiose self representation that accompanies it serve a central defensive role, with multiple functions in relation to narcissism, object relations, painful affects, aggression, and superego conflict, as well as in relation to specifically sexual dangers.

Coen located the origin of sexualization in maternal psychopathology and a consequently pathological mother–child relationship. The typical mother of individuals who later rely on sexualization, he continued, is a depressed woman with a character disorder. Coen noted that such a mother's empathic responsiveness to her child tends to be unpredictable, and that her ability to relate to him as a unique person in his own right tends to be impaired. She characteristically combines teasing overstimulation of the child with relative neglect of his emotional needs. Meanwhile, mother, child, and usually father too collude in protecting the mother from fully acknowledging the extent of her pathology. This pathogenic familial pattern is similar to the pattern that psychoanalytic investigators described in the developmental background of sexual perverts, and similar also to the pathogenic pattern that psychoanalytic investigators described in the early childhoods of drug addicts and bulimics. Thus far, Coen's theory does not indicate what would lead the child later to develop a sexual perversion, instead of drug addiction or bulimia.

Coen then proposed that the future pervert is distinguished by having a mother who relies extensively on sexualization in her defensive activities and in her relationship with her child. She encourages the child in a seductive pregenital relationship with her, which is gratifying to the mother, protects her from her own oedipal conflicts, and obscures her deficiency as a mother. The mother may encourage the child's illusion of his adequacy as her lover. This illusion of adequacy discourages the child from growing up, from identifying with the father in his adult masculine role, and from further differentiating from the mother. The mother's relative neglect of the child's emotional needs and her seductive overstimulation of him combine to give sexual feelings an unusually significant role during his early development. The child then draws on the predominantly available mode of relating with his mother to compensate for her relative unavailability and to stimulate her renewed interest in him. He identifies with the mother's sexualization in order to preserve the object tie with her. Sexual seductiveness eventually becomes the child's predominant mode for relating to others and for expressing his intense object hunger. Coen speculated that the functions of sexualization include: (1) to defend against an unusually large quantity of aggression, which results from early frustration, deprivation, and teasing overstimulation; (2) to counter other painful feelings, such as depression, helplessness, disintegration, and deadness; (3) to enact a fantasy of identification with the comforting mother and, thereby, of restoration of the symbiotic duality; (4) to differentiate oneself from the maternal introject, by hypercathecting the self representation as phallic and masculine; and (5) to provide an illusion of omnipotent control by self-sufficiently producing pleasure through one's own sexual act.

INTEGRATIVE RECAP

While the body of psychoanalytic literature that has been reviewed spans ninety years and a variety of theoretical orientations, the themes around which it crystallizes have remained remarkably stable. The underlying processes that psychoanalytic investigators have described in perversions not only are fairly consistent with each other; they also are fairly consistent with the underlying processes that other psychoanalytic investigators have described in pathological hypersexuality. While the latter have not been addressed as extensively as have the former, the etiologic theories that have been proposed for perversions seem to be applicable, for the most part, to pathological hypersexuality as well. From a psychoanalytic standpoint, then, grouping perversions and pathological hypersexuality together, as Kernberg (1967) and Kohut (1971) did implicitly and Fenichel (1945a) and W. Myers (1995) did explicitly under the rubric of "sexual addiction," seems reasonable. This grouping is further supported by the high rates of comorbidity between paraphilias and nonparaphilic sexual addictions that were reported by Breitner (1973), Carnes (1989), and Kafka and Prentky (1992).

Most psychoanalytic investigators would agree that perverse sexual behavior can occur in individuals at varying levels of character organization; and that the dynamics of perversion, and the distribution of importance among the various psychodynamic functions that perversion can serve in a particular individual, depend on the individual's underlying character organization. The majority of individuals who engage in perverse sexual behavior demonstrate a mixture of neurotic and preoedipal pathology, in varying proportions. When Stolorow (1972), Socarides (1988), and Kernberg (1992) distinguished between perverse behavior that occurs in neurotically organized individuals and perverse behavior that occurs in individuals whose character organization is at the narcissistic or borderline level, I do not believe that any of them intended to define a dichotomy. Freud (1905) focused on the child's failure to successfully negotiate the oedipal crisis; but he also stated that the ego weakness that constitutes the primary etiologic variable in his theory of perversion results from some combination of constitutional factors and pathogenic experiences during the preoedipal period ("situational factors"). In a similar vein, McDougall (1972) observed that, while the crucial factors that set the stage for perversion arise in the oedipal phase, the earlier mother-child relationship establishes the infrastructure of perversion by laying the foundation for how the child will approach the conflicts of the oedipal phase. Meanwhile, as Socarides (1988) indicated, symptom formation is a neurotic process that represents a maladaptive resolution of oedipal dynamics, however much these dynamics and the ego's resolution capacities may have been influenced by preoedipal factors. The triggering of perversion by oedipal processes does not imply that only oedipal processes are causally relevant, and the developmental priority of preoedipal processes does not imply that oedipal processes can be ignored.

Freud (1905) understood perversion to be the libidinal cathexis of a developmentally inappropriate object that emerges as a regressive attempt to cope with castration anxiety that the ego is unable to manage. The crucial precipitant of the process that eventuates in perversion, according to Freud, is castration anxiety that exceeds the regulatory capacity of a child's ego. Such a mismatch could result from ego weakness, from unusually intense castration anxiety, or from some combination of the two. Freud (1905, 1927, 1940) also discussed the psychodynamic and etiologic significance for perversion of the illusion of a maternal phallus and of splitting of the ego. The organization of the present discussion will build on the outline that has been provided by Freud's work. We begin by considering ego weakness, unusually intense castration anxiety, the illusion of a maternal phallus, and splitting of the ego.

Ego Weakness

The ego weakness that characterizes perverts can result from varying combinations of constitutional factors, physiological dysfunctions, and disturbances in the mother–child relationship (Fenichel, 1945a; Bak, 1953; Rosen, 1979a,b). Deficient identification with the father also can be associated with deficits in both ego and identity (Chasseguet-Smirgel, 1974, 1981), and seduction during the latency period can disrupt repression, neutralization, frustration tolerance, and impulse control (Hammer, 1968). Disturbances in the mother–child relationship that have been associated with ego weakness include insufficient maternal availability (Goldberg, 1975), the mother's incapacity to administer doses of life experience that are phase-adequate for the child (Khan, 1979), and early traumatic experiences (Fenichel, 1945b). These features of the child's world can disrupt his transition through the separation–individuation phase (Socarides, 1973, 1988); they can promote a dissociation of ego development and instinctual development (Khan, 1962, 1979); they can give rise to defects in both idealization and grandiosity (Goldberg, 1995); and they can interfere with the process of internalization, which results in defects in the psychic structure (Goldberg, 1975; McDougall, 1986).

The separation–individuation phase (Mahler and Furer, 1968; Mahler, Pine, and Bergman, 1975) is the critical period for the internalization of a number of important self-regulatory ego functions, for the differentiation of a self representation, and consequently for the development of the sense of self and other self-processes. It is thus likely to be a critical period for the disturbances in ego development that eventuate in perversion (Ovesey and Person, 1973, 1976; Socarides, 1973, 1988; Person and Ovesey, 1978; Glasser, 1978, 1979, 1986; McDougall, 1986; Mitchell, 1988). The separation–individuation process may break down specifically at the stage of transitional phenomena, which impedes the child's use of transitional objects in his efforts to separate from his mother and to internalize self-regulatory functions that she had formerly provided for him (McDougall, 1986).

Another factor that can contribute to ego weakness is presuperego weakness; that is, superego-precursor functions that are frail, defective, or poorly integrated, and that consequently fail to provide the ego with the structure that it needs to contain the surging sexual and aggressive drives (Rosen, 1979a,b). Similar to impaired ego functions, impaired presuperego functions can result from varying combinations of constitutional factors and disturbances in the parent–child (and particularly the mother–child) relationship.

Ego weakness can manifest not only in deficient ability to manage castration anxiety, but also in a variety of other functional impairments that are clinically relevant in perversions. Most characteristic is impaired affect regulation, as a result of which affective tension can feel like a threat to survival (Fenichel, 1945a). Separation anxiety consequently tends to be of traumatic intensity, which motivates the child to cling to the mother or to a substitute part of her (Bak, 1953). Affect-laden intrapsychic conflicts may be intensified to the point of being intolerable: for example, the conflict that the little boy experiences, on recognition of the genital difference, between the wish to maintain pregenital identification with his mother and the wish to maintain an intact, uncastrated self. This conflict can be understood as a conflict between separation anxiety and castration anxiety (Bak, 1953). A weak ego is more inclined to rely on primitive defenses, and early defensive processes are exaggerated, particularly projection and introjection (Payne, 1939). The capacity for identification and internalization is impaired, which leads to a fragile sense of self, an excessive fear of losing one's identity or sense of self

(McDougall, 1986), and an exaggerated dependence on introjected objects (Payne, 1939). This exaggerated dependence extends to external objects. Fenichel (1945a) observed that individuals who suffer from perversions demonstrate a desperate need for love, approval, affection, and prestige, which are experienced as necessary for survival; and that they tend to react with violence to frustration of their needs. They experience other human beings in their world, not as persons or whole objects, but as deliverers of needed supplies. Ego weakness is likely also to be associated with (1) disturbed body self schematization; (2) fluid ego boundaries; (3) predominance of primitive mental processes; (4) introjective and projective anxieties; (5) fears of invasion and engulfment; (6) an increase in early aggression; (7) problems with gender identity; and (8) fluctuating states of object relationships (Socarides, 1973, 1988).

Unusually Intense Castration Anxiety

Castration anxiety literally refers to the oedipal phase boy's fear that his father will punish him for his oedipal masturbatory fantasies by depriving him of his phallus. As we considered during our earlier discussion of Freud's theoretical contributions, the psychodynamic implications of castration indicate that castration anxiety can be more comprehensively understood to represent the anxieties that are associated with feelings of being small, inadequate, helpless, and vulnerable to being brutally deprived (1) of one's bodily integrity and hence of the integrity of one's body ego and body self; (2) of one's identity as a male and of the aspects of one's sense of self and sense of belonging that relate to gender identity; and (3) of one's ability to connect libidinally with females. This understanding of castration anxiety, essentially as anxiety about the vulnerability of one's body self to mutilation, enables a richer appreciation of its significance, in both narcissistic and object relational terms. Moreover, it provides a way in which to make sense of the female counterpart of castration anxiety, a concept that may seem questionable when it is understood only literally. Females, as well as males, experience anxiety about the vulnerability of their body selves to mutilation. Much as anxiety of this type in the male characteristically focuses on his penis, which is the distinctive symbol of his identity as a male and of his ability to connect intimately with females, anxiety of this type in the female characteristically focuses on her vagina (Mayer, 1985), which is the distinctive symbol of her identity as a female and of her ability to connect intimately with males. Perhaps "castration anxiety" is a less than optimal name for this anxiety, particularly since castration in the literal sense does not actually mean removal of the penis but removal of the testes (or ovaries). Though, for historical reasons, we would have difficulty parting with "castration anxiety," we might find that "genital mutilation anxiety" or simply "mutilation anxiety" is preferable. (This is not to deny that females may experience feelings of deprivation, narcissistic mortification, envy, or yearning when they discover that males have penises, feelings that could relate also to the power and mastery with which this organ may be associated. I believe that the counterpart of this complex, however, is not male castration anxiety, but similar feelings of deprivation, narcissistic mortification, envy, or yearning that males may feel when they discover that females have wombs and breasts, feelings that could relate also to the generativity and nurturance with which these organs may be associated.)

The unusual intensity of the castration anxiety that perverts experience derives primarily from preoedipal disturbances in their ego development (Bak, 1953; Greenacre, 1953, 1955, 1968, 1970, 1979; McDougall, 1972). Disturbed ego development can intensify castration anxiety in three ways: (1) impaired affect regulation renders any anxiety more intense and destabilizing; (2) the bodily disintegration anxiety of earlier developmental phases persists and fuses with castration anxiety, thereby reinforcing it (Greenacre, 1953, 1955, 1968, 1970, 1979); and (3) castration fear and guilt are amplified when insufficiently metabolized preoedipal aggression or sadism is directed toward the oedipal rival (Greenacre, 1953, 1955, 1968, 1970, 1979; Glasser, 1978, 1979, 1986). Primitive aggression and sadism can also be projected onto the father. The paranoid anxieties that then result merge with castration anxiety, which consequently becomes more primitive and more intense (Gillespie, 1952; Bak, 1965; Kernberg, 1967; Greenacre, 1953, 1955, 1968, 1970, 1979). The boy's father representation is imbued with aggression not only through the boy's projection of his aggressive impulses toward the father, but also by his displacement of oral–aggressive conflicts from his mother to his father (Kernberg, 1967; Ovesey and Person, 1973, 1976; Person and Ovesey, 1978; Glasser, 1978, 1979, 1986). The more aggressive (and the more primitively aggressive) the boy perceives the father to be, the more intense is his castration anxiety.

In addition to impaired ego functions, other factors can contribute to the unusually intense castration anxiety to which perverts are subject. The child can experience his mother as the dangerous, castrating parent, in which case preoedipal anxieties that are related to separation or engulfment can merge with and reinforce castration fears (Kernberg, 1967; Glasser, 1978, 1979, 1986). Castration anxiety can be intensified also by the future pervert's disturbed body image (Greenacre, 1953, 1955, 1968, 1970, 1979), by his unstable self representation with its partial female identification (Bak, 1965; Ovesey and Person, 1973, 1976; Person and Ovesey, 1978), and by the fragility of his male identity (McDougall, 1972). Finally, the excessive stimulation of precocious libidinization or sexualization can lead to amplification of all of the oedipal phase phenomena, including castration anxiety (Rosen, 1979a,b).

The relationship between unusually intense castration anxiety and unusually intense aggression or sadism, as well as the prominence given to aggression and sadism in some theories of perversion (e.g., Stoller, 1970, 1975; Glasser, 1978, 1979, 1986), invites further exploration of how these strong aggressive drives develop. As we saw earlier, ego weakness tends to be associated with impaired modulation of drives in general, and a particular prominence of insufficiently metabolized preoedipal aggression or sadism (Greenacre, 1953, 1955, 1968, 1970, 1979; Socarides, 1988). Preoedipal aggression and sadism also can emerge when regressive defenses against castration anxiety involve drive regression and regressive defusion of libidinal and aggressive drives (Rosen, 1979a,b). The unusual intensity of aggression in perversions may result not only from ego weakness and regression, but also from an underlying level of preoedipal aggressive energy that is abnormally high to begin with. Excessive preoedipal aggression generally develops from some combination of constitutional predisposition and disturbances in the mother-child relationship (Kernberg, 1967). Mother–child disturbances that can potentiate excessive preoedipal aggression include maternal mistreatment, overstimulation, excessive frustration, and deprivation of nurturing or soothing (Glover, 1940–1959, 1964; Bak, 1965; Greenacre, 1953, 1955, 1968, 1970, 1979; Rosen, 1979a,b). Aggressive reactions in the interest of preserving the self also can be provoked by threats of annihilation by merger with the mother (Glasser, 1978, 1979, 1986).

The Illusion of a Maternal Phallus

As I noted earlier, the implications of the fantasy or illusion of the maternal phallus can be understood at two levels. At one level, that a female also has a phallus implies that castration is not an issue. At another level, that females as well as males can possess this sign of maleness suggests either that male and female genders are not differentiated (gender nondifferentiation), or that an individual can be both male and female (gender bipotentiality). While denial of the vulnerabilities that castration can represent is an important theme, the place that the fantasy of the maternal phallus held in Freud's theory of perversion now seems to be occupied by the fantasy of gender bipotentiality: the fantasy that an individual is, or can be, both male and female. This fantasy derives primarily from regression to or abnormal persistence of the primary pregenital identification with the mother. The small boy reverts to or clings to the primary female identification as a means of warding off the intensified separation anxiety that he experiences in the face of pressure to disidentify from his mother, in order to consolidate his male gender identity (Stoller, 1970, 1975; Ovesey and Person, 1973, 1976; Person and Ovesey, 1978; Socarides, 1988). While the intensification of separation anxiety by the pressure to disidentify from the mother is a typical feature of normal male development, some boys are particularly vulnerable to being traumatically overwhelmed by separation anxiety. Such vulnerability can derive from a high antecedent intensity of separation anxiety, as in boys whose basic needs for attachment and maternal contact were not met during the first eighteen months of life (Greenacre, 1953, 1955, 1968, 1970, 1979); or from ego weakness of whatever origin, which impairs the boy's capacity to tolerate anxiety in general (Bak, 1953).

A fantasy of female identification in a male can be reinforced by impaired identification with his father. Hatred of the father, due to any combination of (1) hateful qualities in the actual father and (2) displacement onto the father representation of bad attributes that had been split off from the mother representation, can result in repugnance toward a male or masculine identification (Ovesey and Person, 1973, 1976; Person and Ovesey, 1978). Identification with the father can be impaired also by the boy's disturbed object relations. An attenuated capacity for object relationship and a corresponding increase in narcissistically driven aggression can combine to replace object-related jealousy with envy, spite, and derogation, which in turn interfere with the boy's freedom to identify with his father (Greenacre, 1968).

Splitting of the Ego (or the Self)

Whether or not it is reinforced by impaired identification with the father, a boy's fantasy of maintaining a female identification in order to ward off separation anxiety comes into direct contradiction with his emerging male gender identity. Those boys who will later develop a perversion navigate this contradiction by initiating a process that Freud (1940) described as "splitting of the ego." The core of this process is a defensive disruption of the ego's synthetic function, which manifests primarily as splits or dissociations in the individual's representational world. We may note here that "splitting of the self" is a more correct designation of this process than is "splitting of the ego," since the splitting that this process entails occurs in the representational world, not in the ego. (However, "splitting of the self" is not a wholly adequate term either, since splitting of the object representation also occurs and is of no less importance than is the splitting of the self representation.) Such splitting contributes to further weakening of the ego (Freud, 1940) and to a fundamental disorder of the sense of self (Ovesey and Person, 1973, 1976; Person and Ovesey, 1978). Splitting can be understood (1) as a specific defense to reinforce denial (Freud, 1940; Bak, 1965); (2) as a consequence of defensive regression (Gillespie, 1952); (3) as a result of preoedipal disturbances in ego development that weaken the integrative function of the ego (Greenacre, 1953, 1955, 1968, 1970, 1979); or (4) as a process that at first occurs as a manifestation of impaired integrative capacity and then later is used defensively to prevent or to contain anxiety (Kernberg, 1967).

In the etiology of perversion, the motive for initiating the split can be understood as a need to sustain denial of (1) the perception that a female does not possess a penis (Freud, 1940; Bak, 1965), or (2) the perception that males and females are different and dichotomous (Ovesey and Person, 1973, 1976; Person and Ovesey, 1978). Splitting can be further motivated by a need to maintain a connection with an object who is perceived as self-sustaining (Winnicott, 1952; Goldberg, 1995). In a broader sense, splitting in perversion can be understood to be potentiated by a basic conflict that has been described in a number of ways: as a conflict between separation anxiety and castration anxiety (Bak, 1953); as a "nuclear conflict" between the desire for and the dread of merging with the preoedipal mother (Socarides, 1973, 1988); and as a "core conflict" between a longing for complete merger with the object and a fear of being engulfed and thereby annihilated as a separate identity (Glasser, 1978, 1979, 1986). When ego weakness intensifies the affective components of this basic conflict while undermining the system's capacity to adaptively resolve the conflict, splitting is likely to be adopted as a means of avoiding the overwhelming affects that awareness of the conflict entails.

Superego Pathology

Freud (1905) stated that perverts are not the only individuals who have abnormal sexual instincts. He continued that the key difference between perverts and neurotics is that perverts' abnormal sexual instincts are directly expressed in fantasy and action, while neurotics' abnormal sexual instincts are "diverted from consciousness" (p. 165) and are expressed in neurotic symptoms. Freud recognized that some intrapsychic process initiates the diversion of abnormal sexual instincts from consciousness, and that this process functions more effectively in neurotics than it does in perverts. Not until eighteen years later, in *The Ego and the Id* (1923), did he introduce the term *superego*.

The degree to which perversion infiltrates the character and is expressed in fantasy and action depends partly on the nature of the individual's superego development, particularly its structuralization, integration, and resistance to regression (Greenacre, 1953, 1955, 1968, 1970, 1979; Kernberg, 1992). The primary superego pathology in perversion concerns structural defects or lacunae, which derive primarily from the parents' superego pathology or their tolerance of perverse behavior, and from deficient internalization of the ego ideal (Rosen, 1979a,b). A spotty or defective superego and fragmented ideals can result also from seduction during the latency period (Hammer, 1968). Structuralization and integration of the superego can be additionally impaired by the harshness of the superego that is introjected under the influence of projected aggression (Kernberg, 1967), by the characteristic lack of an idealizable father (McDougall, 1972), and by the individual's fear of identification as an invasive and annihilatory process (Glasser, 1978, 1979, 1986). While the individual may wish to comply with the superego, he may also fear that submission to the superego would result in a total annihilation of his self, in which case he would regard defying the demands of the superego as an act of survival. Individuals whose superego functions are insufficiently structuralized must often employ and evoke object representations to perform for them the controlling, guiding, approving, comforting, and punishing functions that individuals with a structuralized superego are able to do automatically (Socarides, 1973, 1988). Defense against the superego and denial of superego affect (Hershey, 1989) further undermine the superego's capacity to fulfill its self-governing functions. They thus facilitate the infiltration of perversion into the individual's character, and its expression in fantasy and action.

The Functions of Perversion

Perversion is a multiply determined syndrome, and it exemplifies the principle of multiple function (Waelder, 1936). It can fulfill a variety of functions, and the distribution of importance (rank order in the motivational hierarchy) among the various functions in a particular individual depends on the individual's character organization (Stolorow, 1975a,b, 1979).

In terms of classical theory, perversion represents a compromise between instinctual impulses (to discharge sexual tension and to establish a sexual object relationship) and ego defenses (to ward off oedipal anxieties, especially castration anxiety) (Rosen, 1979a,b). It functions also to compensate for inadequate oral gratification and to provide a feeling of security, since it reflects a level of development at which sexual satisfaction, oral gratification, and security are not yet well differentiated (Fenichel, 1945a; M. Klein, 1957). Perversion also represents a compromise between aggressive impulses and ego defenses, which in this case are directed toward protecting the object from being destroyed by the subject's aggression and, ultimately, toward protecting the subject from separation anxiety. This function of perversion is addressed below, in the object relations paragraph.

In terms of ego psychology, perversion serves the related functions of affect defense and provision of a sense of mastery. Perverse sexual behavior can function to defend against, to relieve, or to master intolerable affects, such as depression, anhedonia, anxiety, guilt, loneliness, helplessness, and grief (Fenichel, 1945a; Eisenstein, 1956; Glover, 1940–1959, 1964; Khan, 1964; M. Hoffman, 1964; Kohut, 1971, 1977; McDougall, 1972; Ovesey and

Person, 1973, 1976; Socarides, 1973, 1988; Person and Ovesey, 1978; Mitchell, 1988; Hershey, 1989; Goldberg, 1995; W. Myers, 1995); it can ward off dread by simulating a contradiction of the feared alienation, emptiness, inertia, and deadness (Khan, 1962, 1979; Ovesey and Person, 1973, 1976; Socarides, 1973, 1988; Person and Ovesey, 1978; McDougall, 1986); and, in a similar manner, it can function as a manic defense against threats of despair, ego disintegration, and personality dissolution (Khan, 1979) and as a counterphobic defense against feelings of inadequacy, shame, humiliation, and narcissistic mortification (Kohut, 1971, 1977; Chasseguet-Smirgel, 1974, 1981; Eber, 1981; Shainess, 1983; Mitchell, 1988; Hershey, 1989). In a general sense, perversion can represent both an expression of the ego interests of mastery, power, and control, and a means of enhancing ego interests at the expense of both instinct interests and object interests (Khan, 1962, 1979). It can function as a flight from and a denial of ego weakness and dependency (Khan, 1964). More specifically, perversion can serve as a means by which passively experienced traumatic intrapsychic states that threaten the pervert's ego are transformed into active, ego-directed mastery of objects in external reality (Khan, 1979; Rosen, 1979a,b). A significant aspect of this process of turning active into passive involves doing to others what has been done to oneself, and thereby actively making the object suffer what one once passively endured (Stoller, 1970, 1975; McDougall, 1972; Goldberg, 1975; Rosen, 1979a,b). This process can represent not only an interpersonal reversal of the traumatic experience of victimization, but also an intrapsychic reversal of the traumatic experience of being overwhelmed by painful affects.

In terms of object relations, perversion functions both (1) to express aggression toward the object and to affirm a separate identity, and (2) to preserve the object from being destroyed by the subject's aggression. One aspect of the aggression that perversion can express is revenge for childhood victimization, as we considered in the preceding paragraph. A wish for revenge can be inspired not only by active victimization, but also by early deprivation of needed oral and narcissistic supplies (Rosen,

1979a,b). In such cases, the revenge fantasy may involve "robbing" the frustrating oral mother sexually of what she denied orally (Kernberg, 1967). A second aspect of the aggression that perversion can express relates to the separation–individuation process and the wish to affirm one's own separate identity. Aggression can operate in the service of identity affirmation (1) by defying the overbearing influence of the internal mothering figure; (2) by defining the boundaries of the self; and (3) by protecting against the wish to depend on or to merge with the maternal imago (McDougall, 1972; Khan, 1979; S. Mitchell, 1988). Consequently, aggression may be mobilized when one's sense of identity is threatened, to stem the panic that accompanies a threatened loss of identity sense (McDougall, 1972). Meanwhile, perversion can function also to preserve internal and external objects, especially those that are intrapsychically associated with the oral mother, from primitive aggression and sadism (Glover, 1940–1959, 1964; M. Klein, 1957; Khan, 1964, 1979; Bak, 1965; McDougall, 1972, 1986; Socarides, 1973, 1988; W. Myers, 1995). In so doing, it also preserves those aspects of the self that are identified with the object (Bak, 1953). The simultaneous presence of wishes both to preserve the object from aggression and to express aggression toward the object (and to affirm a separate identity) is in effect a manifestation of the basic conflict that has been described as being between separation anxiety and castration anxiety (Bak, 1953), between the desire for and the dread of merging with the preoedipal mother (Socarides, 1973, 1988), and between a longing for complete merger with the object and a fear of being engulfed and thereby annihilated as a separate identity (Glasser, 1978, 1979, 1986). A constant theme in the psychodynamics of perversion is its function to sustain the denial or disavowal of this basic conflict (Socarides, 1973, 1988), or to provide a spurious resolution to the conflict by converting aggression into sadism, which conveys a sense of connection and control while protecting both the object and the self from destruction (Glasser, 1978, 1979, 1986). Beyond its specific functions in the context of aggression and the basic conflict, perversion also serves more broadly to fill in or to compensate for what is missing or damaged in the individual's internal object world that would regulate feelings and self-processes (Chasseguet-Smirgel, 1974, 1982; McDougall, 1986). In this context, the objects, activities, or bodily states that are associated with the perverse sexual behavior function as "as if" or ersatz transitional objects. The function that these objects, activities, or bodily states are intended to fulfill can be described in terms of object relations (transitional object function), self psychology (selfobject function), or ego psychology (external regulation of affect and identity sense [sense of self]). The relative interchangeability of these descriptions indicates the extent to which these different schools of thought represent not disparate psychologies, but different (and at times overlapping) sets of terms that focus on different aspects of a unitary psychological system.

In terms of self psychology, perversion can function as a splint for an individual's self-esteem or sense of self, as a prosthetic selfobject, or as an attempt to heal the self. Perverse sexual behavior can represent an expression of incorporative longings (1) to fill in missing narcissistic structure in order to regulate self-esteem; (2) to revive a sense of having a cohesive self; (3) to ward off self-depletion and self-fragmentation; and (4) to consolidate and stabilize a sense of self (Fenichel, 1945a; Kohut, 1971, 1977; Socarides, 1973, 1988; Stolorow, 1975a,b, 1979; Goldberg, 1975, 1995; S. A. Mitchell, 1988; Trop and Alexander, 1992). In these cases, the perverse behavior or its object is being employed, in effect, as a "counterfeit selfobject" (Kohut, 1971, 1977) or a "sexual selfobject" (Socarides, 1973, 1988), the function of which is to substitute for self-regulatory intrapsychic structures that are missing or damaged because the selfobject functions that were needed for the internalization of these structures during the developmentally sensitive period were lacking. Perversion can also represent an attempt to heal the self, in two senses. In one sense, perverse sexual behavior can function as an attempt to repair the sense of self (Kohut, 1971, 1977; S. A. Mitchell, 1988), a function that is continuous with the set of narcissistic functions that was described first (the "splint" functions). In a more profound sense, perverse sexual behavior can function as an attempt to achieve a "corrective emotional experience" through which the splits in the pervert's personality and representational world can be healed (Khan, 1962, 1979). The perverse sexual object and scenario then become containers for the individual's split-off parts, which he tries to bring together and master by controlling the object or the scenario (McDougall, 1986). Perversion thus can represent a reparative effort to restore missed opportunities for the integration of ego and self.

Constitutional Contributions to Etiology

Constitutional contributions to the etiology of perversion were not excluded by any of the reviewed psychoanalytic theories, but were specifically mentioned only by Freud (1905) and Bak (1953) as possible factors in the ego's impaired ability to manage castration anxiety, and by Bak (1965) and Kernberg (1967), as a possible source of an excessive intensity of aggression. Epstein (1960) identified cerebral hyperexcitability or dyscontrol as the primary disturbance in fetishism, and it could similarly represent a primary disturbance in all perversions. Epstein did not, however, indicate to what extent he believed this cerebral dysfunction to be constitutional. We cannot take for granted that conditions of the central nervous system are necessarily constitutional and not a result of postnatal processes, since significant development of the human brain occurs after birth and depends on specific kinds of interactions with the environment, particularly with the primary caregiver (neurobiological aspects of the development of perversion are further discussed in chapter 7). Cerebral hyperexcitability or dyscontrol could, in fact, represent a broadly described biological correlate of impaired self-regulatory ego functions.

Contributions of Personal History to Etiology

According to the theory that Freud (1905) presented, the key etiologic factors in perversions are ego weakness and unusually intense castration anxiety. Ego weakness, as we noted, can result from varying combinations of constitutional predispositions, physiological dysfunctions, and disturbances in the mother–child relationship, of which only the latter is typically explored by psychoanalytic investigators. We noted also that unusually intense castration anxiety derives primarily from preoedipal disturbances in ego development, which reflect the same factors that contribute to ego weakness.

Our earlier discussions of ego weakness and unusually intense castration anxiety implicated the following disturbances in the mother–child relationship: insufficient maternal availability; the mother's incapacity to administer doses of life experience that are phase-adequate for the child; and maternal mistreatment, overstimulation, excessive frustration, and deprivation of nurturing or soothing. Most psychoanalytic investigators have agreed that the characteristic historical background of perversion is a long persistence of disturbed interaction with the mother, rather than a single traumatic event or series of events (Greenacre, 1953, 1955, 1968, 1970, 1979; Khan, 1962, 1964, 1969, 1979). Psychoanalytic investigators have tended to focus on the separation–individuation period as the time during which disturbances in the mother–child relationship are most critical in the etiology of perversion. We now consider in more detail "the prototypal case" of the future pervert's early childhood, some but not necessarily all features of which are likely to have characterized the childhood of most perverts.

In the prototypal case, the mother has a character disorder with narcissistic features, and she may also be depressed (Glasser, 1978, 1979; Coen, 1981). She consciously or unconsciously regards the infant either as a narcissistic extension of herself, who is destined to repair her sense of personal inner damage (McDougal, 1986); or as a substitute libidinal object, toward whom she reaches for gratifications that she does not receive from her mate (Ovesey and Person, 1973, 1976; Person and Ovesey, 1978). The mother uses the child as a means of gratifying her own narcissistic and/or emotional needs, and fails to recognize or respond to the child's narcissistic and emotional needs. Her ability to relate to the child as a unique person is impaired, and her empathic responsiveness is unpredictable. In her narcissism, the mother is both overattentive and neglectful. Moreover, to the extent that the mother is responsive, her positive attentions tend to be inconsistent and undependable, often even teasing (Glasser, 1978, 1979; Coen, 1981; Goldberg, 1995). The mother typically idolizes the child, cathecting something special in him and yet not cathecting him as a whole person. The child senses his mother's peculiar experience of him, internalizes the "idolized self" that she has created, and learns to tolerate this discontinuity in his experience of his self. The mother, meanwhile, has a low tolerance for her child's distress and frustration. Furthermore, she has specific difficulty in handling the separateness, defiance, and aggression that he increasingly expresses during his anal phase. These developments evoke in her rage and hate, which she typically disavows. The mother both actively and passively encourages the precocious development of her child's ego. She actively encourages precocious ego development in the child by avidly affirming his nascent ego functions, by encouraging him to channel his pregenital libido into ego processes, functions, and defenses, and by treating him "as if" he were more mature and more integrated than his current development allows. At the same time, she passively encourages the child's precocious ego development by her neglect of his emotional and narcissistic needs. The child must then develop the capacity somehow to take care of these needs himself, however immature his ego infrastructure may be, lest he be overwhelmed by emotional and narcissistic trauma. Often, the mother oscillates unpredictably between actions that actively or passively encourage the child's precocious ego development, and actions that invite regression and seduce the child's id, by providing oversolicitous body contact. Meanwhile, a consequence of her affective dissociation is that, while she continues to comply with the child's body needs in a primitive way, she no longer cathects her participation in these activities. Consistent with her disavowal of aggression, she disavows the deprivation value of her withdrawal of cathexis from the child's body (Khan, 1962, 1979).

The mother–child relationship is not the lone locus of pathogenicity in the future pervert's family of origin. The father–child relationship contributes also, both actively and passively, and so does the mother–father relationship. In the typical case, the mother encourages her son to believe that, with his infantile sexuality, he is a perfect partner for her, and therefore that he has no reason to admire or to emulate his father (Chasseguet-Smirgel, 1974, 1981). The mother denigrates the father's phallic function and gives the child the sense that he is a phallic substitute (McDougall, 1972). For reasons that are both object-relational and narcissistic, the child is usually eager to adopt his mother's version of his relationship to his father. The father, meanwhile, seems to contribute to his own exclusion, whether actively or passively. He typically maintains his distance, he fails to intervene with the mother in behalf of his son or otherwise to protect him against the mother's anxieties and influences, and he colludes in protecting the mother from acknowledging the full extent of her psychopathology (McDougall, 1972; Ovesey and Person, 1973, 1976; Person and Ovesey, 1978; Rosen, 1979a,b; Coen, 1981).

After the infrastructure for perversion has been laid by these earlier disturbances in the parent–child relationship matrix, another crucial step typically occurs during the oedipal phase. This step involves the child's recognition that he is unable to sexually satisfy his mother (McDougall, 1972; Chasseguet-Smirgel, 1974, 1981), or the mother's abrupt withdrawal when she becomes self-conscious about her intensive attachment to and investment in the child (Khan, 1979). This process evokes in the child a combination of castration anxiety, separation anxiety, and narcissistic mortification, which are experienced in the context of the serious preexisting vulnerabilities that were mentioned earlier. The child then develops a perversion, which enables him to maintain a coherent sense of self in the face of these overwhelmingly painful affects.

The foregoing account is helpful, but only up to a point. That point is the account's final sentence, in which the development of a perversion is identified as the outcome of the processes that had been discussed. Up until then, the psychodynamics and history that were described are consistent with a character disorder—most likely in the narcissistic range, but possibly a neurotic character or a frank borderline—that harbors a predilection to develop a perversion, or a psychoactive substance addiction, or an impulsive–compulsive neurosis such as bulimia or pathological gambling. What is not clear, from the foregoing account, is what would lead an individual with psychodynamics and history similar to those that have been described to develop a perversion, rather than one of the other disorders. In other words, the functions that sexual behavior serves in perversions can conceivably be served also by other kinds of behavior, such as taking alcohol or some other drug, or eating, or gambling. What leads the pervert to select sexual behavior to fulfill these functions? The critical factor seems to be the relative influence of sexualization in the individual's psychic life.

Sexualization

Coen (1981) defined sexualization as "the ego's defensive use of sexuality" (p. 907). Sexualization involves the co-opting of a basic drive by the ego for purposes of defense, a process the only other example of which is narcissistic rage. Goldberg (1995) described the complex reciprocal relationship between sexualization and narcissistic rage, noting that either can function to substitute for and defend against the experience of almost every other affect, and that either can substitute for or defend against the other. Not all psychoanalytic investigators of perversion discussed sexualization (or genitalization or libidinization) as a process that is distinct from perversion itself. The following review will include theories that address factors that contribute to the disposition to use sexuality in the service of defense, however this disposition is identified.

Sexualization has been thought to originate in the preoedipal period, as a result of some combination of (1) condensation of oral and sexual trends; (2) inadequate selfobject responsiveness; (3) genital channeling of overflow aggression; (4) maternal seductiveness; and (5) identification with the mother's sexualization.

Fenichel (1945a), M. Klein (1957), Epstein (1960), and Kernberg (1967) associated the development of perversion with a blending or condensation of oral needs with genital sexual feel-ings. One view of such a condensation might predict its outcome to be an alteration of the gratification component of genital sexu-ality, rather than a potentiation of its use for defense. However, a major consequence of the condensation of oral needs with genital sexual feelings is the tendency to use genital sexual fantasy and behavior in attempts to defend against affects, impulses, and pain-ful senses of self that are associated with oral deprivation or frus-tration. Fenichel (1945a) ascribed the blending of oral and genital sexual trends to regression to a fixation point during the oral phase of development, in which oral libido and genital libido are not yet fully differentiated from one another. Klein (1957) and Kernberg (1967) both attributed the condensation of pre-genital and genital needs to premature development of genital strivings. Klein hypothesized that such premature genitality emerges in an attempt to compensate for inadequate oral gratifi-cation that results from interference by the child's excessive envy of the mother. Epstein (1960) did not try to account for it—at least, not in the paper that we have been considering. To whatever extent the condensation of oral needs with genital sexual feelings is associated with sexualization, it may be more useful as a descrip-tion than as an explanation. It does not add significantly to the information that is conveyed in the definition of sexualization, beyond specifying the developmental origin of what is being de-fended against. Moreover, oral–genital condensation and the fac-tors to which it was attributed—regression to a point of oral fixation and inadequate oral gratification—contribute to a broad range of symptomatic and characterological difficulties, and thus are not specific to sexualization.

Kohut (1971, 1977) proposed that sexualization develops as an attempt to reconstitute a sense of self that is crumbling as a result of insufficient empathic selfobject responses from others. Elsewhere, Kohut (1972) observed that the tendency to rely on genital activity to provide selfobject functions derives from the narcissistic as well as the object-libidinal significance of the geni-tals, particularly during the phallic phase. Stolorow's (1975a,b, 1979) contributions expanded and stabilized the foundation of Kohut's account of sexualization. Stolorow noted that, in normal development, psychosexual experiences, fantasies, and enactments serve the function of consolidating the structural cohesion and the temporal stability of self and object representations. He mentioned also that orgasm has the capacity to increase an individual's sense of having a bounded and cohesive self. These developmental functions of sexual fantasy and activity enhance our understanding of the relationship between selfobject deprivation and later reliance on genital activity to serve narcissistic functions. They do not, however, help to explain why sexualization becomes a prominent mode of defense in some but not all individuals who suffer selfobject deprivation.

M. Klein (1957) located the origin of driven sexuality in premature genitality, which emerges from the confluence of (1) a drive to compensate for inadequate oral gratification and (2) a defense against hating and injuring the ambivalently cathected oral mother. Glover (1940–1959, 1964) also alluded to the capacity of libidinization to help in the containment of aggressive impulses. Kernberg (1967) stated that premature genitalization is induced by excessive pregenital (especially oral) aggression, but he did not indicate what might be involved in the induction. Greenacre (1953, 1955, 1968, 1970, 1979) described a process that is initiated when varying combinations of mistreatment, overstimulation, and maternal deprivation evoke aggressive energy that exceeds the infant's capacity for physiological discharge. When this aggressive energy is insufficiently modulated by maternal contact, it can overflow and find discharge in rages, or it can be channeled to the genital zones as premature stimulation of erotized responses for which the child is not maturationally ready. (Incidentally, this interchangeability of rage and genitalization as solutions to the problem of preoedipal aggressive overflow could provide a foundation for the reciprocal relationship between sexualization and narcissistic rage that Goldberg [1995] described.) Greenacre identified four consequences of such precocious genitalization: (1) distortions in body ego development; (2) the emergence of autoerotic behavior that is enacted in order to fulfill transitional object functions; (3) the promotion of sadomasochistic elements in the incipient erotic response; and (4) an intensification of problems of the oedipal period, which is burdened by unresolved narcissistic issues. A likely fifth consequence would be an enduring tendency to automatically channel aggression and tension into genital excitement. Khan (1962, 1979) presented a theory in which precocious ego development, rather than precocious genitalization, is the developmental intermediary between preoedipal aggressive overflow and sexualization. He hypothesized that the precocious heightening of ego processes facilitates exploitation of the erotic potential of the body ego as a means of discharging aggression and other affective tensions. Glasser (1978, 1979), meanwhile, proposed that the child's coming to deal with his aggression through sexualization may be induced by the mother. He hypothesized that the sexually stimulating (and frustrating) behavior of the mother, in the context of the child's ongoing separation–individuation struggle, may predispose the child to sexualize the aggressive components of his conflicts around merging and individuation. A specific consequence of such sexualization, according to Glasser, is the conversion of aggression (the wish to destroy) to sadism (the wish to hurt and control) in an attempt to resolve the basic conflict of separation–individuation and its attendant conflicts and dangers. Greenacre's theory of precocious genitalization, while intuitively sound and clinically meaningful, is characterized by the same lack of specificity that we observed in other approaches to sexualization. It enhances our understanding of the relationships among preoedipal aggression, sexualization, and narcissistic rage, but it does not help to explain why sexualization becomes a prominent mode of defense in some but not all individuals who suffered preoedipal aggressive overflow. Such an explanation would need to specify features of constitutional endowment and/or early caregiving environment that would distinguish those individuals for whom sexualization becomes a prominent mode of defense from those for whom it does not. Khan's theory, as rich in insight as it is, suffers from the same lack of specificity as does Greenacre's theory. Glasser's theory includes the mother's behavior as an independent variable in the process that eventuates in sexualization, and it thus indicates a direction in which our search for etiologic specificity might be more fruitful.

A number of psychoanalytic investigators considered the specific origin of sexualization to be maternal seductiveness. Epstein (1960) characterized the primary disturbance in perversion as a state of increased cerebral excitability or dyscontrol, which amplifies the child's sensoriaffective responsiveness. He proposed that excessive maternal closeness and seductiveness, in the context of heightened excitability, evoke unusually intense sexual feelings in the child. He continued that the child's immature sexual apparatus, however, cannot discharge the sexual excitation, which consequently becomes associated with body tension and anxiety. Later in development, body tension and anxiety may be experienced as sexual excitation, and sexual fantasies and behavior can then be employed (defensively) to reduce tension and anxiety. Ovesey and Person (1973, 1976; Person and Ovesey, 1978) also identified maternal seductiveness as the primary factor that distinguishes the boys who will later develop a perversion. In the typical case, they observed, the mother turns toward her son for gratifications that she does not receive from her mate. She is seductive and overpowering in her closeness to the boy. Ovesey and Person hypothesized that the mother uses the son to gratify herself sexually, but represses (or disavows) the sexual nature of her interest by denying his masculinity. Rosen (1979a,b) traced the origin of perversion to precocious libidinization of early mother–child experience, which he attributed either to actual seduction or to more subtle maternal narcissistic excitement. He observed that pregenital sexual seduction is traumatic because the intensity of the experience is beyond the infant's capacity to endure it. The ego anxiety that is aroused by being out of control is, meanwhile, countered by the hyperlibidinization that accompanies the pleasure in the experience. Rosen noted that precocious libidinization fosters both a high capacity for libidinal excitement and an undue sensitivity to frustration or rejection, which together promote the use of libidinal excitement to defend against the threat of rejection or object loss and the accompanying affects of frustration and rage. He stated that the most important result of childhood seduction is hyperlibidinization or erotization of anxiety, ego defenses, aggressive drives, and the accompanying affects. Rosen added that narcissistic constellations also are libidinized, in order to protect the emerging self from the traumas of being mastered, overwhelmed, and devalued.

Coen (1981) proposed that the development of sexualization is associated with a mother who not only relates to her child in a seductive manner, but also herself relies extensively on sexualization in her defensive activities and in her relationship with her child. Thus, Coen agreed with the investigators who attributed the future pervert's sexualization to maternal seductiveness. He added that the future pervert's sexualization is moreover shaped by identification with the mother's sexualization. In the typical case, Coen observed, the mother encourages the child in a seductive pregenital relationship with her, which is gratifying to the mother, protects her from her own oedipal conflicts, and obscures her deficiency as a mother. She may encourage the child's illusion of his adequacy as her lover, which discourages him from growing up, from identifying with the father in his adult masculine role, and from further differentiating from the mother. Coen continued that the mother's relative neglect of the child's emotional needs and her seductive overstimulation of him combine to give sexual feelings an unusually significant role during his early development. The child then draws on the predominantly available mode of relating with his mother to compensate for her relative unavailability and to stimulate her renewed interest in him. He identifies with the mother's sexualization in order to preserve the object tie with her. Sexual seductiveness, Coen noted, eventually becomes the child's predominant mode for relating to others and for expressing his intense object hunger.

Before we proceed, let us consider the relationship between the cognitive–behavioral theories and the psychoanalytic theories. Overall, the two groups of theories are mutually compatible. For the most part, the cognitive–behavioral theories can be understood as simpler, less detailed versions of the psychoanalytic theories, with four major differences. First of all, the cognitive–behavioral theories place greater emphasis on beliefs as etiologic factors, while the psychoanalytic theories place greater emphasis on affects and psychological functions. Second, the psychoanalytic theories discuss the mother–child relationship as the nucleus of the etiologic matrix, and they explore in detail its pathogenic dynamics. The cognitive–behavioral theories, meanwhile, expand the etiologic matrix to include the entire family of origin and the sociocultural milieu, but they say little about the mother–child relationship or about specific pathogenic interactional patterns other than sexual abuse. Third, the cognitive–behavioral theories hardly mention aggression or sadism at all, while aggression and sadism are prominent as both etiologic and dynamic factors in the psychoanalytic theories. Finally, the psychoanalytic theories emphasize overt sexual abuse less, and covert seduction and narcissistic exploitation more, than do the cognitive–behavioral theories. Also, the pathogenic interactions on which most of the psychoanalytic theories focus occur earlier in life than do those that the cognitive–behavioral theories typically discuss.

5

An Integrated Theory

The human being is both biological and psychological, and the etiology of sexual addiction is likely to be most fully understood through a theory that integrates both biological and psychological understandings. Prior to the 1990s, the theory of fetishism that was proposed by Epstein (1960) was the only coherent attempt to integrate biological theory and psychological theory (in this case, psychoanalytic theory) to account for a form of sexual addiction.

More recently, I proposed an integrated theory of sexual addiction (1993b, 1995a, 1997) that was based on a comprehensive theory of addictive disorders. In my presentation of the comprehensive theory (1995b), I began by conducting an extensive review of research literature concerning conditions that have been grouped together as addictive disorders: alcoholism, drug addiction, bulimia, pathological gambling, and sexual addiction. The review revealed significant lifetime comorbidity, family history relationships, neurobiological similarities (in terms of both the neurochemical correlates of the behaviors that characterize each of these disorders, and the responses of the disorders to pharmacotherapy), and psychometric parallels among these disorders. The research results that were reviewed, considered as a whole, indicated that some significant psychobiological characteristic or characteristics are shared by alcoholism, drug addiction,

143

bulimia, pathological gambling, and sexual addiction. I then reviewed longitudinal and archival studies, and I found them to indicate that specifiable psychometric and psychological abnormalities in individuals who had not yet developed alcoholism or used other drugs of abuse were reliably associated with the later development of alcoholism or addiction to other drugs. The findings of these archival and longitudinal studies indicated that a significant psychobiological abnormality that characterizes alcoholism and drug addiction precedes the onset of these disorders, and is thus not simply caused by substance abuse or by a substance-abusing life-style. The two parts of the review, taken together, suggested (1) that these conditions that I group together as addictive disorders—alcoholism, drug addiction, bulimia, pathological gambling, and sexual addiction—have in common an underlying psychobiological process; and (2) that this psychobiological process precedes the onset of the disorders and is thus not simply a consequence of addictive behavior or an addictive life-style.

For readers who are curious about the studies that were reviewed and the findings from which the above-mentioned conclusions were drawn, the review will now be outlined.

THE ADDICTIVE PROCESS: EMPIRICAL FINDINGS AND CORE HYPOTHESIS

Apparent Similarities and Relationships

I initially was motivated to conduct an extensive review of the research literature by a sense that alcoholism, drug addiction, bulimia, pathological gambling, and sexual addiction are related to one another in a fundamental way. My sense that these conditions are related to one another emerged from my observations of apparent similarities and relationships among these conditions. The similarities included:

1. Characteristic course—the disorder typically begins in adolescence or early adulthood and follows a chronic course with remissions and exacerbations;

2. Behavioral features—narrowing of behavioral repertoire, continuation of the behavior despite harmful consequences;
3. Individuals' subjective experience of the condition—sense of craving, preoccupation, excitement during preparatory activity, mood-altering effects of the behavior, sense of loss of control;
4. Progressive development of the condition—craving, loss of control, narrowing of behavioral repertoire, and harmfulness of consequences all tending to increase as the duration of the condition increases;
5. Experience of tolerance—as the behavior is repeated, its potency to produce reinforcing effects tends to diminish;
6. Experience of withdrawal phenomena—psychological and/or physical discomfort when the behavior is discontinued;
7. Tendency to relapse—that is, to return to harmful patterns of behavior after a period of abstinence or control has been achieved;
8. Relationship between the condition and other aspects of affected individuals' lives—for example, neglect of other areas of life as the behavior assumes priority; and
9. Recurrent themes in the ways individuals with these conditions relate to others and to themselves—including low self-esteem, self-centeredness, denial, rationalization, and conflicts over dependency and control.

The possibility that these conditions have something in common was further suggested by my impressions that the following patterns occurred more frequently than chance would have predicted:

10. Individuals who met diagnostic criteria for addiction to alcohol or to some other drug would at some time in their lives meet diagnostic criteria for addiction to one or more other drugs;
11. Individuals who met diagnostic criteria for addiction to a drug, bulimia, pathological gambling, or sexual addiction would at some time in their lives meet diagnostic criteria for one of the other three conditions;

12. Relatives of individuals who met diagnostic criteria for addiction to one drug would themselves, at some time in their lives, meet diagnostic criteria for addiction to one or more other drugs;

13. Relatives of individuals who met diagnostic criteria for addiction to a drug, pathological gambling, bulimia, or sexual addiction would themselves, at some time in their lives, meet diagnostic criteria for one of the other three conditions;

14. When individuals met diagnostic criteria for two (or more) of these disorders, as behavior that was symptomatic of one disorder came under better control, behavior that was symptomatic of the other disorder would become less manageable;

15. When individuals met diagnostic criteria for only one of these disorders, as behavior that was symptomatic of that disorder came under control, behavior that was symptomatic of one of the other disorders would become a problem for the first time.

I could at this point formulate a hypothesis that these conditions—alcoholism, drug addiction, bulimia, pathological gambling, and sexual addiction—have in common an underlying psychobiological process. I was then able to review the relevant epidemiological, neurobiological, and psychometric research literature and determine the extent to which it supported or refuted the hypothesis.

Epidemiological Findings

Epidemiological findings statistically confirmed the impressions of relationships among the conditions that I mentioned above, particularly items 10 to 13. While interactions among these conditions (items 14 and 15) are often mentioned in the literature (e.g. P. M. Miller, 1979), they have not yet been empirically studied.

Research findings indicate that a person who has been diagnosed with one of these disorders—addiction to alcohol (alcoholism), addictions to other drugs, bulimia, pathological gambling, or sexual addiction—is at a significantly higher risk than is the general population to develop (or to have developed), at some point in his or her life, one of the other disorders:

1. An individual who has been diagnosed with addiction to one type of psychoactive drug (including alcohol) is at a significantly higher risk than is the general population for addiction to one or more other drugs (Hesselbrock, Meyer, and Keener, 1985; Ross, Glaser, and Germanson, 1988; Regier, Farmer, Rae, Locke, Keith, Judd, and Goodwin, 1990; Kosten, Kosten, and Rounsaville, 1991).

2. An individual who has been diagnosed with bulimia is at a significantly higher risk than is the general population for lifetime comorbidity (incidence of another disorder at some time during the person's life) with addiction to a psychoactive drug (including alcohol) (J. E. Mitchell and Goff, 1984; Jones, Cheshire, and Moorehouse, 1985; Mitchell, Hatsukami, Eckert, and Pyle, 1985; Beary, Lacey, and Merry, 1986; Robinson and Holden, 1986; Bulik, 1987; Hudson, Pope, Jonas, and Yurgelun-Todd, 1987; Hudson, Pope, Yurgelun-Todd, Jonas, and Frankenburg, 1987; Johnson and Connors, 1987; Schneider and Agras, 1987; Lacey, 1993), and vice versa (Jonas and Gold, 1986; Jonas, Gold, Sweeney, and Pottash, 1987; Ross et al., 1988; Peveler and Fairburn, 1990; Timmerman, Wells, and Chen, 1990). One study found a significant degree of crossover between bulimia and alcoholism (Pyle, Mitchell, Eckert, Halvorson, Neuman, and Goff, 1983).

3. An individual who has been diagnosed with pathological gambling is at a significantly higher risk than is the general population for lifetime comorbidity with addiction to a psychoactive drug (including alcohol) (Haberman, 1969; Miller, Hedrick, and Taylor, 1983; McCormick, Russo, Ramirez, and Taber, 1984; Ramirez, McCormick, Russo, and Taber, 1984; Linden, Pope, and Jonas, 1986; Lesieur, 1988; Lesieur and Heineman, 1988; Roy, Adinoff, Roerich, Lamparski, Custer, Lorenz, Barbaccia, Guidotti, Costa, and Linnoila, 1988; Steinberg, 1990); and vice versa (Lesieur, Blume, and Zoppa, 1986; Ross et al., 1988; Steinberg, Kosten, and Rounsaville, 1992).

4. An individual who has been diagnosed with pathological gambling is at a significantly higher risk than is the general population for lifetime comorbidity with sexual addiction (Lesieur, 1988; Steinberg, 1990), and vice versa (Kafka and Prentky, 1994).

5. An individual who has been diagnosed with sexual addiction is at a significantly higher risk than is the general population for lifetime comorbidity with addiction to a psychoactive drug, including alcohol (Schneider and Schneider, 1991; Kruesi et al., 1992; Irons and Schneider, 1994; Kafka and Prentky, 1994); and vice versa (Coleman, 1987; Washton, 1989). (Data that were obtained from populations of sex offenders, many but not all of whom would probably have met diagnostic criteria for sexual addiction, are not included in this review.)

6. An individual who has been diagnosed with sexual addiction is at a significantly higher risk than is the general population for lifetime comorbidity with an eating disorder and for lifetime comorbidity with pathological gambling (Schneider and Schneider, 1991).

Family history studies indicate that biological relatives of an individual who has been diagnosed with one of these disorders are at significantly higher risk than is the general population to develop (or to have developed), at some point in their lives, one of the other disorders:

1. First-degree relatives of an individual who has been diagnosed with bulimia are at a significantly higher risk than is the general population for addiction to a psychoactive drug (including alcohol) (Hudson, Laffer, and Pope, 1982; Mitchell et al., 1985; Bulik, 1987; Hudson, Pope, Jonas, and Yurgelun-Todd, 1987; Hudson, Pope, Yurgelun-Todd, Jonas, and Frankenburg, 1987; Jonas et al., 1987; Kassett, Gershon, Maxwell, Guroff, Kazuba, Smith, Brandt, and Jimerson, 1989).

2. First-degree relatives of an individual who has been diagnosed with pathological gambling are at a significantly higher risk

than is the general population for compulsive overeating (Jacobs, 1989) and for addiction to a psychoactive drug (including alcohol); and vice versa (Ramirez et al., 1984; Lesieur, 1988; Roy et al., 1988; Jacobs, 1989).

3. First-degree relatives of an individual who has been diagnosed with sexual addiction are at a significantly higher risk than is the general population for addiction to a psychoactive drug (including alcohol), for an eating disorder, and for pathological gambling (Schneider and Schneider, 1991).

Interestingly, studies have found that alcoholism, addictive use of other drugs, bulimia, pathological gambling, and sexual addiction (paraphilic disorders in most of these studies) are all also associated with frequencies of affective disorders, anxiety disorders, attention deficit disorder, and personality disorders that are higher than their frequencies in the general population.

1. Affective disorders (primarily major depression):
    a. Alcoholism (Powell et al., 1982; Weiss and Rosenberg, 1985; Ross et al., 1988; Regier et al., 1990; Kosten et al., 1991);
    b. Addictive use of other drugs (Hesselbrock et al., 1985; Khantzian and Treece, 1985; Regier et al., 1990; Kosten et al., 1991);
    c. Bulimia (Hudson, Pope, Jonas, and Yurgelun-Todd, 1983; Bulik, 1987; Hudson, Pope, Jonas, and Yurgelun-Todd, 1987);
    d. Pathological gambling (Dell, Ruzicka, and Palisi, 1981; McCormick et al., 1984; Ramirez et al., 1984; Roy et al., 1988);
    e. Sexual addiction (T. N. Wise, 1989; Chalkley and Powell, 1983; Fagan, Wise, Schmidt, Ponticas, and Marshall, 1991; Kafka and Prentky, 1992, 1994; Kruesi et al., 1992).
2. Anxiety disorders:
    a. Alcoholism (Powell, Penick, Othmer, Bingham, and Rice, 1982; Hesselbrock et al., 1985; Weiss and Rosenberg, 1985; Ross et al., 1988);

   b. Addictive use of other drugs (Ross et al., 1988; Regier et
       al., 1990);
   c. Bulimia (Hudson et al., 1983; Hudson, Pope, Jonas, and
       Yurgelun-Todd, 1987);
   d. Pathological gambling (Linden et al., 1986; Roy et al.,
       1988);
   e. Sexual addiction (T. N. Wise, 1989; Fagan et al., 1991;
       Kafka, 1991; Kruesi et al., 1992; Kafka and Prentky,
       1994).
3. Attention deficit disorder:
   a. Alcoholism (Goodwin, Schulsinger, Hermansen, Guze,
       and Winokur, 1975; Wood, Wender, and Reimherr,
       1983);
   b. Addictive use of other drugs (Eyre, Rounsaville, and
       Kleber, 1982);
   c. Pathological gambling (Carlton, Manowitz, McBride,
       Nora, Swartzburg, and Goldstein, 1987);
   d. Sexual addiction (Kavoussi, Kaplan, and Becker, 1988;
       Hunter and Goodwin, 1992).
4. Personality disorders:
   a. Alcoholism (Hesselbrock et al., 1985; Koenigsberg,
       Kaplan, Gilmore, and Cooper, 1985; Ross et al., 1988;
       Mezzich, Fabrega, Coffman, and Haley, 1989; DeJong,
       van den Brink, Harteveld, and van der Wielen, 1993);
   b. Addictive use of other drugs (Koenigsberg et al., 1985;
       Ross et al., 1988; Mezzich et al., 1989; Nace, Davis, and
       Gaspari, 1991; DeJong et al., 1993);
   c. Bulimia (Gartner, Marcus, Halmi, and Loranger, 1987;
       Herzog, Keller, Lavori, Kenny, and Sacks, 1992);
   d. Pathological gambling (Blaszczynski, McConaghy, and
       Frankova, 1989);
   e. Sexual addiction (Blair and Lanyon, 1981; Schmidt,
       Meyer, and Lucas, 1981; Chalkley and Powell, 1983).

Neurobiological Findings

Neurobiological findings concern two areas: the responses of the
disorders that we are considering to pharmacological treatment,

and the relationships of these disorders to neuromodulator systems in the brain. (Neuromodulators are endogenous substances that regulate or alter the function of neurons. In addition to neurotransmitters, neuromodulators comprise certain hormones and peptides, including the endogenous opioids.)

Research indicates that alcoholism, addictive use of other drugs, bulimia, pathological gambling, and sexual addiction respond similarly to antidepressant medications. Antidepressants, particularly those that affect the serotonin system, have been found to reduce craving and/or symptomatic behavior in all of these disorders:

1. Alcoholism (Naranjo, Sellars, and Lawrin, 1986; Gorelick, 1989; Naranjo and Sellars, 1989; Gorelick and Paredes, 1992; Slywka and Hart, 1993);
2. Addictive use of other drugs (Gawin, Kleber, Byck, Rounsaville, Kosten, Jatlow, and Morgan, 1989; Batki, Manfredi, Sorensen, Jacob, Dumontet, and Jones, 1991; Pollack and Rosenbaum, 1991);
3. Bulimia (Pope and Hudson, 1986; Edelstein, Yager, Gitlin, and Landsverk, 1989; Walsh, Hadigan, Devlin, Gladis, and Roose, 1991; Fluoxetine Bulimia Nervosa Collaborative Study Group, 1992);
4. Pathological gambling (Moskowitz, 1980; McCormick et al., 1984; Hollander, Frenkel, Decaria, Trungold, and Stein, 1992);
5. Sexual addiction (Kafka and Prentky, 1992; Stein et al., 1992; Kruesi et al., 1992 [and others, as we note later in chapter 8]).

Research also indicates that the behaviors that characterize each of these disorders—taking into one's body any of the drugs of abuse, eating, gambling, engaging in sexual behavior—have similar activating effects on opioid and dopamine components of the brain reward system. The introduction of opiate drugs into one's body directly stimulates opioid receptors in the brain (Koob and Bloom, 1988; Kreek, 1992), while the behaviors that characterize the rest of these disorders are associated with the release of endogenous opioids:

1. Taking a psychoactive substance (other than an opiate) into one's body:
   a. Ethanol (Schulz, Wuster, Duka, and Herz, 1980; Seizinger, Bovermann, Maysinger, Hollt, and Herz, 1983);
   b. Psychostimulants (cocaine and amphetamines) (Koob and Bloom, 1988; Houdi, Bardo, and Van Loon, 1989; Kreek, 1992);
   c. Nicotine (Hollt and Horn, 1989);
2. Eating (Dum, Gramsch, and Herz, 1983; Kirkham and Cooper, 1988);
3. Gambling (Blaszczynski, Winter, and McConaghy, 1986);
4. Engaging in sexual behavior (Szechtman, Hershkowitz, and Simantov, 1981; Agmo and Berenfeld, 1990).

Similarly, the behaviors that characterize each of these disorders are associated with an increase in the intrasynaptic concentration of dopamine in the brain reward system:

1. Taking a psychoactive substance into one's body:
   a. Ethanol (Di Chiara and Imperato, 1988; Yoshimoto, McBride, Lumeng, and Li, 1991);
   b. Opiates (Gysling and Wang, 1983; R. A. Wise, 1987; Di Chiara and Imperato, 1988; North, 1993);
   c. Psychostimulants (the effects of cocaine seem to result primarily from inhibition of dopamine reuptake) (R. A. Wise, 1987; Ritz, Lamb, Goldberg, and Kuhar, 1987, 1988; Di Chiara and Imperato, 1988; Yoshimoto et al., 1991);
   d. Nicotine (Di Chiara and Imperato, 1988; Mifsud, Hernandez, and Hoebel, 1989);
2. Eating (Hernandez and Hoebel, 1990; Yoshida et al., 1992);
3. Gambling (Blaszczynski et al., 1986);
4. Engaging in sexual behavior (Agmo and Berenfeld, 1990; Pfaus, Damsma, Nomikos, Wenkstern, Blaha, Phillips, and Fibiger, 1990).

Relationships have been discerned also between the behaviors that characterize the disorders that we are considering and the norepinephrine and serotonin systems, but these relationships have not been as clearly delineated. The serotonin system has been the subject of particular interest, since serotonin reuptake inhibitors have been found to be more broadly effective than any other group of medications in decreasing symptomatic behavior and craving in all of the addictive disorders. Research has identified the following relationships between the serotonin system and behaviors that characterize the addictive disorders:

1. Taking alcohol into one's body:
   a. Alcohol intake stimulates the release of serotonin (Khatib, Murphy, and McBride, 1988; Yoshimoto et al., 1991);
   b. Increased serotonergic activity is associated with decreased alcohol intake (Rockman, Amit, Brown, Bourque, and Ogren, 1982);
   c. Administration of antiserotonergic drugs is associated with increased intake of alcohol (R. D. Myers and Tytell, 1972);
   d. Disturbances of brain serotonin metabolism have been reported in alcoholism (Ballenger, Goodwin, Major, and Brown, 1979; Koob and Bloom, 1988).
2. Taking cocaine into one's body:
   Serotonin reuptake is inhibited by cocaine, but the relationship between serotonin reuptake inhibition and cocaine's reinforcing effects is not yet clear (Dunwiddie and Brodie, 1993; Koob, 1993).
3. Eating
   a. Serotonin has been found to play a regulatory role in feeding, particularly in regulating the intake of carbohydrates (Wurtman and Wurtman, 1979; Blundell, 1984; Leibowitz and Shor-Posner, 1986);
   b. Disturbances of brain serotonin metabolism have been reported in bulimia (Kaye, Gwirtsman, Brewerton, George, and Wurtman, 1988; Kaye and Weltzin, 1991)

and in the bulimic subtype of anorexia nervosa (Kaye, Ebert, Gwirtsman, and Weiss, 1984).

4. Engaging in sexual behavior

Serotonin seems to be involved in the regulation of sexual behavior (Fernstrom and Wurtmann, 1977; Gorzalka, Mendelson, and Watson, 1990).

Psychometric Findings

Psychometric findings comprise the results of administering psychological tests to patients who have been diagnosed with the disorders that we are considering. Similar patterns of results have been reported for alcoholics, drug abusers, bulimics, and pathological gamblers on the Minnesota Multiphasic Personality Inventory (MMPI) and on the MacAndrew Alcoholism Scale. Before proceeding, let us be clear that few contemporary investigators would suggest that a single personality profile characterizes all or most patients in any of these diagnostic categories. Rather, the search for characteristic composite MMPI profiles emerges from the belief that identification of such profiles is an important means by which to understand modal features of individuals whose behavior identifies them with these diagnostic categories, and also is a necessary preliminary step to examining potential subclasses of characteristics that are applicable to specific subtypes. Research with the MMPI has demonstrated similar profiles for alcoholics and heroin addicts (reviewed in Barnes, 1983), for women with alcohol or other drug abuse problems and women with bulimia (who have no history of substance abuse) (Hatsukami, Owen, Pyle, and Mitchell, 1982), and for alcoholics and nonalcoholic pathological gamblers (Lowenfeld, 1979; Ciarrocchi, Kirschner, and Fallik, 1991). In the typical profile, the highest scales were 2 (Depression) and 4 (Psychopathic Deviate), both above 70; next highest were 7 (Psychasthenia) and 8 (Schizophrenia), both above 65. In a comprehensive review, Sutker and Archer (1979) concluded that alcoholics, opiate addicts, and abusers of other illicit drugs share common constellations of MMPI features; but they noted that alcoholics, as abusers of a socially sanctioned (and even encouraged) drug, differ from abusers of illicit drugs on dimensions of social nonconformity and neurotic symptomatology.

Since MMPI profiles for these groups of patients are not homogeneous, some investigators have attempted to delineate homogeneous MMPI profile subgroups with the help of multivariate cluster analysis. Almost all studies of this nature have been conducted with alcoholics. A review of these studies (Sutker and Archer, 1979) found that they consistently delineated two major subtypes or clusters, a neurotic subtype and a sociopathic subtype. One study of opiate addicts (Berzins, Ross, English, and Haley, 1974) identified two homogeneous subtypes, the larger of which showed elevations on scales 2, 4, and 8 (2-4-8-7 for males, 4-8-2 for females), while the smaller was characterized by a single peak on scale 4 (both males and females). The authors of the study noted that these subtypes corresponded to the two largest profile subtypes that S. G. Goldstein and Linden (1969) had delineated for male alcoholics (with the minor difference that the rank order of scales for the larger subtype group of alcoholics was 2-4-7-8). Glen (1979, cited in McCormick and Taber, 1979) and Lowenfeld (1979) each delineated four MMPI profile subtypes in pathological gamblers. In order of frequency, Glen's subtypes were 2-7-8, 2-4-7, 4-9 (9 is Mania), and 4, while Lowenfeld's were 4-9, 8-7-2-4, 2-7-4-3, and 2-8-7. If Glen's first two subtypes were grouped together to form one neurotic subtype, and her third and fourth subtypes were grouped together to form one sociopathic subtype, her results would be comparable to those that were obtained with alcoholics and opiate addicts. Similar comparability could be obtained by grouping together Lowenfeld's last three subtypes to form one large neurotic subtype, which would leave one remaining as a sociopathic subtype. Whether this pattern of findings can be repeated with addictive users of other drugs, with bulimics, and with sex addicts remains to be investigated.

Using the MacAndrew Alcoholism Scale, researchers have found the same range of scores for problem drinkers, heroin addicts, massively obese individuals, and smokers (Kranitz, 1972; Burke and Marcus, 1977; Leon, Kolotkin, and Korgeski, 1979).

Assessments of field dependence have yielded similar results of greater field dependence (poorer performance on the Rod-and-Frame Test) for alcoholics (reviewed in Barnes, 1983), for heroin addicts (Arnon, Kleinman, and Kissin, 1974), and for obese individuals (Karp and Pardes, 1965; Brown and Williams, 1975). A related condition, overdependence on external cues and impaired ability to recognize or correctly to interpret internal cues, has been found to be associated with both alcoholism (Brown and Williams, 1975; Lansky, Nathan, and Lawson, 1978) and obesity (Brown and Williams, 1975; Nisbett and Storms, 1974).

Correlations between these behavioral syndromes and patterns of psychological test results raise questions about their causal relationship. Do biological and social consequences of the behavioral syndromes cause the abnormalities of psychological functioning that are indicated by the test results? Or do abnormalities of psychological functioning predispose to development of the behavioral syndromes? Archival studies found elevations in the MMPI and MacAndrew scale scores of young individuals who later became alcoholics, which were similar to the score elevations of alcoholics and drug addicts. The results for subjects who were tested again at the time of alcoholism treatment correlated well with their prealcoholic test results (Kammeier, Hoffman, and Loper, 1973; Loper, Kammeier, and Hoffman, 1973; H. Hoffman, Loper, and Kammeier, 1974). Another study found the MMPI profiles of college entrants who later become heavy users of drugs other than alcohol to be similar to those of alcoholics and drug addicts (Goldstein and Sappington, 1977). In the case of field dependence, early studies determined that this tendency antedated the onset of drinking (Witkin, Karp, and Goodenough, 1959), and that the degree of field dependence was not related to duration of drinking, which it presumably would have been if it were a consequence of alcohol intake (Karp and Kronstadt, 1965).

In line with the question about psychological predisposition to addiction, a number of longitudinal and archival studies have addressed the question of whether any relationship exists between pre-existing personality characteristics and the likelihood of developing alcoholism or addictive use of some other drug. While no particular personality disorder is specifically predictive of alcoholism, several prealcoholic personality traits have been found to be associated with the later development of alcoholism, including: aggressiveness, nonconformity, rejection of societal values, antisocial behavior, impulsivity, extroversion, emphasis on independence, and hyperactivity (McCord and McCord, 1960, 1962; Robins, 1966; Robins, Bates, and O'Neal, 1962; Jones, 1968, 1971; Goodwin, Schulsinger, Hermansen, Guze, and Winokur, 1973; Kammeier, Hoffman, and Loper, 1973; Jessor and Jessor, 1977, 1978; Kandel, 1978, 1980; Zucker, 1979; Kellam, Ensminger, and Simon, 1980; Wingard, Huba, and Bentler, 1980; Jessor, Chase, and Donovan, 1980; Zucker and Noll, 1982; Vicary and Lerner, 1983; Labouvie and McGee, 1986). While Vaillant and Milofsky (1982) reported that ethnicity and the number of alcoholic relatives accounted for most of the variance in adult alcoholism and that childhood emotional problems explained no additional variance, their data did not include emotional or personality characteristics, but only ratings of environmental weaknesses, poor infant health, and school behavior problems. Vaillant and Milofsky also observed that premorbid antisocial behavior contributed significantly to the risk for alcoholism. This observation was very much in accord with the findings of the other investigators. Moreover, Vaillant (1975) himself wrote in a classic paper that antisocial (sociopathic) behavior typically expresses characterological defenses that develop to cope with painful affects, particularly painful affects that are associated with impaired object relations.

Other studies have focused on the differences between individuals who later in life frequently used drugs other than alcohol and those who did not. (Not all individuals in this group would necessarily become drug addicts, but all drug addicts would come from the group of frequent users.) Prior to any drug experience, frequent or heavy users tended to be more unconventional or nonconformist, depressed, insecure in their personal identity, anxious with other people, alienated, pessimistic, dependent, extroversive, overreactive, undercontrolled, impulsive, aggressive, rebellious, low in self-esteem, and labile or erratic in mood than their abstaining or infrequently-using peers (Sadava, 1973; Gulas and King, 1976; Goldstein and Sappington, 1977; Sadava and Forsyth, 1977; G.M. Smith, 1977; Jessor and Jessor, 1977, 1978; Ginsberg and Greenley, 1978; Smith and Fogg, 1978; Brook, Lukoff, and Whiteman, 1980; Kandel, 1980; Kellam, Ensminger, and Simon, 1980; Wingard, Huba, and Bentler, 1980; Huba and Bentler, 1982; Kellam, Brown, Rubin, and Ensminger, 1983a,b; Brook, Whiteman, Gordon, and Cohen, 1986; Labouvie and McGee, 1986; Block, Block, and Keyes, 1988; Shedler and Block, 1990; Kellam, 1991).

Core Hypothesis: The Addictive Process

The body of epidemiological, neurobiological, and psychometric research findings that was just summarized provided support for my hypothesis that these conditions—addiction to alcohol (alcoholism), addictions to other drugs, bulimia, pathological gambling, and sexual addiction—have in common an underlying psychobiological process that precedes the onset of the disorders and is thus not simply a consequence of addictive behavior or an addictive life-style. The apparent similarities and relationships between these conditions in turn suggested the utility of grouping them together as addictive disorders, or addictions.

Extrapolating from these findings, I hypothesized that all addictive disorders, whatever the types of behavior that characterize them, share an underlying psychobiological process, which I designated the *addictive process*. The perspective that was provided by this hypothesis suggested that the category of addictive disorders is most accurately described, not as a collection of distinct disorders, but as an underlying pathological process that can be expressed in one or more of various behavioral manifestations. I suggested that the addictive process could be understood as compulsive dependence on external action as a means of regulating one's internal (or subjective) states, one's feelings and sense of self. I continued that it involves compulsively depending on something outside, which the individual believes that he or she can control, as a means of dealing with problems that are within.

I would now define the addictive process as an enduring, inordinately strong tendency to engage in some form of pleasure-producing behavior as a means of relieving painful affects and/or regulating one's sense of self. (I have replaced "feelings" with "affects" in the definition because *affects* is a more accurate term in this context. In agreement with Novey [1959], I understand *affect* to designate a complex emotional process that has subjective, physiological, behavioral, and interpersonal aspects, while *feeling* designates the subjectively experienced aspects of an affect.)

Similar to the theories that were presented by Coleman (1986, 1987) and Carnes (1983, 1989), my theory of addictive disorders identifies two sets of factors and predisposing conditions: those that concern the underlying addictive process, and those that relate to the selection of a particular substance or behavior as the one that is preferred for addictive use. Similar again to Coleman and Carnes, I consider the former set to be the more important, both in terms of etiological significance and as a guide in treatment.

According to my theory, the addictive process is both psychological and biological, and it can be described and understood in either psychological or biological terms. While Epstein (1960) developed his integrated psychobiological theory within a framework of mental–physical interaction, I developed mine within a framework of mental–physical identity, in which mind and body are understood to be not distinct forms of reality but distinct ways of describing and understanding a unitary human organism (Goodman, 1991, 1994a, in press a, in press b). Accordingly, I introduced the addictive process in two complementary formulations, a psychological formulation and a neurobiological formulation.

The next two sections present psychological and neurobiological formulations of the addictive process. The bipartite theory that these formulations constitute is proposed as a general way to organize our understanding of addiction, and as a prototype for characterizing the process that is hypothesized to underlie some significant proportion of all types of addictive disorder. The theory is not claimed to completely account for all cases of addictive disorders. We can keep in mind that the diagnostic label for an addictive disorder designates not a homogeneous syndrome but a heterogeneous class of conditions that share a specified set of descriptive features. Different subtypes of each addictive disorder can be expected to vary in the psychological dynamics, neurobiological processes, and etiologic pathways with which they are associated.

PSYCHOLOGICAL FORMULATION OF THE ADDICTIVE PROCESS

The addictive process was defined as an enduring, inordinately strong tendency to engage in some form of pleasure-producing behavior as a means of relieving painful affects and/or regulating one's sense of self. It is thus constituted by two components: (1) impairment of the self-regulation system, the internal psychobiological system that regulates one's subjective (sensory, emotional, and cognitive) states and one's behavioral states; and (2) a tendency to depend on external action to cope with the effects of impaired self-regulation, which reflects a relative incapacity to utilize other, more healthy and adaptive means of coping. This simple formulation of addiction reflects a convergence of various psychoanalytic theories of alcoholism, addiction to other drugs, bulimia, pathological gambling, and sexual addiction. It also is consistent with formulations of addiction—generally, addiction to alcohol or other drugs—that are based in learning theory.

In the present section, I present overviews of psychoanalytic theories and learning theory-based theories of the addictive disorders. I then outline an integrated psychological formulation of the addictive process. Readers may notice that the overview of psychoanalytic theories of addictive disorders is considerably longer and more detailed than is the overview of learning theory-based theories of the addictive disorders. The primary reason for this imbalance is that much more psychoanalytic theoretical material than learning theory-based theoretical material on addictive disorders is available. The larger volume of psychoanalytic theoretical material results partly from the characteristically greater detail and complexity of psychoanalytic theory. Another, more substantial factor was mentioned by Blair and Lanyon (1981) in their review of psychological theories of exhibitionism: learning theory approaches are concerned less with explaining how behavioral symptoms developed than with altering the symptoms in the present. Psychoanalytic investigators are thus typically more interested in etiology than are behaviorally oriented investigators, and they have a broader and deeper range of etiologically relevant concepts with which to work.

Overview of Psychoanalytic Theories of Addictive Disorders

The following overview summarizes comprehensive reviews of psychoanalytic theories of psychoactive substance addiction (alcoholism and addictions to other drugs), bulimia, pathological gambling, and sexual addiction, which I am presenting in a separate book. While the details of the theories that are included in these reviews are valuable, both in their own right and in support of my thesis that these disorders share significant psychodynamic and developmental features, their inclusion here would have overshadowed the rest of the chapter. The summary of each disorder below is followed by a list of the sources that are included in the comprehensive reviews.

Psychoactive Substance Addiction (Alcoholism and Addictions to Other Drugs)

Current psychoanalytic theory understands psychoactive substance addiction to be fundamentally a disorder of the self-regulation system. This disorder involves impairments in affect regulation, self-soothing, sense of self, self-esteem, and self-care functions, of which impairment in affect regulation seems to be the most central. Impaired affect regulation involves affect regression tendencies, deficient ability to utilize anxiety or affect as a signal, and impaired tolerance of painful affect. These deficits leave addicts vulnerable to the psychic trauma of being over-whelmed with painful affect in circumstances that would not be potentially traumatic to others. Other psychodynamic factors that seem to be significant in psychoactive substance addiction in-clude: claustrophobia, superego pathology, characteristic primi-tive defenses, alexithymia, and a basic fusion–individuation conflict.

Claustrophobia is a potentially traumatic anxiety that is asso-ciated with the general idea of being closed in, trapped, engulfed, or smothered. It is characteristically displaced onto external struc-tures, as a result of which addicts tend to experience phobic anxi-ety when they are faced by limitations of any kind. (Limitations can be experienced also as an affront to omnipotence and hence as a narcissistic injury, which the narcissistically vulnerable indi-vidual can associate with traumatic anxiety.)

The superego pathology that is usually associated with psy-choactive substance addiction consists of insufficient structural-ization, integration, and differentiation. A split in superego functioning, which results from insufficient integration and from inability to sufficiently resolve crucial conflicts, promotes a corres-ponding split in the individual's self representation and in his object representations. Superego pathology affects not only the punitive, critical superego functions but also the approving, car-ing, self-esteem regulating, and protective superego functions.

The defenses that are typically employed by individuals who use psychoactive substances addictively are denial or disavowal, externalization, turning passive into active, and the narcissistic characterological defenses. The latter most often include grandi-osity, entitlement, fantasies of omnipotence, and pseudo-self-suf-ficiency (denial of their longings for nurturance and of their needs for help); but they can also include idealization, submis-sion, and fantasies of having an omnipotent protector.

Alexithymia—the difficulty that drug addicts characteristi-cally have in recognizing, identifying, and naming their af-fects—can derive from impaired affect regulation or from impaired symbolization function (or from both). Whatever its origin, it interferes with the development of affect tolerance and affect signal function.

While the association between psychoactive substance addiction and an unusually intense fusion–individuation conflict was noted only by Woollcott (1981), early as well as contemporary psychoanalytic investigators have discussed the drug addict's intense wish to merge with the primal love object, and a number of contemporary theorists have described the addict's intense fear of being controlled, of being smothered, or of losing his identity. Recognition of the polarization or even the dissociation of the inner life that can result when such a wish–fear conflict is intense—intensified, perhaps, by the addict's impaired affect regulation—helps us to understand many of the phenomena that we observe clinically in individuals who use psychoactive substances addictively.

The addictive use of alcohol or other drugs primarily represents an attempt to compensate for self-regulatory functions that are impaired: to fill in the defects in psychological structure and the gaps in the inner object world with which these impairments are associated. The functions that psychoactive substance use is intended (often unconsciously) to fulfill can include: (1) modulation or regulation of intense and painful affects, such as tension, depression, loneliness, superego affects, paranoid anxieties, and the affects that are associated with narcissistic injury; (2) containment of aggressive energies that threaten the integrity of the self; (3) management or circumvention of painful intrapsychic conflicts; and (4) restoration of narcissistic balance. Psychoactive substance use additionally can function to support and to express the narcissistic defenses of pseudo-self-sufficiency and omnipotent control. The drug user assumes both the role of the one who needs and the role of the one who satisfies the need: he is able to take care of his needs by himself. More specifically, addicts use psychoactive substances not only to relieve affects, but also to control them. Use of alcohol or other drugs enables the user intentionally to alter his own affective state. This ability provides addicts with a sense of control or omnipotence that can counter traumatic feelings of helplessness or powerlessness, to which they are particularly sensitive as a result of their narcissistic pathology. Use of psychoactive substances can moreover function as an expression of the narcissistic rage that powerlessness can produce.

At the same time, addicts are driven to control their affects, not only as a means of defending against the distress of feeling powerless, but also as an attempt to master painful affect states for which they lack symbolic representation, by turning passive into active. Finally, the use of psychoactive substances can represent an attempt to gratify primitive oral–sexual longings for undifferentiated food-love-security, for merger with the archaic maternal object. Alcohol and other drugs not only permit and reinforce an experience of blissful fusion of the self and object worlds, they also do so in a way that enables avoidance of the various persecutory and claustrophobic anxieties that could accompany real closeness with another person. They thus provide an illusory but compelling solution to the basic fusion–individuation conflict.

While psychoanalytic investigators have produced abundant material on the psychodynamic factors that are associated with psychoactive substance addiction and on the dynamic functions that it can serve, they have thus far provided relatively little material on the factors that contribute to the development of psychoactive substance addiction. The impairments of self-regulatory function that underlie substance addiction primarily reflect defects in psychological structure and in the inner object world. Disavowal and externalization of self-care, self-comforting, and superego functions can further contribute to self-regulatory impairments. The critical structural and representational defects seem to result from disturbances in internalization, the developmental process whereby regulatory functions that had been provided to the child by the caregiver gradually become assimilated into the child's autonomous functional system through interactions between the maturing child and the responsive caregiver. Other than Kohut's (1971) allusion to traumatic disappointments during early childhood that interfere with the internalization of experiences of being soothed, none of the reviewed publications specifically considered the etiology of the pathogenic disturbances in internalization. Meanwhile, Hartocollis and Hartocollis (1980) and Woollcott (1981) attributed the development of psychoactive substance addiction to a basic disturbance of separation–individuation. An association between the development of psychoactive substance addiction and disturbed separation–individuation is not inconsistent with an association between the development of psychoactive substance addiction and disturbed internalization. The separation–individuation phase of development is contemporaneous with the period during which many important self-regulation functions are internalized, and disturbances in the mother–child relationship that are likely to interfere with separation–individuation are likely to interfere also with internalization, and vice versa. Hartocollis and Hartocollis (1980), whose discussion focused on alcoholics' denial of their need for help, hypothesized that alcoholics' denial of their needs originates in the rapprochement subphase of separation–individuation. According to the Hartocollises' hypothesis, the typical mother of the future alcololic denies the rapprochment child's needs. The child, in response, regresses to the hypomanic mode of functioning that characterizes the earlier practicing subphase, in which mode the child also denies his needs.

The following sources are included in the comprehensive review of psychoanalytic theories of psychoactive substance addiction: Abraham, 1908; Brill, 1922; Freud, 1905; Glover, 1932; Rado, 1933; Fenichel, 1945a; Bergler, 1946; Kohut, 1959, 1971; Rosenfeld, 1965; D. Hartmann, 1969; Wieder and Kaplan, 1969; Krystal and Raskin, 1970; Ritvo, 1971; Krystal, 1974, 1975, 1982, 1995; Khantzian and Treece, 1977; Milkman and Frosch, 1977, 1980; Wurmser, 1977, 1978, 1980a,b, 1981, 1982, 1984, 1987, 1988, 1995; Khantzian, 1978, 1980, 1981, 1982, 1985, 1987, 1990, 1995; Hartocollis and Hartocollis, 1980; Meissner, 1980–1981; Woollcott, 1981; Wurmser and Zients, 1982; Khantzian and Mack, 1983; Blatt, Rounsaville, Eyre, and Wilber, 1984; Grotstein, 1984; and Dodes, 1990, 1996.

Bulimia

Most of the psychoanalytic writing on the subject of bulimia is of recent vintage, published in the 1980s or later. The majority of the psychoanalytic theories of bulimia focus on disturbed object

relations and impaired self-regulation, particularly impaired affect regulation, deficient self-soothing and self-enlivening, and
pathological self-experience (which includes the experience of
one's own body). Other theories allude to the dynamic importance of externalization and of a bisexual identification that involves the fantasy of an "unlimited potential" to be both male
and female. Bulimic individuals have been noted to lack particular ego and self functions, and consequently to seek substitutes
for these missing functions in selfobjects over which they have
control, such as food. From another perspective, bulimics are
noted to be characterized by an impaired ability to use objects as
true transitional objects, as a result of which they use food in
attempts to fulfill transitional object functions.

Bulimic symptoms are understood to be defensive reparative
maneuvers that attempt (1) to alleviate intolerable inner tensions;
(2) to soothe oneself; (3) to counteract anguished feelings of
emptiness or deadness; (4) to restore narcissistic equilibrium or
to provide a temporary sense of self-organization; (5) to compensate for what is felt to be missing inside; or (6) to recreate the
archaic, self-sustaining self-selfobject tie through a selfobject
transference to food. Preceding a binge, bulimic individuals usually experience a sense of discomfort. Their ability to recognize
and distinguish different affects and bodily sensations is typically
impaired, so they may be able to identify nothing more specific
than an uneasy dysphoria. Some bulimics do not even experience
the underlying emotional discomfort at all, but are aware only of
an urge to binge.

While far fewer pages of psychoanalytic writing have been
devoted to bulimia than to psychoactive substance addiction, bulimia has been the subject of considerably more discussion of
developmental antecedents and pathways. Bulimia is believed to
develop out of underlying vulnerabilities that result from derailed
separation–individuation and from inadequate internalization of
self-regulatory functions during early childhood. Most psychoanalytic theories attribute the future bulimic's impairments to a mismatch between the infant's emerging psychobiological needs and
the available environmental provisions. Such a mismatch could
be due to extraordinary demands on the part of the infant, to

inadequate maternal care of or responsiveness to the infant (which seems to be more likely), or to both in combination. In the typical case, the mother views the child as a narcissistic extension of a part of her own self, as a compensatory means of repairing her self-esteem, rather than as a separate individual with needs and feelings of her own. The result is a prolonged disturbance in empathic connectedness that is characterized by unmet needs, experiences of abandonment, and traumatic disappointments. These experiences are likely to be small, multiple, and cumulative over time, rather than singular and massive. The outcome of such a background that specifically predisposes an individual to bulimia is conceptualized to be disruptions of the separation–individuation process and of the internalization process. Disrupted separation–individuation leaves the child unable to use external inanimate objects as transitional objects, and stunts the development of her object relations. Disrupted internalization of parental selfobject or self-regulatory functions impedes the child's development of an effective capacity to modulate intense affective states and scrambles her development of a cohesive sense of self.

In the presence of these underlying vulnerabilities, bulimics seem to select the eating of food as their prosthetic self-regulatory behavior primarily because food is unconsciously identified with the mother. Food may thus become the unconsciously determined repository for dissociated aspects of representations of the mother or of the self-in-relation-to-mother. Conflicting emotions toward the mother are readily displaced onto food, and can then be expressed in the child's behavior toward the food. The selection of eating may be influenced also by (1) the significance of the oral cavity in the initial development of the self; (2) the subjective connection between eating and filling an inner emptiness; and (3) the symbolic equation of eating (incorporation) with the process by which psychic structure and the representational world first begin to develop.

The following sources are included in the comprehensive review of psychoanalytic theories of bulimia: Fenichel, 1945a; Sperling, 1949, 1983; Sours, 1974; Sugarman and Kurash, 1982; Goodsitt, 1983; Hogan, 1983; Ritvo, 1984; Swift and Letven, 1984;

Chessick, 1985; Rizzutto, 1985; H. J. Schwartz, 1986, 1988a,b; Ceasar, 1988; Krueger, 1988; Geist, 1989.

Pathological Gambling

Pathological gambling has received less attention in the psychoanalytic literature than have the other addictive disorders. Its dynamics have been discussed in less depth, and little has been written about possible factors in its etiology. In contrast to the psychoanalytic literature on bulimia, most of which was published in the 1980s and after, nearly all of the literature on pathological gambling was published in 1970 or earlier. As a result, most of the psychoanalytic theories about gambling are framed in drive theory or structural terms, and little has been written about pathological gambling from the perspective of object relations or self psychology.

The predominant psychodynamic factors in pathological gambling seem to be orality, narcissistic pathology, and masochism, of which narcissistic pathology is the most central. Pathological gambling has been thought to originate in the oral level of development, at which hunger, sexuality, need for love, and striving for security are not differentiated from one another. Gambling expresses a yearning to recapture the feeling of primary omnipotence that is associated with a fantasied fusion with the oral phase mother. The most prominent theme in psychoanalytic theories of pathological gambling is the gambler's narcissistic pathology, which is characterized by grandiosity, an entitled expectation of special privilege, a sense of omnipotence, frantic attempts at oral–narcissistic replenishment, and a tendency to aggressively control potential sources of supplies. The core dynamic process is a fantasy of omnipotence, an illusion of power and control, that functions to defend against: (1) depression, loneliness, and grief; (2) separation anxiety; (3) castration anxiety (which, as we considered in chapter 4, refers to anxiety about the vulnerability of one's body self to mutilation); (4) feelings of fragmentation, nothingness, and emptiness; and (5) the limitations that the reality principle forces one to confront, which include uncertainty and the inevitability of death. A recurrent counterpoint to the narcissism theme is the theme of bisexuality or female identification, which is associated with a wish to be overwhelmed and with unusually intense castration anxiety. A hypermasculine form of omnipotence may be adopted as a defense against one's female identification and the castration anxiety that it entails. On the other hand, a bisexual form of omnipotence, with the potential to be both male and female, enables denial of the reality limits that force a choice between castration and loss of the female identification. The third of the predominant dynamics in pathological gambling, masochism, has components of both moral and erotogenic masochism. The moral component derives from guilt for the aggressive aspects of omnipotence: challenging the oedipal father, robbing the preoedipal mother, and transgressing the boundaries of reality. Guilt for triumphing over reality can be reinforced by the anxiety that can accompany the sense that one's power is unlimited. The erotogenic component derives both from anal sadism and from a sadomasochistic relationship between the superego and the self, in which the individual seeks punishment because that is how his self experiences being loved by his superego. Masochism leads gamblers unconsciously to seek or to provoke situations in which they are defeated, rejected, or refused.

The primary functions of pathological gambling mirror the functions of the fantasy of omnipotence from which it emerges: affect regulation, or defense against painful affects, anxieties, and moods; and restoration or bolstering of a fragile narcissistic equilibrium. A number of psychoanalytic investigators characterized gambling as a plea to or demand of Fate—the externalized parental representative, primarily of the preoedipal mother—for a show of favor and for narcissistic validation. Gambling can function also as an attempt to win reparation for the gambler's mother's narcissistic damage. The psychodynamic complexity of pathological gambling is indicated by the paradox that the only sure bet in the game is that the gambler's plea for validation and his attempt to win reparation will fail.

Psychoanalytic investigators thus far have said little about possible factors in the origin of pathological gambling. Galdston

(1951) attributed pathological gambling to a developmental arrest that results from early and severe deprivations in future gamblers' affective relations with their parents, especially their mothers. He noted also that, during their childhood, these individuals do not receive adequate validation of their self-worth. Geha (1970) stated that the primary determinant of the gambling impulse is a disturbed preoedipal mother–child relationship, in which the mother refuses to feed. The remainder of Geha's discussion did not indicate whether he intended "refuses to feed" to be understood literally, or whether he meant the phrase metaphorically, to include a mother's impaired ability to nurture her child emotionally.

The following sources are included in the comprehensive review of psychoanalytic theories of pathological gambling: Simmel, 1920; Freud, 1928; Bergler, 1936, 1943, 1958; Fenichel, 1945a; Greenson, 1947; Galdston, 1951, 1960; Tyndel, 1963; Niederland, 1967; Bolen and Boyd, 1968; Geha, 1970; and Rosenthal, 1985, 1987.

Sexual Addiction

Psychoanalytic theories of sexual perversion and pathological hypersexuality, the conditions most similar to conditions that now would meet the diagnostic criteria for sexual addiction, were reviewed in chapter 4. The following paragraphs represent a brief summary of the integrative recap that concluded chapter 4.

The psychodynamic and etiologic factors in perversion and pathological hypersexuality can be considered in two categories: nonspecific factors that promote the development of addictive patterns in general, and specific factors that foster sexualization and thus promote the development of sexual addiction in particular.

The primary nonspecific factors are ego weakness, unusually intense castration anxiety (anxiety about the vulnerability of one's body self to mutilation), the fantasy of gender bipotentiality, splitting, and superego pathology. These factors are interrelated, and are understood to originate in some combination of constitutional factors and disturbances in the mother–child relationship. The central difficulty is seen to concern deficiencies and distortions in the mother's responsiveness to the child's needs, which result from the mother's narcissistic pathology and her use of the child as a means of meeting her own narcissistic and emotional needs. While different authors emphasized different aspects of the etiologic process, three consequences of deficient and distorted maternal responsiveness seem to promote the development of addictive behavior patterns in general: (1) impaired internalization of a variety of self-regulatory ego and superego functions; (2) a disrupted transition through the separation–individuation process; and (3) abnormally high levels of aggression, which derives primarily from the frustration of early needs. The sequelae of these factors can then be summarized as: (1) deficits in psychic structuralization and development, with specific impairments in affect regulation, self-comforting, superego functions (including ego ideal), object relations, and self-system; and (2) reliance on some form of pleasure-producing behavior as an attempt to regulate affects and self-esteem, to repair narcissistic balance, to manage aggression, and to compensate for missing pieces in the psychic structure and in the inner object world.

The specific factors that typically foster sexualization, and that thus promote the development of sexual addiction in particular, are seductiveness and sexualization on the mother's part, which induce precocious genitalization and identification with the mother's sexualization. Maternal seductiveness can be either overtly sexual or more subtly narcissistic, and the sexual nature of the mother's interest is usually repressed or disavowed.

Conclusion of the Overview

The psychoanalytic theories of psychoactive substance addiction, bulimia, pathological gambling, and sexual addiction share so many features that they resemble variations on a theme, rather than separate themes (Goodman, 1993a). The thesis that these four disorders should be grouped together as addictive disorders is thus supported not only by the empirical data that were reviewed earlier in this chapter, but also by the core psychodynamic and etiologic factors that the four disorders share. A number of earlier psychoanalytic investigators also recognized the psychodynamic commonalities among psychoactive substance addiction, bulimia, pathological gambling, and sexual addiction; and my thesis that these disorders should be grouped together is not original. Similar thoughts were presented by Freud (1892–1899, 1928), Rado (1933), Fenichel (1945a), Bergler (1958), McDougall (1972), Chasseguet-Smirgel (1974), and Tolpin and Kohut (1985).

In chapter 1, I presented a series of arguments in favor of designating as sexual addiction a condition in which some form of sexual behavior is employed in a pattern that is characterized by recurrent loss of control and continuation of the behavior despite significant harmful consequences. The basis of those arguments was more empirical than psychoanalytic, and more semantic than clinical. The material that I have presented in this chapter has, I believe, rectified the balance by providing a more psychoanalytic and clinical perspective on the appropriateness of grouping this pattern of sexual behavior with the psychoactive substance addictions.

Overview of Learning Theory-Based Formulations of Addictive Disorders

Learning theory-based formulations of addiction can be divided into two groups, simple and complex. Simple learning theory formulations of alcoholism and drug addiction attribute the use of alcohol and other drugs to their reinforcing properties, and they emphasize their negative reinforcing consequences—their ability to relieve anxiety, tension, and other uncomfortable affects (Conger, 1956; Teasdale, 1973; Jarvik, 1977; Russell, 1977; Schachter, 1978; Barrett, 1985). Individual differences in the strength of this response are linked to the degree of threat that the individual experiences, which depends on the interaction between the level of environmental stress and the emotional vulnerability of the individual (Vogel-Sprott, 1972). The consumption of alcohol or other drugs is then influenced by their availability and by the availability of alternative reinforcers (Vuchinich and Tucker, 1988). Similar theories have been proposed for bulimia (Mitchell et al., 1985) and for pathological gambling (Ferrioli and Ciminero, 1985; Lyons, 1985; Blaszczynski, Wilson, and McConaghy, 1986; Blaszczynski and McConaghy, 1989). Craving and withdrawal are understood to be the results of learning processes in which craving sensations and withdrawal symptoms are conditioned to aversive mood states that the drug has been used to relieve. Craving sensations and withdrawal symptoms are then triggered by external stimuli that have become associated with these mood states (Wikler, 1971, 1973, 1980a,b; Ludwig and Wikler, 1974; O'Brien, 1975; Leventhal and Cleary, 1980; Sideroff and Jarvik, 1980; Childress, McLellan, and O'Brien, 1986; Childress, McLellan, Natale, and O'Brien, 1987; Sherman, Jorenby, and Baker, 1988). The external cues that are associated with the various behavioral and chemical addictions are seen to differ according to the syndrome, while the internal cues that condition to addiction are similar across the various syndromes (Marks, 1990).

Complex learning theory formulations of addiction, which derive from social learning theory, cognitive–behavioral theory, decision-making theory, and social cognitive theory, include expectations as relevant motivational factors and take interpersonal influences into account as well. Their basic principle is that addictive behavior (most of these theories address only addiction to alcohol or other drugs) results from aversive emotional states, plus expectations that engaging in the behavior will provide relief from the emotional distress, plus low self-efficacy beliefs; that is, expectations that other means of responding to the emotional distress will be less likely to provide relief. According to the formulations of addiction that are based in complex learning theory, predisposing individual-difference factors interact with socializing agents and situations to determine the initial patterns of the behavior, which are then modified according to contingencies of reinforcement, environmental stress, and expectations. Addiction develops out of the reciprocal interaction among three interlocking sets of factors: behavior, cognition (beliefs and expectations), and environment, primarily the social environment

(Bandura, 1977a,b, 1982; Marlatt, 1978, 1985; Cummings, Gordon, and Marlatt, 1980; Marlatt and Rohsenow, 1980; Edwards, Arif, and Hodgson, 1981; Adesso, 1985; Orford, 1985; Abrams and Niaura, 1987; R. I. F. Brown, 1987; Cox and Klinger, 1988; Marlatt, Baer, Donovan, and Kivlahan, 1988; Niaura, Rohsenow, Binkoff, Monti, Pedraza, and Abrams, 1988; A. T. Wilson, 1988).

A Unified Psychological Theory of the Addictive Process

The similarities between the psychoanalytic theories of the various addictive disorders are consistent with the hypothesis that the disorders share an underlying pathological process, a hypothesis with which the learning theory-based formulations of addiction also are consistent. Differences in terminology and in conceptual constructs between the psychoanalytic and the learning theory-based formulations may obscure the fact that they do not contradict but complement one another, that they are mutually compatible. The psychoanalytic theories discuss in considerable detail the nature and origins of the "predisposing individual-difference factors": (1) an individual's emotional and psychological vulnerabilities; (2) the prevalence and intensity of the individual's painful affects or mood states; (3) the functional status of the individual's alternative means of managing vulnerabilities and emotional pain; and (4) the individual's background set of beliefs and expectations, including beliefs about self-efficacy. The learning theory-based formulations begin at a point where the predisposing individual-difference factors are already established, and they focus on how addictive patterns of behavior develop when individual predisposing factors and social environment factors combine to extraordinarily reinforce the occurrence of a particular kind of behavior.

A unified psychological theory of addiction can be woven from the common threads in these formulations. Two sets of factors can be seen to influence the development of addictive disorders: those that concern the underlying addictive process, and those that relate to the selection of a particular form of behavior as the one that is preferred for addictive use. The remainder of this section is devoted to outlining a psychological theory of the addictive process. It is framed primarily in psychoanalytic terms, which provide the most information about individual predisposing factors and about individuals' subjective experience. The matter of how a particular form of behavior is selected as the one that is preferred for addictive use is addressed later in this chapter. Before I proceed, I would like to note that what I am doing in this section is not presenting a complete psychological theory of the addictive process, which would require a book of its own, but only sketching the outline of such a theory. My intention here is only to indicate that a psychological or psychoanalytic theory of the addictive process is feasible and potentially useful, and to suggest a form that such a theory could take.

Impairment of the Self-Regulation System

The central thesis of the theory that I am presenting is that the addictive process originates in an impairment of the self-regulation system, the internal psychobiological system that regulates one's subjective (sensory, emotional, and cognitive) states and one's behavioral states. Impaired internal regulation of their subjective states leads individuals to depend on external actions to regulate their subjective states and to cope with the subjective consequences of internal dysregulation. Impaired internal regulation of their behavioral states limits individuals' capacity to modulate or to inhibit urges to engage in such compensatory actions. Addictive behavior thus represents both an attempt to cope with the subjective consequences of impaired self-regulatory functioning, and an overt manifestation of impaired self-regulatory functioning.

In my formulation, the terms *impairment of the self-regulation system* and *impaired self-regulatory functioning* serve the purpose that in more classical psychoanalytic formulations was served by the term *ego weakness*. Though the meanings of *self-regulation system* and *ego* overlap considerably, they are not identical, and I find the former term to be the more useful in the present context. First of all, the addictive process often involves the impairment

of a number of functional subsystems that are constituents of
the self-regulation system but are not usually considered to be
constituents of the ego. These functional subsystems include the
superego, the ego ideal, and processes that regulate the sense of
self. Second, some functions of the ego that are not part of the
self-regulation system, such as motility and intellectual ability, are
typically not significantly impaired in addiction. Finally, the Latin
word *ego*, which was introduced into the English translation of
Freud's work in a misguided attempt to make his "Ich" more
scientifically respectable than it would have been were it simply
translated into English as "I," is more obscure in meaning than
is "self-regulation system" or "self-regulatory functioning," and
it is also more prone to being reified.

The self-regulation system is a complex system of functions
that are interrelated both functionally and developmentally. It
can be understood to consist of three primary components: affect
regulation functions (the most basic and significant), self-care
functions, and self-governance functions. Various combinations
of genetic and environmental factors can interfere with the development of the self-regulation system, and each of the three primary components may be impaired to varying degrees.

Affect regulation functions include self-soothing, self-enlivening, keeping affects in balance, and tolerating affects without being overwhelmed. Impaired affect regulation involves (1) affect
regression tendencies; (2) deficient ability to utilize anxiety and
other affects as signals; and (3) impaired tolerance of painful
affect. To the extent that affect regulation is impaired, emotional
states tend to be unstable, intense, and disorganizing. Affect-dysregulated individuals are often subject to affect regression, in
which affects become amorphous, somatic, and global. In the
context of low affect tolerance and deficient affect signal function, these regressive affects can be experienced as impending
organismic catastrophe. Affect-dysregulated individuals are thus
vulnerable to being traumatically overwhelmed by affects that an
intact individual does not experience as potentially traumatic.
Especially threatening are separation anxiety, castration (mutilation) anxiety, superego affects, depressive affects, and affects that

are associated with narcissistic injury. But almost any intense affect, including excitement and love, can be experienced by these individuals as threatening.

Self-care functions include self-protection and self-nurturing. Self-protection involves the capacity to recognize, to assess, to warn oneself of, and to protect oneself against danger. Self-nurturing involves the capacity to recognize, to assess, to set priorities among, and to take care of one's needs. Self-care is a multiplex functional system that involves a variety of affective and cognitive processes, defensive operations, reality testing, judgment, control, delay, synthesis, cause-consequence reasoning, and relatively stable superego functions. A critical component of self-care is the ability to use affects as signals or guides for appropriate action. To the extent that self-care is impaired, individuals are deficient in their abilities to avoid danger, to protect themselves, and to take care of their needs. The dangers to which they expose themselves include physical, emotional, and narcissistic dangers. Similarly, the needs to which they fail adequately to attend include physical, emotional, and narcissistic needs. As a result, they are particularly susceptible to getting hurt and to being chronically dissatisfied, on all three levels.

Self governance functions include values, standards, self-esteem, self-punishment, and maintenance of a stable and cohesive sense of self. Self-governance thus subsumes (1) the superego, in its approving, encouraging, and loving aspects as well as its prohibiting, condemning, and punishing aspects; (2) the ego ideal; and (3) the processes that are involved in regulating the sense of self. The superego pathology that is usually associated with addictive disorders consists of (1) insufficient structuralization and integration; (2) structural defects or lacunae; and (3) a split in superego functioning. Defenses against the superego and denial of superego affects further undermine the superego's capacity to fulfill its self-governing functions. The ego ideal tends also to have been deficiently structuralized and integrated, and it is often infiltrated by grandiose fantasies that derive from the pathological narcissism of the subject and/or his parents (usually his mother). In addictive disorders, the processes that are involved in healthy regulation of the sense of self typically have not been sufficiently internalized. Often, processes of regulating the sense of self that are ultimately maladaptive, such as sexualization, are internalized in their stead. Regulation of the sense of self may be further handicapped by the split in the self representation that can result from split superego functioning, and by the disorganizing intensity and instability of affect that is associated with impaired affect regulation. To the extent that self-governance is impaired, individuals lack a stable self-esteem, a consistent sense of self, and a clear sense of direction. They may have skewed or fragmented values, ideals, and sense of meaning. Their behavior tends to oscillate between extremes, and they may swing from actions that violate their values to actions that are self-injurious or that invite punishment from the environment.

Impaired self-regulation thus leaves individuals abnormally vulnerable to being overwhelmed by intense affect states and by loss of self-coherence, a danger that they experience as a threat to their very existence. They consequently turn to a variety of self-protective mental and behavioral processes in order to attenuate or to avoid this danger. Such individuals typically must evoke and employ object representations to perform for them the functions that individuals with an intact and well structuralized self-regulation system are able to do automatically. They then externalize these self-regulation endowed object representations, or selfobject representations, onto persons, institutions, nonhuman objects, substances, activities, or bodily states, which thereby come to function for the individuals as selfobjects: that is, nonself entities or processes that serve self-regulatory functions. These individuals are subsequently inclined to depend on their artificial selfobjects for the provision of self-regulatory functions that they are not sufficiently able to provide for themselves. Insofar as these individuals experience (consciously or unconsciously) their deficient or missing self-regulatory functions to be necessary for their survival, they are highly motivated (1) to control their artificial selfobjects, and (2) to externalize their self-regulatory potential onto, and thereby to create artificial selfobjects of, objects over which they believe (consciously or unconsciously) that they have control. Furthermore, insofar as these individuals experience their deficient or missing self-regulatory functions to be necessary for their survival, their urges to engage in behavior that conjures (or attempts to conjure) self-regulatory functions from their artificial selfobjects are typically so imperative that their patterns of engaging in such behavior are likely to be characterized by impaired control and by relative imperviousness to the restraining influence of harmful consequences. This, then, is the essence of the addictive process: (1) due to some combination of genetic and environmental factors, individuals' self-regulatory functions are impaired; (2) impaired self-regulation leaves these individuals abnormally vulnerable to being overwhelmed by intense affect states and by loss of self-coherence; and (3) in attempts to attenuate or to avoid the danger of being thus overwhelmed, these individuals externalize their self-regulatory potential onto nonself entities or processes over which they believe that they have control. Individuals whose externalizations of this type lead them to engage in some form of behavior in a pattern that is characterized by recurrent loss of control and by continuation of the behavior despite significant harmful consequences, can then be characterized as "addicts," whatever the behaviors in which they addictively engage. Many such addicts learn to ward off overwhelming affect states and traumatic self states by engaging in a rewarding activity: for example, eating, or taking a mood-altering substance into their bodies, or gambling, or engaging in some form of sexual behavior. With practice, this response can evolve into a self-protective way of being. External or internal cues that are associated with intense affect states or with loss of self-coherence can then become conditioned to particular craving sensations or can become discriminative stimuli for particular addictive-behavioral responses. As a result, these cues can trigger or can be experienced as urges to engage in addictive behavior.

Other important psychodynamic factors that are associated with the addictive process include: (1) a failure to resolve the basic merger–individuation conflict; (2) unusually intense castration anxiety (anxiety about the vulnerability of one's body self to mutilation); (3) high levels of preoedipal aggression or sadism; (4) alexithymia; (5) bisexual (bi-gender) identification; (6) masochism; and (7) characteristic primitive defenses.

Failure to Resolve the Basic Merger–Individuation Conflict

Addictive disorders are characterized by a failure to resolve what I call the "basic merger–individuation conflict," and consequently also a failure to adaptively manage the conflicts that evolve from it. The basic merger–individuation conflict is one between two fundamental sets of wishes and fears, which derive from the small child's fantasies about the preoedipal mother. It is continuous with conflicts that have been described by a number of psychoanalytic investigators: (1) the conflict that Bak (1953) described between separation anxiety and castration anxiety; (2) the conflict that Socarides (1973, 1988) described as a "nuclear conflict" between the desire for and the dread of merging with the preoedipal mother; (3) the conflict that Sours (1974) described between a longing for passive submission to the overpowering maternal object and a fear of the regressive fusion and dedifferentiation that such submission would entail; (4) the conflict that Glasser (1978, 1979, 1986) described as a "core conflict" between a longing for complete merger with the object and a fear of being engulfed and thereby annihilated as a separate identity; (5) the conflict that Woollcott (1981) described as the "fusion–individuation conflict"; and (6) the conflict that Sugarman and Kurash (1982) described between the wish for and the dread of fusion with the archaic mother. On one side of the conflict is the wish for merger or union with the object, which is combined with the fear of being separated from or abandoned by the object. On the other side of the conflict is the wish or (biologically determined) drive for individuation, mastery, and wholeness (inactness), which is combined with the fear of being engulfed, controlled, or damaged (mutilated or intruded into). Each side of this conflict involves one branch of the developmental bifurcation of annihilation anxiety, or fear of loss of self, into two antithetical components: claustrophobia, a potentially traumatic anxiety that is associated with the general idea of being closed in, intruded into, trapped, engulfed, or smothered; and agoraphobia, a potentially traumatic anxiety that is associated with the general idea of fragmenting or disintegrating due to a lack of supporting structure.

The basic merger–individuation conflict, then, can be understood as being between a basic pull toward another person and
a basic push away from another person. A diagrammatic outline
of the basic merger–individuation conflict is presented in Table
5.1.

TABLE 5.1
THE BASIC MERGER–INDIVIDUATION CONFLICT

Merger	vs.	Individuation
Basic Pull Toward Another Person		*Basic Push Away From Another Person*
Wish for Merger or Union with the Object		Wish or Drive for Individuation, Mastery, and Wholeness (intactness)
+		+
Fear of Being Separated from or Abandoned by the Object		Fear of Being Engulfed, Controlled, or Damaged (mutilated or intruded into)

The basic merger–individuation conflict is not limited to addicts; it is part of the human condition. In healthy development,
this conflict is resolved, in the sense that some stable form of
dynamic equilibrium is achieved and maintained. Individuals who
develop addictive disorders have particular difficulty resolving the
basic conflict (i.e., achieving and maintaining equilibrium),
which results from some combination of (1) a fundamental defect
in integrative function; (2) the emotional component of the conflict being overwhelming due to impaired affect regulation; (3)
reliance on "dis-integrating" defenses (such as splitting and denial or disavowal); and (4) splits and defects in the self-governance system. When the basic merger–individuation conflict
remains unresolved, the individual's inner life becomes organized
in terms of the conflict's polarities. Object relations, superego
functions, identity processes, and defenses become polarized by
the intensity of this basic conflict; and the resulting polarization
of the inner life further compounds the individual's difficulty in
resolving the basic conflict.

The basic merger–individuation conflict is manifested in derivative conflicts that emerge under the influence of developmental factors. The subsequent development of conflicts is both

diachronic (linear) and synchronic (concurrent): from the basic merger–individuation conflict evolves a succession of derivatives that reflect emerging developmental issues, while the basic conflict and each of its successive derivatives continue to operate in their original forms. Examples of such derivatives that are familiar in clinical practice include the conflict between the wish to be taken care of and the fear of being controlled, and the conflict between the wish to be competent and the fear of being abandoned. Failure to resolve the basic merger–individuation conflict promotes reliance on the primitive defenses of denial, splitting, projection, and externalization. Addicts characteristically displace their phobic anxieties onto external entities. As a result, they tend to experience claustrophobic anxiety when they are faced by limitations of any kind, and to experience agoraphobic anxiety when they perceive an insufficiency of supporting structure.

Unusually Intense Castration Anxiety

Addicts, or individuals who engage addictively in one or more forms of behavior, are typically subject to unusually intense castration anxiety: that is, anxiety about the vulnerability of their body self to mutilation. Intense castration anxiety makes negotiation of the oedipal period more difficult; it enhances the appeal of regression as a solution to oedipal conflicts; and it can have lasting sequelae in terms of superego functioning, feelings of adequacy, stability of the sense of self, and various aspects of interpersonal relationships with both males and females. As we considered in chapter 4, the psychodynamic meaning of castration extends far beyond removal of the phallus (or the gonads). Castration anxiety can be more comprehensively understood to represent the anxieties that are associated with feelings of being small, inadequate, helpless, and vulnerable to being brutally deprived (1) of one's bodily integrity and hence of the integrity of one's body ego and body self; (2) of one's gender identity and of the aspects of one's sense of self and sense of belonging that

relate to gender identity; and (3) of one's ability to connect libidinally with individuals of the other gender. This understanding of
castration anxiety enables a richer appreciation of its significance
(a) for females as well as males, and (b) in both narcissistic and
object relational terms.

The unusual intensity of the castration or mutilation anxiety
to which addicts are subject can derive from any combination of
several potential factors: (1) a persistence of body-related anxiety
from earlier developmental phases, which fuses with castration
anxiety and thereby reinforces it; (2) a distorted body image;
(3) an unstable self-representation; (4) fragile gender identity,
perhaps due to a bisexual (bi-gender) identification; (5) impaired
affect regulation, which renders any anxiety more intense and
destabilizing; and (6) projection of insufficiently metabolized preoedipal aggression or sadism onto a potentially castrating (muti-
lating) parent.

High Levels of Preoedipal Aggression or Sadism

The frequent persistence in addicts of high levels of preoedipal
aggression or sadism is itself worth examining. Impaired self-regulation tends to be associated with impaired modulation of drives
in general, and with a particular prominence of primitive aggression or sadism. Preoedipal aggression and sadism can also emerge
when regressive defenses against castration anxiety involve drive
regression and regressive defusion of libidinal and aggressive
drives. The unusual intensity of aggression in addicts may result
not only from regression and impaired self-regulation, but also
from an underlying level of preoedipal aggressive energy that is
abnormally high to begin with. Excessive preoedipal aggression
generally develops from some combination of constitutional predisposition and disturbances in the mother–child relationship.
Mother–child disturbances that can potentiate excessive preoedipal aggression include maternal mistreatment, overstimulation,
excessive frustration, and deprivation of nurturing or soothing.
In addition, aggressive reactions in the interest of preserving the

self can be provoked by threats of annihilation by merger with the mother.

Alexithymia

"Alexithymia" (literally, inability to read emotions) is a term that was coined by Sifneos (1967) to describe a characteristic pattern that he observed in patients with psychosomatic disorders. These patients demonstrated an impaired ability to recognize, to name, and to verbalize their emotions. They typically experienced their affects as physical bodily states, rather than as meaningful emotions, and they demonstrated a general disturbance of symbolic function that interfered not only with their ability to symbolize emotions but also with their ability to fantasize. Sifneos noted that these disturbances were often accompanied by anhedonia, impaired self-care, diminished emotional involvement in whole object relationships, and a lowered capacity for empathy. The ability to recognize and to identify emotions is a critical component of affect tolerance and affect signal function. Consequently, alexithymia tends to be associated with a significant impairment of affect regulation. The experience of affects as physical bodily states moreover disposes the individual to address them by physical means, by action—and particularly by action that directly affects the body.

Alexithymia has been found to characterize not only individuals with psychosomatic disorders, but also individuals with post-traumatic stress disorders and individuals with addictive disorders. The affects of individuals with addictive disorders tend to emerge in an undifferentiated, global, primarily somatic way, with particular prominence of an affect that combines anxiety and depression. This relatively undifferentiated, primarily somatic, potentially overwhelming affect may reflect empty depression, loneliness, separation anxiety, castration (mutilation) anxiety, guilt, shame, envy, narcissistic deflation, disappointment, or disillusionment. These individuals, however, are frequently out of touch with their internal states, and they have great difficulty identifying their emotions. Preceding an episode of addictive behavior, an addict typically experiences a nonspecific sense of dysphoria—a vague restlessness, an uneasiness, an unpleasant sense of tension. Some addicts do not experience the underlying emotional discomfort at all, but are aware only of an urge or a craving to engage in addictive behavior.

We can note that alexithymia is not an explanatory concept that accounts for addicts' impaired ability to recognize, name, and verbalize emotions, but a descriptive term. It conveys no specific information about the origin of the condition that it designates. Alexithymia can result from one or more of the following factors: (1) a primary developmental deficit; (2) a regression to a more primitive mode of symbolic and/or affective functioning; (3) a defense against affects or symbolic processes; and (4) a "walling off" of affect regulation functions in deference to the maternal object representation.

I would like to append another thought to our consideration of alexithymia. While addictive behavior is external action, it is precipitated by internal sensations that are often experienced as states of bodily need: craving by a drug addict, hunger by a bulimic, lust by a sex addict. As inquiry deepens, boundaries seem to blur between externalization onto the body (Ritvo, 1984), conversion of affect into somatic function (Wurmser, 1981), and the somatic quality of affective experience that characterizes affect regression (Krystal, 1974, 1975, 1995). Wurmser's (1980a) idea that addicts are "today's version of conversion hysterics" (p. 71) seems to be worthy of consideration.

Bisexual (Bi-Gender) Identification

Bisexual identification refers to an individual's unconscious fantasy that he or she is, or can be, both male and female. While *bisexual identification* is the term by which this fantasy is usually designated in the psychoanalytic literature, *bi-gender identification* may in fact be a more accurate designation. In the male, this fantasy derives primarily from a regression to or an abnormal persistence of the primary pregenital female identification. Both girls and boys begin life in a state of subjective identification with their mothers: they have not yet developed the representational capacities that are involved in differentiating a sense of self that is separate from their sense of their mothers. Since their mothers are female, the original or primary identification of both girls and boys is generally considered to be female. The primary identification could perhaps more accurately be described as "generic human," for which the mother represents the infant's prototype. Only later, with awareness of the genital difference, does the concept of female (or male) become meaningful. When girls and boys begin to develop gender identities, their developmental paths bifurcate. In the course of the differentiation and consolidation of her female gender identity, the girl can maintain her primary identification with her mother. Her primary female identification does not conflict with her emerging female gender identity. The boy, on the other hand, can differentiate and consolidate his male gender identity only by disidentifying from his mother, since his primary female identification (primary identification with a person who turns out to have been female) conflicts with his emerging male gender identity. The developmental pressure on boys to disidentify from their mothers intensifies the separation anxiety that they experience in the course of the separation–individuation process. Boys may then attempt to ward off this separation anxiety by clinging to or reverting to the primary female identification.

While the intensification of separation anxiety by the pressure to disidentify from the mother is a typical feature of normal male development, some boys are particularly vulnerable to being traumatically overwhelmed by separation anxiety. Such vulnerability can derive from a high antecedent intensity of separation anxiety, as in boys whose basic needs for attachment and maternal contact were not met during their first eighteen months of life; or from impaired affect regulation of whatever origin, which impairs the capacity to tolerate anxiety in general. The fantasy of a bisexual (bi-gender) identification represents a variation on the theme of "unlimited potential" that characterizes fantasies of omnipotence. In this case, the "unlimited potential" to be both female and male enables the boy to deny the reality-imposed limits that force him to choose between either clinging to his female identification (which can imply castration and/or loss of self) and giving up his female identification (which can imply an irremediable separation from the life-giving maternal object). A fantasy of female identification in a male can be further reinforced by impaired identification with the father. Hatred of the father, which may be due to (1) hateful qualities in the actual father, or (2) displacement onto the father representation of bad attributes that had been split off from the mother representation, can result in repugnance toward a male or masculine identification. Identification with the father can be impaired also by the boy's disturbed object relations. An attenuated capacity for object relationship and a corresponding increase in narcissistically driven aggression can combine to replace object-related jealousy with envy, spite, and derogation, which in turn interfere with the boy's freedom to identify with his father.

Bisexual (bi-gender) identification in females is given little attention in the psychoanalytic literature on addictive disorders, to a great extent, because females are given little attention in this literature, other than in the literature on bulimia. While the psychoanalytic investigators of bulimia mentioned bisexual identification in females, they did not discuss it in the depth that characterizes the discussion in the perversion literature of bisexual identification in males. Schwartz (1986, 1988b), the only one of these investigators who explored the dynamics of bisexual identification in females, hypothesized that it denies the humiliation of having been excluded from the primal scene, that it undoes castration, and that it reverses passive (masochistic) oedipal impregnation wishes. He continued that bisexual forms of masturbation enable the acting out on one's own body of the imagined roles of both the sadistic phallic father and the suffering castrated mother. I believe that preoedipal factors also contribute to a bisexual (bi-gender) identification in females, and I suspect that they are more fundamentally important, as they are in males, than are the oedipal factors that Schwartz identified. Preoedipal factors that could contribute to a bisexual (bi-gender) identification in females include: (1) an inability to relinquish the mother

as the primary love object (when, for example, basic oral or narcissistic needs have remained unmet); (2) fear of the potential
consequences of turning toward the father as a love object, which
the little girl might imagine to entail abandonment by or destruction of the mother; (3) identification with a mother who is psychotic and has a disturbed gender identity; or, conversely,
defense against identification with a psychotic mother; and (4)
narcissistic pathology that is expressed in omnipotent fantasies
of total self-sufficiency; for example, fantasies in which the girl
imagines that she can be both man and woman, that she can
complete the sexual union within herself, and that she thus needs
no one else.

Masochism

Masochism in addictive disorders has components of both moral
and erotogenic masochism. The moral component involves a
seeking of punishment in order to expiate guilt. This guilt may
derive from oedipal fantasies, or it may derive more generally
from the aggressive aspects of omnipotent fantasies: fantasies of
robbing the preoedipal mother and of transgressing boundaries,
including the boundaries of reality, as well as fantasies of challenging the oedipal rival. Guilt for triumphing over reality may
be reinforced by the anxiety that can accompany the sense that
one's power is unlimited: an agoraphobic type of anxiety about
fragmenting or disintegrating due to lack of supporting structure.
    The erotogenic component of masochism in addictive disor-
ders can derive from one or more of several sources: (1) bisexual
(bi-gender) identification in males, when sexual relations are
seen in sadomasochistic terms and the female identification is
associated with a masochistic role; (2) repressed or disavowed
anal sadism, which is externalized and then experienced vicariously by submitting to it and identifying with the perpetrator; (3)
a sadomasochistic relationship between the superego and the self,
in which the individual seeks punishment because that is how his
or her self experiences being loved by the superego; and (4) a
wish to be overwhelmed, which can reflect, in addition to the

factors that were just listed, a conflicted wish to break through the defensive shell that separates the individual from other people or from his or her own inner vitality. Masochism undermines or sabotages self-care, and it often leads addicts unconsciously to seek or to provoke situations in which they are punished, defeated, rejected, or refused. This dynamic may in some cases be difficult to distinguish from provocation of the environment to assume the role of a punitive superego that has been disavowed and externalized.

Characteristic Primitive Defenses

The defenses that are typically employed by individuals who engage addictively in one or more forms of behavior are denial or disavowal, splitting, externalization, turning passive into active, and the defenses that constitute the narcissistic defensive system.

Denial or disavowal can be defined as a defensive failure either (1) to recognize the reality of what is perceived (Laplanche and Pontalis, 1967), or (2) to appreciate the significance or implications of what is perceived (Trunnel and Holt, 1974). In addictive disorders, the chief operands of denial are: (1) painful affects, particularly affects that relate to superego functions or that violate superego standards; (2) inner conflict, particularly the basic merger–individuation conflict and its derivatives; (3) narcissistic vulnerability and limitations; and (4) impulses that have been associated with severe trauma.

Splitting can be understood as both a defense and a manifestation of impaired integrative capacity. The core of this process is a disruption of the synthetic function of the ego, which manifests primarily as splits or dissociations in the individual's representational world. Such splitting contributes to a further weakening of the ego and to a fundamental disorder of the sense of self. Splitting can be understood (1) as a specific defense to reinforce denial (disavowal); (2) as a descriptive term for reciprocal denial as a means of coping with severe inner conflict (and not as a separate defense per se); (3) as the consequence of a defensive regression to a developmental period in which contradictory aspects of representations are not yet integrated; (4) as a result of preoedipal disturbances in ego development that weaken the integrative function of the ego; or (5) as a process that at first occurs as a manifestation of impaired integrative capacity and then later is used defensively. In addictive disorders, splitting is promoted by varying combinations of the following factors: (1) the overwhelming intensity of the affective component of inner conflicts, as a result of impaired affect regulation; (2) a split superego, which is associated with extreme and contradictory demands; (3) insufficient resolution of the basic merger–individuation conflict; and (4) reliance on a defensive system that is based on denial and on narcissistic or counterphobic fantasies that may in fact be antithetical (e.g., grandiose fantasies of omnipotence, juxtaposed with fantasies of being taken care of by an omnipotent protector); as well as (5) developmental defects in integrative function, which can result from any combination of constitutional vulnerabilities and deficiencies in the internalization matrix.

Externalization is the defense that is most specific to addictive disorders. Wurmser (1977, 1978, 1980b) described externalization as the defensive effort to resort to external action in order to support the denial of internal conflict, and thereby to transform internal into external conflict. Elsewhere, he noted that externalization converts anxiety about a vague, internal danger into anxiety about a tangible, external danger (Wurmser and Zients, 1982). Relief from anxiety about inner dangers could then be expected to be obtainable by action that evades or defeats dangers in the external world. Wurmser's use of the term *externalization* differs from customary usage, according to which it is nearly a synonym of projection. Moore and Fine (1968) defined externalization as "the tendency to project into the external world one's instinctual wishes, conflicts, moods, and ways of thinking (cognitive styles)" (p. 45). Meissner (1985) similarly defined externalization as "the tendency to perceive in the external world and in external objects components of one's own personality, including instinctual impulses, conflicts, moods, attitudes, and styles of thinking" (p. 389). He added that externalization is a more general term than is projection, and that it correlates with internalization while projection correlates with introjection. Externalization was not mentioned by Laplanche and Pontalis (1967), nor by Anna Freud (1937). Nonetheless, what Wurmser described as externalization is a significant process in addiction and, more generally, in narcissistic and borderline character pathology. It thus merits a specific term by which to be designated. I believe that externalization would be more useful as a psychodynamic concept if it were assigned a definition that is distinct from the definition of projection and that is consistent with Wurmser's usage. I suggest that externalization be distinguished as a process of action, while projection remains a process of perception. Projection would continue to be defined as the attribution to an object (human or nonhuman) of an impulse, affect, superego function, or other psychic process that in fact belongs to the subject's self; that is, perceiving as part of one's psychic representation of another person or thing what properly belongs with one's self representation. Externalization, then, would be defined as action that is based on the projection of an impulse, affect, superego function, or other psychic process onto an object. This proposed definition of externalization would be consistent with the definition that was indicated by Sandler, Kawenoka, Neurath, Rosenblatt, Schnurmann, and Sigal (1962) in their Hampstead Index work: "Externalization of the superego here means the process of investing an external figure with the qualities of the introject *and reacting to it* as if it were the introject" (p. 108; emphasis added). In addition, the proposed definition would echo Meissner's (1985) correlation of externalization with internalization. According to the proposed definition, externalization not only would indicate a process within the representational world. Like internalization, it also would connote an alteration of function. The action in externalization can function additionally as an (unconsciously directed) attempt to induce or to compel the object to act in a manner that is consistent with the projected material. Externalization, according to the proposed definition, is thus a complex process that combines elements of both projection and acting out. It can be seen, moreover, to represent a significant component of projective identification.

Externalization can function in one or more of several ways: (1) to support the denial of an internal conflict by assigning one pole of the conflict to an external agent, and thereby transforming the internal conflict into an external conflict; (2) to take magical, omnipotent control over the inner life by converting a passive, traumatic inner state into a tangible, external problem that can then be resolved through ego-directed mastery and concrete action; (3) to neutralize potentially overwhelming, primitive sadistic and aggressive impulses through the libidinization of activity; and (4) to mitigate the deadness in the addict's internal world that results from archaic, excessive defenses, particularly defenses against unconscious sadism and aggression. Externalization represents the essence of the process whereby substances, objects, activities, or bodily states are endowed in fantasy with self-regulatory capacity and thus become the artificial selfobjects around which addictive disorders revolve.

The defense of turning passive into active involves actively recreating an intrapsychic situation of affects and self states that one has in the past suffered passively and experienced as traumatic. The intended recipient of this intrapsychic situation can be either another person or oneself. Turning passive into active can serve (1) to defend against narcissistic mortification (A. Freud, 1937); (2) to express aggressive and sadistic impulses, particularly those that were generated, directly or indirectly, by the traumatic experience; (3) as a counterphobic demonstration of control; and/or (4) as a means of gaining ego mastery. Turning passive into active is a normal process in ego and superego development. Its operation in addictive disorders indicates a striving for mastery that can represent a critical resource in the therapeutic process.

The narcissistic defensive system in addictive disorders is characterized by grandiosity, entitlement (an entitled expectation of special privilege), a sense of omnipotence, and pseudo-self-sufficiency, which is associated with denial of longings for nurturance and of needs for help. This system can be described also as a manic defense system or as a counterphobic system. An alternate aspect within the narcissistic system involves idealization and fantasies of an omnipotent protector, with whom the individual enjoys a special relationship. The narcissistic defensive system functions to defend against: (1) depression, loneliness, and grief; (2) separation anxiety; (3) castration (mutilation) anxiety and the associated feelings of helplessness, powerlessness, vulnerability, inadequacy, and shame; (4) feelings of fragmentation, nothingness, and emptiness; and (5) the limitations that the reality principle forces one to confront. Individuals whose character is structured by the narcissistic defensive system tend desperately to seek and aggressively to control potential sources of oral–narcissistic supplies, and to relate to external entities primarily in terms of their capacity to provide or to interfere with access to supplies. Addictive behavior patterns can be understood as a natural expression of narcissistic character pathology, of the characteristic modes of adaptation that individuals with such pathology employ to deal with their underlying vulnerabilities and impairments. In addictive disorders, denial, externalization, and narcissistic defenses support, reinforce, and promote each other, so that in effect they operate as one characterological system.

The Functions of Addictive Behavior

Addiction is a multiply determined syndrome, and it exemplifies the principle of multiple function (Waelder, 1936). Addictive behavior can fulfill a variety of functions, and the distribution of importance (the rank order in the motivational hierarchy) among the various functions in a particular individual depends on the individual's character organization.

In terms of classical theory, addiction represents a compromise between instinctual impulses and ego defenses. Addictive behavior functions to gratify primitive oral–sexual longings for undifferentiated food-love-security, for blissful merger with the archaic maternal object. It also functions to ward off oedipal anxieties, especially castration (mutilation) anxiety. In addition, addiction can represent a compromise between aggressive impulses, particularly reactive rage, and ego defenses, which in this case are directed primarily toward protecting the object from being destroyed by the subject's aggression (and, ultimately, toward protecting the subject from separation anxiety). The function of addiction that relates to conflicts around aggression is addressed below, in the object relations paragraph.

In terms of ego psychology, addiction serves the related functions of affect defense and provision of a sense of mastery. Addictive behavior can function to defend against, to relieve, or to master intolerable affects, such as depression, anhedonia, tension, superego affects (primarily guilt and shame), separation anxiety, paranoid anxieties, loneliness, helplessness, disappointment, and disillusionment. It can ward off dread by simulating a contradiction of the feared alienation, emptiness, inertia, and deadness. In a similar manner, addictive behavior can function as a manic defense against threats of despair, ego disintegration, and personality dissolution; and as a counterphobic defense against castration (mutilation) anxiety and feelings of inadequacy, shame, humiliation, and narcissistic mortification. Meanwhile, it can serve also to contain or to channel aggressive energies that threaten to overwhelm the ego. Addiction can furthermore function to provide a sense of mastery. In a general sense, it represents both an expression of the ego interests of mastery, power, and control, and a means of enhancing ego interests at the expense of both instinct interests (motivation to satisfy instinctual needs) and object interests (motivation to form connections with other persons). Addictive behavior can function to support and to express the narcissistic defenses of pseudo-self-sufficiency and omnipotent control. When the addict engages in addictive behavior, he assumes both the role of the one who is in need and the role of the one who satisfies the need: he is able to take care of his needs by himself. More specifically, addicts use addictive behavior not only to relieve affects, but also to control them. Addictive behavior enables addicts intentionally to alter their own affective states. This ability provides addicts with a sense of control or omnipotence that can counter traumatic feelings of helplessness or powerlessness, to which they are particularly sensitive as a result of their narcissistic pathology. At the same time, addicts are driven to control their affects, not only as a means of defending against the distress of feeling powerless, but also as an attempt to master painful affect states for which they lack symbolic representation, by turning passive into active.

In terms of object relations, addiction functions both (1) to express aggression toward the object and to affirm a separate identity, and (2) to preserve the object from being destroyed by the subject's aggression. One aspect of the aggression that addiction can express is revenge for childhood victimization or for early deprivation of needed oral and narcissistic supplies. A second aspect relates to the separation–individuation process and the wish to affirm one's own separate identity. Aggression can operate in the service of identity affirmation by defying the overbearing influence of the internal mothering figure, by defining the boundaries of the self, and by protecting against the wish to depend on or to merge with the maternal imago. Aggression may thus be mobilized when one's sense of identity is threatened, to stem the panic that accompanies a threatened loss of identity sense. Meanwhile, addiction can function also to preserve internal and external objects, especially those that are intrapsychically associated with the oral mother, from primitive aggression and sadism. In so doing, it also preserves those aspects of the self that are identified with the object. The simultaneous presence of wishes both to preserve the object from aggression and to express aggression toward the object (and to affirm a separate identity) is, in effect, a manifestation of the basic merger–individuation conflict. A constant theme in the psychodynamics of addiction is its function to sustain denial or disavowal of this basic conflict, or to provide an illusory resolution to the conflict. Addictive behavior not only permits and reinforces an experience of blissful fusion of the self and object worlds, it also does so in a way that enables the avoidance of the various persecutory and claustrophobic anxieties that could accompany real closeness with another person. It thus provides a spurious but compelling solution to the basic merger–individuation conflict. Beyond its specific functions in the context of aggression and the basic conflict, addictive behavior also serves more broadly to fill in or to compensate for what is missing or damaged in the individual's internal object world that would regulate affects and self-processes. In this regard, the substances, objects, activities, or bodily states that are

associated with the addictive behavior function as "as if" transitional objects; that is, prototransitional objects of the symbolic-
equation type (Segal, 1957, 1978), with which the individual attempts to fulfill the function of a true transitional object. This
latter function, which can be described in terms of object relations (transitional object function), ego psychology (externalized
affect regulation), or self psychology (selfobject function), indicates the extent to which these different schools of thought represent, not disparate psychologies, but different (and at times
overlapping) sets of terms that focus on different aspects of a
unitary psychological system.

In terms of self psychology, addiction can function as a splint
for an individual's self-esteem or sense of self, as a prosthetic
selfobject, or as an attempt to heal the self. Addictive behavior
can represent an expression of incorporative longings (1) to fill
in missing narcissistic structure in order to regulate self-esteem;
(2) to revive a sense of having a cohesive self; (3) to ward off
self-depletion and self-fragmentation; and (4) to consolidate and
stabilize one's sense of self. In these cases, the addictive process
artificially recreates the archaic, self-sustaining self-selfobject tie
through a selfobject transference to the substances, objects, activities, or bodily states with which the addictive behavior is associated. These artificial selfobjects then serve to substitute for self-
regulatory intrapsychic structures that are missing or damaged
because the selfobject functions that were needed for the internalization of these structures during the developmentally sensitive period were lacking. Addiction can also represent an attempt
to heal the self, in two senses. In one sense, addictive behavior
can function as an attempt to repair the sense of self, a function
that is continuous with the set of narcissistic functions that was
described at the beginning of this paragraph (the "splint" functions). In a more profound sense, addictive behavior can function
as an attempt to achieve a "corrective emotional experience"
through which the splits in the addict's personality and representational world can be healed. The substances, objects, activities,
or bodily states with which the addictive behavior is associated
then become containers for the individual's split-off aspects,
which he tries to bring together and master by controlling the

substances, objects, activities, or bodily states. Addiction thus can represent a reparative effort to restore missed opportunities for the integration of ego and self.

In addition to the general addictive or self-regulatory functions that have been summarized, other functions also are likely to be served by a specific form of behavior in the individual case. The nature of and need for these particular functions are determined by the psychodynamics and personal history of the individual. The addictive process is never the only psychodynamic determinant of an addictive pattern of behavior. In other words, the identification of a pattern of behavior as an addictive disorder implies that the addictive process is a necessary explanatory factor, but not that it is a sufficient one.

Development of the Addictive Process

Contributions of Personal History to Etiology

The addictive process originates in a disorder of self-regulation. Approaches to formulating how disorders of self-regulation develop begin most productively with an understanding of how the self-regulation system forms in healthy development. The self-regulation system develops through the interaction of multiple systems that involve both genetic endowment and the child's relationship with his or her primary caregiver during the first years of life. The essential process in the development of self-regulatory functions is internalization, a dialectical process whereby regulatory functions that had been provided for the child by the caregiver gradually become integrated into the child's autonomous functional system through interactions between the maturing child and the responsive caregiver. A survey of the relevant literature indicates that all aspects of the self-regulation system, including affect regulation, self-care, and self-governance functions, develop through the gradual internalization of caregiver functions and their assimilation into unfolding, constitutionally determined infrastructures. Affect regulation functions develop through internalization of the mother's holding or container function (Bion, 1962; Winnicott, 1965; Modell, 1978; Grotstein, 1980) and internalization of her responses to the infant's affective behavior (Krystal, 1974). The former is the basic matrix for affect tolerance, while the latter is the template for the development of affect signal function. These affect regulation functions are ultimately indistinguishable in their development and in their operation (Krystal, 1975; Grotstein, 1984). Self-care functions become internalized in the context of caregivers' nurturing and protective behavior, accompanied by internalization of the message that the child is valued and worth taking care of (Khantzian and Mack, 1983). Superego functions, the self-governance functions that have been most thoroughly studied, are also generally recognized to develop through introjection and then internalization of parental functions (Reich, 1954; Beres, 1958; Spitz, 1958; Sandler, 1960; Furer, 1967; Hammerman, 1965; Kohut, 1971; Meissner, 1980; Brickman, 1983; Westen, 1986). The central unifying concept in these processes of functional development is developmental internalization, or transmuting internalization (Kohut, 1968, 1971), which was described by Tolpin (1971) as "bit-by-bit accretion of psychic structure from innumerable fractionated internalizations of specific maternal functions" (p. 318). (We can note that the relationship with the mother is usually the primary matrix for internalization, but it is not the only one.)

Consistent with this understanding of self-regulatory function development is the principle that disorders of the self-regulation system develop as a result of disturbances in the process of developmental internalization. These disturbances have been variously attributed to failure of parental container function (Bion, 1962), impingements or failures of empathic response (Winnicott, 1965), traumatic disappointments (Kohut, 1966, 1968, 1971), a mismatch between the infant's emerging psychobiological needs and the available environmental provisions (Balint, 1968), inadequacy of maternal stimulus barrier function (Krystal and Raskin, 1970), insufficient maternal availability (Goldberg, 1975), the mother's incapacity to administer doses of life experience that are phase-adequate for the child (Khan, 1979), and faulty patterns of affective interchange between the child and the caregiver (Emde, 1983, 1988). Most psychoanalytic investigators have agreed that the characteristic historical background of addictive disorders is a long persistence of disturbed interaction with the primary caregiver, not a single traumatic event or series of events. The pathogenic experiences are likely to be small, multiple, and cumulative over time, rather than isolated and massive.

A number of investigators have emphasized disturbances in separation–individuation as central in the development of addictive disorders. Some investigators have in particular focused on the rapprochement subphase of separation–individuation, proposing that the core problem in addiction is either a failure to progress to rapprochement, an inability to negotiate rapprochement, or a defensive regression from rapprochement to practicing.[1]

The separation–individuation phase of development is the critical period for the internalization of a number of important self-regulatory functions, for the differentiation of a self representation, and consequently for the development of the sense of self and of other self-processes. It is thus likely to be a critical period for the developmental disturbances that eventuate in addictive disorders. The separation–individuation process may break down

---

[1]Separation–individuation is a developmental process through which children gradually differentiate out of the symbiotic mother–child matrix (Mahler and Fuhrer, 1968; Mahler, Pine, and Bergman, 1975). Although its stages are often described in terms of their association with observable and/or interpersonal events, separation–individuation is an intrapsychic process that primarily involves the development of the child's inner representational system. The practicing subphase of the separation–individuation process, which generally corresponds to the chronological age of 10 to 16 months, is initiated by the attainment of free upright locomotion. During the practicing subphase, children initiate activities in which they actively move away from their mothers to explore a new world that they formerly were unable even to see on their own, let alone to move through. The rapprochement subphase, which generally corresponds to the age of 16 to 18 months, is initiated by children's dawning awareness that they still need and depend on their mothers. They moreover realize that their increasing separateness from their mothers entails that their mothers are becoming less available to them. These realizations evoke separation anxiety, which opposes the children's practicing subphase fantasies of autonomy and omnipotence, and thereby generates intrapsychic conflict. The rapprochement subphase is characterized by ambivalence and by the first indications of depressive moods.

specifically at the stage of transitional phenomena. In such cases, the child fails to develop the ability to use external objects as transitional objects. Transitional objects not only facilitate the child's efforts to separate from the mother; they also function as training wheels or stepping stones on the way to internalizing self-regulatory functions that the mother had formerly provided for the child. Impairment of the child's ability to use external objects as transitional objects thus can disrupt the child's internalization of self-regulatory functions, as well as distorting the development of his object relations.

We now consider in more detail "the prototypal case" of the future addict's early childhood, some but not necessarily all features of which are likely to have characterized the childhood of most addicts. For ease of writing and reading, I am assigning the child in this prototypal case a male gender. The historical-dynamic antecedents of addiction in males and females are likely to differ less in the early and middle preoedipal (oral and anal) periods, and to differ more in the later preoedipal (phallic) and oedipal periods. I refer to the child's primary and secondary care-givers as the child's mother and father, respectively, for reasons that I noted in the Preface.

In the prototypal case, the mother has a character disorder with narcissistic features, and she may also be depressed. She consciously or unconsciously regards the infant either as a narcissistic extension of herself, a compensatory means of repairing her self-esteem and her sense of inner defectiveness; or as a substitute libidinal object, toward whom she reaches for gratifications that she does not receive from her mate. The mother uses the child as a means of gratifying her own narcissistic or emotional needs, and she fails to recognize or respond to the child's narcissistic and emotional needs. Her ability to relate to the child as a unique person is impaired, and her empathic responsiveness is unpredictable. The result is a prolonged disturbance in empathic connectedness that is characterized by unmet needs, experiences of abandonment, and traumatic disappointments. In response to the mother's denial of the child's needs, the child learns also to deny his needs.

In her narcissism, the mother is both overattentive and ne-glectful. Moreover, to the extent that the mother is responsive, her positive attentions tend to be inconsistent and undependable, often even teasing. The mother typically idolizes the child, ca-thecting (investing emotional energy in) something special in him and yet not cathecting him as a whole person. The child senses his mother's peculiar experience of him, internalizes the "idolized self" that she has created, and learns to tolerate this discontinuity in his experience of his self. The mother, mean-while, has a low tolerance for her child's distress and frustration. Furthermore, she has specific difficulty in handling the separate-ness, defiance, and aggression that he increasingly expresses dur-ing his anal phase. These developments evoke in her rage and hate, which she typically disavows.

The mother both actively and passively encourages the preco-cious development of her child's ego. She actively encourages precocious ego development in the child by avidly affirming his nascent ego functions, by encouraging him to channel his pregen-ital libido into ego processes, functions, and defenses, and by treating him "as if" he were more mature and more integrated than his current development allows. At the same time, she pas-sively encourages the child's precocious ego development by her neglect of his emotional and narcissistic needs. The child must then develop the capacity somehow to take care of these needs himself, however immature his ego infrastructure may be, lest he be overwhelmed by emotional and narcissistic trauma. Often, the mother oscillates unpredictably between actions that actively or passively encourage the child's precocious ego development, and actions that invite regression and seduce the child's id, by provid-ing oversolicitous body contact.

Meanwhile, a consequence of the mother's affective dissocia-tion is that, while she continues to comply with the child's body needs in a primitive way, she no longer cathects her participation in these activities. Consistent with her disavowal of aggression, she disavows the deprivation value of her withdrawal of cathexis from the child's body. These features of the child's world can disrupt his transition through the separation–individuation phase; they can promote a dissociation of ego development and instinctual development; they can give rise to defects in both the idealization and the grandiosity components of narcissistic development; and they can interfere with the process of internalization. To the extent that the process of internalization is disrupted, defects can develop in the child's psychic structure. Interference with internalization can result also when the child's defenses against dangerous wishes or needs disrupt the accessibility upon which internalization depends. Denial or disavowal of affect-regulation, self-care, or self-governance functions can further contribute to self-regulatory impairments. Such denial typically occurs when the child unconsciously reserves self-regulation functions for the maternal object representation out of fear that the exercise of these functions himself will result in his abandonment by the mother, or in her destruction.

The mother–child relationship is not the lone locus of pathogenicity in the future addict's family of origin. The father–child relationship contributes also, both actively and passively, and so does the mother–father relationship. In the typical case, the mother encourages her son to believe that, with his infantile sexuality, he is a perfect partner for her, and therefore that he has no reason to admire or to emulate his father. The mother denigrates the father's phallic function and gives the child the sense that he is a phallic substitute. For reasons that are both object relational and narcissistic, the child is usually eager to adopt his mother's version of his relationship to his father. The father, meanwhile, seems to contribute to his own exclusion, whether actively or passively. He typically maintains his distance, he fails to intervene with the mother in behalf of his son or otherwise to protect him against the mother's anxieties and influences, and he colludes in protecting the mother from acknowledging the full extent of her psychopathology. Deficient identification with the father can be associated with deficits in self-care, self-governance, and identity.

After the infrastructure for addiction has been laid down by these earlier disturbances in the parent–child relationship matrix, another crucial step typically occurs during the oedipal phase. This step involves the child's recognition that he is unable to sexually satisfy his mother, or the mother's abrupt withdrawal when she becomes self-conscious about her intensive attachment to and investment in the child. This process evokes in the child a combination of castration (mutilation) anxiety, separation anxiety, and narcissistic mortification, which are experienced in the context of the serious preexisting vulnerabilities that were mentioned earlier.

Seduction during the latency period can further disrupt repression, neutralization, frustration tolerance, and impulse control.

Constitutional Contributions to Etiology

In the preceding subsection, I noted that the self-regulation system develops through the interaction of multiple systems that involve both genetic endowment and the child's relationship with his or her primary caregiver during the first years of life. Near the beginning of this chapter, I mentioned that impairment of the self-regulation system can result from various combinations of genetic and environmental factors. Psychoanalytic investigators have focused almost exclusively on the environmental or personal history contributions to impaired self-regulation. Constitutional contributions to the etiology of addiction are not excluded by any of the reviewed psychoanalytic theories, but are specifically mentioned only in a few of the psychoanalytic theories of perversion (and in none of the psychoanalytic theories of the other addictive disorders): in the theories of Freud (1905) and Bak (1953), as possible factors in the ego's impaired ability to manage castration anxiety; and in the theories of Bak (1965) and Kernberg (1967), as a possible source of an excessive intensity of aggression. Epstein (1960) identified cerebral hyperexcitability or dyscontrol as the primary disturbance in fetishism, and such cerebral dysfunction could similarly represent a primary disturbance in all addictive disorders. Epstein did not, however, indicate to what extent he believed this cerebral hyperexcitability or dyscontrol to be constitutional. We cannot take for granted that conditions of the central nervous system are necessarily constitutional and not a result of postnatal processes, since significant development of the human brain occurs after birth and depends on specific kinds of environmental input. Cerebral hyperexcitability or dyscontrol could, in fact, represent a broadly described biological correlate of impaired self-regulatory ego functions.

NEUROBIOLOGICAL FORMULATION OF THE ADDICTIVE PROCESS

The empirical research that was reviewed earlier in this chapter provided substantial support for the hypothesis that addiction to alcohol (alcoholism), addictions to other drugs, bulimia, pathological gambling, and sexual addiction have in common an underlying psychobiological process that precedes the onset of the disorders. I proposed that this process be designated the addictive process. In this section, we explore what a neurobiological formulation of the addictive process might look like.

At the outset, we can recognize that this venture will be more speculative than definitive. Far fewer neurobiological than psychological theories of psychoactive substance addiction, bulimia, pathological gambling, or sexual addiction have been published; and few among those have much to offer a nascent neurobiological theory of the addictive process. Psychological theories are closer to our experience, and they employ concepts that are more similar to the language in terms of which we ordinarily discuss and understand addiction. Moreover, the constructs of neurobiological theories generally represent an elementary level of the neurobiological system, while the more familiar psychological constructs typically represent a more complex or molar level of the psychological system; so meaningful correspondence between constructs in neurobiological theories and constructs in psychological theories is difficult to achieve. Whatever emerges from the ensuing discussion is, at best, an oversimplification.

In any case, this section begins with the premise that the research findings that were reviewed in the first section of this chapter sufficiently support the hypothesis of the addictive process: that all addictive disorders, whatever behaviors they involve, share an underlying pathological process. My intention in the present section is not to prove that the addictive process exists by explicating its neurobiology, but to stimulate further thought and to demonstrate that a neurobiological theory of the addictive process is possible.

A number of neurobiological theories of addictive disorders have been proposed, most of which concern alcoholism or addiction to other drugs. Some of these theories—for example, those that concern the metabolism of alcohol or another drug—apply to one specific substance or behavior and cannot be extended to others. They thus might enhance our understanding of why a person who is predisposed to addiction by virtue of the addictive process prefers to use one substance or behavior rather than another, but they contribute little to our understanding of the addictive process itself. Substance-specific and behavior-specific theories are unable to account for the clinical relationships and the epidemiological, neurobiological, and psychometric findings that we considered in the first section of this chapter. Meanwhile, a number of other theories are concerned primarily with the neurobiology of drug tolerance and neuroadaptation (physiological dependence). Tolerance and neuroadaptation can contribute to maintaining or increasing drug use, but they are neither necessary nor sufficient for the development of addiction (N. S. Miller et al., 1987; Goldstein, 1989; Jaffe, 1992). More to the point, knowledge of the neurobiology of drug tolerance and neuroadaptation does not help us to understand the addictive process, or otherwise to account for research findings that indicate significant relationships among the various addictive disorders. In a more technical paper (Goodman, 1996a), I critically reviewed current neurobiological theories of addiction and, with the aid of additional research data, developed a set of hypotheses about the neurobiology of the addictive process. In this section, I summarize the neurobiological formulation that emerged.

Framework

Temperament

We begin by outlining a framework for understanding the neurobiology of the addictive process. Like other aspects of the personality system, healthy and pathological, the addictive process begins with genetically based temperamental tendencies and develops as the maturing central nervous system interacts with the environment. Temperamental disturbances that have been associated with the addictive process include: high emotionality (susceptibility to become easily and intensely distressed); low soothability (difficulty being calmed after experiencing emotional distress); high activity level; impaired attention span persistence; and a superficial sociability that reveals a disinhibited, labile, self-centered, and impulsive disposition (Tarter, Alterman, and Edwards, 1985). Genetic contributions to the addictive process can be understood also in terms of: (1) innate components of sensory processing, integration, and differentiation (Greenspan, 1989); (2) endogenous predispositions to affective dysregulation and perhaps also to schizotypal traits (Grotstein, 1987); (3) temperamental variables that influence the "goodness of fit" between the infant and the caregiver (Thomas and Chess, 1980; Chess and Thomas, 1986); (4) innate elements of self-regulatory and adaptational functions, including the processes that are involved in learning and in forming interpersonal connections; and (5) the timetable of development for different systems within the brain, the specific kinds of environmental input to which development is responsive during sensitive or critical periods, and the range of developmental responses of which a particular system is capable (Greenough, Black, and Wallace, 1987; Greenough and Black, 1992; Schore, 1994). The most important aspect of the environment for the human infant is its primary caregiver, and parent–child interactions can modify temperamental traits and reduce or exacerbate the child's inherited vulnerability to developing addictive pathology.

Spectrum Disorder Theories

Researchers in biological psychiatry have associated addictive conditions with two families of disorders, the affective spectrum disorder family (Winokur, 1972; Hudson and Pope, 1990; McElroy et al., 1992) and the obsessive–compulsive spectrum disorder family (Stein et al., 1992; Hollander, 1993). Affective spectrum disorder theory, which was initially formulated by Winokur (1972) and was later extended by the Hudson and Pope group (Hudson and Pope, 1990; McElroy et al., 1992), identifies alcoholism (Winokur, 1972), bulimia (Hudson and Pope, 1990; McElroy et al., 1992), pathological gambling (McElroy et al., 1992), and sexual addiction (paraphilias and "compulsive sexual behaviors") (McElroy et al., 1992), as affective spectrum disorders, a family of conditions that includes major depression, obsessive–compulsive disorder, panic disorder, and attention deficit disorder. According to this theory, these conditions are not separate diseases but rather are different manifestations of the same genetically based diathesis. Which of the manifestations develops in a genetically predisposed individual is then determined by environmental (familial and cultural) factors. These disorders are hypothesized to have in common an underlying physiological abnormality that constitutes a necessary (but not sufficient) step in the etiologic chain of steps that are required for their expression. McElroy and her colleagues (1992) hypothesized that this shared abnormality involves a disturbance of serotonergic function.

Obsessive–compulsive spectrum disorder theory, which was developed primarily by Hollander (1993) and his colleagues (Stein et al., 1992), identifies pathological gambling and sexual addiction as obsessive–compulsive spectrum disorders, a family of conditions that overlap with obsessive–compulsive disorder in terms of clinical symptoms, associated features (age of onset, clinical course, and comorbidity), presumed etiology, familial transmission, and response to selective pharmacological or behavioral treatments. These disorders usually involve an inability to delay or inhibit repetitive behaviors, and they respond preferentially to serotonin reuptake blockers rather than to norepinephrine reuptake blockers. The core members of this family, in addition to obsessive–compulsive disorder, include Tourette's syndrome, trichotillomania, and body dysmorphic disorder. According to this theory, these conditions can be viewed along a dimension of harm avoidance, from the most compulsive to the most impulsive. Hollander (1993) noted that some patients demonstrate both compulsive and impulsive features.

These two theories, obsessive–compulsive spectrum disorder theory and affective spectrum disorder theory, have much in common, from the manner in which the theories were presented to their emphasis on abnormalities in serotonergic function. Each theory defines a family of disorders that share a genetically based diathesis, which interacts with environmental factors (and other genetic factors) to result in one or more of the specific disorders. How are we to organize these family relationships? We can begin by hypothesizing that obsessive–compulsive spectrum disorders could represent a subset of affective spectrum disorders, a relationship that was implied in the paper by McElroy's group (1992) and that does not seem to be contradicted in the reviewed papers by Hollander and his colleagues (Stein et al., 1992; Hollander, 1993). I suggest a model in which a large group of psychiatric disorders can be visualized as two overlapping ovals (refer to Figure 5.1).One of the ovals defines the family of affective spectrum disorders, the members of which are characterized by impaired affect regulation. Impaired affect regulation renders individuals chronically vulnerable to painful affect states and affective instability. Overlapping this large oval is another that defines the family of "driven behavior spectrum disorders," which, as I described in chapter 1, includes obsessive–compulsive disorders, impulse-control disorders, and addictive disorders. Members of this family are characterized by impaired behavioral inhibition. Impaired behavioral inhibition increases the likelihood that an urge for some form of reinforcement (positive, negative, or both) in the short term will override consideration of longer term consequences, both negative and positive. The driven behavior spectrum disorders oval itself consists of two overlapping zones, one of which represents impulse-control disorders while the other represents obsessive-compulsive disorders. Among driven behavior spectrum disorders, impulse-control disorders are distinguished by behavioral symptoms that function primarily to produce pleasure or gratification: they are maintained primarily by positive reinforcement (reward). These disorders are characterized by aberrant function of the motivational-reward system, as well as impaired behavioral inhibition. Aberrant function of the motivational-reward system subjects the individual to unsatisfied states of restless

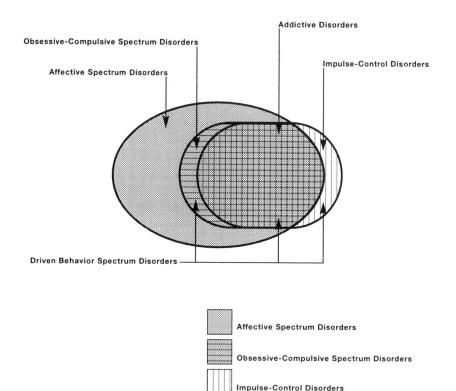

Figure 5.1 Relationships Between Affective Spectrum Disorders and "Driven Behavior Spectrum Disorders" (Obsessive–Compulsive Spectrum Disorders, Impulse-Control Disorders, and Addictive Disorders)

anhedonia or emptiness. In the context of aberrant motivational-reward function, behaviors that are associated with activation of the reward system are more strongly reinforced than they otherwise would have been. Impaired behavioral inhibition then increases the likelihood that such behaviors will occur precipitately, without regard for their longer term consequences. Some portion of the impulse-control disorders zone lies outside the area of overlap with the affective spectrum disorders oval, while all of the obsessive–compulsive spectrum disorders zone, including its area of overlap with the impulse-control disorders zone, lies within the area of overlap between the two large ovals that represent affective spectrum disorders and driven behavior spectrum disorders. Among driven behavior spectrum disorders, obsessive–compulsive spectrum disorders are distinguished by behavioral symptoms that function primarily to relieve anxiety or other painful affects: they are maintained primarily by negative reinforcement (relief of discomfort). These disorders are characterized by impaired affect regulation, as well as impaired behavioral inhibition. Individuals who suffer from these disorders are chronically vulnerable to painful affect states, and they experience strong urges to engage in behaviors that enable escape from or avoidance of these painful affect states. Impaired behavioral inhibition increases the likelihood that states of dysregulated affect will be associated with occurrences of behaviors that are reinforced by relief or avoidance of the distress that dysregulated affect entails. The area of overlap between the obsessive–compulsive spectrum disorders zone and the impulse-control disorders zone represents addictive disorders. These disorders combine features of both impulse-control disorders and obsessive–compulsive disorders, and they involve behavioral symptoms that function both to produce pleasure and to relieve painful affects. Addictive disorders are characterized by impaired affect regulation, impaired behavioral inhibition, and aberrant function of the motivational-reward system. Impaired affect regulation and aberrant motivational-reward system function combine to subject the individual to painful states of dysregulated affect and restless anhedonia or emptiness, in which behaviors that are associated with relief of dysregulated affect and with activation of the reward system are (abnormally) strongly reinforced. Impaired behavioral inhibition then increases the likelihood that such behaviors will occur, despite their longer term harmful consequences.

Meanwhile, the model that I am proposing is not entirely adequate. Addictive disorders cannot be understood simply as a subset of obsessive–compulsive spectrum disorders. As I noted in chapter 1, pharmacological studies have indicated some significant differences in symptomatic response to affect-regulating agents between sexual addiction and obsessive–compulsive disorder (Kafka, 1991; Kruesi et al., 1992). The response of other addictive disorders to medications seems to fit the pattern of sexual addiction, though it has not yet been systematically investigated in the same way. The details of this difference in response to pharmacological treatment between obsessive–compulsive disorders and addictive disorders remain to be fleshed out, and their implications remain to be elucidated.

The model that was just sketched provides a framework for understanding the neurobiology of the addictive process, but it does not yet have much to say about what happens in the brain. The functioning of the brain can be described in two ways, neurochemically and neuroanatomically. We proceed now to explore possible neurochemical and neuroanatomical formulations of the addictive process.

Neurochemical Formulation

The preceding discussion concluded that addictive disorders are characterized by impaired affect regulation, impaired behavioral inhibition, and aberrant function of the motivational-reward system. Accordingly, the addictive process can be hypothesized to involve this combination of impairments. On the basis of a broad range of research findings (which are summarized below), we can speculate that impaired affect regulation, impaired behavioral inhibition, and aberrant function of the motivational-reward system are primarily associated (but not in a simple one-to-one fashion) with dysfunctions in the norepinephrine, serotonin, and dopamine systems, and that dysfunction in the endogenous opioid system can contribute to all of these functional aberrations.

The Norepinephrine System

Activity of the norepinephrine system is associated with affect regulation and ability to manage emotional stress. Recent work by Post and his colleagues (Post, 1992; Post, Rubinow, and Ballenger, 1984, 1986), by Gold, Goodwin, and Chrousos (1988a,b), and by Kraemer and his colleagues (Kraemer, 1985, 1986; Kraemer, Ebert, Lake, and McKinney, 1984; Kraemer, Ebert, Schmidt, and McKinney, 1989, 1991) suggests that affective dysregulation may originate in neuroaffective sensitization of the norepinephrine system; that is, hypersensitivity of postsynaptic receptors to norepinephrine, particularly in the limbic system, which can result from overactivity of the stress response system. This body of research indicates that stress response system overactivity, which involves prolonged release of norepinephrine from the locus ceruleus and secretion of corticotropin releasing hormone from the hypothalamus, leads to supersensitivity of postsynaptic norepinephrine receptors in critical limbic sites and pathways, perhaps through its effects on gene transcription factors.

The limbic system is most susceptible to neuroaffective sensitization in the critical periods of the first years of life, during which the development of the brain is most sensitive to environmental influences. Overactivity of the stress response system results from the interaction among genetic vulnerabilities, stressors that can be external (such as cold or loud noise) or internal (such as hunger or anxiety), and the primary caregiver's failure to modulate sufficiently the stress to which the infant is subject. Having not yet developed their own autonomous means of regulating their physiological–affective states, human infants depend on their caregivers to provide such regulation. Optimal provision of physiological–affective regulation by the caregiver facilitates the elimination of superfluous synapses and the growth of neural connections that will provide the neurobiological substrate for the infant's developing affect-regulatory functions (Schore,

1994). When caregiver-provided regulation is inadequate or lacking, however, the infant's stress response system can easily be overstimulated. Such overstimulation during critical periods of central nervous system development can stunt the growth of catecholamine (norepinephrine and dopamine) synapses, or it can exaggerate the experience-dependent elimination of overabundant neural connections between the limbic system and the neocortex (Edelman, 1987; Greenough, Black, and Wallace, 1987; Greenough and Black, 1992; Schore, 1994; Tucker, 1992). Maternal deprivation in primate infants has been associated with subsequent inadequate cortical catecholamine innervation and with persistently low levels of norepinephrine in the cerebrospinal fluid (Pearson, Teicher, Shaywitz, Cohen, Young, and Anderson, 1980; Kraemer, Eber, Lake, and McKinney, 1984; Kraemer, 1985, 1986; Gold, Goodwin, and Chrousos, 1988a). Inadequate catecholamine innervation and persistently low levels of norepinephrine could then result in denervation supersensitivity of postsynaptic norepinephrine receptors (Prescott, 1971). (Parenthetically, since dopamine also is a catecholamine, the dopamine system is likely to develop through processes that are similar to those through which the norepinephrine system develops. Neuroaffective sensitization in the dopamine system, which would be characterized by low basal firing rates of dopaminergic neurons and greater sensitivity of postsynaptic receptors to dopamine, might then develop in a manner analogous to that in which neuroaffective sensitization in the norepinephrine system is thought to develop.)

The process of neuroaffective sensitization to norepinephrine is associated with an enduring vulnerability to affective dysregulation. The stress response systems of individuals who are thus affected react more intensely to environmental stressors, such as separations, losses, and narcissistic injuries (i.e., injuries to one's self-esteem or sense of self). Episodes of overwhelming affect can be triggered in these individuals by degrees of psychosocial stress that are readily managed by intact individuals. Since individuals with sensitized norepinephrine systems are subject to the discomfort of dysregulated affect and to the threat of being overwhelmed by stress more often and more intensely than are individuals with normal norepinephrine systems, the reinforcing properties of behaviors that provide relief from the discomfort of dysregulated affect, or from physiological states that have become conditioned stimuli for overwhelming stress, are greater for them. Such individuals would consequently be predisposed to develop addictive patterns of engaging in behaviors that relieve emotional distress.

The Serotonin System

Serotonin has been found to have a diffuse regulatory function in appetite modulation (Blundell, 1992), sensory reactivity (Sheard and Aghajanian, 1968), pain sensitivity (Harvey and Yunger, 1973; Akil and Liebeskind, 1975), emotional stabilization (Mandell and Knapp, 1979; van Praag, Kahn, Asnis, Wetzler, Brown, Belich, and Korn, 1987), and behavioral inhibition (Coccaro, Siever, Klar, Maurer, Cochrane, Cooper, Mohs, and Davis, 1989; Stein, Hollander, and Liebowitz, 1993). Dysfunction of the serotonin system is thus likely to be associated with impaired appetite modulation, impaired emotional stabilization, and impaired behavioral inhibition. Some research suggests that serotonin might also function as a modulator of the brain reward system and as a facilitator of satiety function (Hoebel, Hernandez, Schwartz, Mark, and Hunter, 1989). Subnormal levels of serotonin seem to be correlated with a general impairment of affect regulation that results in irritability, hypersensitivity, and a propensity to be overwhelmed by emotional states. When behavioral inhibition functions are impaired, these overwhelming affective states can trigger driven behaviors. Chronic states of dysregulated affect, particularly when overwhelming, can result in depression, perhaps through chronic stress and consequent overactivity of the norepinephrine-CRH stress system, or through learned helplessness. To the extent that driven behaviors alleviate the stress of dysregulated affect, even temporarily, they might thereby also serve to avert or to postpone a depressive episode. Reduced serotonin activity can thus contribute to the addictive process in its association with both impaired affect regulation and impaired behavioral inhibition.

The Endogenous Opioid and Dopamine Systems

Both the endogenous opioid system and the dopaminergic system are components of the brain reward system. Low basal activity in either the opioid system or the dopamine reward system may be associated with anhedonia or dysphoria, which could motivate affected individuals (via negative reinforcement) to engage in behaviors that evoke release of these neuromodulators or that stimulate their receptors (R. A. Wise, 1987; Ramsey and Van Ree, 1992). Supersensitivity of postsynaptic receptors, a result of low basal activity in the case of dopamine and possibly also in the case of opioid receptors, could mean greater responsiveness of the reward system to occurrences of behaviors that are associated with activation of the reward system. Behaviors that are associated with activation of the opioid system or the dopamine system would thus be more strongly reinforced (both negatively and positively) when engaged in by individuals whose reward systems functioned at a low basal rate than they would be when engaged in by individuals with normal reward system function. We can recall from the discussion earlier in this chapter of neurobiological commonalities among the addictive disorders, that the behaviors that characterize each of these disorders—taking into one's body any of the drugs of abuse, eating, gambling, and engaging in sexual behavior—all are associated with (1) activation of opioid receptors in the brain, either by directly stimulating opioid receptors or through association with the release of endogenous opioids; and (2) an increase in the intrasynaptic concentration of dopamine in the brain reward system.

The endogenous opioid system and the dopamine system could contribute to the addictive process in other ways as well. Endogenous opioids seem to be involved in the regulation of feeding in general (Morley and Levine, 1985; Baile, McLaughlin, and Della-Fera, 1986), of stress-induced feeding (Morley, Levine, and Rowland, 1983), of sexual behavior (Pfaus and Gorzalka,

1987), and of defensive behavior and related emotions (Graeff, 1994). Low basal levels of opioid activity thus could undermine behavioral or emotional regulation, either directly or through a diminished capacity to compensate for a dysfunction in another neuromodulator system that is involved in self-regulation. An additional feature of the opioid system is that endogenous opioid activity is associated both with reward (positive reinforcement) and with relief of pain or distress (negative reinforcement), whether the distress is of somatic or psychosocial origin (Panksepp, Herman, Conner, Bishop, and Scott, 1978; Amir, Brown, and Amit, 1980). A behavior that is associated with the release of endogenous opioids could thus be particularly strongly reinforced when it is engaged in by individuals who are experiencing psychosocial distress, especially if they have not developed other, more adaptive means of relieving such distress.

Activity in the mesolimbic dopamine system seems to correspond to a range of processes that are understood psychologically as components of motivation: incentive, motor activation, and reward. Low basal firing rates of dopaminergic neurons and greater postsynaptic sensitivity to dopamine could promote increased behavioral activation and novelty seeking (Cloninger, 1987), which most likely would particularly include seeking for opportunities to engage in behaviors that are associated with the release of dopamine. The pattern of low basal dopaminergic activity and supersensitivity of postsynaptic dopamine receptors in mesolimbic regions also leads to a greater tendency to lose control of behavior after an occurrence of a behavior that raises the intrasynaptic concentration of dopamine (Modell, Mountz, and Beresford, 1990). As we recall, the class of behaviors that are associated with increases in the intrasynaptic concentration of dopamine includes the behaviors that characterize all of the addictive disorders.

Primary Defect: Low Basal Activity

We can hypothesize that the addictive process may develop concurrently with a similar primary defect in each of these systems:

low basal activity of the neuromodulator, which is associated with supersensitivity of postsynaptic receptors in the cases of norepinephrine and dopamine, and perhaps also in the case of endogenous opioids. Dysfunction of the serotonergic system may be the most critical neurochemical correlate of the addictive process. Serotonin is released from all of the axonal varicosities where it is concentrated, not only from those that make typical synaptic contacts (Beaudet and Descarries, 1976; Chan-Palay, 1977). Such widespread release suggests that serotonin diffuses as a neurohumoral agent to reach relatively distant targets. The serotonergic system is moreover characterized by tonic activity, with serotonergic neurons firing at rates of about one spike per second (Aghajanian and Wang, 1978). These findings suggest that the serotonergic system serves a widespread pacemaker or homeostatic regulatory function (B. H. Smith and Sweet, 1978).

The preceding schema is at best preliminary, since it treats neuromodulator systems as though they were functionally homogeneous units that are self-contained and independent from one another. In the living brain, a single neuromodulator can have diverse functional roles at different receptor types and in different anatomical locations, and neuromodulator systems are complexly interrelated. Discussing these systems as though they were homogeneous and self-contained is a heuristic technique that lays the groundwork for understanding, but leaves the structure incomplete.

Neuroanatomical Formulation

A number of brain regions appear to be involved in the addictive process. Research findings suggest that the areas in which a functional abnormality is most likely to be associated with the addictive process are the prefrontal cortex and the limbic system, which together constitute a functionally integrated system (Tarter et al., 1985). Within this larger system, the subsystem that seems to be most centrally involved in the functions of affect regulation and behavioral inhibition consists of the orbitofrontal cortex, the septum, and the hippocampus (Eyzaguirre and Fidone, 1975;

Gorenstein and Newman, 1980; Schore, 1994). Dysfunction in this subsystem could thus be sufficient to account for two of the major dimensions of the addictive process, impaired affect regulation and impaired behavioral inhibition, which addictive disorders share with obsessive-compulsive disorders. The regions that are most likely to be involved in the motivational-reward system dysfunction that characterizes addictive disorders are the ventral tegmental area and the substantia nigra, perhaps specifically the neural pathways from these regions to the nucleus accumbens (Modell et al., 1990). The nucleus accumbens, a region that seems to have a central role in organizing behavioral responses to emotional states (Louilot, Taghzouti, Simon, and Le Moal, 1989; S. J. Watson, Trujillo, Herman, and Akil, 1989), is probably also involved in the addictive process. Dysfunction in the nucleus accumbens, or in projections that modulate nucleus accumbens activity, could be involved in the behavioral component of impaired affect regulation.

We can thus hypothesize that the neuroanatomical correlates of the addictive process may involve dysfunctions in two systems within the brain: one that is constituted by the orbitofrontal cortex, the septum, and the hippocampus; and one that includes the nucleus accumbens, the ventral tegmental area, and related structures. Dysfunction in the former system may be primarily associated with impaired affect regulation and impaired behavioral inhibition (Eyzaguirre and Fidone, 1975; Gorenstein and Newman, 1980; Tarter et al., 1985; Modell et al., 1990; Schore, 1994). Dysfunction in the latter system may be primarily associated with aberrant function of the motivational-reward system (Louilot et al., 1989; Watson et al., 1989) and with dysregulation of the orbitofrontal cortex (Modell et al., 1990), which is the cortical component of the former system.

Impairments in neurochemical and neuroanatomical functioning of the types that we have been considering develop out of the interaction between genetic propensities and deficiencies in the child's early caregiving environment. This interaction is particularly important in the developmentally critical periods of the first years of life, during which the maturing brain is most sensitive to environmental influences and depends on particular qualities of environmental interchange for its healthy development (Kraemer, 1985, 1986; Edelman, 1987; Greenough et al., 1987; Kraemer et al., 1989, 1991; Greenough and Black, 1992; Tucker, 1992; Schore, 1994).

While this formulation brings us a step closer to understanding the neurobiology of the addictive process, we can note that it represents a considerable oversimplification. Each neuromodulator involves a diverse system of connections and receptors, and interactions among the neuromodulator systems are complex. Functional neuroanatomy also is more complex than this formulation can accommodate. Brain regions are interconnected by tangled networks through which they influence each other, and serious questions have been raised by neuroscientists about the extent to which functions can be meaningfully localized within the brain (Luria, 1973; Gorenstein and Newman, 1980; Kiernan, 1981; L. Miller, 1986).

Neurobiological and Psychological Formulations: A Unitary Process

We can see that the psychological formulation of the addictive process and the neurobiological formulation of the addictive process are consistent with each other; and that they are moreover, to a great extent, isomorphic with each other. The psychological and neurobiological formulations of the addictive process are not antagonistic or mutually exclusive, but complementary and mutually enhancing. While each type of formulation is expressed in a different set of terms and is investigated by different methods, they both address a unitary process. The integrated understanding of the addictive process that emerges from these formulations exemplifies the principle that the human organism is a unitary reality; and that "psychological" and "neurobiological" represent not two different kinds of reality, but two languages, each of which is associated with a different way of knowing, that we use to describe this unitary human reality (Rado, 1946, 1949; Feigl, 1967, 1981; Globus, 1973; Booth, 1978; Maxwell, 1978; Reiser,

1984; Macdonald, 1989; Goodman, 1991, 1994a, in press a, in press b). Our challenge now is not the philosophical challenge of choosing between these formulations, but the practical challenge of delineating conditions under which one formulation or the other is more effective in fulfilling our objectives of understanding, treating, and preventing addictive illness.

THE ADDICTIVE PROCESS: FURTHER CONSIDERATIONS

We now briefly consider three additional areas of theoretical interest that concern the addictive process: the contribution of heredity or constitution, the self-perpetuating nature of addictive disorders, and the relationship between the addictive process and the concept of an "addictive personality."

Hereditary (Constitutional) Contribution

The findings of family history studies indicate that hereditary factors play a significant part in the development of addictive disorders. Some investigators of psychoactive substance addiction have presented these findings as evidence that substance addiction is a biological disorder, rather than a psychological disorder. Arguments that hereditary transmission indicates a biological rather than a psychological disorder are predicated on an erroneous equation of genetic with biological and of psychological with environmental, as well as an erroneous dichotomization of biological and psychological. Concerning psychopathology and personality in general, what are inherited are genetically encoded predispositions for the development of processes that can be described in terms of either biological or psychological concepts. A number of extensive reviews of literature on genetic factors in personality development are available (e.g., Scarr and Kidd, 1983; Goldsmith, 1983; Buss and Plomin, 1984; Plomin, 1986), and specific studies of hereditary influences in personality disorders have also been published (including Torgerson, 1980, 1984; Loranger, Oldham, and Tulis, 1982; Cadoret, Cain, and Crowe, 1983; Baron,

Gruen, Asnis, and Lord, 1985; J. H. Reich, 1989; Cadoret, Troughton, Bagford, and Woodworth, 1990).

Meanwhile, the equation of environmental with psychological in a way that excludes biological is clearly erroneous. Numerous environmental factors that are involved in the etiology of nonpsychiatric illnesses (such as toxins and infectious agents) are usually described in biological or physical terms, and some of these factors also contribute to psychiatric syndromes (including toxic psychosis and syphilitic paresis). A more salient example of the importance of environmental factors in the genesis of conditions that are described in biological terms is provided by the critical role in central nervous system development of the primary caregiver's modulation of the infant's physiological-affective stress (which we considered in the section "Neurobiological Formulation of the Addictive Process").

The discussion in earlier sections suggests that hereditary contributions to the addictive process operate primarily by influencing the development of functions that can be described either in terms of self-regulation, ego, and superego, or in terms of affect regulation, behavioral inhibition, and motivation-reward. Constitutional factors are likely to include: (1) endogenous predispositions to affective dysregulation and perhaps also to schizotypal traits (Grotstein, 1987); (2) innate components of sensory processing, integration, and differentiation (Greenspan, 1989); (3) temperamental variables that influence the "goodness of fit" between infant and caregiver (Thomas and Chess, 1980; Chess and Thomas, 1986); (4) innate elements of self-regulatory and adaptational functions, including the processes that are involved in learning and in forming interpersonal connections; and (5) the timetable of development for different systems within the brain, the specific kinds of environmental input to which development is responsive during sensitive or critical periods, and the range of developmental responses of which a particular system is capable (Greenough et al., 1987; Greenough and Black, 1992; Schore, 1994). Notably absent from this list is genetic factors that determine the specific effects of exogenous substances. Such factors may affect the choice of which substances will be preferred for addictive use, but they contribute little to the addictive process.

The Self-Perpetuating Nature of Addictive Disorders

Among the factors that make addictive behavior patterns so tenacious is the self-perpetuating nature of addictive disorders: their tendency to create conditions that deepen the addict's dependence on addictive behavior. The most obvious example of this process is the neuroadaptation and tolerance that occur with recurrent ingestion of alcohol and other drugs. Addictive syndromes that involve behaviors other than the ingestion of psychoactive substances also have been associated with the development of tolerance (as the behavior is repeated, its potency to produce reinforcing effects tends to diminish) and with withdrawal symptoms (psychological and/or physical discomfort when the behavior is discontinued). We have reason to believe that changes in an organism's hedonic–motivational responses, and changes in an individual's baseline level of psychological discomfort, are both correlated with changes in the functional status of the brain. We can therefore presume that some kind of neuroadaptation and neurobiological tolerance, which correlate with the psychological adaptation (dependence) and psychological tolerance that individuals report, operate in nonpharmacological as well as in pharmacological addictive disorders.

The next most obvious level of self-perpetuation concerns the responses of the environment to addictive patterns of behavior. A key feature of addiction is continuation of the behavior despite significant harmful consequences. For most individuals who engage addictively in one or more forms of behavior, the most overtly harmful consequences of their addictive behavior concern the responses of their environment. Pressures from financial obligations, work troubles, legal entanglements, and strained interpersonal relationships that result from addictive behavior can add to anxiety and other painful affects; while losses of friends, organizational connections, spouse, home, and job can undermine and eventually demolish social supports that help the individual to manage disturbing affects and their precipitants. Increasing levels of anxiety and other painful affects, combined with a decreasing availability of nondestructive means for managing disturbing affects and their precipitants, promotes an increasing reliance on addictive behavior to cope with anxiety and affective distress.

The least obvious but most pervasive means by which addictive disorders perpetuate themselves is through their effects on addicts' psychological functioning, which are multiple. First of all, the recurrent experience of loss of control erodes addicts' self-esteem, self-confidence, and sense of self-efficacy. Wounded narcissism, shame, and feelings of inadequacy are common triggers for addictive behavior, particularly when individuals lack confidence in their capacity to restore a positively toned sense of self by other means. Second, addictive behavior, which results from impaired self-regulatory ego and superego functions, can exacerbate ego and superego impairments, and thus further potentiate the addictive process. Addictive behavior can support or enable defensive functions that otherwise are inadequate, and thus can weaken existing adaptive options and impede the development of more healthy self-regulatory functions. The short-term effectiveness of addictive behavior in regulating individuals' affects undermines their motivation to develop healthier means of coping, or even to use the healthier means that they already possess. "Disuse atrophy" of their adaptive self-regulatory functions can then result in further deterioration of self-regulation, and hence deeper dependence on addictive behavior to fulfill self-regulatory functions. Psychoanalytic investigators have identified a number of mutually reinforcing pairs of pathological processes that are often associated with the addictive process. For example, Gillespie (1952) described the process in which anxiety triggers defensive regression, which in turn intensifies the anxiety; and Kernberg (1967) and others have observed the mutually reinforcing relationship between splitting and ego weakness. Finally, addiction involves a high level of what Rangell (1968) termed "tertiary gain": the process by which a chronic symptom comes to function as part of the self or identity, even becoming the central organizing event in a person's life. This process further deepens the addict's dependence on the addictive behavior.

The self-perpetuating nature of addictive disorders helps to explain their tenacity and their characteristically chronic and progressive course. It also indicates how a chronic addictive disorder can to some extent become functionally autonomous from the factors that originally determined the addictive behavior.

The Addictive Process and the Concept of an "Addictive Personality"

The concept of the addictive process, a psychobiological process that underlies all addictive disorders, may seem to represent an attempt to resurrect the concept of the "addictive personality," which many investigators consider to have been discredited. Pattison (1979), however, reminded us of the importance of differentiating between the attempt to define a uniformity among addicts, which has failed, and the attempt to define a number of personality factors that might predict individual vulnerability to addiction. Critics of the addictive personality concept have typically presented it to be a claim for a specific personality type that is unique to addicts and uniform among addicts, a presentation that some investigators (e.g., Blane [1968]) have identified as a straw man, a deliberate misrepresentation of a theoretical stance in order to more easily discredit it. Researchers' inability to demonstrate a specific personality type that is unique to and uniform among addicts does not preclude the existence of a cluster of personality features that are significantly correlated with addictive disorders and that predict individual vulnerability to developing an addictive disorder.

The addictive process—an enduring, inordinately strong tendency to engage in some form of pleasure-producing behavior as a means of relieving painful affects and/or regulating one's sense of self—is a personality feature that characterizes individuals who suffer from addictive disorders. It represents character pathology, but it does not in itself constitute a type of personality disorder. It can be associated with a broad range of character organizations that vary (1) in cognitive style; (2) in personality traits; (3) in the degree to which ego functions, object relations, and self-processes are impaired; and (4) in the availability of personality assets and inner resources. The addictive process is not unique to individuals who suffer from addictive disorders; but it is stronger, more enduring, and more pervasive in their personalities than in the personalities of individuals who do not suffer from an addictive disorder. In effect, the addictive process represents a level of analysis that is intermediate in specificity between a symptom pattern and a personality disorder. It is more focal than is the personality disorder level, and it conveys more clinically relevant information than does the symptom level. It also provides us with a framework for understanding the relationships among symptomatically discrete but phenomenologically related clinical syndromes.

THE "DRUG OF CHOICE" QUESTION

Two sets of factors influence the development of addictive disorders: those that concern the underlying addictive process, and those that relate to the selection of a particular form of behavior (and further, in the case of psychoactive substance use addiction, a particular substance) as the one that is preferred for addictive use. This book has focused on the former set because it is the more important, both in terms of etiologic significance and as a guide in treatment. Before we conclude part II, however, we consider the "drug of choice" question: Given a sufficient degree of predisposition to develop addictive behavior patterns, as represented in the addictive process, what determines which substances or behaviors are selected for addictive use?

In general, the selection of a substance or a behavior for addictive use seems to depend both on factors of learning and on genetic factors. Three components of the learning process may be particularly influential in the selection of an addictive means: affect, expectancy, and exposure. The affect(s) from which an individual is most motivated to seek relief are those that he or she experiences as most painful or dangerous. The substance or experience that brings relief from the affects that an individual experiences as most painful or dangerous is thereby most strongly reinforced (via negative reinforcement). Meanwhile, learned expectations about how a substance or a behavior will alter one's affective state or sense of self are an integral part of the substance's or behavior's effects, and controlled studies have found the subjective and behavioral effects of psychoactive substances to be determined as much by expectancies as by the pharmacological properties of the substances (Hull and Bond, 1986; Cooper, Russell, and George, 1988; G. T. Wilson, 1988). The third component, exposure, can consist of either direct experience or modeling of (identification with) another person who engages in the behavior. Direct experience can occur through either experimentation or adventitious contact. Exposure gives the contingencies of reinforcement a chance to operate.

The selection process is influenced also by genetic factors, especially those that affect the hedonic quality of specific experiences. The sensitivity of the reward system to different substances is subject to genetically based variation (Besnard, Kempf, Fuhrmann, Kempf, and Ebel, 1986; Fadda, Colombo, and Gessa, 1991). Greater sensitivity of the reward system to a particular substance (or behavior) enhances its positive reinforcement value, relative to other substances and behaviors. Genetically based biological variations can also render an individual more or less sensitive to the immediate aversive consequences of a substance or a behavior, such as standing ataxia or flushing after ingestion of alcohol (Schuckit, 1985; Schuckit, Li, Cloninger, and Deitrich, 1985). The immediate aversive consequences that an individual experiences then influence the frequency and extent to which he or she ingests the substance or engages in the behavior. Finally, the negatively reinforcing properties of a substance or a behavior (e.g., its capacity to attenuate physiological responses to stress) may also be subject to genetically based variation (Levenson, Oyama, and Meek, 1987).

The addictive process is not separable from the addict's personality and character organization, except by theoretical abstraction, and neither is the addict's selection of a particular substance or behavior for addictive use. An addict's drug of choice or behavior of choice is typically an agent or action that is congruent with his or her characteristic modes of adaptation: one that facilitates the addict's preexisting means of managing and integrating affective, behavioral, and cognitive responses. The selection of a particular substance or behavior is facilitated also by its capacity to enhance the individual's adaptation, by compensating for defects or weaknesses in his or her adaptational system. An individual's affective, behavioral, and cognitive response tendencies, and the ego processes that function to manage and to integrate them, also are the products of the interaction between genetic factors and factors of learning.

The development of a particular addictive disorder thus seems to have three components: (1) an individual is predisposed to depend on some form of pleasure-producing behavior to regulate his or her (dysregulated) affects and sense of self, by virtue of the addictive process; (2) the individual takes a mood-altering substance into his or her body, or engages in some other rewarding behavior; and (3) the effects of the substance or behavior (negatively reinforcing, positively reinforcing, and aversive), the individual's expectations about its effects in the future, and the fit between the substance or the behavior and the individual's characteristic modes of adaptation, combine to determine the likelihood that the individual will select that substance or behavior as his or her addictive "drug of choice." These effects and expectations are determined by both genetic and environmental factors. Meanwhile, the adaptive human organism, once having developed the capacity to use an external action as a means of regulating internal states, can shift among different behaviors (and substances) or combine them, according to the opportunities and limitations of the situation.

THE SELECTION OF SEXUAL BEHAVIOR

The "drug of choice" theory suggests that sexual addiction develops in addictively predisposed individuals who experience some form of sexual stimulation, either directly or through identification with a parental figure (usually the mother) who sexualizes, and who learn to expect that sexual behavior not only will provide pleasure but also (1) will relieve the affects that they experience as most painful or dangerous, through (2) means that are congruent with their characteristic modes of adaptation. Children naturally explore their bodies with their hands and their physical surroundings with their bodies, so exposure to sexual sensations is virtually inevitable. Yet, not all addictively predisposed individuals become sex addicts. The selection of sexual behavior as an addictive preference thus seems to depend not only on exposure to sexual stimulation, but also on the interpersonal context of the exposure. The kind of exposure that leads to the development of sexual addiction in addictively predisposed individuals typically results from sexual seduction, which, as a number of investigators have noted, can be overt or covert (A. M. Johnson and Robinson, 1957; Ovesey and Person, 1973, 1976; Person and Ovesey, 1978; Khan, 1979; Rosen, 1979a,b; Coen, 1981; Carnes, 1989). In addition to overt or covert seduction, other characteristics of the mother–child relationship that promote sexualization, including the mother's reliance on sexualization in her defensive activities and in her relationship with her child (Coen, 1981), are likely also to contribute to the predisposed individual's selection of some form of sexual behavior as his or her addictive "drug of choice."

The higher prevalence of sexual addiction in men than in women suggests that gender-related factors play a significant role in its development. A critical component seems to be the developmental crisis that the little boy undergoes during the separation–individuation period, when stabilization of his nascent male gender identity requires the dissolution of his primary pregenital identification with his mother (Bak, 1953; Stoller, 1970, 1975; Ovesey and Person, 1973, 1976; Socarides, 1973, 1988; Person and Ovesey, 1978). The ensuing conflict between separation anxiety and castration anxiety (anxiety about the vulnerability of one's body self to mutilation) is then superimposed on the basic merger–individuation conflict: the wish to merge plus the fear of separation or abandonment, versus the wish for individuation, mastery, and wholeness plus the fear of being engulfed, controlled, or damaged. In addiction, the mother's narcissistic bond with a male child may be more sexually infiltrated than it is with a female child, and her tendency to sexualize may emerge more strongly or with a more genital tinge when the child is a boy. Open to speculation is what symmetries and complementarities might obtain between the development of sexual addiction in males and the development of bulimia in females (beyond their sharing the addictive process).

In short, if we had to sum up the etiology of sexual addiction in one brief equation, it would be: sexual addiction = the addictive process + sexualization.

Part III.

Diagnosis and Treatment of Sexual Addiction

Since the clinical vignettes with which the Introduction began, our discussion has proceeded almost entirely on a theoretical plane. In part III, our focus returns to clinical issues. Chapter 6 begins with a definition of and diagnostic criteria for sexual addiction, which are followed by the differential diagnosis of sexual addiction and epidemiological data. In chapter 7, a range of approaches to treating sexual addiction are reviewed, including medication, behavior modification, cognitive–behavioral therapy, therapeutic groups, couples and family therapy, psychodynamic psychotherapy, and integrated treatment. In chapter 8, a version of integrated treatment is suggested as a general guideline for formulating individualized treatment plans. The book then concludes, in chapter 9, by bringing us back to the five individuals whom we met in the Introduction. Illustrative narratives are presented that include each individual's personal history, a discussion of the development and dynamics of the individual's disorder, and a description of the course of the individual's treatment.

6

Diagnosis and Epidemiology

DIAGNOSIS OF SEXUAL ADDICTION

The diagnostic criteria for sexual addiction (Goodman, 1992, 1993b, 1995b, 1997) can be derived from the behaviorally nonspecific criteria for addictive disorder that were presented in chapter 1, by replacing "behavior" with "sexual behavior" (as we keep in mind that both sets of diagnostic criteria are provisional):

Sexual Addiction
A maladaptive pattern of sexual behavior, *leading to clinically significant impairment or distress,* as manifested by three (or more) of the following, occurring at any time in the same 12-month period:
(1) tolerance, as defined by either of the following:
    (a) a need for markedly increased amount or intensity of the sexual behavior to achieve the desired effect
    (b) markedly diminished effect with continued involvement in the sexual behavior at the same level of intensity
(2) withdrawal, as manifested by either of the following:
    (a) characteristic psychophysiological withdrawal syndrome of physiologically described changes and/or psychologically described changes upon discontinuation of the sexual behavior

(b) the same (or a closely related) sexual behavior is engaged in to relieve or avoid withdrawal symptoms

(3) the sexual behavior is often engaged in over a longer period, in greater quantity, or at a higher level of intensity than was intended

(4) there is a persistent desire or unsuccessful efforts to cut down or control the sexual behavior

(5) a great deal of time is spent in activities necessary to prepare for the sexual behavior, to engage in the behavior, or to recover from its effects

(6) important social, occupational, or recreational activities are given up or reduced because of the sexual behavior

(7) the sexual behavior continues despite knowledge of having a persistent or recurrent physical or psychological problem that is likely to have been caused or exacerbated by the behavior

A definition of sexual addiction, which facilitates preliminary diagnosis of the disorder, can similarly be derived from the simple definition of addiction by replacing "behavior" with "sexual behavior." Accordingly, sexual addiction is defined as a condition in which some form of sexual behavior that can function both to produce pleasure and to relieve painful affects is employed in a pattern that is characterized by two key features: (1) recurrent failure to control the sexual behavior, and (2) continuation of the sexual behavior despite significant harmful consequences. In sum, sexual addiction is a syndrome in which some form of sexual behavior relates to and affects an individual's life in such a manner as to accord with the simple definition of addiction or to meet the diagnostic criteria for addictive disorder.

Significantly, as I noted earlier in the review of arguments against the concept of sexual addiction, no form of sexual behavior is in itself defined as sexual addiction. A pattern of sexual behavior is designated sexual addiction, not on the basis of what the behavior is, but on the basis of how the behavior relates to and affects a person's life. Any sexual behavior has the potential to be engaged in addictively, but constitutes an addictive disorder only to the extent that it occurs in a pattern that meets the diagnostic criteria or accords with the definition. The diagnostic criteria for sexual addiction do not discriminate, for example, between heterosexual behavior and homosexual behavior. Behaviors of either type can be practiced in addictive ways that meet the diagnostic criteria for sexual addiction, or in nonaddictive ways that do not meet the criteria. Whether a pattern of sexual behavior qualifies as sexual addiction is determined not by the type of behavior, its object, its frequency, or its social acceptability, but by the relationship between this behavior pattern and an individual's life, as indicated in the definition and specified in the diagnostic criteria. The features that distinguish sexual addiction from other patterns of sexual behavior are: (1) that the individual is not reliably able to control the sexual behavior; and (2) that the sexual behavior has significant harmful consequences and continues despite these consequences.

The concept of sexual addiction is often understood to group together, in the same diagnostic class, both paraphilias and "nonparaphilic sexual addictions" (the latter being conditions in which socioculturally acceptable sexual behaviors are used addictively; for example, masturbation or sexual activity between consenting adults that is out of control and continues despite harmful consequences). This understanding is both correct and incorrect. The incorrect aspect concerns an important difference between the definition of sexual addiction and the definition of paraphilia, as it is specified in DSM-IV:

> The essential features of a Paraphilia are recurrent, intense sexually arousing fantasies, sexual urges, or behaviors [sic] generally involving 1) nonhuman objects, 2) the suffering or humiliation of oneself or one's partner, or 3) children or other nonconsenting persons, that occur over a period of at least 6 months (Criterion A). For some individuals, paraphilic fantasies or stimuli are obligatory for erotic arousal and are always included in sexual activity. In other cases, the paraphilic preferences occur only episodically (e.g., perhaps during periods of stress), whereas at other times the person is able to function sexually without paraphilic fantasies or stimuli. The behavior, sexual urges, or fantasies cause clinically significant distress or impairment in social, occupational, or other important areas of functioning (Criterion B) [pp. 522–523].

If we compare the two key features in the definition of sexual addiction to the two essential criteria of a paraphilia that are identified in DSM-IV (Criterion A and Criterion B), we can notice that the second key feature of sexual addiction—continuation of the sexual behavior despite significant harmful consequences—is quite similar to Criterion B of DSM-IV paraphilia, "The behavior, sexual urges, or fantasies cause clinically significant distress or impairment in social, occupational, or other important areas of functioning" (p. 523). On the other hand, the first key feature of sexual addiction—recurrent failure to control the sexual behavior—has nothing in common with Criterion A of DSM-IV paraphilia, namely, that the sexual fantasies, urges, or behaviors involve "1) nonhuman objects, 2) the suffering or humiliation of oneself or one's partner, or 3) children or other nonconsenting persons, that occur over a period of at least 6 months" (pp. 522–523). Criterion A of a paraphilia in DSM-IV is a categorical formula that defines specific types of sexual behavior as paraphilias (when Criterion B also is met). The first key feature of sexual addiction, meanwhile, is a functional formula that emphasizes the "how" of a pattern of sexual behavior, rather than the "what." That the definition of sexual addiction focuses on recurrent failure to control the behavior reflects sexual addiction's relationship with substance dependence, pathological gambling, and bulimia, the DSM-IV diagnostic criteria for all of which also include impaired control (in bulimia, "a sense of lack of control").

Meanwhile, the concept of sexual addiction does group together (1) conditions in which paraphilic behaviors are used addictively, and (2) conditions in which socioculturally acceptable sexual behaviors are used addictively. Support for grouping these conditions together was provided by a recent study, in which Kafka and Prentky (1992) found that men with nonviolent paraphilias were similar to men with nonparaphilic sexual addictions in most measures of both sexual functioning (including parameters of frequency, desire, intensity, and temporal patterns of activity) and nonsexual functioning (comparable impairment in social, occupational, and psychological functioning as well as medical risk-taking and financial cost that could be attributed directly to sexual behaviors). The authors concluded that men with nonviolent paraphilias and men with nonparaphilic sexual addictions were similar in the most clinically significant measures of sexual and nonsexual functioning, and that "the difference between the groups may lie primarily in the operational distinction of sexual preferences and the relationship of specific sexual preferences to cultural norms" (p. 348). Grouping together paraphilic sexual addictions and nonparaphilic sexual addictions in the same diagnostic category thus fulfills a primary purpose of a psychiatric diagnostic classification system, which is to provide a basis for describing important similarities and differences among psychiatric disorders (Blashfield and Draguns, 1976). A system for categorizing psychiatric disorders is most useful when conditions that share many clinically significant features are grouped together; and important questions in nosology tend to be determined according to pragmatic considerations of usefulness (Panzetta, 1974; Kendler, 1990). These considerations are relevant also to the reorganization of the diagnostic classification system that is entailed in the grouping of sexual addiction with alcoholism, drug addiction, bulimia, and pathological gambling in the superordinate category, addictive disorders (reasons for grouping these conditions together were considered in detail in chapter 5).

Differential Diagnosis

The paraphilic behavior and hypersexual behavior that characterize sexual addiction can occur also as manifestations of underlying organic pathology, and occasionally are its earliest or most prominent symptoms. Paraphilic or hypersexual behavior can be a symptom of a brain lesion, particularly a lesion in the medial basal-frontal, diencephalic, or septal region. Anomalous sexual behavior can occur also in the context of a seizure disorder, especially in association with temporal lobe epilepsy (Epstein, 1960, 1961; Kolarsky et al., 1967; Blumer, 1970; Mohan et al., 1975; Hoenig and Kenna, 1979). Among the paraphilic and nonparaphilic sexual addictions, fetishism and transvestism are the types that are most frequently associated with temporal lobe epilepsy (Epstein, 1961; Blumer, 1970). In one interesting report,

hypersexuality was described as the presenting symptom of a seizure disorder that was caused by a tumor in the right parietal
parasagittal region (Erickson, 1945). Both hypersexual and paraphilic behavior have been observed in persons who suffer from
degenerative disorders of the brain, such as Alzheimer's disease
and Huntington's chorea (Dewhurst, Oliver, and McNight, 1970),
or from mental retardation, in which cases they probably reflect
a general debility of inhibitory processes. More broadly, any disorder that is associated with an impairment of cerebral functioning
can weaken normal inhibitory controls and thereby allow the expression of sexual behaviors that ordinarily are suppressed. Hypersexual behavior can occur also as a side effect of medication,
particularly antiparkinsonian agents. Finally, pathological sexual
behavior can be a symptom of endocrine abnormality. Exhibitionism has been reported in the context of diabetic hyperglycemia
and hypoglycemia (Evans, 1970), and sexually aggressive behavior
has been associated with abnormally elevated levels of testosterone (Raboch, Cerna, and Zemek, 1987; Seim, 1988). The differential diagnosis is usually facilitated by the presence of additional
symptoms or circumstances that suggest the underlying etiology,
although altered sexual behavior may be the earliest manifestation in some cases of brain pathology. Clues that invite an organic
evaluation include: onset in middle age or later, regression from
previously normal sexuality, excessive aggression, report of auras
or seizurelike symptoms prior to or during the sexual behavior,
abnormal body habitus, and presence of soft neurological signs.
Cases that present for the first time in middle or old age should
be examined for exclusion of arteriopathic or neoplastic organic
brain illness (P. Snaith, 1983), though some first-time presenta-
tions in older men may be explained entirely by psychosocial
factors (Hucker and Ben-Aron, 1985). Also of value in determining whether a case of paraphilia or hypersexuality represents sexual addiction are the diagnostic criteria for sexual addiction.
Tolerance, psychophysiological withdrawal symptoms on discontinuation of the sexual behavior (usually affective discomfort, irritability, or restlessness), and a persistent desire to cut down or
control the behavior, are generally not observed in patterns of

paraphilic or hypersexual behavior that are not part of the sexual addiction syndrome.

Obsessions and compulsions with sexual content can occur in obsessive–compulsive disorder. Sexual obsessions are fairly common in OCD, and were reported in 32 percent of the patients who were studied by Rasmussen and Tsuang (1986). The content of these obsessions, however, consisted most often not of sexual fantasies, but of fears of acting on sexual impulses or fears of being a pervert. Moreover, in contrast with sexual addiction, sexual obsessions and compulsions typically are not accompanied by sexual arousal, and they typically do not provide or lead to sexual pleasure. Psychophysiological assessment in cases of obsessive–compulsive disorder with sexual content normally fails to reveal erection responses to the obsessive thoughts (Abel, 1989). One case report presented the occurrence of inappropriate penile erections in two OCD patients with sexual obsessions (Warwick and Salkovskis, 1990). However, in neither case did the patient act out the sexual obsession and in both cases they experienced a profound fear and repugnance of doing so. In short, the symptoms of sexual addiction differ from sexual obsessions and compulsions in that the former are associated with sexual arousal and sexual pleasure, while the latter typically are not. Meanwhile, as we noted earlier, the distinction between sexual addiction and obsessive–compulsive disorder with sexual content is more dimensional than categorical.

A syndrome that meets the diagnostic criteria for sexual addiction can occur in the context of other psychiatric disorders, including manic–depressive disorder and its variants, schizophrenia, borderline personality disorder, narcissistic personality disorder, and substance dependence. When the diagnostic criteria for both sexual addiction and another psychiatric disorder are met, both diagnoses are warranted, regardless of whether sexual addiction might be secondary to the other psychiatric disorder. The diagnosis of sexual addiction is a descriptive designation of how a pattern of sexual behavior relates to and affects an individual's life. It does not presume a particular etiology, nor is it precluded by the presence of other conditions that may be etiologically relevant.

EPIDEMIOLOGY

Prevalence

Data on the prevalence of sexual addiction in the general population are scarce, to some extent, because such data are difficult to collect. Random sampling of the general population is unlikely to be reliable, since shame as well as fear of legal repercussions may lead to significant underreporting. Meanwhile, data from arrest records, victim assessments, or treatment programs, however informative they may be, are unlikely to be representative of the general population.

Carnes (1989) reported that 3 to 6 percent of Americans suffer from sexual addiction, and Coleman (1992) reported that approximately 5 percent of the population meet diagnostic criteria for "sexual compulsivity." Neither report indicated how the data were obtained. Templeman and Stinnet (1991) questioned sixty undergraduate males about child molestation and other forms of paraphilic interest. Three percent reported a history of sexual contact with girls under 12, 42 percent reported voyeurism, 8 percent reported obscene phone calls, 35 percent reported frottage (sexual rubbing against a nonconsenting person), 2 percent reported exhibitionism, 5 percent reported coercive sex, and a total of 65 percent reported some category of paraphilic behavior. Conclusions about the prevalence of sexual addiction cannot, however, be reliably drawn from data about the history of paraphilic activity, which could reflect isolated instances of behavior. Sexual addiction is a chronic pattern of sexual behavior, paraphilic or nonparaphilic, that involves impaired control and harmful consequences. We would expect the prevalence of paraphilic sexual addiction to be much less than the lifetime prevalence of paraphilic activity, and the prevalence of paraphilic or nonparaphilic sexual addiction to be greater than the prevalence of paraphilic sexual addiction alone. A literature review at the end of 1995 revealed no further data on the prevalence of sexual addiction.

Gender and Age Features

The majority of individuals who use sexual behavior addictively are men. Gender differences in prevalence are greater for paraphilias than for nonparaphilic sexual addictions. In the majority of cases of paraphilia, onset is prior to age 18 (Abel and Rouleau, 1990; Abel and Osborn, 1992a). While sexual addiction tends to be a chronic, lifelong disorder, the frequency of addictive sexual behavior typically peaks between the ages of 20 and 30, and then gradually declines. The "modal subject" in a cohort that responded to an advertisement for evaluation and treatment of sexual addictions and compulsive sexual behaviors (Kafka and Prentky, 1992) was characterized as a 34-year-old, white, married, Catholic college graduate earning a middle-class income.

Comorbidity and Familial Patterns

Researchers have noted significant comorbidity among different forms of sexual addiction; that is, individuals who engage addictively in one form of sexual behavior are likely also to engage addictively in other forms of sexual behavior. High frequencies of comorbidity have been observed not only within the category of paraphilias (Rooth, 1973; G.D. Wilson and Gosselin, 1980; Chalkley and Powell, 1983; Kruesi et al., 1992), but also between paraphilias and nonparaphilic sexual addictions (Breitner, 1973; Carnes, 1989; Kafka and Prentky, 1992).

The remainder of this section is prefaced by the observation that little research has actually been conducted specifically with individuals who use sexual behavior addictively. For a variety of reasons, most of the reviewed research studied sex offenders who had engaged in sexually aggressive behavior. The applicability to sex *addicts* of findings that were obtained from sex *offenders* may, however, be limited. Many sex offenders are not sex addicts (Blanchard, 1990) and many sex addicts do not engage in sexually aggressive behavior. A number of researchers have concluded that the nosology and characteristic features of sexual assault are closer to those of nonsexual assault than they are to those of other forms of deviant sexual behavior (Scott et al., 1984). In view of the significant comorbidity and shared clinical features between paraphilic and nonparaphilic patterns of addictive use of sexual behavior (Carnes, 1989; Kafka and Prentky, 1992), research with paraphilic subjects is likely to be more applicable to sexual addiction in general than is research with sex offenders. Nonetheless, caution is advised in extrapolating research findings to groups that differ from the subject cohort.

A variety of psychiatric disorders have been reported to be comorbid with sexual addiction at a rate that is significantly higher than their prevalence in the general population. These disorders include mood disorders, anxiety disorders, personality disorders, psychoactive substance dependence, and other addictive disorders. The disorder that has been most widely reported to be comorbid with sexual addiction is substance dependence. Coleman (1987) noted preliminary findings that chemically dependent individuals have a higher frequency of sexually compulsive behavior patterns than is prevalent in the general population, but the results of his study have not yet been published. Washton (1989) reported that about 70 percent of the cocaine addicts who entered an outpatient treatment program were found to engage addictively in sexual behavior as well. In an anonymous survey of seventy five sex addicts, Schneider and Schneider (1991) found that 39 percent were recovering from chemical dependency. Irons and Schneider's (1994) study of health professionals who were assessed for sexual impropriety revealed concurrent chemical dependency in 38 percent of those who did use sexual behavior addictively and in 21 percent of those who did not. Kruesi and his colleagues (1992) noted that 53 percent (8) of fifteen paraphilic subjects in a drug study met the diagnostic criteria for alcoholism and that 13 percent (2) met the criteria for drug abuse. Kafka and Prentky (1994) reported that 47 percent (16) of thirty four men with paraphilias and 46 percent (12) of twenty six men with "paraphilia-related disorders" also suffered from psychoactive substance use disorders.

A number of researchers have noted that sex offenders have rates of alcohol addiction and drug abuse that are significantly higher than those in the general population (Rada, 1975, 1978;

Anderson, Kunce, and Rich, 1979; Knight, Rosenberg, and Schneider, 1985; Langevin, 1985; Langevin et al., 1985; Mio, Nanjundappa, Verleur, and Rios, 1986; Langevin and Lang, 1988, 1990). However, the significance of these data is not clear. Lack of closely matched comparison groups leaves unresolved the question of whether this extent of substance abuse is characteristic of sex offenders specifically, of a general prison population, or of a population of men that share similar demographic features, irrespective of criminal history.

Addictive disorders other than substance dependence also have been found in association with sexual addiction. Schneider and Schneider (1991) reported that 32 percent of the sex addicts in their survey had an eating disorder, 13 percent characterized themselves as compulsive spenders, and 5 percent were compulsive gamblers. Travin and Protter (1993) mentioned that a significant proportion of paraphilic patients in their practice suffered also from "cross addictions," such as gambling, eating disorders, and nonparaphilic sexual compulsivity. They did not, however, provide any statistics. Kafka and Prentky (1994) found that 9 percent (3) of thirty four paraphilic men were also pathological gamblers. Meanwhile, studies of compulsive gamblers found that they are at a significantly higher risk than is the general population for lifetime comorbidity with sexual addiction (Lesieur, 1988; Steinberg, 1990).

Several other psychiatric disorders have been found in association with sexual addiction. Kafka and Prentky (1992) studied a group of twenty men, ten diagnosed with paraphilias and ten diagnosed with nonparaphilic sexual addictions (only), and reported that nineteen of the twenty (95%) met diagnostic criteria for dysthymia and that eleven of the twenty (55%) met criteria for current major depression. A larger study by Kafka and Prentky (1994) found that 41 percent (14) of thirty four men with paraphilias suffered from major depression, 68 percent (23) suffered from dysthymia, and 47 percent (16) suffered from an anxiety disorder (social phobia in 21%, generalized anxiety in 18%, OCD in 12%, and panic disorder in 12%). Meanwhile, the same study found that 62 percent (16) of twenty six men with nonparaphilic sexual addictions suffered from major depression, 62 percent

(16) suffered from dysthymia, and 46 percent (12) suffered from an anxiety disorder (social phobia in 47%, generalized anxiety in 12%, OCD in 12%, and panic disorder in 8%). In another study, however, Kafka (1994) reported that only three of twenty one sexually addicted men met diagnostic criteria for major depression. Kruesi and his colleagues (1992) found that nine of fifteen paraphilic men (60%) met RDC diagnostic criteria for depression (5 unipolar depression and 4 minor depression), and that six of the fifteen (40%) met diagnostic criteria for an anxiety disorder (panic disorder in 2, general anxiety disorder in all 6). Kafka (1991) determined that four of ten sexually addicted patients met diagnostic criteria for social phobia. Chalkley and Powell (1983) assessed contemporaneous comorbidity in forty eight sexual fetishists and diagnosed three with paranoid schizophrenia, seven with a depressive disorder, two with an anxiety disorder, thirteen with a personality disorder, and nine with another sexual deviation or a sexual dysfunction. Focusing on transvestites, Fagan and his colleagues (Fagan, Wise, Derogatis, and Schmidt, 1988) found that 38 percent of those whom they studied merited formal Axis I diagnoses, primarily mood, anxiety, and adjustment disorders. In an earlier study, T. N. Wise and Meyer (1980) observed that 80 percent of gender dysphoric transvestites qualified for a concurrent Axis I diagnosis. The authors commented that whether the presence of an Axis I diagnosis was an independent phenomenon, or a reaction to an adverse consequence of transvestism, or an effect of the same factors that led to transvestism, was not known. Neither of these studies mentioned whether subjects were assessed for Axis II disorders. In a review article, Blair and Lanyon (1981) identified six studies that assessed the presence in exhibitionists of other psychopathology. Two studies found a high rate of nonpsychotic Axis I disorders and a very high rate of character or personality disorders in exhibitionists, two found a moderately high rate of nonpsychotic disorders, and two found a rate of psychopathology that was not significantly different from that in the general population. Other studies found a high prevalence of conduct disorder and attention deficit disorder in adolescent sex offenders (Kavoussi, Kaplan, and Becker, 1988; Hunter and Goodwin, 1992).

Carnes (1989) alluded to a significant family history of substance addiction as well as sexual addiction in first-degree relatives of sex addicts, but he did not cite any supportive data. In their survey study, Schneider and Schneider (1991) found that 36 percent of seventy five sex addicts reported that one or both parents were sex addicts, 40 percent reported that one or both parents were chemically dependent, 33 percent reported that one or both parents had an eating disorder, and 7 percent reported that one parent was a compulsive gambler. They did not mention whether the family history of other psychiatric disorders was assessed.

In sum, the reviewed body of comorbidity and family history studies is more suggestive than conclusive. Significant comorbidity of sexual addiction with other addictive disorders, particularly substance abuse disorders, is the strongest trend that this research reveals. Significant comorbidity between sexual addiction and mood disorders, anxiety disorders, personality disorders, and schizophrenia is suggested by the literature as well, though less robustly than is comorbidity with other addictive disorders. The single family history study that was reviewed indicated a significant history of sexual addiction and of other addictive disorders in parents of individuals who use sexual behavior addictively. Clearly, more research needs to be conducted in the areas of sexual addiction comorbidity and family history, particularly in light of the usefulness of such findings in understanding etiology and in formulating treatment plans. Studies that assess lifetime comorbidity, such as those that were conducted by Lesieur (1988) and by Steinberg (1990), are likely to be especially instructive.

7

Overview of Treatment Modalities

ASSESSMENT OF EFFICACY

An overview of modalities that can be employed in the treatment of sexual addiction begins properly with a series of caveats. First of all, most of the reported studies that assessed the efficacy of these treatment modalities were conducted with sex offenders, not with sex addicts. As I noted earlier, while the two groups share a significant number of members, each of the groups also contains a significant number of members who do not fit in the other group. The degree to which findings that were obtained with sex offenders are applicable also to sex addicts is indeterminate, and this indeterminacy complicates the difficulty of evaluating and selecting methods for the treatment of sexual addiction. Moreover, a number of investigators, including Wakeling (1979), Gelder (1979), Blair and Lanyon (1981), and Marshall and his colleagues (Marshall, Jones, Ward, Johnson, and Barbaree, 1991), have raised questions about the methodology of the reported studies that assessed the efficacy of particular methods for treating paraphilias and sexual aggression. Among the problems that

247

these investigators identified were: (1) small number of subjects studied; (2) nonrepresentativeness of the sample, as a result of patient selection factors; (3) failure to identify patient variables that have significant prognostic value; (4) failure to compare the outcome with a suitable control group; (5) insufficiently clear description of the treatment procedures that were utilized; (6) failure to specify the levels of therapist experience; (7) contamination of major dependent variables by variations in therapist experience; (8) lack of clear and meaningful criteria by which to measure improvement; (9) lack of knowledge about the natural course of the condition when it is not treated; and (10) inadequate duration of posttreatment follow-up. Such methodological weaknesses limit the confidence with which conclusions about the efficacy of treatment modalities can be drawn from these studies. Marshall's group (1991) cautioned against setting standards for methodological rigor that could not reasonably be expected to be met in so immature a field. However, they also observed that to ignore certain criteria in reviewing the literature would not encourage any reader to have confidence in the conclusions that could be drawn from the review.

While we are on the subject of research methodology, we can note that the majority of studies in which the methodology is sound by empirical standards concern behavioral treatments or medication treatments. These relatively simple, impersonal, objective, technologically oriented methods of treatment are much more readily studied by empirical methodologies than are the more complex, personal, subjective, psychotherapeutically oriented methods. The reasons for this difference have been considered elsewhere (Docherty, 1984; Goodman, 1994b, in press b) and are beyond the scope of the present discussion. The difference is, however, worth keeping in mind, lest we prematurely interpret the scarcity of sound empirical studies that report positive results for treatment modalities in the latter group to indicate that these treatment modalities lack merit (as did, for example, Berlin and Meinecke [1981]).

The modalities that have been employed in treating sexual addiction include medication, behavior modification, cognitive–behavioral therapy, therapeutic groups, couples or family therapy, and psychodynamic psychotherapy. Most programs or systems for treating sexual addiction combine two or more of these modalities, so classification of treatment systems in categories that are defined by particular modalities misrepresents many of the treatment systems. On the other hand, the specific details of the different therapeutic modalities are most clearly presented when the material is organized by modality; and, while most of the treatment systems employ a combination of modalities, they also tend to emphasize one modality or another as their primary core.

MEDICATION

The category of medication comprises two different kinds of pharmacological treatment, antiandrogenic agents and affect-regulating agents (antidepressants and mood stabilizers).

Antiandrogenic Agents

Antiandrogenic agents have been studied in the treatment of paraphilias, and particularly in the treatment of paraphilic behaviors in sex offenders. Early investigations included clinical trials of estrogens (Whittaker, 1959; Symmers, 1968). While they were reported to be successful in reducing deviant sexual behavior, estrogen treatments were associated with undesirable side effects, such as feminization and an increased incidence of breast cancer. In a similar manner, antipsychotic agents appeared to reduce deviant sexual behavior (Sterkmans and Geerts, 1966; Field, 1973), but their side effects of dyskinesias, drowsiness, and slowed thinking, as well as the long-term risk of tardive dyskinesia, limit their usefulness in treating nonpsychotic individuals.

Antiandrogenic agents that are currently in use include medroxyprogesterone acetate (MPA) and cyproterone acetate (CPA). The former is available throughout North America, although it has not been approved in the United States for reduction of sex drive; the latter is available only outside the United

States. Medroxyprogesterone acetate has been reported to influence the synthesis, transport, metabolism, and activity of testosterone (Walker and Meyer, 1981; Bradford, 1990; Kravitz, Haywood, Kelly, Wahlstrom, Liles, and Cavanaugh, 1995). It can displace testosterone from its plasma transport protein, testosterone-binding globulin, but it does not seem to compete significantly with androgens at androgen receptors (Bradford, 1990). The reduction of sex drive by MPA seems to be associated primarily with its induction of testosterone-A reductase in the liver, which then accelerates the metabolism of testosterone. Besides decreasing serum testosterone levels, MPA appears also to act centrally on the brain. This hypothesis is supported by three observations. First, MPA seems to decrease erotic fantasies even at doses that are not associated with a decrease in serum testosterone levels. Second, when MPA is administered, production of LH (luteinizing hormone) and FSH (follicle stimulating hormone) by the pituitary gland does not increase in response to lowered serum levels of testosterone production, while LH and FSH production do increase when the origin of a testosterone decrease is peripheral (Berlin and Meinecke, 1981). Finally, neurons in brain regions that are involved in sexual behavior (the preoptic nucleus and the hypothalamus) have been found to accumulate MPA in monkeys (Rees, Bonsall, and Michael, 1986). A number of clinical studies have demonstrated that MPA can reduce sex drive, sexual thoughts, sexual behavior, and aggressiveness (Money, 1968, 1970, 1972; Freund, 1980; Hermann and Beach, 1980; Gagne, 1981; Berlin and Meinecke, 1981; Berlin, 1983; Cordoba and Chapel, 1983; Wincze, Bansal, and Malamud, 1986; Bradford, 1988, 1990; Maletzky, 1991; Kravitz et al., 1995). Kravitz and his colleagues (1995), however, raised a number of questions about the validity of these MPA research findings, including the lack of controlled, double-blind studies (due to medicolegal and ethical concerns) and the difficulty in distinguishing MPA effects from (1) the effects of other, concurrently employed treatment modalities, and (2) the effects of factors that are not directly related to treatment. Kiersch (1990) conducted a double-blind within-subjects study, and he found that both MPA and placebo were associated with decrements in self-reported deviant fantasies. Possible adverse effects of MPA include fatigue and drowsiness, weight gain, hot and cold flashes, nausea and vomiting, headaches, hyperglycemia, sleep disturbances, leg cramps, pulmonary embolism, and thrombophlebitis. In addition, some patients experience the global reduction of sex drive as undesirable.

Cyproterone acetate (CPA) has antiandrogenic, antigonadotropic, and progestational effects. Its principal mode of action is on the androgen receptors. It blocks testosterone receptor binding, intracellular testosterone uptake, and intracellular metabolism of the androgens (Bradford, 1988). In controlled trials, CPA has produced a decrease in (reported) erotic fantasies, but not a significant reduction in erectile response to erotic slides and film (Bancroft, Tennent, Loucas, and Cass, 1974; Murray, Bancroft, Anderson, Tennent, and Carr, 1975; A. J. Cooper, 1981). Administration of CPA has been associated with decreases in sexually driven aggression and in the recidivism rates of various forms of sexual aggression and pedophilia (Laschet, 1973; Laschet and Laschet, 1975; A. J. Cooper, 1986; Gilby, Wolf, and Goldberg, 1989). One large study noted that aggressive behavior that did not involve sexual deviation did not respond at all to CPA (Laschet and Laschet, 1975). In a single case report of a double-blind placebo crossover study, Bradford and Pawlak (1993a) found that CPA significantly reduced sexual arousal responses to pedophilic and coercive sexual stimuli, but did not reduce arousal to mutually consenting adult sex scenes. Possible adverse effects include liver dysfunction, adrenal suppression, fatigue, hypersomnia, depression, weight gain, and feminization.

In sum, while antiandrogen medications seem to be effective in decreasing sex drive, sexual thoughts, and sexual behavior, their clinical usefulness is limited by a number of significant drawbacks. Unpleasant side effects are frequent and serious side effects occasionally occur. Noncompliance also is a considerable problem, and one study had a dropout rate of greater than 50 percent (Berlin and Meinecke, 1981). Moreover, while antiandrogen agents lower the sex drive, they do nothing to alter the deviation itself, and the patient's deviant behavior has been reported to recur soon after the medication is discontinued (Travin, Blu-estone, Coleman, Cullen, and Melella, 1985). (However, Bradford [1990] suggested that these characteristics may be less true for CPA than for MPA.) Finally, "chemical castration," however temporary, can be attended by a variety of social and political difficulties.

Most reviewers have agreed that antiandrogen agents alone do not constitute adequate treatment for paraphilias or sexual aggression, but that they can be a valuable adjunct to behavior modification, group therapy, or individual psychotherapy with some patients, particularly during early stages of treatment (Reid, 1989; Bradford, 1990; Marshall et al., 1991). Although these medications do not change the direction of the paraphiliac's sexual interest, they decrease the intensity of his sexual drive, so he is more in control and less likely to act on his paraphilic interest. Their primary therapeutic function is not to eliminate maladaptive sexual behavior, but to reduce sex drive to manageable levels in those individuals whose ability to control their behavioral impulses is so severely impaired as to put them at serious immediate risk either to injure themselves or others, or to render them unresponsive to psychological interventions. Antiandrogenic agents can lower the risk of problematic sexual behavior during the interval between the initiation of treatment and the consolidation of the changes that behavior modification, group therapy, or psychotherapy induce.

Affect-Regulating Agents

A number of reports have provided evidence for the efficacy of affect-regulating agents in the treatment of paraphilias, even in patients who are not suffering from a major affective disorder. Agents that have been found to be effective include:

1. Fluoxetine [Prozac] (Bianchi, 1990; Jorgensen, 1990; Emmanuel, Lydiard, and Ballenger, 1991; Kafka, 1991; Lorefice, 1991; Perilstein, Lipper, and Friedman, 1991; Kafka and Prentky, 1992; Stein et al., 1992).

2. Sertraline [Zoloft] (Kafka, 1994; Bradford and Gratzer, 1995).
3. Fluvoxamine [Luvox] (Zohar, Kaplan, and Benjamin, 1994).
4. Imipramine [Tofranil and others] (Snaith and Collins, 1981; Kafka, 1991).
5. Desipramine [Norpramin and others] (Kruesi et al., 1992).
6. Clomipramine [Anafranil] (Wawrose and Sisto, 1992; Casals-Ariet and Cullen, 1993; Clayton, 1993; Torres and de Abreu Cerquiera, 1993).
7. Lithium (Ward, 1975; Bartova, Nahumek, and Svestke, 1978; Cesnik and Coleman, 1989; Kafka, 1991).
8. Sertraline plus lithium (Rubenstein and Engel, 1996).
9. Buspirone [Buspar] (Federoff, 1988).
10. Electroconvulsive therapy (Eyres, 1960).

The author of one of the earliest of these reports (Ward, 1975) explained his findings with the hypothesis that paraphilic behavior had been maintained by mood-dependent motives, and that pharmacological treatment of the underlying mood disorder consequently eliminated the paraphilic behavior by alleviating the mood conditions that motivated it. Kafka (1991, 1994) and Kafka and Prentky (1992) treated nonparaphilic sexual addictions as well as paraphilias with affect-regulating agents, and found that both conditions responded favorably.

While such a large number of positive findings is encouraging, the confidence with which conclusions can be drawn from these findings is limited by the paucity of controlled studies. The study that was reported by Kruesi and colleagues (1992) was a double-blind crossover comparison, and all of the rest were either clinical case reports or open trials. A double-blind, placebo-controlled study that evaluates the efficacy of a serotonin reuptake inhibitor in the treatment of sexual addiction would be a welcome addition to the literature.

Different investigators have observed that paraphilias respond almost equally well to different kinds of affect-regulating agents: fluoxetine, imipramine, and lithium for Kafka (1991), clomipramine and desipramine for Kruesi and his colleagues (1992). The latter group of investigators noted that this pattern of similar response to serotonergic and noradrenergic antidepressants more closely resembles the response pattern of affective disorders than that of obsessive–compulsive disorders. A single case of paraphilia that was reported by Bradford and Gratzer (1995) responded to sertraline but not to clomipramine. While Bradford and Gratzer had initially considered paraphilias to be part of the obsessive–compulsive disorder spectrum, they hypothesized that "depression may have been a disinhibiting factor which caused (the patient) to act on his paraphilic fantasies" (p. 5). Stein and his colleagues (1992) also observed that paraphilias respond to medication in patterns more similar to those of affective disorders than to those of obsessive–compulsive disorders. They found that serotonin reuptake inhibitors were helpful in treating paraphilias, but that they were less effective than they typically are with sexual obsessions and compulsions that occur in the context of obsessive–compulsive disorder. They noted that paraphilic patients with comorbid depression showed concurrent improvement in sexual addiction when depressive symptoms improved, while patients with comorbid OCD often had improvement in OCD without improvement in sexual behavior. Kafka (1991) also reported that the target symptoms of sexual behavior improved concomitantly with depressive symptoms. Meanwhile, Kafka and Prentky (1992) observed that the response of paraphilias and of nonparaphilic sexual addictions to fluoxetine was independent of the baseline level of depression. They did not, however, indicate whether improvement of sexual behavior symptoms coincided with improvement of depressive symptoms.

Shifting to consider issues of theory, the reviewed findings of pharmacological treatment—that the symptoms of sexual addiction respond to medications in a pattern that resembles the response pattern of affective disorder symptoms—make sense when the biopsychological process that underlies sexual addiction (the addictive process) is understood to originate in impaired affect regulation, impaired behavioral inhibition, and aberrant function of the motivational-reward system. Addictive urges can then be recognized to represent both (1) expressions of dysregulated affect, and (2) conditioned stimuli for coping responses (responses to cope with dysregulated affect) that have been learned in the context of impaired behavioral inhibition and aberrant motivational-reward function. Interventions that enhance affect regulation and behavioral inhibition can thus be expected to diminish addictive craving and addictive behavior.

BEHAVIOR MODIFICATION

Behavioral methods have been employed in the treatment of paraphilias, but not in the treatment of nonparaphilic sexual addictions. They are oriented toward assisting individuals to reduce the erotic quality of their paraphilic interests, or to shift the balance of erotic arousal potential from paraphilic interests to nonparaphilic interests. The primary forms of behavioral treatment for paraphilias are aversion conditioning, covert sensitization, masturbatory training, and imaginal desensitization. Some behavioral methods also teach patients a self-administered treatment that they can perform on their own. Such methods can help not only to diminish paraphilic behavior but also to enhance feelings of self-control.

Aversion Conditioning

In aversion conditioning, unwanted patterns of sexual behavior are linked repeatedly with unpleasant stimuli. This classical or Pavlovian conditioning procedure is intended to transform stimulus features of the sexual behavior into conditioned stimuli or triggers for the aversive responses to the unpleasant stimuli. In the original version of aversion conditioning, the unpleasant stimulus was nausea that was induced by apomorphine or emetine. This method was associated with a variety of problems (Rachman and Teasdale, 1969), and it is rarely recommended any more. The preferred aversive stimuli nowadays are foul odors and electric shock, which are easier to control and can be used for operant punishment of responses as well as for classical conditioning to stimuli.

A number of uncontrolled studies (Marks, Rachman, and Gelder, 1965; Evans, 1968, 1970; Fookes, 1969; Abel, Lewis, and Clancy, 1970; Marks, Gelder, and Bancroft, 1970; Birk, Huddleston, Miller, and Cohler, 1971; MacCulloch, Williams, and Birtles, 1971; Wijesinghe, 1977) found that aversion conditioning yielded positive results, while one study (Quinsey, Bergersen, and Steinman, 1976) found no significant effects and another (Feldman and MacCulloch, 1968) found that the success of aversion conditioning depended on the availability of appropriate sexual outlets and the absence of severe nonsexual pathology. Three controlled studies of aversion conditioning treatment for exhibitionism (Evans, 1968, 1970; MacCullock et al., 1971) yielded positive results, but two employed follow-up intervals of six months or less. One investigation that compared aversive therapy with a placebo and attempted to control for expectancy effects (Birk et al., 1971) found that, at one-year follow-up, significantly more subjects who had received the aversive procedure reported an increased ability to control sexual behaviors that they wished to avoid carrying out.

A number of investigators have found that the sexual arousal that is elicited by different sexually deviant themes varies independently, so that aversion conditioning for arousal to one class of deviation does not necessarily generalize to other classes (Quinsey and Earls, 1990). For example, Earls and Castonguay (1989) found that pairing an aversive odor with arousal to homosexual themes involving children reduced arousal to homosexual pedophilic stimuli, but that arousal to heterosexual pedophilic themes remained unaffected until it was directly targeted in treatment.

Bandura (1970) criticized the theory but not the method of aversion conditioning treatment, noting that its behavioral effects in clinical practice lasted much longer than was typical for aversive conditioning in the laboratory. He stated that too little attention had been paid to cognitive variables in aversion therapy, and he suggested that aversion therapy is a technique for learning self-control, which depends on cognitive, as well as automatic reflexive, learning. He proposed that aversion conditioning is effective because it activates covert self-stimulation, in which the patient rehearses to himself the unpleasant experiences of the treatment sessions, and continues to do so long after the sessions have finished. To the extent that Bandura was correct, the ease of rehearsal may be more crucial to the success of aversion conditioning than are the stimulus qualities or their timing. In support of Bandura's arguments that emphasized the importance of cognitive factors, Quinsey, Chaplin, and Carrigan (1980) found that a signaled punishment plus biofeedback procedure was considerably more effective than was a classical conditioning aversion therapy procedure.

Covert Sensitization

Covert sensitization was developed as an imaginary form of aversion conditioning, in which fantasies of paraphilic arousal are paired with fantasies of aversive events in order to promote a learned association between paraphilic themes and unpleasant feelings. In covert sensitization, patients are first led through a relaxation exercise, which enhances their receptiveness to vivid mental imagery and helps them to focus their attention on the imagery rather than on external events. They then are instructed to visualize themselves engaging in some aspect of their paraphilic behaviors, and they are encouraged to feel personally involved. At that point, patients are told to imagine either an unpleasant event, such as nausea and vomiting (which can be reinforced by a nauseating odor), or an aversive consequence that could follow the behavior in reality, such as public humiliation or shame at being discovered by a superego figure (a parent or a clergyperson, for example).

Studies have found covert sensitization to be effective in the treatment of exhibitionism and pedophilia (Callahan and Leitenberg, 1973; Barlow and Able, 1976; Maletzky, 1974, 1980; Brownell, Hayes, and Barlow, 1977; Hayes, Browness, and Barlow, 1978; Alford, Webster, and Sanders, 1980; Lamontagne and Lesage, 1986; Abel and Osborn, 1992b). Unlike aversion conditioning, covert sensitization neither involves the infliction of physical discomfort on the patient, nor does it require expensive technology. Consequently, in the absence of clear evidence that aversion therapy is more effective than covert sensitization (Callahan and Leitenberg, 1973), many behavior therapists prefer to begin with covert sensitization, turning to aversion therapy only for patients who do not respond to covert sensitization. Maletzky (1974, 1980) described a method that was actually a modification of covert sensitization, in which the aversive valence of the imagined noxious scene was amplified by simultaneously presenting a malodorous substance at the subject's nostrils. Maletzky (1980) found that this method, which he called "assisted covert sensitization," was as effective as electrical aversion conditioning and was superior to covert sensitization.

A treatment program for sex offenders that was described by Marshall and Barbaree (1990b) added a self-training technique to aversive conditioning and covert sensitization. The patient was given smelling salts, which he could use in his everyday life as a way of countering deviant thoughts or urges. Each patient also carried several pocket-sized cards on which were written covert sensitization scripts that described in detail the typical sequence of specific behaviors that led up to his offending, and that also described the associated negative consequences. The patient was instructed to read each card at least three times a day, in various situations. This practice and the patient's use of smelling salts were meant to increase the likelihood of generalization from therapy to the patient's everyday life.

In a review of behavior therapy, Gelder (1979) observed that the effect of covert sensitization depends more on cognitive processes than on associative learning. He cited a study by Marks et al. (1970), in which the final clinical outcome of covert sensitization was correlated not with the amount of conditioned anxiety that was induced during treatment sessions, but with the extent to which attitudes toward deviant sexual behavior changed during the course of treatment.

Masturbatory Training

Masturbatory training attempts to shift paraphilic patients' arousal patterns in the conventional direction by controlling the fantasies or visual stimuli that they experience while masturbating. The two main forms of masturbatory training are satiation and fading.

Satiation, the more common of the two, involves instructing male patients to masturbate to orgasm with conventional sexual stimuli or fantasies, and then to continue masturbating while visualizing their deviant objects. The idea is that masturbating after orgasm will extinguish erotic arousal to paraphilic fantasies. Hunter and Goodwin (1992) employed this method with juvenile sex offenders and reported mild success after six to nine months of treatment. Little about masturbatory satiation can be concluded from this study, however, since other therapeutic modalities were provided at the same time, the study did not include a control group, and no posttreatment follow-up was reported.

In the fading technique, paraphilic patients' fantasies are gradually shifted from deviant to conventional during periods of sexual arousal. Patients may be provided with visual stimuli on which to focus, such as photographic slides that automatically fade from one kind of scene to another; or they may be instructed to gradually alter the scenario that they fantasize while they masturbate.

Imaginal Desensitization

The technique of imaginal desensitization is based on the theory that, once an individual has developed a sequence of sexual activity, which begins with a sexual thought or fantasy and ends with overt behavior, interruption of the sequence results in anxiety that then motivates completion of the sequence. Imaginal desensitization uses the methods of systematic desensitization to diminish the anxiety that is aroused by interruption of the sequence that leads to paraphilic behavior. In the procedure that was described by McConaghy, Armstrong, and Blaszczynski (1985), the patient describes a scene in which he is stimulated to carry out the sexual activities for which he sought treatment. After relaxation is induced, the patient visualizes performing a sequence of behaviors that lead to noncompletion of the act. Relaxation is allowed to develop with each visualized behavior before the patient proceeds to the next behavior in the sequence. The patient is thus trained to visualize not completing the sexual act, while remaining relaxed. The procedure can then be repeated with other scenes that the patient has described. No aversive physical stimulus or traumatic imagery is employed. A study that was conducted by McConaghy et al. (1985) reported imaginal desensitization to be more effective than covert sensitization.

COGNITIVE–BEHAVIORAL THERAPIES

Marshall and his colleagues observed in 1991 that, over the preceding fifteen years, the field of sex offender treatment in general had shifted away from a strictly behavioral approach that focused on changing sexual behavior, and toward a more cognitive–behavioral and social learning theory approach that focused on intrapsychic and interpersonal as well as behavioral issues. By the time that the field of sexual addiction emerged in the 1980s, the cognitive revolution in psychology was well under way. Cognitive–behavioral therapies conceptualize psychological problems primarily in terms of maladaptive learning, and are oriented toward assisting the individual to learn more adaptive patterns of thinking and acting. They typically rely on interventions that are directive, practical, task-oriented, and educative in nature.

Quadland (1985), Schwartz and Brasted (1985), and Carnes (1983, 1989) described programs for treating sexual addiction that were predominantly cognitive–behavioral (or social–cognitive–behavioral) in their approach. In addition to their cognitive–behavioral orientation, the three programs shared a reliance on group therapy as their primary form of treatment.

Quadland (1985) described a group therapy program for treating "compulsive sexual behavior." The program was intended to help group members both (1) to change their sexual behavior, and (2) to recognize and understand the factors that drove their sexual behavior. Quadland identified two cognitive–behavioral techniques that the program employed, self-monitoring and contracting. In the self-monitoring component, participants kept journals of their sexual thoughts, feelings, and experiences. They then talked in group sessions about what they had entered in their journals. In the contracting component, participants made contracts with the group about changes that they wanted to make each week. Group sessions then usually began with a review of contracts from the previous week, and individuals shared their thoughts and feelings about their various successes and failures. As they were described by Quadland, the group sessions seemed to be fairly unstructured, other than the structure that was involved in self-monitoring and contracting. Quadland noted that the group process was a significant therapeutic factor in his program. He specifically identified the benefits of mutual support and of confrontation by peers of participants who seemed to be less than honest with themselves or with the group.

M. F. Schwartz and Brasted (1985) presented a cognitive–behavioral treatment program that involved six stages. The first stage focused on stopping the undesired sexual behavior. Behavior modification techniques and/or pharmacotherapy were employed, as needed, to modify patients' sexual drives. The goal of the second stage, which the authors identified as the "admission" stage, was for the patient to accept the existence of a problem and to promise to keep no secrets from the therapist or from fellow group members. In the third stage, patients were taught anxiety reduction techniques, such as progressive relaxation, so they would no longer need to rely on sexual behavior to alleviate their anxiety. The fourth stage represented the core of Schwartz and Brasted's program. It consisted of cognitive therapy that was directed toward modifying the irrational beliefs that Schwartz and Brasted hypothesized to underlie the sexual addiction. In the fifth stage, patients were trained in such skills as assertiveness and problem solving, in order to facilitate their adaptive social functioning. Finally, the sixth stage focused on resolving whatever residual problems the individual had in establishing a primary sexual relationship. This stage most often involved couples therapy with the pretreatment sexual partner.

The program for treating sexual addiction that was developed by Carnes (1983, 1989) shared with Schwartz and Brasted's program an initial focus on stopping the addictive sexual behavior and a subsequent emphasis on altering the maladaptive core beliefs that were thought to underlie the patient's addictive system. It differed from the programs that were described by Quadland and by Schwartz and Brasted in several ways that reflected the more complete adoption by Carnes of the addiction model. Carnes developed a structured, intensive program that resembled the traditional substance addiction ("chemical dependency") treatment program. A series of lectures and workshops were interwoven with group therapies and homework assignments. The program incorporated principles and methods from the 12-step approach, and participants were encouraged to regularly attend meetings of a 12-step fellowship for recovering sex addicts after they had completed the program (in much the same way as participants in traditional substance addiction treatment are encouraged to attend meetings of Alcoholics Anonymous). Carnes' program also directly involved members of sex addicts' families, who were invited to participate in special lectures and groups. Finally, Carnes' program was distinguished from the others by its inclusion of relapse prevention techniques. Participants were guided in compiling an inventory of their relapse risk factors, and then in preparing for what could be done before a "slip" (an episode of symptomatic behavior), during a slip, and after a slip had occurred. They learned to anticipate slip-inducing possibilities and to devise a series of action steps that could serve to prevent a slip. Participants were then instructed to rehearse the slip prevention steps so thoroughly that, when a potentially seductive situation occurred, they would be able to perform the steps automatically. Carnes added that an effective relapse prevention plan must also build in rewards, in order that the addict would not wind up feeling deprived.

Quadland (1985) reported that participants in his program indicated a decrease in the frequency of their compulsive sexual behavior at follow-up six months after treatment. No other studies have been published that specifically assessed the efficacy of cognitive–behavioral treatment for sexual addiction. This research deficit may be due to any one of a number of factors: (1) the use of other modalities in addition to cognitive–behavioral therapy in the treatment programs; (2) the difficulty of identifying a suitable control group; (3) a belief that the success of a particular program depends at least as much on the individuals who comprise the treatment staff as it does on the techniques of the program; and (4) the fact that the individuals who conduct these programs typically have a clinical rather than a research orientation, which leads them to devote their time and energy to patient care issues rather than to the design and implementation of empirical studies. In a review of treatment outcomes with sex offenders (a category that overlaps but is not identical with the category of sex addicts), Marshall and his colleagues (1991) concluded that evaluations of comprehensive cognitive–behavioral programs were encouraging, at least for the treatment of child molesters and exhibitionists. However, they noted, the programs were not uniformly effective.

THERAPEUTIC GROUPS

Many clinicians believe that group therapy and self-help groups are the most effective modalities for the treatment of individuals who use sexual behavior addictively. Travin and Protter (1993) observed that therapeutic groups can offer a variety of nonspecific beneficial effects, such as ventilation, support, positive identification, empathic bonding, and facilitative confrontation.

The types of therapeutic group that have been employed in treating individuals who use sexual behavior addictively include cognitive–behavioral groups, psychodynamic psychotherapy groups, and support groups. While group therapy can range from highly structured to relatively unstructured, most investigators have concluded that individuals who use sexual behavior addictively seem to do best in groups that are at least moderately structured. Mathis and Collins (1970) and Truax (1970) emphasized the importance of treating paraphilic patients in groups that consist of individuals with similar problems, where shared experiences and needs can help to dissolve rationalization, isolation, and denial. Ganzarain and Buchele (1990) observed that, for many paraphilic patients, groupmates and the group peer culture become a surrogate benign superego. Group members often can more readily receive guidance, confrontation, and support from groupmates than from therapists or other individuals in their lives. Travin and Protter (1993) similarly mentioned the importance of confrontation in helping group members to develop a sense of responsibility for their paraphilic activity. They moreover noted the therapeutic benefit that is available to group members who use the group community as a selfobject that can provide mirroring and empathic functions to the struggling self. The benign superego and selfobject functions of groups can assist members in working through issues of guilt and shame that are often central to their character pathology. Three studies reported positive results from psychodynamic group psychotherapy treatment of patients who suffered from perversions (Rosen, 1964; Witzig, 1968; Ganzarain and Buchele, 1990). A study of a treatment program for nonviolent offenders that included group therapy and other therapeutic modalities (but not individual psychotherapy) found positive change in a variety of psychological and psychosocial problems. The patients rated all therapeutic techniques in the moderately to very helpful range, except for group therapy, which was rated extremely helpful (Dwyer and Myers, 1990).

Self-help support groups typically are not led by professional therapists and are open-ended. The most common self-help groups for individuals who use sexual behavior addictively are the 12-step groups that are modeled on Alcoholics Anonymous. Herman (1990) observed that a group of peers who are reliably available on demand and who are committed to the goal of recovery through abstinence from addictive sexual behavior provides all four of the factors that Vaillant (1983) identified as being associated with achievement of stable sobriety in alcoholism: a constant reminder of the harmful consequences of the addictive behavior, social support, a new source of hope and self-esteem, and "a substitute addiction." (We can note here that, unless an individual's involvement in a self-help group is characterized by loss of control and continuation despite significant harmful consequences, the designation of such involvement as "addiction" is inappropriate.)

Since the 1970s, four 12-step fellowships of recovering sex addicts have developed, each based on the model of Alcoholics Anonymous and adapted for sexual addiction: Sex Addicts Anonymous (SAA), Sex and Love Addicts Anonymous (SLAA), Sexaholics Anonymous (SA), and Sexual Compulsives Anonymous (SCA). The primary differences between the four fellowships are encapsulated in their definitions of sobriety. Sobriety in SAA is defined as no "out-of-bounds" sex. In consultation with their sponsors and fellow group members, sex addicts in SAA identify the sexual behaviors that are likely to lead to harmful consequences, and they then define "boundaries" that exclude these behaviors (Sex Addicts Anonymous, 1986). In SLAA, sobriety is similarly defined as no "bottom-line" sex: "Define your bottom-line behavior . . . any sexual or emotional act which, once engaged in, leads to loss of control over rate, frequency or duration of its recurrence, resulting in worsening self-destructive consequences" (Augustine Fellowship, 1986, p. 4). Sobriety in SA is more strictly defined as no sexual activity other than with a spouse: "Any form of sex with one's self or with partners other than the spouse is progressively addictive and destructive" (Sexaholics Anonymous, 1989, p. 4). In SCA, members are encouraged to define sexual sobriety for themselves, to develop sexual recovery plans that are consistent with their own values (Sexual Compulsives Anonymous, 1989). The differences between the 12-step fellowships may, however, be less important than the differences between individual groups. Since the fellowships lack formal leadership structures and internal controls, the characteristics of a particular group are determined primarily by the individuals who attend it.

COUPLES AND FAMILY THERAPY

As discussed earlier, the sexual addiction treatment programs that were presented by M. F. Schwartz and Brasted (1985) and by Carnes (1983, 1989) both involved couples or family therapy. The inclusion of couples or family therapy in the treatment of sexual addiction has been recommended also by psychiatric and psychoanalytic clinicians. Gabbard (1994) observed that marital therapy can often help to delineate how perverse sexual activity reflects sexual and emotional difficulties in the marital dyad. Reid (1989) suggested that an exploration of marital discord may reveal that paraphilic activity is a container or "scapegoat" that deflects the focus from other, more problematic areas in the marriage. T. N. Wise (1979) emphasized that marital therapy not only can elucidate pathogenic factors in the marital relationship, but also can engage the spouse and the energy in the relationship as agents of therapeutic change. Little has been written about the use of family therapy specifically in the treatment of sexual addiction, paraphilias, or perversions. Both the cognitive–behaviorally oriented therapists and the psychodynamically oriented therapists, while noting that couples or family therapy can be important in the treatment of sexual addiction, accorded it a supplemental or adjunctive status. No published data are available that assess the efficacy of marital or family therapy in the treatment of sexual addiction.

PSYCHODYNAMIC PSYCHOTHERAPY

A number of psychoanalytically oriented clinicians have stated that intensive psychodynamic psychotherapy is the treatment of choice for paraphilias (Rosen, 1979c; Wakeling, 1979; T. N. Wise, 1989; Gabbard, 1994). The primary focus of psychodynamic treatment is on patients' character pathology, rather than on their pathological behavior. Thus, as Rosen (1979c) noted, the more pronounced the accompanying personality disorder, the greater the need for psychodynamic therapy that emphasizes transference work. T. N. Wise (1989) observed that dynamic psychotherapy, in addition to being the most effective modality for addressing character pathology, may also be the most appropriate treatment to help individuals cope with life stresses and painful affect states that may contribute to urges to engage in addictive sexual behavior. Meanwhile, he cautioned, therapists who treat perversions with psychodynamic psychotherapy must understand the nuances of treating individuals with borderline personality organization and must watch for the regression and fragmenting that may occur. However the focus of treatment may change from moment to moment, the paraphilic individual's character pathology continues to deserve the clinician's respect. All of the investigators who recommended psychodynamic psychotherapy qualified their recommendations with statements to the effect that the general criteria of suitability for psychodynamic psychotherapy apply as well in the treatment of individuals who use sexual behavior addictively.

Rosen (1964) presented the results of a study in which six exhibitionists, all referred by the courts, were treated in weekly psychoanalytic psychotherapy for an average of twenty one sessions. Rosen reported that five of the six lost all urges to expose themselves, and that no indications of relapse were detected at the twenty four–month follow-up. The one individual who did relapse was reported to have improved later, after treatment with inpatient psychotherapy.

INTEGRATED TREATMENT

Clinicians from different perspectives agree that the overdctermined, multicausal nature of sexual addiction precludes the possibility that a simple, unitary psychopathology underlies the disorder (M. Cox, 1979; Wakeling, 1979). As Wakeling (1979) observed, "In the absence of a full understanding of etiology, there are no specific treatments for particular conditions, no penny-in-the-slot diagnostic and treatment formulations." Many investigators have concluded that no single treatment is effective for all paraphilic patients, and that the best approach for most patients seems to be to provide individually tailored combinations of behavioral, psychosocial, psychodynamic, and pharmacological modalities (Wakeling, 1979; Kilmann, Sabalis, Gearing, Bukstel, and Scovern, 1982; Reid, 1989; Adson, 1992; M. F. Schwartz, 1992; Gabbard, 1994). Reid (1989) and Wakeling (1979) emphasized psychodynamic psychotherapy, either individual or group, as the main arm of treatment, with pharmacotherapy, behavior therapy, cognitive–behavioral treatment, and marital–family therapy serving adjunctive or supplemental roles. Meanwhile, researchers

who were not primarily oriented toward psychodynamic psychotherapy have observed that the beneficial effect of antidepressant
medications in sexual addiction "may only be seen in combination with intensive psychotherapy" (Stein et al., 1992, p. 270),
and that the success of behavioral treatments depends to a great
extent on the relationship between the patient and the therapist
and on how the issues that emerge in the context of this relationship are managed (Meyer and Gelder, 1963).

A number of clinicians have presented programs for treating
sexual addiction that combined two or more therapeutic modalities. Interestingly, those multimodality programs that had a cognitive–behavioral core were usually described by their authors as
"cognitive–behavioral," while those multiple-modality programs
that had a psychodynamic core were described as "integrated."
At this time, no outcome studies that assess the efficacy of integrated programs for treating sexual addiction have been published.

Protter and Travin (1987) were the first to introduce an integrated paradigm for the treatment of paraphilic disorders, which
they termed a "bimodal approach." They later described this
treatment paradigm in more detail in a book, *Sexual Perversion:
Integrative Treatment Perspectives for the Clinician* (Travin and Protter, 1993). Travin and Protter described their bimodal approach
as a synthesis of cognitive–behavioral and focused psychodynamic
treatment modalities, with which could be integrated other modalities, such as medication, family therapy, and longer term psychodynamic psychotherapy. They understood cognitive–behavioral
treatment and psychodynamic treatment to be complementary
and mutually enhancing. Travin and Protter identified the domain of cognitive–behavioral techniques as overt behavior and
consciously accessible fantasy, and they noted that such techniques can enable the individual to have more control of his
perverse sexual behavior. They characterized psychodynamic
treatment, meanwhile, as being oriented toward developing insight into the unconscious meaning of the symptomatic behavior.
Travin and Protter cited Wachtel's (1977) findings, in his integration of psychoanalysis and behavior therapy, that alterations in

overt behavior can lead to changes in insight and self representation, while increased understanding of unconscious dynamics can lead to changes in overt behavior. They observed, "This reciprocal interaction of the two modalities, which addresses both the conscious and unconscious aspects of the sexual perversion, can have a synergistic therapeutic impact on the patient" (p. 158).

The cognitive–behavioral protocol that Travin and Protter recommended consists of (1) measures that enhance behavioral control, which include covert sensitization or masturbatory satiation, and (2) measures that address social–interpersonal deficits, which include stress management, assertiveness training, and social–communicative skills training. While relapse prevention was included among the self-control techniques that were identified in the authors' book (1993), it was not further discussed in the book, and it was not mentioned at all in the initial paper by Protter and Travin (1987) or in a more recent paper by Travin (1995). Travin and Protter described the psychodynamic component of their approach as more active, more directive, and more focused on symptoms than is psychoanalytic psychotherapy. The goal of this focal dynamic psychotherapy is to reach "a comprehensive understanding of the nature, purpose, function, and meaning of the patient's perverse sexuality" (p. 160). Travin and Protter focused on sexual fantasy both as a bridge that links the cognitive–behavioral and psychodynamic components, and as an organizing schema for treatment intervention. In the psychotherapy component of their approach, the therapist treats the patient's conscious fantasy productions and ritualized sexual behavior as symbolic transformations of the unconscious perverse fantasy that organizes the patient's sexual life.

Travin and Protter noted that the way in which the various components of their treatment approach are implemented depends on a variety of factors that concern the patient, the severity of the disorder, and the treatment context. With patients who have little behavioral control and are at risk for victimizing others, covert sensitization and masturbatory satiation are initiated immediately, in order to promote the development of self-control. Until symptomatic control stabilizes, psychodynamic intervention assumes a secondary role. Such patients are likely also to require fairly comprehensive social rehabilitation. Meanwhile, the treatment of patients whose disorder is less severe and whose behavior is less likely to be harmful to others consists primarily of psychodynamic psychotherapy that addresses characterological issues. Specific cognitive–behavioral interventions are then added, as they are needed.

More recently, Travin (1995) fine-tuned his bimodal approach in a few ways. He singled out Kohut's self psychology as a particularly useful framework for the psychodynamic psychotherapy of patients with "compulsive sexual behaviors"; and he observed that, among the medications that are available, serotonergic agents seemed to be the most effective. Travin also identified group therapy as the primary means of treatment in his approach, noting that patients were seen individually as well when such treatment was deemed to be appropriate.

Another integrated system for treating sexual addiction was developed by me (Goodman, 1992, 1993b, 1995b, 1996b, 1997). It will be presented in the next chapter.

8

Integrated Treatment

My integrated system for treating sexual addiction (1992, 1993b, 1995b, 1996b) developed in the context of the theory that sexual addiction represents an expression through sexual behavior of the addictive process: an enduring, inordinately strong tendency to engage in some form of pleasure-producing behavior as a means of regulating affects or self states that are painful and potentially overwhelming due to impaired self-regulation. Consequently, the treatment system was designed to address both the addictive sexual behavior and the underlying addictive process. It brings together psychodynamic psychotherapy, cognitive–behavioral treatment, therapeutic groups, and psychiatric pharmacotherapy in one theoretically coherent, clinically unified approach. Before I proceed, I would like to note that this system for treating sexual addiction has not yet been the subject of outcome studies. The presentation of my treatment system in this chapter is thus intended to be a theoretically informed, clinically oriented proposal, rather than an empirically proven prescription.

My presentation of this integrated treatment system begins with a consideration of assessment issues and then addresses in turn each of the major components of treatment.

ASSESSMENT

Diagnosis of Sexual Addiction

The first step toward effective treatment is accurate diagnosis. The diagnosis of sexual addiction proceeds according to the diagnostic criteria that were introduced in chapter 6. The definition of sexual addiction that was presented in chapter 6, which reflects the essence of the diagnostic criteria, can also be used in diagnostic assessment, and is often more practical in the clinical situation than are the diagnostic criteria.

Diagnosis of Concurrent Conditions

Accurate diagnosis of concurrent conditions is also of critical importance, since they often determine treatment priorities and the likely course of the illness. Our discussion of comorbidity in chapter 6 indicated high frequencies of comorbidity both within the category of paraphilias and between paraphilias and nonparaphilic sexual addictions. Thus, a patient's addictive use of one form of sexual behavior should alert the clinician to the possibility that the patient is using or could use other forms of sexual behavior in a similar manner. The discussion in chapter 6 further indicated high frequencies of comorbidity between sexual addiction and a number of other psychiatric disorders: psychoactive substance addiction, other addictive disorders, affective disorders, anxiety disorders, and personality disorders.

Psychoactive substance addiction is common in individuals who have been diagnosed with sexual addiction. Consequently, a history of substance use should be actively elicited. If the patient addictively uses alcohol or other drugs, treatment for sexual addiction is most likely to be effective when the substance addiction is addressed first. Significant comorbidity has been reported also between sexual addiction and other addictive disorders. In the initial evaluation prior to beginning treatment, specific inquiry about other behaviors that may have been engaged in addictively is good practice. Comorbid addictive disorders tend to flare up as the addictive sexual behavior comes under control. The earlier they are addressed, the less problematic they are likely to become. Moreover, asking about other behaviors alerts patients to their importance, and increases the likelihood that patients will notice and report if they begin to use any other behaviors addictively.

Individuals who have been diagnosed with sexual addiction frequently suffer from affective or anxiety disorders. Depressive, manic–depressive, or anxiety symptoms often require pharmacological treatment from the beginning, usually with antidepressants or mood stabilizers (or a combination of both). They also may emerge for the first time or become more severe as treatment progresses. Accurate initial assessment must thus be followed by sensitive monitoring of symptomatic status throughout the course of treatment. We can note, in passing, that a history of addictive use of sexual behavior that precedes by years the onset of an affective or anxiety disorder does not necessarily imply that the affective or anxiety disorder was caused by the addictive behavior or its consequences. The natural course of affective and anxiety disorders is characterized by an average age of clinical onset in the twenties and thirties, while the average age of onset for sexual addiction is in the teens or early twenties. Even if the conditions were entirely unrelated, we would expect that addictive sexual behavior might begin years before affective or anxiety symptoms become clinically significant. Moreover, affective and anxiety disorders do not suddenly emerge out of nowhere. They evolve over years in a developmental interaction between unfolding genetic propensities, vulnerabilities that were occasioned by deficiencies in the early caregiving environment, and emotionally significant life events. The processes that result in these disorders begin long before the disorders come to clinical attention, and the relationship between their development and the development of addictive behavior patterns is complex and variable. (I believe that the foregoing point about the relationship between affective or anxiety disorders and sexual addiction applies equally to the relationship between affective or anxiety disorders and other addictive disorders.)

The theoretical perspective that was presented in chapter 5 suggests that personality or character disorders are not truly comorbid conditions, but rather are the ground from which sexual addiction emerges and which, through its emergence, sexual addiction expresses. The personality of virtually every individual who uses sexual behavior addictively could be accurately characterized by the description, "an enduring pattern of inner experience and behavior that deviates markedly from the expectations of the individual's culture, is pervasive and inflexible, has an onset in adolescence or early adulthood, is stable over time, and leads to distress or impairment," which is the definition of personality disorder in DSM-IV (APA, 1994, p. 629). Schmidt et al. (1981) concluded a study of paraphilic patients by noting that "all the sexually deviant patients presented had some degree of personality disorder. . . . The degree of sexual deviancy was not a function of the severity of the personality disorder and the Paraphilias were not associated with any one particular type of personality disorder" (p. 285). The integrated system for treating sexual addiction that is presented in this chapter has three main components: management of behavioral symptoms; pharmacotherapy for affective, anxiety, and psychotic symptoms; and treatment of the addictive process itself. The third component, treatment of the addictive process, is treatment of a disorder of the personality system. The diagnostic issue, then, is not whether a personality disorder is present, but what are its predominant flavors (narcissistic, obsessive–compulsive, dependent, and so on) and how severe is it: that is, how severely impaired are the person's ego functions, object relations, and self-processes.

Psychotic symptoms occur somewhat more frequently among individuals who use sexual behavior addictively than they do in the general population. Sexual addiction is a fairly common complication of psychiatric conditions that are associated with psychosis, particularly manic–depressive disorder and its variants. In addition, some individuals who use sexual behavior addictively are characterologically unstable and may develop psychotic symptoms in response to overwhelming stress ("micropsychotic episodes"). Psychotic symptoms usually require medication, and they often indicate limits to what treatment can achieve. Psychotherapy may need to be more supportive than exploratory-expressive, with more emphasis on providing structure and managing symptoms.

Initial Treatment: Institution or Office?

A question that occasionally arises during the evaluation is whether treatment should be initiated in an institution (a hospital or a treatment center) or in the clinician's office. In general, individuals benefit more when they are able to work on mastering self-regulatory and life management problems in the actual settings in which they are having difficulty. Office treatment promotes patients' capacity for tolerating emotional distress and handling it adaptively, it facilitates the integration of their progress in treatment with their daily reality, and it avoids disrupting their lives. Therefore, exhausting all possibilities of office treatment before recommending admission to an institution is usually the preferable course. Indications for hospitalization or admission to an appropriate treatment facility include: (1) significant medical difficulty; (2) significant risk of harm to self; (3) significant risk of harm to others; (4) demonstrated inability to provide self-care; (5) unavailability of a living arrangement in which improvement can occur; and (6) need to interrupt a cycle of addictive behavior when office treatment has been unsuccessful. While attention to these considerations is particularly important at the time of the initial evaluation, monitoring the patient's status throughout the course of treatment is frequently necessary, especially the likelihood that he or she might act out in a way that would pose a risk of harm to others.

One consideration that concerns inpatient treatment may be self-evident, but it is nonetheless worth mentioning. While an inpatient setting, whether a hospital or a specialized treatment center, sometimes provides the necessary conditions without which treatment can not begin, it does not in itself provide sufficient treatment for sexual addiction. No treatment program, however well designed and well implemented, can resolve in a few weeks or even in a few months pathology of the personality or character system that developed over many years.

OVERVIEW OF THE TREATMENT SYSTEM

The understanding of addiction that was presented in chapter 5 entails that treatment for sexual addiction is most likely to be effective when it addresses not only the addictive sexual behavior but also the underlying addictive process. Addictive sexual behavior can be addressed through behavioral symptom management, which consists primarily of relapse prevention and other cognitive–behavioral techniques. On rare occasions, particularly at the beginning of treatment, an individual may be unable to modulate his sexual behavior unless the treatment regimen includes behavior modification or antiandrogen pharmacotherapy or both. The addictive process can be addressed through treatments that promote self-regulation and the development of meaningful interpersonal connections. Such treatment include psychodynamic psychotherapy and therapeutic groups. At times, direct intervention is needed to enhance affect regulation, to modulate psychotic symptoms, or to stabilize psychobiological functioning. Such intervention is effected by means of psychiatric pharmacotherapy. The integrated treatment for sexual addiction that I present here brings these various modalities together in one theoretically coherent, clinically unified system.

What follows is, of course, only the outline of a system for treating sexual addiction, not a comprehensive discussion of each treatment modality. Treatment of the addictive process through psychodynamic psychotherapy, for example, is continuous with psychodynamic treatment of character pathology; and I would not presume to cover in a few paragraphs a subject to which experienced clinicians have devoted entire books. Neither can a few paragraphs do justice to an area as broad and ever-changing as the pharmacological treatment for affective and anxiety disorders. My discussion focuses, with varying degrees of specificity, on how these treatment modalities can be employed in treating individuals who use sexual behavior addictively. A disproportionate amount of space is devoted to psychodynamic psychotherapy, since it is given little attention by most contemporary approaches to treating sexual addiction or related conditions.

We proceed now to consider the components of treatment for sexual addiction, how they can be integrated with each other, and how their implementation is integrated with the individual patient's course of recovery. (Incidentally, my use of the term *recovery* in this context is not intended to imply an unqualified endorsement of the 12-step approach to understanding or treating sexual addiction. I am using this term because, of the terms that are available, it seems to best convey the meaning that I intend.)

BEHAVIORAL SYMPTOM MANAGEMENT

The goals of behavioral symptom management are twofold: (1) to prevent the initial occurrence of symptomatic behavior (slips); and (2) if symptomatic behavior does occur, to prevent progression to relapse. As I noted earlier, behavioral symptom management consists primarily of relapse prevention and other cognitive–behavioral techniques.

What Is Symptomatic Behavior?

Before we discuss behavioral symptom management, let us consider the question of what constitutes symptomatic behavior. Even in alcoholism and drug addiction, the answer is neither easy nor absolute. For example, symptomatic behavior in psychoactive substance use addictions has sometimes been defined as any use of mood-altering chemicals. This definition is impractical, because the category of mood-altering chemicals is excessively broad. It includes caffeine, a psychostimulant the use of which is rarely described as symptomatic behavior. Moreover, it includes all psychiatric medications, many of which have no association with addictive use and may be therapeutically necessary. At the furthest extreme, any substance that is taken to relieve a condition that affects mood (such as hypothyroidism, allergy symptoms, or hunger) can be considered a mood-altering chemical. Ultimately, no categorical description is suitable across the board for defining symptomatic behavior in psychoactive substance use addictions. We can expect that defining symptomatic behavior categorically in sexual addiction would be no less difficult.

Rather than attempting to define specific behaviors as symptomatic, a more useful approach defines symptomatic behavior functionally, according to how it affects a person's life. Such an approach borrows from the definition of addiction that we considered in chapter 1, and its emphasis on the two key features of addictive behavior: (1) recurrent failure to control the behavior, and (2) continuation of the behavior despite significant harmful consequences. Symptomatic behavior in sexual addiction can then be defined as sexual behavior that, for the person under consideration, is likely to become out of control and to lead to harmful consequences. Unlike the categorical definitions of specific behaviors as symptomatic, this functional definition is not a black-or-white rule, but a guideline that is helpful in making decisions.

Relapse Prevention

Relapse prevention consists of three primary components: risk-recognition, urge-coping, and slip-handling (for a more comprehensive discussion of relapse prevention, see Marlatt and George, [1984]; Marlatt [1985]; Brownell, Marlatt, Lichtenstein, and Wilson [1986]; Johnson and Connors [1987]; Johnson, Connors, and Tobin [1987]; Marlatt et al. [1988]; Carey and McGrath [1989]; Daley [1989]; George [1989]; George and Marlatt [1989]; Pithers [1990]; Mackay and Marlatt [1990–1991]). Relapse prevention strategies help individuals who use sexual behavior addictively (1) to recognize factors and situations that are associated with an increased risk of acting out sexually; (2) to cope more effectively with sexual urges; (3) to recover rapidly from episodes of symptomatic behavior; and (4) to use such "slips" as opportunities to learn about how their recovery plans can be improved.

Symptomatic behavior is more likely to occur under some conditions than others. *Risk-recognition* teaches the individual who uses sexual behavior addictively to be aware of factors that increase the likelihood of symptomatic sexual behavior, and to recognize these factors before they overwhelm his or her ability to cope with them. A carefully obtained history can often illuminate sequences of steps that culminate in episodes of symptomatic behavior, key features or patterns that different sequences share, and triggers that precipitate the sequences. Recognition of risk factors is also facilitated when the patient practices self-monitoring; for example, by keeping a daily diary of situations, times of day, moods, people, activities, and thoughts that are associated with urges to engage in symptomatic behavior. The earlier in the process leading up to symptomatic behavior that the patient's healthy resources can be mobilized, the less likely is he or she to engage in symptomatic behavior. Consequently, a critical component of risk-recognition is identification of early warning signs; that is, indicators of risk that can be detected early in the process that leads up to symptomatic behavior. Among the most important early warning signs to recognize are "apparently irrelevant decisions" (Marlatt, 1985) by which sex addicts unconsciously set themselves up for relapse. Such recognition not only decreases the likelihood of relapse, but also fosters a sense of responsibility and personal effectiveness.

During the course of recovery from sexual addiction, urges to engage in symptomatic behavior are inevitable. *Urge-coping* skills help the individual who uses sexual behavior addictively to manage these urges without lapsing into symptomatic behavior. These skills comprise behavioral and cognitive strategies. Behavioral strategies involve actions that can be put into practice. They include: (1) avoidance of identified risk factors and (2) specific protective responses that the individual can enact when he or she is exposed to a risk factor; for example, physically leaving the location, or engaging in an activity that precludes the next step toward sexually acting out, or contacting a peer and talking about the situation. Behavioral strategies are most effective when planned in advance and rehearsed to the point where they become second nature, since the concentration that formulation of an unfamiliar behavioral plan requires may not be available in the midst of a strong addictive urge. Cognitive strategies for coping with urges to engage in symptomatic sexual behavior involve options for modifying one's thoughts. They include: (1) accepting urges to fantasize about and to engage in symptomatic sexual behavior as natural accompaniments of the recovery process; (2) recognizing that urges are not imperatives to act, but surface manifestations of affects—and that the affects are not in themselves lethal and will eventually subside; (3) reviewing the benefits of abstaining from symptomatic sexual behavior and the potential negative consequences of engaging in symptomatic sexual behavior; and (4) when fantasies of engaging in the behavior persist, prolonging the fantasies beyond the pleasurable experiences and imagining the harmful consequences that could ensue, especially those that entail shame, humiliation, or guilt. Particularly in the early phases of recovery, cognitive strategies are most likely to be effective in practice when they have been verbally rehearsed with others.

Some forms of sexual behavior, such as pedophilia and rape, are so harmful to others that zero tolerance of the behavior is the only reasonable treatment stance. If the treating clinician believes that an individual who uses sexual behavior addictively will not reliably be able to restrain himself from acting on urges to engage in such seriously harmful sexual behavior, then the clinician should recommend that the treatment plan include behavior modification or antiandrogen pharmacotherapy or both, until such time as the clinician believes that the patient will reliably be able to restrain himself. If a sexually addicted individual whom a clinician believes to be unable to reliably restrain himself from acting on urges to engage in seriously harmful sexual behavior does not accept the clinician's recommendation for behavior modification and/or antiandrogen pharmacotherapy, then the clinician should not consent to undertake the treatment of this individual. The risks are considerable, and if the patient is not sufficiently motivated to cooperate with a recommendation of this type, then the likelihood of significant progress in treatment is too small to justify such risks. The discussion of slip-handling that follows thus applies only to the treatment of sexually addicted individuals whose sexual behaviors, while far from benign, are not so seriously harmful to others.

Slip-handling skills are developed in order to prevent progression to relapse after an episode of symptomatic sexual behavior, or a slip, has occurred. Even when motivation is genuine and therapeutic management is competent, slips can happen. However much an individual who has used sexual behavior addictively may consciously wish to abstain from the addictive behavior, a strong motivation to resume the behavior, which derives from the self-regulating functions that the behavior had served, persists unconsciously, if not at a conscious level. Some combination of emotional stress, narcissistic injury, weakening of internal behavioral controls, and gaps in the external support structure can converge momentarily to shift the motivational balance in favor of resuming the behavior. If such a motivational shift happens to coincide with the availability of an opportunity to engage in the behavior, then a slip can occur. Like urge-coping skills, slip-handling skills consist of behavioral and cognitive strategies. Behavioral strategies are action responses that limit the progression of symptomatic behavior and reinstitute recovery. Examples include communicating with the therapist, getting together with a supportive friend, and attending a 12-step meeting. Similar to the behavioral strategies of urge-coping, those of slip-handling are most effective when they are planned in advance and rehearsed. Cognitive strategies for handling slips involve reframing the slip, or reconceptualizing what it means to have engaged in symptomatic behavior. A slip is most usefully understood, not as a sign of failure or as the beginning of relapse, but as a signal that a change in the program is indicated. It represents a risk situation for which the individual had not yet developed an appropriate coping strategy. A slip thus reframed becomes an opportunity to learn and to improve the therapeutic program. A problem-solving approach is ultimately more effective in containing slips and promoting recovery than is judgmental reproof or self-reproach. In the case of both behavioral and cognitive strategies for slip-handling, the sooner after a slip that an intervention occurs, the greater the probability of preventing relapse.

Relapse prevention conceptualizes urges to engage in addictive sexual behavior as signals of disruptive affect states that the addict needs to develop healthier, more adaptive means to manage. In thus shifting the focus from controlling the behavior to understanding the affects, relapse prevention provides a natural bridge from behavior management to psychodynamic psychotherapy.

Other Cognitive–Behavioral Techniques

Cognitive–behavioral techniques other than relapse prevention have a variable role in the treatment of sexual addiction, depending on the patient's needs and limitations. They comprise directive, didactic procedures that focus not on the symptomatic sexual behavior itself, but on other aspects of a person's life that predispose to reliance on symptomatic behavior as a means of coping with distressful affects and unmet needs. Applicable cognitive–behavioral techniques may be divided into two groups, skill training and life-style regeneration.

Skill training consists of a broad range of interventions that help patients to learn thoughts and behaviors that will result in more effective management of their affects and meeting of their needs. These include communication skills, assertiveness training, relaxation training, stress management, anger management, general social skills, and problem solving. Cognitive restructuring, which involves modifications of thinking patterns that serve to justify addictive sexual behavior, can also be helpful. Skill training often utilizes structured learning techniques such as bibliotherapy, instructional videos, modeling, role-playing, and homework assignments.

Life-style regeneration focuses on helping patients learn to achieve and maintain a healthy, balanced life-style. It is based on the principle that a healthy, balanced life-style decreases one's vulnerability to covert antecedents of relapse and promotes mental and physical well-being in general. Issues that are addressed include diet, exercise, rest, recreation, and the balance between work and play.

PSYCHODYNAMIC PSYCHOTHERAPY

General Principles

The psychodynamic psychotherapy component of treatment for sexual addiction is, in essence, the psychodynamic psychotherapy treatment of the character pathology from which the sexual addiction emerges. The symptomatic behaviors of sexual addiction and their associated conscious and unconscious fantasies constitute a productive initial focus for psychodynamic understanding. Moreover, they provide direct entry to the psychodynamic understanding of the patient's character pathology, which they reflect in microcosm. Rather than attempting to review the vast literature on psychodynamic treatment of character pathology, I have decided to present a brief and simple overview that may be helpful for readers who are not as familiar with psychodynamic psychotherapy as they are with other types of treatment, and who thus may have less of an idea how it can be useful in treating sexual addiction. As I mentioned earlier, a few paragraphs that summarize the literature are unlikely to do the subject justice. Nor would readers who are already knowledgeable about psychodynamic treatment of character pathology be likely to find in so brief a summary any material that would be new to them.

The primary goals of psychodynamic psychotherapy in the treatment of sexual addiction are to enhance individuals' self-regulation and to foster their capacity for meaningful interpersonal connections. Psychotherapy serves these goals by facilitating the development of healthy, adaptive means for managing affects, for getting needs met, for resolving inner conflicts, and for taking care of oneself. The core processes by which effective psychotherapy operates can be identified as intellectual understanding, integration, and internalization. In the psychotherapeutic situation, these three processes are interwoven and interdependent. Each enhances and, in turn, is enhanced by the others. In the following discussion, however, for purposes of clarity, they are considered separately.

Intellectual Understanding

Intellectual understanding in psychodynamic psychotherapy is, essentially, a form of cognitive therapy. As such, its domain overlaps with that of the cognitive components of behavioral symptom management. It focuses on fostering patients' appreciation that their subjective experiences and their behavior have identifiable relationships with meaningful mental or psychological processes. Such an appreciation provides a framework for working productively with the psychotherapeutic process. In the psychotherapeutic treatment of sexual addiction, the focus of understanding is on the addictive process and the process of recovery.

Addictive disorders involve the use of some form of pleasure-producing behavior as a means of relieving painful affects and/or regulating one's sense of self. As we considered earlier, addictive disorders originate in an impairment of the internal system that regulates one's affects and sense of self. When this system, which I call the self-regulation system, is impaired, affected individuals are abnormally vulnerable to being overwhelmed by intense emotional states and by loss of self-coherence. In their attempts to attenuate or to avoid the danger of being thus overwhelmed, some of these individuals develop fantasies, which are often outside their awareness, that the potential for regulating their affects and sense of self resides in something outside themselves, over which they believe that they have control. Individuals whose fantasies of this type lead them to engage in some kind of behavior in a pattern that is characterized by recurrent loss of control and by continuation of the behavior despite significant harmful consequences, can then be characterized as suffering from an addictive disorder. When a form of sexual behavior is employed in this manner, the addictive disorder (or one of the addictive disorders) from which the individual suffers is sexual addiction.

The therapeutic approach that I am describing begins with the recognition that an urge to engage in symptomatic sexual behavior is not simply the first step in an experience of being out of control or an evil force that must be either resisted or submitted to, but an indication that the individual's coping system is trying to ward off a disruptive affect state that is not being effectively managed. An urge to engage in symptomatic behavior is thus a signal of an affect state that the individual needs to manage in a healthier, more adaptive manner.

Individuals who suffer from addictive disorders typically are not aware of any connection between their behavioral urges and the underlying emotional states. Sometimes they are aware of a vague, restless discomfort, but more often they are aware only of urges to engage in their symptomatic behaviors. A key element in the psychotherapeutic treatment of individuals who suffer from addictive disorders entails engaging them in a basic paradigm shift, from (a) oscillating between resisting and submitting to the behavioral urge as a *force-in-itself,* to (b) becoming interested in the feelings and mental processes, of which the behavioral urge is an *indication.*

The question then becomes, what to do with these painful feelings, of which the individual is now becoming aware? A person's natural tendency when beset by painful feelings is to try to get rid of them. This tendency is reinforced by cultural messages: (1) that we should be in control of our feelings; and (2) that all significant problems, including emotional distress, are most appropriately addressed by technological methods that will "fix" them. The view that painful feelings are an enemy that must be vanquished or subdued, however, fails to take into account that these feelings might be serving an important function. The human organism is a very complex, elegant, highly developed, and sensitive system that has been shaped by millennia of evolution. That something as prevalent as painful feelings would occur by chance in a system as highly developed as the human organism is very unlikely. Much more likely is that the human capacity for such affects developed and persisted through evolution because it had significant adaptive value.

What would be the adaptive value of painful affects? Affects are signals (Basch, 1976; Campos, Campos, and Barrett, 1989). Their outwardly observable expressions, which are sometimes called "affect" in the narrow sense of the term, are interpersonal signals, an important means of communicating information about our emotional states. Their inner or subjective expressions are signals that we send to ourselves, signals of something that an automatic process within us interprets as psychologically important. Painful affects are not only painful; they are also meaningful, and their painful aspects are arrows that direct our attention toward their meanings. Getting rid of an important signal because our experience of it is uncomfortable is like shutting off the fire alarm because it makes an ugly sound. We do better in the long run to find the fire, address the fire directly, determine how the fire started, and then take steps to decrease the likelihood of another fire. If we consider the fire alarm to be a metaphor for painful affects, then the referent for the complex metaphor of finding the fire, addressing it, determining how it started, and taking steps to decrease the likelihood of another one would be psychodynamic psychotherapy. Psychotherapy enables us to discover the relationships between painful affects and the complexes of needs, wishes, fears, inner conflicts, core beliefs, and self-protective processes that have been triggered by current events.

The framework of our intellectual understanding can be summarized in a simple formula: addictive urges are indications of underlying painful affects; and painful affects, in turn, are signals of something that is psychologically important. Our therapeutic task, thus, is to discover the painful affects that underlie the addictive urges, and then to discern the psychologically significant meanings toward which the affects point. In effect, this approach begins where relapse prevention leaves off, in shifting the therapeutic focus from behavior to affects: What affects are emerging? What events triggered the affects? What core beliefs, inner conflicts, and personal history are involved? What alternative responses would be more healthy; that is, less self-damaging and ultimately more gratifying?

I have described this framework in some detail because it can both (1) guide the therapist's initial approach to a psychotherapeutic situation; and (2) constitute an important aspect of what the intellectual understanding component of psychotherapy initially conveys. This component typically includes an educational element, in which patients are provided with some elementary understanding of the conditions from which they suffer, and of how psychotherapy works. They are taught about the addictive process and about how addictive sexual behavior represents an attempt to modulate dysregulated inner states. Such instruction can be provided either in a brief "minicourse" at the beginning of treatment, or gradually in the course of therapeutic dialogue about the dynamics of patients' urges to engage in symptomatic behavior. The understanding that results not only enables patients to evolve more effective and productive relationships with their painful affects and their addictive urges; it also provides them with an infrastructure for the development of self-observatory capacity. First of all, having words to describe inner states and processes gives the conscious mind a handle, a more ready means by which to apprehend inner realities. Second, being able to name one's affects and sense of self provides perspective: the part of the mind that names, in so doing, steps back from the part of the mind that feels. The individual's emotional states and self-states thus no longer occupy the totality of his or her subjective psychic space, and he or she is much less likely to be overwhelmed by them. As this perspective becomes established, a capacity for self-observation develops naturally.

Meanwhile, the kind of understanding that can be provided by theories, such as those that were discussed in part II, is too generic to lead to significant therapeutic change. These theories represent a framework within which to organize (1) the information that the patient presents and (2) the therapist's subjective experience of being with the patient. They are not a set of formulas that can be consulted like a horoscope. The kind of understanding that is most likely to lead to enduring therapeutic change emerges from interpretations in the midst of the therapeutic action that remain close to the patient's affective experience in the here-and-now. If they stray too far in the direction of theory, they may, even if accurate, inadvertently conspire with the patient's tendencies to intellectualize, to isolate ideas from affects, and to believe that through intellectual knowledge he or she can control his or her affective life without actually having to feel it. As Protter and Travin (1987) wrote, "It is vital in the psychotherapy to stay close to the patient's actual experience as he lives and recounts them [sic]. For only by the patient reintegrating his own personal narrative can he emotionally gain the insight regarding the derivation and meaning of his symptomatology" (p. 291).

Integration

Integration in psychodynamic psychotherapy refers to integration of the patient's personality. The personalities of individuals who use sexual behavior addictively tend to be characterized by splits, or deficits in integration, on several levels. A central component of psychotherapeutic treatment is promoting personality integration by bringing together under the light of consciousness the split, denied, dissociated, and repressed aspects of the sex addict's mental functions.

Various psychic functions of individuals who use sexual behavior addictively are subject to splitting, which can represent both a defense—that is, a self-protective process—and a manifestation of impaired integrative capacity. The defense of splitting is generally understood as a division of people into "all good" and "all bad," along with oscillation between contradictory self-concepts and between contradictory concepts of significant others. Some individuals have great difficulty tolerating the awareness of themselves or others as both "good" and "bad," and splitting protects them from the intense distress that this awareness would cause them. Splitting can be potentiated when the normal capacity to integrate positive and negative aspects of a person into an experience of the person as a whole has not developed properly. When this integrative capacity is developmentally vulnerable, it is more susceptible to breaking down in the face of unbearable inner conflicts that could be alleviated by splitting. Sex addicts tend to experience a split identity (based on a split self representation) and split perceptions of others (based on split object representations), which often are organized in terms of all-good versus all-bad. They also typically are governed by a split superego that is characterized by conflicting values, commandments, and self-evaluations. On a broader level, important affects, needs, wishes, fears, inner conflicts, and core beliefs are shut out of sex addicts' awareness by a combination of self-protective processes that may include disavowal or denial, dissociation, repression, and auxiliary defenses (such as projection, externalization, and isolation of affect). Finally, sexual addiction is associated with a failure to integrate the basic merger–individuation conflict (which we considered in chapter 5) between (1) the wish to merge with the object plus the fear of being abandoned, and (2) the wish for individuation, mastery, and wholeness plus the fear of being engulfed, controlled, or damaged.

In sexual addiction, deficits in integration and impairment of self-regulation deepen and intensify each other. Analogously, recovery from sexual addiction involves a dialectical process in which improved integration potentiates the enhancement of self-regulation, which in turn promotes further integration.

The cornerstone of integration in psychotherapeutic treatment is the fostering of patients' awareness of their feelings, their needs, their wishes, their fears, their inner conflicts, their core beliefs, and their defenses (i.e., their automatic ways of protecting themselves from inner pain)—particularly when these processes arise in the context of interpersonal relationships. As aspects of psychic function that had been hidden from consciousness come into view, they can be integrated into the healthy, adaptive dimension of the personality system.

The closer to the here-and-now that the subject being addressed in a psychotherapy session is, the more emotionally "hot" or salient it is, and the more likely is work on that subject to lead to improved integration and enhanced self-regulation. Particularly important to track are patients' responses to what they experience as injuries to their sense of self or their sense of connection with a significant person. In psychotherapy, the most here-and-now relationship issues are those that concern the patient's relationship with the therapist. Hence, these issues are the most productive issues to address.

Early in life, we develop our basic inner models for how we perceive, experience, and respond to significant others, and also for how we perceive and experience ourselves in relationships with others. Typically, our models emerge from our interactions with our caregivers, especially our primary caregivers. The psychoanalytic term that approximately corresponds to what I have identified as our basic inner models is *object relations*. These "models" are more than mental representations: they are also functional predispositions, enduring tendencies to perceive, experience, and respond in characteristic ways, which are activated automatically in relationship contexts. These models include our affects, our needs, our wishes, our fears, our inner conflicts, our core beliefs, and our automatic self-protective processes, as they emerge in the context of significant relationships. When we then proceed through our lives and develop other significant relationships, we do not have to learn from scratch each time how to perceive, to experience, and to respond to others and to ourselves, because we have our basic inner models to guide us. This system is, thus, very adaptive; but it can have maladaptive consequences if significant aspects of our basic models do not fit the relationship world in which we currently live. We might say that much of our psychological pain derives directly or indirectly from aspects of our basic inner models that were adaptive in the relationship contexts in which they developed during our childhood, but that do not fit our current relationship world. While this statement is an oversimplification, it provides a useful framework for understanding and treating psychological pain.

In the course of psychotherapeutic treatment, a significant relationship develops between the patient and the therapist. The patient's inner models for perceiving, experiencing, and responding to significant others then become activated, and the affects, needs, wishes, fears, inner conflicts, core beliefs, and automatic self-protective processes that influence the patient's other significant relationships begin to affect how the patient perceives, experiences, and acts toward the therapist. In this sense, the therapeutic relationship resembles other significant relationships in the patient's life. The therapeutic relationship, however, differs from other relationships in a crucial respect. Rather than reacting behaviorally to the content of the patient's verbalizations and actions, the therapist provides a safe environment in which the patient and the therapist together can explore the meaning of the patient's responses in terms of defenses, affects, needs, wishes, fears, inner conflicts, and core beliefs. This collaborative exploration expands the patient's awareness of these processes, and of how they relate to his or her personal history and current difficulties. The resulting incremental expansion of awareness affords patients increasingly more opportunity to employ their resources of conscious reason to challenge and amend maladaptive core beliefs, to resolve inner conflicts, to get needs met, to manage affects, and to take care of themselves. Bringing together in consciousness the various split, denied, dissociated, and repressed aspects of the sex addict's psychic processes gradually heals the personality and enables it increasingly to function as an integrated whole. On a behavioral level, broader access to important information improves the likelihood that actions that are initiated on the basis of that information will have positive consequences. The net result is more conscious choice, more flexibility, and more freedom.

Internalization

The function of internalization in psychotherapy derives from its role in the development of self-regulation. As we considered in chapter 5, the essential process in the development of all aspects of the self-regulation system, including affect regulation, self-care, and self-governance functions, is the gradual internalization of caregiver functions and their assimilation into unfolding, constitutionally determined infrastructures. The capacity for such developmental internalization is greatest during early childhood; but it continues throughout life, particularly in situations that evoke mental states that are similar to those of early childhood. A primary means by which psychotherapy promotes the healing of impaired self-regulation is by providing new opportunities for the patient to internalize self-regulatory functions that were not adequately internalized during childhood. Characterization of this function of psychotherapy as "restorative" is not entirely accurate, since psychotherapy does not restore missing internal structures of the self so much as provide a matrix for them to develop de novo. Affect regulation functions can develop through internalization of (1) the therapist's provision of a holding environment (i.e., his or her ability to tolerate the patient's affects without suppressing them, withdrawing, acting out, or being overwhelmed); (2) the therapist's soothing and enlivening functions; and (3) the therapist's treatment of affects as indications of internal states that deserve attention. Self-care functions can develop through internalization of the therapist's nurturing and protective functions, accompanied by internalization of the message that the patient is valued as a person and worth taking care of. Healthy superego and other self-governance functions can develop through internalization of the therapist's integrity, respectfulness, nonjudgmental acceptance, and general stabilizing function.

Psychotherapy is not the only context in which self-regulatory functions can be internalized. Internalization can occur in any significant relationship, and also in groups. What distinguishes psychotherapy is (1) the depth of the relationship; (2) the therapeutic frame of a dyadic relationship with a figure who combines caregiving attributes and authority attitudes; (3) the therapist's ability to facilitate the patient's personality integration, and thus to minimize the extent to which the patient's projections distort the internalization process; and (4) (as we have the right to expect) the therapist's level of psychological and emotional health.

Therapeutic internalization is facilitated by sex addicts' tendency to form selfobject transferences: to externalize their self-regulation, to experience their self-regulatory functions as being located in the external world. This tendency is continuous with the addictive process itself. Paradoxically, the very process that determines addictive dependence on sexual behavior is thus an important factor in this critical component of the psychotherapeutic process.

The Relationship between Interpretation and Internalization

A number of psychoanalytic investigators have recommended that the treatment of perversions should begin by fostering the internalization of psychic structures and should only later proceed to interpreting intrapsychic conflicts. Stolorow (1979) advised that the analyst should not interpret what the patient has needed to ward off, but rather should permit the unfolding of the primitive selfobject transferences that the patient has needed to recreate. In such cases, he continued, the aim of the analyst's interpretations should be "to promote sufficient consolidation of self and object representations to make possible a subsequent analysis of the defensive functions of the patient's sexual pathology in terms of intrapsychic conflicts that it serves to ward off" (p. 44). Socarides (1988) suggested that treatment should at first focus on promoting structuralization of ego functions, self representation, and object representations by understanding and repairing within the transference what was missed or prematurely lost. He continued that exploration of instinctual (oedipal) and structural conflicts should be deferred until after the ego has been assisted in its belated development: "It is necessary to deal first with what the arrested ego needs to achieve, and only later what the ego needs to ward off" (p. 14). I believe that these investigators were not advocating that interpretation and integration should wait until after therapeutic internalization of psychic structures has been completed, but rather that the developmental level of an interpretation, and of the integration that it is intended to promote, should be congruent with the patient's current level of structural development. Interpretation of splitting and associated defenses, and interpretation of intrapsychic conflicts that derive from the basic merger–individuation conflict, may often, in fact, be necessary prerequisites for the integration on which further structuralization depends. When such interpretations are presented to a patient at a time and in a way that he or she can assimilate them, the patient not only acquires the understanding that the interpretations convey, but also internalizes (fractionally) the holding or containing capacities and the integrative functions that the process of interpretation represents. Integration and internalization are interdependent, mutually constitutive processes, both in normal development and in the development that occurs through psychoanalysis or psychodynamic psychotherapy.

Psychotherapeutic Treatment for a Biological Disorder?

A question is sometimes raised: If the addictive process is a biological disorder, as our neurobiological formulation in chapter 5 indicated, then is not a biological treatment, such as medication, a more appropriate therapeutic modality for treating addictive disorders than is psychotherapy, which is a psychological treatment? Such a question reflects a number of assumptions that merit scrutiny.

First of all, the question implies that the addictive process, if it is a biological process, is not a psychological process. It presumes an either–or relationship between biological and psychological: if a disorder is one, then it is not the other. Meanwhile, my introductory comments identified the addictive process to be not biological *or* psychological, but biological *and* psychological. The human organism is a unitary reality. "Biological" and "psychological" represent not two different kinds of reality but two languages, each of which is associated with a different way of knowing, that we use to describe this unitary human reality (Rado, 1946, 1949; Feigl, 1967, 1981; Globus, 1973; Booth, 1978; Maxwell, 1978; Reiser, 1984; Macdonald, 1989; Goodman, 1991, 1994a, in press a, in press b). That the addictive process can be described and understood in biological terms does not preclude that it is also a psychological process. The assumption of an ontological dichotomy between biological and psychological is erroneous.

Second, the question implies that psychotherapy is not a biological treatment. Mohl (1987) reviewed a broad range of literature, which included empirical research in neuroscience and in developmental neurobiology, and concluded: "Thus . . . psychotherapy *is* a biological treatment that acts through biological mechanisms (interneuronal synaptic facilitation, provision of external physiological regulation, exploration of hippocampal memory processing) on biological problems (deficits in gene-environment interactions, erroneous synaptic facilitation, inappropriate locus ceruleus gate activity)" (p. 325). Indirect support for Mohl's argument has been provided by recent findings that responders to behavior therapy treatment for obsessive–compulsive disorder demonstrated similar changes in rates of local cerebral glucose metabolism (measured with positron emission tomography) as did responders to pharmacological treatment (Baxter, Schwartz, Bergman, Szuba, Guze, Mazziotta, Alazraki, Selin, Ferng, and Munford, 1993; J. M. Schwartz, Stoessel, Baxter, Martin, and Phelps, 1996).

Additional assistance in recognizing that the processes and effects of psychotherapy are both psychological and biological is provided by the unity perspective that was mentioned in the preceding paragraph. A set of events occurs in a person during and after psychotherapy. These events can be described in psychological terms or in biological terms, they can be known subjectively or empirically: but they remain a single set of events. We can be more specific. Critical regulatory and integrative functions of the central nervous system develop through experience-dependent growth processes (Greenough et al., 1987; Greenough and Black, 1992). During genetically programmed critical periods in the first years of life, the developing brain is particularly sensitive to inputs from the caregiving environment. These inputs from the caregiving environment shape the incipient neurobiological substrates of affect regulation, behavioral inhibition, and motivational-reward functions. While experience-dependent growth processes occur at their highest rates during early life, they continue long after developmental critical periods have ended, and they may become particularly active when conditions are favorable (Schore, 1994). Recent neurobiological investigations indicate that adults retain the potential for plasticity in some neuronal systems. Central catecholaminergic neurons, including dopaminergic mesolimbic neurons, exhibit considerable capacities for regeneration (Reis, Ross, Gilad, and Joh, 1978). Prefrontal areas are known to continue maturing well into adulthood, perhaps throughout the lifespan. Schore (1994) observed that affect-regulatory interactions in psychotherapy can induce structural change in the form of new patterns of corticolimbic connections, especially in the right hemisphere, which he noted, contains neural circuits that are associated with self and object representations. The neurobiological concept of a continued potential for plasticity and regeneration in limbic and cortical neurons seems to correspond to the psychological concept of a continuing capacity for developmental internalization.

Third, the question with which this section began implies that medication is the best, if not the only, biological treatment for the addictive process. Our discussion of neurobiological theory in chapter 5, though condensed and simplified, was sufficiently detailed to enable us to conclude that the neurobiology of addiction is not a matter of a simple defect in one neuromodulator system. It seems rather to be a dynamic process that emerges from a system of complex intractions among various components of neuromodulator networks in diverse anatomical locations. We have little reason to expect that such a dynamic, complex, and multifarious process could be redressed by the widespread application of a single molecule. Put another way, the addictive process is more likely to be a system problem than a unit problem, and remedies at the unit level are unlikely, by themselves, to resolve a problem that operates at the system level. Means of addressing the addictive process are more likely to be effective when they operate at the same level of organization as does the addictive process. While medication is helpful in addressing specific components of the addictive syndrome and may in many cases be necessary, psychotherapy could conceivably be the form of biological treatment that is most specifically and comprehensively capable of addressing a neurobiological system dysfunction that is as dynamic and complex as is the addictive process.

The Relationship between Behavioral Symptom Management and Psychotherapy

Before proceeding to therapeutic groups, let us briefly consider the relationship between behavioral symptom management and psychodynamic psychotherapy in the treatment of sexual addiction.

Effective psychotherapy in patients who use sexual behavior addictively often depends on effective management of behavioral symptoms. Psychotherapy requires awareness of the inner life, particularly awareness of affects. Meanwhile, addictive sexual behavior (i.e., sexual behavior that is being used addictively) functions specifically to distort or ward off such awareness. It is thus directly antagonistic to the psychotherapeutic process. Moreover, cessation of addictive sexual behavior allows the self-regulatory functions that it had fulfilled to be transferred to the psychotherapist, an essential step in the process by which these functions are gradually internalized. Consequently, the more consistent the patient's abstinence from addictive sexual behavior, the more effective psychotherapy is likely to be.

By the same token, effective management of behavioral symptoms often depends on effective psychotherapy. Addictive sexual behavior that has served important self-regulatory functions is generally not relinquished without a great deal of resistance, which can diminish or disrupt the effectiveness of behavioral symptom management. Resistances to symptom management interventions can be explored psychotherapeutically, just as can other resistances that interfere with the therapeutic process, and understanding the nature of a resistance may attenuate its effect and allow the symptom management to proceed. In addition, the symptom management itself requires a therapeutic alliance that is strong enough to overcome resistance, and a strong therapeutic alliance depends on appropriate psychotherapeutic management of transference responses.

Psychotherapy and behavioral symptom management can thus be recognized to be interdependent, mutually constitutive components of integrated treatment for sexual addiction.

Indications

Psychodynamic psychotherapy is not universally effective in treating individuals who suffer from sexual addiction. Sexual addiction is often comorbid with other conditions, some of which may respond to psychotherapy less robustly than do others. Significantly, the distinctions between what does and what does not respond well to psychodynamic psychotherapy, like the distinctions between what does and what does not respond well to psychiatric medications, do not correspond to the diagnostic distinctions in DSM-IV. Psychiatric medications treat symptoms or constellations of symptoms—such as anhedonia, panic anxiety, insomnia, impaired ability to concentrate, or psychosis—regardless of the DSM category in which the patient's general disorder is classified. Similarly, psychodynamic psychotherapy treats character pathology—such as may be expressed in extreme sensitivity to criticism, inordinate need to be in control, or impaired capacity to empathize with others—regardless of the DSM category in which the patient's general disorder is classified.

What is character pathology? Its definition can be approached in a variety of ways. We begin by considering separately the two words that constitute the concept, *character* and *pathology*. Character can be defined as enduring patterns of psychological and emotional processes (of which we may or may not be aware) that shape our inner experience and our behavior, primarily by structuring how we perceive, think about, and relate to the interpersonal environment and to ourselves. Pathology is more tricky to define, since its definition involves values. I am inclined to borrow from the DSM-III-R definition of personality disorder, according to which personality traits constitute a personality disorder when they are "inflexible and maladaptive and cause either significant functional impairment or subjective distress" (American Psychiatric Association, 1987, p. 335).[1] Accordingly, I would define character pathology as enduring patterns of psychological and emotional processes that shape inner experience or behavior that is relatively inflexible and that is maladaptive; i.e., that causes either significant functional impairment or subjective distress. Personality disorder is, of course, not a synonym for character pathology. A personality disorder is the functional manifestation of character pathology, much as the operation of a word processing application is the functional manifestation of the algorithms in its program. Character pathology constitutes the inner emotional and psychological conditions that manifest as maladaptive personality traits. It can range from severe, as we see in borderline and antisocial personality disorders, to mild, as we see

---

[1]I do not agree with the addition in DSM-IV of the criterion, "deviates markedly from the expectations of the individual's culture" (American Psychiatric Association, 1994, p. 629). If a personality trait is inflexible and maladaptive and cause either significant functional impairment or subjective distress, then it represents character pathology, regardless of whether it deviates markedly from the expectations of the individual's culture. Meanwhile, if a personality trait deviates markedly from the expectations of the individual's culture, but it is not inflexible or maladaptive and it does not cause either significant functional impairment or subjective distress, then I would be reluctant to label it as pathological. I believe that the criterion of deviation from cultural expectations is superfluous, at best, and that it moreover could be dangerous.

in neurotic and normal individuals. Character pathology can be associated with any type of psychiatric disorder. As we considered in our discussion of assessment of concurrent conditions, sexual addiction is almost invariably associated with significant character pathology.

Not only do some conditions respond better to psychodynamic psychotherapy than do others; some individuals respond to it better than do others. Those who experience some distress about their symptoms, who are motivated to make changes in themselves, who are psychologically minded, and who are curious about the origins of their difficulties are likely to do better than those who lack such qualities. Individuals who are psychotic, who are cognitively disabled, who are true antisocial personalities, or who are otherwise severely impaired in their capacity to form a human relationship, are generally not suitable candidates for psychodynamic psychotherapy. These statements, however, are only generalizations; they are not rules. Some individuals who are motivated, bright, and psychologically minded benefit little from psychotherapy, because they are virtually unable to form a human relationship. And some psychotic individuals who are able to make a connection with their therapists can benefit considerably.

Meanwhile, therapists as well as patients differ in their capacity to form relationships and to work effectively with different individuals. Some therapists, for example, are unusually gifted in their abilities to make meaningful connections with sociopathic individuals. A sociopathic person who consults a therapist who possesses such gifts is more likely to benefit from psychotherapy than is one who consults a therapist who lacks them. How much an individual benefits from psychotherapy depends not only on the personal characteristics of the patient but also on the personal characteristics of the therapist, and on the nature of the relationship that these two individuals can develop. Consequently, a therapist's assessment of an individual's suitability for psychodynamic psychotherapy includes an assessment of the individual's suitability for a relationship with that particular therapist: an assessment of their goodness of fit. In this context, an important consideration is that psychodynamic psychotherapy is not simply a therapeutic method that employs relationship as its means; it is a relationship that serves therapeutic ends.

THERAPEUTIC GROUPS

Individuals who use sexual behavior addictively have particular difficulty with interpersonal relationships, due to fears about dependency and closeness, feelings of personal inadequacy, inner conflicts concerning anger, problems with the basic merger–individuation conflict and its derivatives, and other factors. A crucial component in the process of recovery from sexual addiction is the development of abilities to make meaningful connections with others and to turn to people in times of need instead of turning to addictive behavior. Therapeutic groups fulfill a valuable function in facilitating this development.

Yalom (1975) identified as particularly helpful a number of processes that often occur in group therapy: experiencing a chance to help others, which facilitates the development of altruism; group cohesiveness and a sense of belonging; universality (the "I'm not the only one" experience); interpersonal learning, in terms of improving skills and receiving feedback; guidance; catharsis; learning by identification; family reenactment; self-understanding; instillation of hope; and existential factors, particularly the experience of limitations and of personal responsibility. Some of these processes are more likely to occur in therapeutic groups than in individual psychotherapy.

A number of different types of therapeutic group can be helpful for individuals who use sexual behavior addictively. These include psychoeducational groups, cognitive–behavioral groups, psychodynamic therapy groups, process groups, couples groups, and self-help groups. Both relapse prevention and psychodynamic psychotherapy can be conducted in either individual or group therapy settings. Relapse prevention is likely to be not only more resource-efficient in a group setting, but also, in many cases, more effective. Group members can learn from one another's struggles; and they can, through identification, acquire tools to deal with problems that they have not yet had to face. Psychodynamic psychotherapy in a group setting offers some advantages that are missing in individual therapy, but the breadth and depth of character change tends to be proportional to the intensity of transference involvement, which is likely to be greater in individual than in group therapy. Thus, treatment for sexual addiction may be most effective when relapse prevention is conducted in a group therapy setting, while psychodynamic psychotherapy is conducted in a one-to-one setting. Meanwhile, we can note that psychodynamic issues are likely to arise and to need to be addressed in the course of relapse prevention group therapy; and that elements of relapse prevention will probably need to be integrated into the individual psychodynamic psychotherapy, particularly early in treatment and during times of stress or regression.

The most common and easy-to-access therapeutic groups are the 12-step groups, a family of self-help networks or "fellowships" that includes Sex Addicts Anonymous (SAA), Sex and Love Addicts Anonymous (SLAA), Sexaholics Anonymous (SA), and Sexual Compulsives Anonymous (SCA). Twelve-step groups can potentially provide all of the factors that Yalom (1975) identified as helpful in group therapy (see p. 300). In addition, they offer free membership for as long as the individual wishes, round-the-clock support, and connection with a worldwide support network. They present a coherent framework for approaching addictive problems and life in general, including acceptance of limitations, honesty with self, and transcendence of the customary dichotomy of in-control versus out-of-control (Bateson, 1972). In addition, 12-step groups offer (but do not impose) a nonjudgmental, nondogmatic, spiritual foundation. Meanwhile, as I mentioned in my earlier discussion of the 12-step fellowships for sex addicts, individual 12-step groups vary considerably one from another, even different groups within the same fellowship. Since the fellowships lack formal leadership structures and internal controls, the characteristics of a group are determined primarily by the individuals who attend it. For example, a few judgmental and dogmatic group members can make a particular group feel judgmental and dogmatic, however accepting and open-minded the fellowship as a whole may be. Moreover, sexual addiction develops in the context of a broad range of character pathology, and some groups contain seriously disturbed members who have not had the treatment that they need. Recovering sex addicts are well advised to decide whether or not to attend a particular group on the basis of the goodness of fit between themselves and the individuals who attend that group, rather than on the basis of their perceived fit with the fellowship as a whole.

PSYCHIATRIC PHARMACOTHERAPY

General Approach

Socarides (1988) observed that the cessation of perverse activity may precipitate an eruption of intolerable anxiety, which in turn can lead the patient to withdraw from treatment. He continued that the need to engage in perverse activity should be treated as a manifestation of an arrested developmental phase: "In a sense, as a developmental necessity, at least for the time being, and not as a resistance" (p. 16). I agree that the need to engage in perverse activity should be treated as a manifestation of an arrested developmental phase and not as a resistance—at least, not only as a resistance, since it often can be both. I do not believe, however, that Socarides intended to imply that the threat of intolerable anxiety compels us and our patients to sanction perverse activity as the price for continuing the treatment. We are fortunate to live in a time when a variety of safe and effective pharmacological agents are available to assist patients in the regulation of their painful affects. Addictive behavior is not the only available alternative to affects that a patient is unable to tolerate. Occasionally, we and our patients will decide that the affects that emerge after cessation of addictive sexual behavior, though painful and destabilizing, are tolerable. At times, we and our patients may decide that sporadic episodes of addictive sexual behavior are less disruptive of ultimate therapeutic goals than would be reliance on psychiatric medication. More often, though, we and our patients will opt for the use of psychiatric medication to regulate the painful affects that emerge with cessation of addictive sexual behavior.

Psychiatric pharmacotherapy, or treatment with psychiatric medication, is direct intervention to enhance affect regulation, to stabilize psychobiological functioning, or to modulate psychotic symptoms, as well as to treat other symptoms of comorbid psychiatric disorders. We can note that psychiatric medication does not treat sexual addiction per se, but addresses conditions that either contribute to the addictive process or interfere with the process of recovery.

Research has determined that antidepressant medications, particularly the serotonin reuptake inhibitors, can reduce the frequency of addictive sexual behavior and the intensity of urges to engage in addictive sexual behavior, even when the patient is not suffering from major depression (Bartova et al., 1978; Snaith and Collins, 1981; Cesnik and Coleman, 1989; Bianchi, 1990; Jorgensen, 1990; Emmanuel et al., 1991; Kafka, 1991; Lorefice, 1991; Perilstein, Lipper, and Friedman, 1991; Kafka and Prentky, 1992; Kruesi et al., 1992; Stein et al., 1992; Wawrose and Sisto, 1992; Casals-Ariet and Cullen, 1993; Clayton, 1993; Torres and de Abreu Cerquiera, 1993; Kafka, 1994; Zohar, Kaplan, and Benjamin, 1994; Rubenstein and Engel, 1996). Such findings make sense when the biopsychological process that underlies addictive disorders is understood to originate in impaired affect regulation, impaired behavioral inhibition, and aberrant motivational-reward function. Addictive craving and addictive urges arc then recognized to be both (1) expressions of dysregulated affect, and (2) conditioned stimuli for coping responses (responses to cope with dysregulated affect) that have been learned in the context of impaired behavioral inhibition and aberrant motivational-reward function. Accordingly, to the extent that affect regulation is enhanced, the frequency and intensity of addictive urges are likely to diminish. Meanwhile, greater stability of psychobiological functioning is associated with better behavioral control and improved assessment of reality. Interventions that enhance affect regulation and behavioral inhibition can thus be expected to reduce the symptomatic expression of sexual addiction.

In nontechnical terms, the impairment of affect regulation that underlies addiction can be seen as an imbalance between individuals' affects, particularly their painful affects, and the capacity of their built-in coping systems. Painful affects, such as anxiety and depressed mood, are not bad in themselves: they are signals that we send to ourselves to call our attention to something that is important for our survival. Painful affects become a problem when their intensity overwhelms or threatens to overwhelm the individual's coping system. The affects can then no longer be used as signals, but are experienced as extreme dangers that must be escaped or avoided. An individual who has learned that certain self-initiated behaviors can quell such dangerous affects and prevent the system from being overwhelmed will experience strong urges to engage in these behaviors whenever such affects threaten. Often, the individual will not consciously experience the painful affects, or even the threats of these affects, and will feel only a vague unease; or the individual may be completely shut down to affects, and may experience only bodily states that he or she interprets as urges to engage in symptomatic behavior.

Psychiatric medication works by restoring or reinforcing the brain chemistry that is associated with individuals' built-in coping systems. While psychodynamic psychotherapy also can enhance the capacity of individuals' coping systems, individuals' accessibility to psychotherapy and to what it can offer may be limited when they are emotionally overwhelmed. When psychiatric medication is effective in establishing a more stable balance between individuals' affects and the capacity of their coping systems, the coping systems are less likely to be overwhelmed, and individuals can better tolerate experiencing their painful affects as affects. Not only will urges to engage in self-medicating behaviors consequently become less frequent and intense. These individuals will also, as a result, have more conscious access to their inner states. Enhanced conscious access provides them with more opportunity to work with their inner states in psychotherapy. Subsequent psychotherapeutic work can then help individuals to develop healthier, more adaptive ways of regulating and responding to their inner states, which may eventually enable them to manage without the psychiatric medication. Psychiatric medication and psychotherapy can thus be seen to be, not antagonistic or mutually exclusive, but interdependent and mutually enhancing.

Indications

The basic parameters that guide decisions of when to initiate or to alter medication treatment are not markedly different in the context of sexual addiction from what they are in the context of psychiatric disorders in general. In general psychiatry, such decisions are guided by the presence, intensity, and duration of particular patterns of symptoms, the degree to which a patient's functioning is impaired by these symptoms, and the overall goals of treatment. Primary indications for psychiatric pharmacotherapy include (1) significant impairment of functioning that results from depression, anxiety, psychosis, or psychobiological instability, and (2) emotional discomfort that is intolerable for the patient. We can recognize that these criteria are to some degree subjective and context-relative. Impairment of functioning is difficult to assess without knowledge of the patient's premorbid functional baseline, and what constitutes significant impairment may vary from person to person and from situation to situation. Even more subjective and context-relative is the degree of emotional discomfort that the patient is able and willing to tolerate. A variety of factors, in addition to the severity of the symptoms, enter into the determination of how tolerable is a state of emotional disorder. These factors include the patient's strengths and coping resources, the availability and degree of connection with other individuals who can provide emotional support (including the clinician), and the patient's cognitive set or expectations. The decision whether to prescribe medication is influenced also by the nature of the psychotherapy in which the patient is involved (if any). With respect to the latter, an individual in twice-a-week psychodynamic psychotherapy is likely to tolerate and even to benefit from working through states of emotional distress that might merit pharmacotherapy in a person who is unable or unwilling to be involved in psychotherapy. When all is said and done, the patient is the ultimate expert on how much emotional discomfort he or she is able and willing to tolerate. Assessment of the tolerability of a patient's state of emotional discomfort is thus most effectively conducted as a dialogue.

Some cases of depression, anxiety disorder, manic–depressive spectrum disorder, and (more rarely) psychotic symptoms can be managed effectively without medication. More often, though, recovery from sexual addiction is facilitated when treatment for these other psychiatric conditions includes appropriate medication.

A general principle that often is helpful to keep in mind is that some symptoms of psychiatric disorders may be more responsive to pharmacotherapy, while other symptoms may be more responsive to psychotherapy. Let us consider depression, for example. The following symptoms, in my experience, tend to respond preferentially to medication: (1) fatigue, low energy, and psychomotor retardation; (2) sleep and appetite disturbances; (3) irritability and restlessness; (4) anhedonia (loss of pleasure or ability to enjoy); (5) cognitive impairments, such as problems with memory or concentration and difficulty thinking; and (6) psychotic symptoms. Meanwhile, other symptoms of depression may be more likely to respond to psychotherapy: (1) loneliness; (2) inappropriate feelings of guilt or shame; (3) problems with motivation; (4) interpersonal difficulties; (5) social withdrawal; and (6) negativistic and self-defeating patterns of thinking.

Also worth considering are the patient's thoughts and feelings about using psychiatric medication, and they are often particularly salient in patients with addictive disorders. For example, some patients may be concerned about "becoming addicted" to the psychiatric medication. Discussion of the definition of addiction, with clarification that use of the medication as prescribed does not entail loss of control or significant harmful consequences, often allays the rational aspect of this concern. Other patients who object to medication as a "crutch" can be invited to further explore the metaphor of a device that enables the individual to remain active and effective, while the impaired function is relieved of excessive pressure and thereby permitted to heal. Occasionally, further dialogue may then be needed to clarify and to work through a patient's deeper anxieties about the issues of dependence and control that can be evoked by the prescription of psychiatric medication (Goodman, 1993c, 1995c,d).

Parameters that are more specific to the treatment of sexual addiction include: (1) with patients who have been using psychoactive substances that acutely or subacutely affect mental status, the question of whether to defer initiation of pharmacotherapy until a sufficient period of abstinence from psychoactive substances allows assessment of the individual's affective and cognitive baseline; (2) a relatively greater reluctance to use medications that are more frequently abused, such as antianxiety drugs and psychostimulants; and (3) the use of antidepressant medications for the specific purpose of reducing the frequency and intensity of addictive urges, even when the patient is not suffering from a major affective or anxiety disorder.

Finally, decisions about whether and how to use medications are influenced by personal and philosophical as well as practical considerations. The likelihood of a positive outcome is enhanced when the prescriber and the patient communicate well, respect each other, and have congruent understandings of the medication's function and purpose.

The Importance of Integrating Psychotherapy and Psychiatric Pharmacotherapy

We complete this discussion of psychiatric pharmacotherapy by noting that, for cases of sexual addiction in which psychiatric medication as well as psychotherapy is indicated, treatment tends to be most effective when one clinician is responsible both for conducting psychotherapy and for prescribing medication.

First of all, the prescriber of psychiatric medication should be psychotherapeutically adept. Patients often have responses to medications and to the prescriber that are determined by psychodynamic factors, by the meanings that taking medication has for them, and by the affects that these meanings stir up (Goodman, 1993c, 1995c). Such responses can interfere with a patient's compliance or response to medication, unless they are dealt with psychotherapeutically.

Second, the psychotherapist should be pharmacotherapeutically adept. Indications for initiating or changing pharmacological treatment often emerge during the course of psychotherapeutic treatment. Accurate reading of these indications generally requires sensitive pharmacotherapeutic acumen, as well as an ongoing therapeutic alliance and a finely tuned, empathic sense of subtle changes in the patient.

Third, patients who use sexual behavior addictively tend to employ splitting and externalization in attempts to cope with inner conflicts that they are (often unconsciously) afraid to face. A split in the therapeutic functions potentiates this tendency and renders it more difficult to explore in psychotherapy, even when good communication prevails between the prescriber and the psychotherapist.

Finally, sexual addiction itself cannot readily be compartmentalized into "behavior and personality part" and "emotion part." Behavior, personality, and emotion are interdependent, mutually constitutive aspects of a person, in illness and in health. In an analogous manner, psychotherapy and psychiatric pharmacotherapy are generally interdependent, mutually determining aspects of treatment for sexual addiction. A clinical split between them is thus artificial, and undermines the integrative intent of the treatment.

When psychotherapy and psychiatric medication are provided by different clinicians, mutual consultation, collaboration, and good communication between the two clinicians is mandatory. When more than one mental health clinician is treating a patient who uses sexual behavior addictively, the relationship between the clinicians is no less important than is their ability to exchange information. Both psychotherapy and pharmacotherapy are likely to be most effective when the relationship between the treating clinicians is characterized by honesty, open-mindedness, trust, and respect (Goodman, 1995d).

TAILORING AND TIMING

The specific functional impairments, needs, and inner resources that individuals who use sexual behavior addictively bring to the treatment situation are far from uniform. They vary not only from individual to individual, but also within the same individual, from one point during treatment to another. Treatment for sexual addiction is thus most likely to be effective when the treatment plan for each patient is individually tailored and is designed to evolve, in terms of both therapeutic focus and primary modalities employed, as the patient progresses through recovery. Recovery from sexual addiction is a developmental process that can be understood to proceed in four stages (more or less): Stage I,

Initial Behavior Modulation; Stage II, Stabilization (of behavior and affect); Stage III, Character Healing; and Stage IV, Self-Renewal.

During stage I, most individuals who use sexual behavior addictively can begin to modulate their addictive behavior by means of a combination of inner motivation, psychological support, and affect-regulating medication. Many sex addicts do not require affect-regulating medication; but some who are able to modulate their behavior without medication may still benefit from the medication's attenuation of addictive urges and from its alleviation of the affective distress that often accompanies the initial modulation of addictive behavior. While the core of treatment for sexual addiction is constituted by relapse prevention, psychodynamic psychotherapy, and therapeutic groups, the benefit that sex addicts derive from these treatment modalities is likely to be limited until a significant degree of control has been achieved over addictive sexual behavior. For some individuals who use sexual behavior addictively, the combination of inner motivation, psychological support, and affect-regulating medication may be insufficient to enable achievement of behavioral control. In such cases, behavior modification and/or antiandrogen pharmacotherapy may be a necessary foundation of the entire treatment. Worthy of note is that the functions of these two modalities are different and complementary. The main function of behavior modification is to shift the predominant direction of sexual urges, while the main function of antiandrogen pharmacotherapy is to decrease the intensity of sexual urges.

The progressive modulation of addictive sexual behavior marks the transition from stage I to stage II. At this point, the therapeutic focus can shift to relapse prevention as the primary modality for stabilizing abstinence from addictive behavior. Supportive psychotherapy may be helpful at this time, but exploratory–expressive psychotherapy is likely to be more beneficial in most cases if it is deferred until the latter part of stage II, when behavior and affect are more stable. Meanwhile, psychodynamically oriented interventions may be needed during stages I and II to address psychodynamically based resistances to pharmacological, behavioral, and cognitive–behavioral interventions, lest the entire treatment be disrupted. Moreover, unlike psychoactive substance addictions, sexual addiction involves the addictive use of a kind of behavior that is part of normal living. Consequently, recovery from sexual addiction is not a matter of complete abstinence from sexual behavior, but of learning (1) to distinguish between those forms of sexual behavior that are high risk (for loss of control and harmful consequences) and those that are low risk, and to refrain from engaging in high risk forms of sexual behavior; and (2) to engage in sexual behavior in ways that are healthy rather than pathological. Learning of the first type can usually be addressed in relapse prevention, but learning of the second type often requires psychodynamic psychotherapy. Early in recovery, when the sex addict's judgment is still significantly distorted by a combination of denial, rationalization, vague or fragmented identity, and superego pathology, distinguishing healthy from pathological sexual behavior can be exceedingly difficult. This difficulty has led some clinicians (e.g., Carnes, 1983, 1989) to recommend an initial period of total abstinence from any kind of sexual behavior. The rationale for initial abstinence is that, early in recovery, individuals who have been using sexual behavior addictively may be incapable of selectively eliminating the self-regulatory functions from their sexual behavior; and, to the extent that they continue to use sexual behavior to regulate their affects and/or self-states, the degree to which they are likely to benefit from treatment diminishes. Meanwhile, refraining from behaviors that could be used addictively forces the individual into greater self-awareness. Therapeutic use of this enhanced self-awareness to undermine denial and rationalization, to stabilize identity and sense of self, and to integrate healthy superego functions then brings the individual to a point where he is more capable of distinguishing healthy from pathological sexual behavior. Abstinence from sexual behavior, though not a goal of treatment for sexual addiction, can thus on occasion be a helpful therapeutic technique.

Stage III is the period during which the therapeutic focus can turn to psychodynamic psychotherapy as the therapeutic modality that is most effective in treating character pathology. Psychodynamic psychotherapy, however, is not equally effective in all cases.

Both the need for and the capacity for psychodynamic therapy vary considerably among individuals who use sexual behavior addictively. In addition, the effectiveness of psychodynamic treatment often depends also on the "goodness of fit" between the patient and the therapist, and on the nature of their relationship (Strupp and Hadley, 1979; Luborsky, McLellan, Woody, O'Brien, and Auerbach, 1985; Karasu, 1986; Elkin, Pilkonis, Docherty, and Sotsky, 1988). Initiation of psychodynamic psychotherapy does not, of course, entail that relapse prevention is no longer needed. Urges to engage in symptomatic sexual behavior can be evoked or exacerbated by affects that emerge in the course of psychodynamic psychotherapy. Relapse prevention skills not only help to limit undesirable behaviors, but also enhance the effectiveness of psychotherapy by increasing the likelihood that inner states will be communicated in words rather than acted out. The therapist must thus be able to shift sensitively among exploratory psychodynamic therapy, supportive psychodynamic therapy, and relapse prevention, in response to the changing needs of the patient. Couples or family therapy, when it is indicated, is most likely to have positive results if it is deferred at least until stage III. (I prefer to describe conjoint therapy with a mate as "couples therapy" rather than "marital therapy," since the latter term seems to exclude gay, lesbian, and unmarried heterosexual couples.) In the present view, couples therapy and family therapy are considered to be treatments not for sexual addiction per se, but for the interpersonal issues and dysfunctional patterns that are likely to be associated with sexual addiction. Indications for couples or family therapy in the context of sexual addiction are then not significantly different from what they are in the context of other psychiatric disorders, unless the addict's addictive sexual behavior directly involves the couple or another member of the family. As is the case when treating individuals who suffer from psychiatric conditions other than sexual addiction, couples therapy and family therapy are likely to be most helpful after the individual's major disorder has stabilized and, if significant character pathology was part of the presenting picture, after character healing is well under way. The identified patient's mate or children often also require time to stabilize, and occasionally some individual psychotherapy as well, before they can productively engage in conjoint therapy. However, some form of couple or family intervention may be necessary earlier in treatment if the couple or family system is in crisis. Such crises are not unusual with sexual addiction, particularly since a relationship or family crisis that was related in some way to addictive sexual behavior is often one of the main forces that push the sex addict into treatment. Self-help groups, such as 12-step groups, are typically most helpful during stages I and II and early in stage III. A good self-help group—one that is composed of relatively healthy, growing individuals with whom the patient fits well—can be helpful also later in stage III and stage IV.

COUNTERTRANSFERENCE

The subject of countertransference is considered in its own section, rather than in the middle of the psychodynamic psychotherapy section, because even though countertransference responses are most clearly evident in psychodynamic psychotherapies, they occur in all forms of treatment. Discussions of countertransference properly include both (1) the ways in which the therapists' inner responses to their patients who use sexual behavior addictively can interfere with treatment, and (2) the ways in which the therapists' inner responses to their patients can be used to enhance treatment. Since the methods of using countertransference to enhance treatment are applicable primarily in psychodynamic psychotherapy, while the potential of countertransference to interfere with treatment is shared by all therapeutic modalities, the present discussion will focus on ways in which countertransference responses can interfere, particularly if they remain outside the therapist's awareness.

Many theorists have stated that we all harbor perverse sexual fantasies, as well as fantasies of being able to engage freely in sexual activity without inhibition or restraint. We need not be surprised, then, that many of us respond to sex addicts in ways that are influenced by our fantasies and by our automatic ways of dealing with our fantasies. Some of us may experience anxiety, disgust, or contempt. We may recoil in horror at the thought of anyone allowing full rein to perverse sexual impulses, which we ourselves control so scrupulously that many of us are hardly even aware of them. Some of us might even envy such individuals, in the midst of our disgust and horror. In response to such affects, our natural impulse may be to withdraw from or to punish the patient. Withdrawal may be expressed as collusion with the patient's avoidance of emotionally loaded issues, including the sexual addiction itself. In addition, some therapists have themselves been sexually exploited, either overtly or covertly, and the affects that are stirred up by certain sexually exploitative patients—pedophiles, in particular—may prevent the therapists from functioning effectively. In such instances, referral of the patient elsewhere is usually the best plan.

Factors that contribute to countertransference responses include not only the personal history and dynamics that therapists bring to the therapeutic situation, but also the dynamics, character pathology, and behavioral tendencies that the patients bring. While Khan (1964) was discussing psychoanalytic treatment of perversion when he wrote the following, it seems applicable to any form of treatment for sexual addiction.

> In every piece of acting out the patient is expressing hostility and defiance on the one hand and yet staking maximal claim on our understanding and support. The denial of dependency, the presence of very archaic ego-id processes, the phallic emphasis on action and activity, all directed at the transference, are bound to evoke hostility in the analyst. Perverse sexuality adds to this attack on the analytic process by being by its nature contrary to our normal social morality. It is easier to sympathize with a suffering inhibited human being trapped in his or her conflicts than to empathize with an antisocial person who has gone ecstatically berserk with his or her primitive sexuality, and is flaunting it in one's face. . . . To weather such clinical crises and storms one has to be able to sense and deal with one's hate and distaste. . . . If the analyst's "angry reactions" are intruded into by his moral bias or envy or his incapacity to tolerate violation of his "omnipotent control of the patient's emotions" then the clinical picture gets confused and the patient can only react with either panic and withdrawal or confusion and neurotic submissiveness [p. 276].

PROGNOSIS

The data that could provide an empirical basis for most statements about the prognosis of sexual addiction are not yet available. While the long-term response of sexual addiction to various types of treatment cannot at this time be reliably predicted, a number of factors have been identified that seem to influence the prognosis. These factors can be clustered in three groups: (1) illness factors (that complicate the prognosis), which include early age of onset, high frequency of symptomatic sexual behavior, concomitant use of alcohol or other drugs, and absence of anxiety or guilt about the behavior; (2) recovery support factors (that improve the prognosis), which include a stable job, a stable primary relationship, a supportive social network, availability of appropriate sexual outlets, and environmental monitoring; and (3) personality factors (that improve the prognosis), which include intelligence, creativity, self-observatory capacity, sense of humor, capacity to form interpersonal connections, and motivation for change—which is a function of one's ability to experience oneself as responsible, as well as one's degree of subjective distress. Prognosis is influenced also by comorbidity with other psychiatric disorders and by the degree of associated character pathology.

Many clinicians agree with Herman (1990) that significant recovery from sexual addiction, as from any other addictive disorder, requires a considerable period of time. As Herman observed, addiction interferes with normal development and destroys social relationships. These problems remain after the addictive behavior has ceased, and only then can they begin to be addressed. Moreover, addiction is a chronic condition and, as we have seen, the core pathology in addiction is not readily separable from the affective and characterological matrix from which it arises. However much they may have benefited from treatment, most addicts (of all behavioral types) will to some extent remain vulnerable to being overwhelmed by intense affect states and loss of self-coherence in situations that would be neither traumatic nor disorganizing for individuals whose self-regulation systems are intact.

And sex addicts, in particular, will remain vulnerable to experiencing threats of being overwhelmed by these internal states as urges to engage in sexual behavior. Even after stable recovery has been achieved, ongoing maintenance activity may be required indefinitely to prevent relapse. We might recall from our discussion in chapter 1 that the most appropriate disease model for addictive disorders is not the acute disease that effective treatment can cure, but the chronic disease that effective treatment can, with the patient's active collaboration, bring into remission. Sexual addiction, like other addictive disorders, does not typically get "cured." Nonetheless, as Camus (1955) observed in "The Myth of Sisyphus" (an apparently unrelated context), "The important thing . . . is not to be cured, but to live with one's ailments" (p. 38).

9

Illustrative Clinical Vignettes

The illustrative vignettes that are presented in this chapter concern the same five individuals to whom we were introduced in the book's Introduction. For ease of tracking, the narrative for each of the five individuals begins with a repetition of the "history of present illness," which was originally presented in the Introduction.

HAROLD

History of Present Illness

Harold was a fast-track executive in his middle thirties. Handsome, athletic, bright, and likeable, he seemed destined for a highly successful career. His Achilles' heel was, as he would say, his "weakness for the fair sex." Women often found Harold to be attractive; and when an attractive woman indicated to him that she was interested in him sexually, he found himself unable to resist—or, more accurately, he found himself unable to want to resist. He experienced himself almost as a victim, sexually drawn by women against his will. He was unaware that his banter with

317

women was flirtatious, and that his general manner was seductive in a way that invited women to approach him sexually. Harold's college sweetheart had ended their engagement after he repeatedly broke promises to her that he would stop fooling around with other women. The company that employed Harold had leased an apartment in the city so he could stay over when he was working late. He began to use the apartment for midday sexual liaisons, and his lunch breaks stretched longer and longer. His formerly superior work performance began to slacken, and he did not receive an expected promotion. Harold was convinced that he was passed over because his immediate boss, whom he believed to be jealous of him for his successes with women, had bad-mouthed him to the higher-ups. Harold's senior boss, who was also a mentor to him, warned him that he could lose his job if he was unable to keep his business and pleasure separate. Harold resolved that he would turn over a new leaf, and for six weeks he engaged in sexual activity with no one other than his girl friend. Then, he was out of town on business and had just finished dinner with his work team after a difficult but successful negotiation. He commented that he was feeling mellow from the wine, but that his neck and back were still tight. When his secretary offered to give him a back rub, he accepted the offer without a moment's thought, and they wound up in bed together. After his return, Harold continued to engage in sexual activity with his secretary. She noticed that he was also meeting with another woman who worked in the office, and she began to pressure Harold for an exclusive relationship. When he then rebuffed her, she filed a suit against him for sexual harassment. He was fired immediately.

Personal History

Harold's mother came from a wealthy family of businessmen and heavy drinkers. Harold's father was raised in foster homes until he was adopted at age 6 by a childless farm couple. Harold's parents met in college, where Harold's father had a football scholarship, and they got married when Harold's father graduated. Harold's mother did not stay to complete her degree but left to set up the household, and Harold's father started a business with money that he borrowed from his new father-in-law.

Harold was the first of three children, with two younger sisters. Before he was born, his mother had had a miscarriage at five months gestation. Harold described his mother as very deceitful, warm and inviting one moment and rejecting the next: "She was the type of person you could never trust but were always tempted to." She idolized Harold. He was the apple of her eye, her pride and joy, and he could do no wrong. Harold recalled that she did not see him as a person: "I was an event. A precious jewel." Harold's mother gave him the message that he was special, that he could do anything, and that the rules that applied to ordinary people did not apply to him. In later years, she would make use of her friends in high places to get him out of trouble. Meanwhile, she demanded of him as a little boy that he be neat and clean, soft spoken, well mannered, and well groomed, "as befits a young gentleman." When he failed to meet her standards, she would tell him with contempt that he was noisy or dirty or boorish, and that people would think that he was raised in a barn. She would then send him to his room with the comment that she would not tell him anything that was not for his own good. As a child, Harold often feared that he would be sent away to a farm if he did not behave right. One of his strongest memories was of a time when he was 10 years old and had been told that they were going to be dropping his cousin off at the Boy Scout camp. When his mother also dropped Harold off, he was surprised and terrified. He cried continuously until his mother came and picked him up, on the following day. During the entire ride home she did not speak to or look at him, and when they got home she sent him to his room and called him "a goddamned baby."

Harold recalled that his mother had "horrendous" attitudes toward men and would often complain that men were animals: rough, loud, dirty, and interested only in sex. Meanwhile, she would often dress and undress in front of Harold, and would leave the bathroom door open when she showered or bathed. She also bathed Harold until he was 11, ostensibly in order to keep him from getting water in his ears. When he was a little boy and woke up at night scared, he would crawl into bed with his parents. This behavior continued after his parents' divorce when he was 9 years old, and his mother would wear a flimsy nightgown to bed with nothing underneath. Harold recalled one time when he was 11 or 12 years old, that he was lying in bed with her in a nestled position and had an erection against her buttocks. Thereafter, he was not allowed back into her bed. Harold reported that he always had sexual thoughts about his mother; and that even now, when she touched him, it felt sexual.

Harold's father was a kind, sensitive, and depressive man, when he was sober. When he was under the influence of alcohol, however, he was loud, boisterous, and "supermacho"—which typically progressed to being argumentative and sadistic. His alcohol use increased steadily after his marriage, and by the time that Harold was 3 years old, his father was rarely sober when he was at home. Harold's father was emotionally abusive to the whole family when he was under the influence of alcohol, but he was particularly mean and belittling toward Harold. He occasionally mentioned that when Harold was born, he was neither planned nor wanted. In Harold's presence, he would joke to his friends that Harold had been found in a cabbage patch or left on the front steps. Harold understood his father to be saying that Harold was not really his. Once, when Harold was a small child, his father held him by his ankles over Hoover Dam. On another occasion, he threw Harold into a swimming pool, though Harold was deathly afraid of water. He often criticized Harold, in front of others, for spending too much time in the bathroom and for using too much toilet paper. Harold observed that his father "always made sure I knew what an asshole I was."

Harold's father presented himself as a "new breed" of businessman: brash, dynamic, not afraid to rock the boat or to take a risk. A fortuitous combination of circumstances led to his making a lot of money in his first year of business, which confirmed his belief that he had a brilliant intuitive business sense. In fact, he was as confidently self-destructive in business as is a gambler at the racetrack. After his first year of success he piled failure on top of failure, and he had to continually "borrow" money from his father-in-law in order to make ends meet. Nonetheless, at the bar and at home, he maintained his image as an unconventional business genius who was being shut out and sabotaged by the "old boys club," of which he identified his father-in-law as a prominent member. Harold reported that his father was at one time his greatest hero, until Harold "realized that it was all a lie." He continued that he had always wanted a father figure.

The person to whom Harold was closest during his childhood was his nanny, who was suddenly dismissed when Harold was 7 years old. Harold was unable to recall anything about her. He suspected that she was black, because he would often experience mixed feelings of warmth, longing, and sadness when he saw large black women.

Although Harold's father was louder and more physically intimidating, his mother was the more dominant parent. She would often put Harold's father down and put Harold up on a pedestal. In a variety of ways, both of Harold's parents gave him messages that he should not grow up to be like his father. Harold was 9 years old when his father left the home. He felt abandoned by his father, and he also feared that his father would come back and shoot them all. At the same time, he felt responsible for the breakup of his parents' marriage, a feeling that was reinforced when his mother told him that he was now the man of the house and responsible for his sisters. Harold did not see his father again until three years later, after his father had quit drinking and had begun to lead a stable life.

Harold had his first sexual experiences at age 12, when his high school age (female) baby-sitter engaged him in playing "house." He became sexually active in eighth grade, and his physical attractiveness and athletic talents combined to attract many willing female partners. Harold reported that he received mixed messages from his father about his sexual activity; his father encouraged Harold to "sow his wild oats," but yelled at him for being out all night. Harold recalled that the only time that he ever sensed his father to be proud of him was when he went with his father to a doctor to be treated for a condition that turned out to be gonorrhea, and he heard his father say to the doctor, "That kid of mine, he can't keep it in his pants."

Discussion

Harold demonstrated a number of personality features that are characteristic of a narcissistic disorder. He felt a strong sense of being special, and he believed that he possessed a kind of irresistable attractiveness, which allowed him the illusion of an omnipotence that was free of aggressiveness. His sense of entitlement was closely related to his sense of omnipotent attractiveness. His fantasy was that nothing bad could ever really happen to him, because he would be able to charm a powerful person into rescuing him. This fantasy seemed to be genetically related to his mother's pattern of bailing him out of trouble, and to deeper fantasies of merging with an omnipotent (maternal) object. Harold consistently had difficulty with boundaries and limits. He knew what the rules were; he knew that they were intended to apply to him; and he even endorsed the reasoning behind some of the rules, such as keeping business and pleasure separate; but he somehow felt that the rules did not really apply to him. Not only did Harold's mother give him the message that he was above the rules; she also modeled for him a disregard for intergenerational boundaries, and for the material boundaries of doors and clothes.

While Harold felt that he was special, he also felt that he had "no self." He described himself as being hollow, like a balloon; and he felt that the only thing that kept him from being blown away was a string that represented his sexual connections with women. Harold needed to go out and lure women into seducing him in order to prove his specialness and to reassure himself that he was not about to be blown away. When he was not actively engaged in his work or his sexual pursuits, Harold felt lifeless and empty, devoid of energy, interest, or capacity for enjoyment. A sexual encounter made him feel alive and gave him a sense of direction. Harold had recurrent nightmares about an advertising poster that he once saw as he passed a photography shop. The poster's caption was "Image is everything"; and in his mind, Harold kept adding, "If you have no substance."

As far back as he could remember, Harold suffered from an intense fear of being abandoned, which he associated with being sent back to the farm—the kind of place his father came from.

His fantasy was that he would be left in a delapidated barn that would be empty except for dirty straw and animal excrement. Harold's memory of the Boy Scout camp incident may have been a microcosmic snapshot of (screen memory for) his mother's empathic failure and dishonesty, and of her pattern of encouraging his excessive dependence on her and then punishing him for his neediness with rage and contempt. Harold did not trust women, and he would not entrust himself to anyone. He always needed to have at least two sexual relationships going at once, so if one woman rejected him he would not be alone.

Harold's low self-esteem and his vacuous sense of self derived partly from his sense that his father neither wanted nor valued him, partly from his mother's erratic and narcissistic responsiveness to him, and partly from his split and sometimes amorphous sense of identity. Harold had what amounted to two fathers: a sober father who was kind, sensitive, and depressive; and an under-the-influence father who was loud, boisterous, "supermacho," argumentative, and sadistic. The father that Harold had for most of his childhood was the loud and sadistic one. Harold's mother complicated Harold's task of developing a healthy male identity by devaluing his father, criticizing Harold when he acted like his father, and railing at men in general. She encouraged Harold to be a gentleman, soft spoken and emasculated, not a crude and animalistic man like his father. Harold consequently developed a self representation that was split into a charming gentleman, whom women adored, and a crude, lusty, sadistic brute who was disavowed and rigorously defended against. The gentleman, in fact, to some extent derived from a female identification. On one level, Harold's sexualization, his seductive behavior, and his reliance on denial or disavowal reflected an identification with his mother's personality traits. On another level, Harold's presentation suggested the early operation of intense separation anxiety that can be associated with an abnormal persistence of the primary female identification.

Harold's narcissistic pathology was accompanied by superego pathology that included (1) lacunae, particularly in areas of sexual and monetary exploitation, and (2) a deep split between a

sadistic, punitive, and contemptuous part and a permissive, disor-
ganized, boundaryless part. Harold's superego pathology derived
from (1) his mother's inconsistencies, mixed messages, disregard
of boundaries, and disavowed sadism; (2) his father's sadism, ex-
ploitativeness, and mixed messages; and (3) Harold's massive disillusionment in his father, which crippled his identification with
his father. As a result of his impaired superego functions, Harold
was often exploitative, and he often betrayed people who trusted
him. Meanwhile, he would also often set himself up to get caught
and then to be punished, or else to be himself exploited and
betrayed. This pattern reflected an externalization of superego
function and a masochism that had both moral and erotogenic
components. The moral component reflected Harold's unconscious guilt, which derived from various sources, including his
having displaced his father from his mother's bed. The erotogenic component related both to his yearning for a father figure
and to his partial female identification. For example, Harold often spoke indiscreetly about his sexual exploits, primarily when
they involved a boundary violation, such as using the company-
provided apartment for daytime liaisons. On one level, Harold
secretly wanted other men to know of his exploits and to admire
his "cocksmanship." The one time that he sensed his father to
be proud of him had to do with his sexual promiscuity. On another level, he was unconsciously seeking punishment for his sexual and exploitative transgressions. On a third level, Harold
unconsciously wished to be held and loved by a kind man. He
wished that a strong and caring man would save him from being
eaten alive by these women. The occasion that brought Harold
and his father to the doctor's office was Harold's contraction of
gonorrhea, a castration-symbolizing punishment for his sexual
transgressions. Harold's masochistic leaking of information and
leaving himself open to being hurt reflected also a counterpart
to his father's sadism—anal sadism that also humiliated Harold
for his anality—and a defense against his own anal sadism, which
he nonetheless gratified in his soiling of his employer's reputation by provoking a situation that led to the company being his
codefendent in a lawsuit.

Harold's relationship with his sexuality was full of conflict. In response to his sexual impulses, he feared not only his father's retaliation but also his mother's contempt and rejection. Harold's mother teased him sexually and acted in sexually provocative ways, yet she made clear that she despised men who were sexually interested in her. Harold was always on guard when he was with a woman, and he always waited for the woman to make the first move so he would not be humiliated. At the same time, perhaps as a result of his mother's sexualization of him and her sexually provocative behavior during his childhood, Harold felt that his sexuality did not really belong to him but to women: he felt that women controlled his sexuality and consequently had a power over him that he could not resist but could only submit to, masochistically.

Harold's addictive use of normal heterosexual behavior thus served several interrelated functions, which included: (1) to counter feelings of emptiness, deadness, anhedonia, dread, and directionlessness; (2) to ward off separation anxiety and castration (mutilation) anxiety; (3) to defend against his own sadism and sexual aggressiveness; (4) to restore his sense of narcissistic equilibrium, to stabilize his sense of self, and to ward off fragmentation anxiety; (5) to confirm his sense of specialness, the power of his attractiveness, and his entitlement fantasy that he could violate "the rules" without harmful consequences; (6) to find the limits to his omnipotence, to provoke the environment into providing the structure that he was not able to provide for himself; (7) to win the admiration of other men; (8) to bring on himself punishment and thereby to expiate his guilt; and (9) to call out for a strong and caring man who would save him from being destroyed by the castrating, devouring women.

Course of Treatment

Harold initially sought psychiatric care for the treatment of depression. He presented as a trim, well-groomed man in a well-tailored suit. He looked several years younger than his stated age of 36 and he seemed to be overeager. Harold reported symptoms of an irritable depression and mild vegetative signs. He attributed his depression to the loss of his job two months earlier and his inability to find work since then. He blamed his having been fired on his envious boss and his vindictive secretary, and he suspected that he had been unable to find another job in his field because his former boss had spread false rumors about him throughout the industry. My initial diagnostic impression was of a depressive reaction (an apparent adjustment disorder that met the diagnostic criteria for major depression) in the context of a narcissistic personality disorder. Harold and I collaboratively decided to begin treatment with individual psychotherapy, and to defer the decision about antidepressant medication until we had a chance to observe how the depressive symptoms responded to psychotherapy alone. Psychotherapy sessions were weekly for the first eight months, and then twice per week thereafter.

The content of the psychotherapy sessions during the first few months of treatment to a great extent focused on practical matters: helping Harold to develop a healthier life-style, to find suitable employment, and to cope with interpersonal conflicts or tensions that arose outside the therapeutic setting. Harold avoided areas in which he was affectively vulnerable, and he deftly ignored my allusions to his avoidance. After one month of treatment, Harold was more motivated and less irritable. His sleep and concentration improved, and he felt much better after he found employment. Harold seemed to enjoy being listened to and having my undivided attention. He was affable, charming, and engaging, at a superficial level; but, under the surface, he was seamlessly controlled and impermeably guarded. Even after his sexual history had unfolded, Harold maintained that his sexual behavior had nothing to do with his work difficulties or his depression. He was ambivalently proud of his "weakness for the fair sex," and he accused me of "pathologizing" his sexual successfulness out of envy. However, further incidents during the first few months of treatment forced Harold to recognize that his sexual behavior did indeed lead to consequences that were harmful to him, and that his resolutions to rein in his sexual behavior were inordinately difficult for him to keep. These recognitions were accompanied by a slide into another state of depression.

Harold's new depressive state was more desperate, more lonely, and more empty than the earlier one, and it was associated with more prominent vegetative signs and with recurrent suicidal ideation. I recommended to Harold that he begin a trial of an antidepressant, but he declined, stating that he wanted to develop his potential, not to be tranquilized. He added that drugs are a crutch, and that he could still run on his own legs. However, after being rejected by a woman whom he had thought was interested in him, Harold took an overdose of over-the-counter sleeping pills and wound up in a hospital emergency room. After this incident, he was ready to acknowledge that his affect regulation needed reinforcement, and he agreed to a trial of medication. Antidepressant pharmacotherapy with paroxetine (Paxil) was initiated, and Harold began to feel better than he had in years. Five weeks after he started the paroxetine, Harold told me that he was going to discontinue his treatment with me, and that he would get his prescriptions from his family doctor. I encouraged Harold to talk about what had led him to this decision, and our exploration revealed his fantasy that I would punish and humiliate him for having "failed" after having been so sure of himself. Further work indicated relationships between this fantasy and (1) Harold's shame about his fall from grandiosity and his need for help; (2) his envy and resentment of me; and (3) a number of emotionally significant childhood experiences with both of his parents. This dialogue marked the first time that Harold and I explored the dynamics of something that was happening in our relationship. It was followed by a deepening of Harold's motivation for treatment and by a shift in his emotional experience of me. In general, he experienced me less as a bully who threatened to take away from Harold the one thing about himself that he felt to be valuable, and more as a stable and stabilizing mentor who might be able to help him out of the tangled mess that he now knew to be his inner life. Shortly thereafter, we increased the frequency of psychotherapy sessions to twice per week.

Harold's depressive symptoms responded positively but not completely to the antidepressant medication. Harold and I decided to keep the paroxetine dosage at the minimum that could help him from being overwhelmed by his emotional states, even though it did not completely alleviate his symptoms. When he tried taking a higher dose, Harold felt more generally comfortable and more free of symptoms. However, he then also felt "too smooth," and he believed that, at the higher dose, he could not feel feelings that he should have been feeling. Harold continued to take paroxetine for two years.

With the shift to twice-weekly sessions, the psychotherapy became both more cognitive–behavioral and more psychodynamic than it had been during the first months of treatment. The cognitive–behavioral component was oriented primarily around relapse prevention. In addition to helping Harold become aware of how he set himself up to act out sexually, relapse prevention helped him to recognize his urges and fantasies, which previously had been operating at a virtually preconscious level. It moreover enabled him to understand his urges as signals of inner distress. The cognitive–behavioral component thus provided Harold with a structure within which he could more readily observe and verbalize his inner states, rather than simply responding to them with physical action. Since Harold's symptomatic behavior—sexual relations with a consenting adult—did not differ descriptively from normal sexual behavior, the emphasis of relapse prevention was less on preventing behavior of a general type than on sorting out healthy instances of the behavior from unhealthy instances. Relapse prevention was integrated into the ongoing individual psychotherapy, rather than being provided in a separate therapeutic group. Although some advantages accrue from integrating relapse prevention with individual psychodynamic psychotherapy, particularly when the behavior that is used addictively is a socioculturally normal behavior, the overriding reason for doing so in the case of Harold (and in the other clinical vignettes that follow, except the last one) was that no relapse prevention group was available.

During the course of our reassessment of the treatment plan, after Harold had slid into the deeper depression, I mentioned the 12-step group, Sex and Love Addicts Anonymous (SLAA), as an available resource. About one month later, when his depression had become less overwhelming, Harold attended his first meeting of SLAA. His initial response was not positive. He felt little in common with the other members of the group, most of whom were less well off financially than he was, and he found the 12-step philosophy and rituals to be alien and irritating. Harold also felt uncomfortable that the group included several women, who represented for him both temptations and threats. Nonetheless, he followed the recommendation of a group member to come to the meeting six times before making his decision to discontinue; and he wound up attending the meeting regularly for over a year. Harold observed that he benefited from the support, the encouragement, and the suggestions that the other group members offered, and from the recognition that his problem with sex was shared by others who in other ways functioned as responsible adults. Perhaps even more importantly, he reported, he was learning how to be himself and to be comfortable with himself in social situations. After the first year, Harold's frequency of attendance at SLAA meetings began to diminish. However, he maintained his friendships with two men whom he had met in the SLAA group.

The psychodynamic component of the individual psychotherapy was oriented primarily around exploring (1) the motivational dynamics and the fantasies that were associated with Harold's sexual attractions and inclinations, and (2) the thoughts, fantasies, and feelings that he was experiencing in the context of current interpersonal relationships—including, of course, his relationship with me. Of all the themes that emerged in Harold's relationship with me, the one that was perhaps the most difficult to deal with in the therapeutic situation, and that generated the greatest threat to the therapeutic process, concerned the overdetermined conflict between Harold's wish for and his fear of being passive. A typical sequence would begin when I would mention that I had noticed that Harold seemed withdrawn or distant in our interactions, or that he seemed to be behaviorally compliant with but emotionally disengaged from the therapeutic process, or that he seemed more slow or forgetful with the relapse prevention practices than he could have been. Harold would at first deny the validity of my observation; and then, later in the session, he would flare with rage for no apparent reason. Exploration then usually would reveal that Harold's rage had been triggered by my earlier comment, and that it originally developed in response to some aspect of the treatment that Harold unconsciously had experienced as an attempt to dominate him, to make him passive. Harold then had withdrawn or had become slow as a passive–aggressive compromise that functioned both to bury his rage and to defeat, through passivity, what he experienced as my attempt to dominate him. Eventually, Harold and I were able to recognize that his overperception that I was trying to dominate him, and his intense emotional reaction to such overperceptions, derived not only from his childhood experiences of being dominated, but also from his multiply determined wishes that I would guide him to manhood, would rescue him from dangerous women (including his female identification), would control him (sadistically, if necessary), and would fill him with substance.

As treatment progressed, Harold became more deliberate and less impulsive about his sexual relations. He began to realize that a transient sexual encounter, even if it did not entail explicitly harmful consequences, was not what he was really looking for, since it would not satisfy him or meet his needs for intimate connection. This realization initially emerged at a superficial, intellectual level, and then gradually deepened as Harold occasionally pursued such encounters and then later processed his subsequent emotional experience, which typically consisted of disappointment, emptiness, disgust, and rage. Harold developed a series of committed but brief relationships with disturbed, needy, exploitative women whom he fantasized about rescuing. While all of the women in this series were troubled, each one seemed to be less severely troubled than her predecessor. At the time of treatment termination, Harold had been living for almost one year with a female mental health professional who was herself in psychoanalytic psychotherapy and who seemed, from Harold's report, to be benefiting from treatment. Harold occasionally experienced strong feelings of attraction for other women, which were accompanied by sexual fantasies and urges to pursue seductive agendas. He was able, however, to step back and reasonably to consider whether this other woman represented a potential for a truly fulfilling relationship, and whether what he stood to gain by pursuing this woman was worth the sacrifice of his current relationship. These considerations did not necessarily dissolve his attraction and fantasies, but they helped him to refrain from impulsively acting on them. He was then able to explore what characteristics of the woman had evoked in him such strong feelings of attraction.

Even after Harold was able to maintain a separation between his sex life and his work life, he continued to have difficulties at work, which were related primarily to his extreme sensitivity to narcissistic injury. Gradually, he became more able to recognize his feelings of narcissistic injury, and to step back from them in order to formulate more adaptive responses to the situations that had evoked them. Harold went through a period during which he felt dissatisfied with business, and he considered changing his career to psychology. His identification with me was explored, and heretofore hidden aspects of Harold's identification with his father emerged. Harold decided to buy a farm in a neighboring state, where he would frequently go on weekends to engage in physical work and to relax.

JOE

History of Present Illness

Joe was an electrician in his midtwenties who had used alcohol and other drugs heavily in high school. He dropped out of college in his freshman year and went to work in his uncle's electrical contracting business. After a serious accident on the job while he was intoxicated, Joe quit using alcohol and other drugs. Over the next several months, he found that his sexual fantasies and urges to masturbate were becoming more frequent and more intense than they previously had been. Since his middle teens, Joe had masturbated nearly every night before going to sleep, unless he was having sex with a girl friend or a woman he had picked up. Some mornings during his first year of being drug-free, Joe would get strong urges to masturbate. He found that if he did not act on these urges, he would remain "horny" all day, which would make him restless, distracted, and irritable. Consequently, he started to masturbate in the mornings also, even though he would sometimes be late for work as a result. Some months later, Joe began to get urges to masturbate when he was at work, particularly if he saw a woman at the job site. Again, he found that if he did not masturbate, he would become very uncomfortable and would be unable to focus on his work. No longer sufficiently excited by his fantasies, Joe began to purchase pornography. He also discovered "channel cruising": compulsively flipping through the television channels in search of images by which to masturbate. Before long, Joe was masturbating five or six times a day, even more when he felt under stress. He was chronically tired from lack of sleep, he had received a second warning about tardiness and inattentiveness at work, and he felt disgusted with himself; but each time he tried to stop masturbating, he would fail. Sexual fantasies accompanied by arousal would intrude into his consciousness throughout the day, and he would feel as though he were going to explode. When he began a new sexual relationship, he would throw away his collection of pornography and he would resolve to quit masturbating, or at least to cut down to once a day. Within a few months, though, he would lose control of his masturbation, his sexual interest in his girl friend would fade, and the relationship would fall apart. Frustrated by channel cruising, Joe acquired a VCR and began to buy pornographic videos. He also started using telephone sex services. When he had "maxed out" his credit cards, he applied for new ones and then ran them also up to their limits. He got behind on his rent, and the power company threatened to cut him off unless he paid his bill. Socially isolated, deeply in debt, and about to lose his job, Joe realized that his preoccupation with masturbation and pornography was ruining his life, but he felt powerless. Meanwhile, he also was beginning to sense that pornography and phone sex no longer excited him as much as they used to. He started going to shopping malls specifically for the purpose of looking at women and girls, whom he would later fantasize about raping while he masturbated. When he began to feel compelled to study the patterns of the women who worked in the malls and to compile schedules of their comings and goings, he became scared that he was in danger of acting on his fantasies. At that point, he sought help.

Personal History

Joe was the second of two children, with a sister who was one year older than he was. Joe's mother was sexually abused when she was a child, and she had been treated with antidepressants and other psychiatric medications for most of her life. Joe described his mother as a "compulsive liar" who lived in a fantasy world. He continued that he could never really trust what she said, because she would act differently from one moment to the next, and she gave him a lot of mixed messages. Joe's mother was a perfectionist who imposed her perfectionism on her children. When Joe and his sister were 4 and 5 years old, their mother had them do the dishes and clean the house, and she would obsessively scan the glasses for fingerprints and check the tub to see if water would bead on it. What Joe said was most disturbing to him as a child was his mother's rage attacks, which were unpredictable and could be triggered by almost anything. He experienced his mother's rages as horrifying, and he was in an almost constant state of fear throughout his childhood. He recalled an occasion when he was 5 years old and he forgot to lower the seat on the toilet after urinating. His mother descended on him almost immediately, slapped his ears, pulled his hair, and screamed at him that he was a bad child. Joe could not remember his mother ever hugging or holding him. He could not recall ever going to her for comfort, nor ever feeling comforted by her. He said that his mother pretended to be accepting of him and his sister, but that underneath she despised them. Joe mentioned that he had recently learned that he stayed with a woman for a year when he was an infant, probably because his mother was in and out of psychiatric hospitals. He was told that the woman potty-trained him at 15 months because she could not stand to change diapers.

Joe's father worked in the hardware store that his father (Joe's grandfather) had started and had successfully run until he sold it to cover his gambling debts. Joe's father had intended to save his money and eventually either to buy out the hardware store's current owner or else to open his own store. After many years, however, he was still working for little more than minimum wage, while the store's owner would regularly rebuke him for not having his father's knack for hardware. Joe's father was not ready to have a child when Joe was born. Joe heard that his father had been planning to divorce his mother, but that when he learned that she was pregnant again, he could not bring himself to leave her on her own with two small babies. Joe said that he believed this story when he heard it, and that even before then he had somehow blamed himself for his father having had to stay with his mother. He continued that he realized later that his father would not have had the guts to leave. Joe noted that his father never stood up for himself or for his family, and that he never stood up to Joe's mother. Joe's mother was severely critical of his father and would often taunt his father with belittling comments about his manhood. Joe said, "Mother could do anything, and Dad would never fight back. I told myself I'd never be like that." Joe's father also never intervened to protect Joe from his mother's rages. Joe sometimes used to believe that he was paying the price for his father's lost freedom to leave. At other times, he believed that he was saving his father from being mistreated, and he then felt like a hero. More recently, Joe concluded that his father did not want his wife's rage directed at him; and that rather than stepping into the line of fire, he preferred to sacrifice his son. Joe recalled another disillusioning experience with his father that did not directly involve his mother. When Joe was 6 or 7 years old, he was not allowed to go anywhere out of the house unless he was accompanied by his sister. One time, Joe wanted to go skating, and his sister told him that she would take him if he did the dishes for the whole family. After he had completed the dishes, his sister told him that she had changed her mind and had decided not to go. Joe complained to his father, who shrugged his shoulders and said that he could do nothing about it. Joe stated that from that episode he learned that he "could not trust Dad to make life more fair." Joe recalled that his father was often bitter, irritable, and withdrawn, and that when he was angry he would usually pretend that he was not. During these times, he occasionally would make harsh and cutting remarks to Joe when Joe tried to engage him. Afterward, he typically would cry and apologize to Joe. Joe noted that a depressive atmosphere often surrounded his father, and that he wished that he would get hit so the depressive atmosphere would disappear. Joe recalled that he and his father were close until Joe was 11 years old. At that time, the family moved to a new city, and Joe began to spend time with and look up to a male neighbor. After Joe's father found out about Joe's connection with the neighbor, he withdrew from Joe and shut him out. When Joe would then try to engage his father or to get his advice, his father would bitterly tell him to go ask the neighbor. Joe reported that he had recently heard from his sister, who had sought treatment for bulimia, depression, and self-mutilation, that she had been sexually molested by their father from age 4 to age 13. Joe did not recall being aware that such activity was occurring, but he did remember that his father would sometimes sit in the living room in his underwear and masturbate. While all this was going on, Joe added, his family was staunchly Roman Catholic, and every Sunday they would get dressed up and "parade around the church."

Joe's mother had a nervous breakdown and was hospitalized for a few weeks when Joe was 7 years old. Around that time, Joe began sneaking into his father's room and looking at the *Playboy*s and other sexually explicit magazines that his father kept hidden there. Several times during his third and fourth grade years, Joe got into trouble at school for masturbating in class. While he masturbated, Joe would often look at comic books in which he had erased the clothes from the women and had drawn in pubic hair. Joe recalled that, although he had difficulty with reading and spelling, he was a fairly good student and got straight As in math and science until he was 15 years old. However, he felt that he was never accepted socially. He attributed his social alienation to his having been seductive with his elementary school teachers and having received a lot of attention from them.

Joe had his first steady sexual relationship when he was 17. A pattern developed in this relationship that then recurred in his subsequent relationships. When Joe sensed that his girl friend was displeased with him or that she was withholding herself, he began to experience obsessive fantasies of watching while his girl friend was having sex with other guys or was being raped. In these fantasies, he perceived that this was being done in order to humiliate him. The masturbation fantasy that Joe experienced as most intensely arousing was a fantasy of raping a woman. When he would find himself becoming depressed or discouraged, his fantasies would become more violent and more degrading of women.

Joe said of himself, "I felt like the black sheep in my family, and I acted that out. In every relationship I get into, I wind up being the bad guy. I believe I'm good enough, but I feel I have to prove to everyone else that I am. . . . My problem is I trust too much, and most people are not trustworthy."

Discussion

Joe's early childhood was chronically traumatic. His mother was emotionally and behaviorally unstable, unreasonably demanding, unpredictably rageful, physically abusive, and unaffectionate. Joe did not recall his mother ever touching him, except to hit him. She also was intermittently absent, sometimes emotionally (during depressions and dissociative episodes) and sometimes also physically (during psychiatric hospitalizations). Joe sensed that his mother wished to be rid of him, and that she despised him and found him to be disgusting. Joe did not recall ever feeling angry at his mother. However, the first time he got drunk, at age 14, he demolished his mother's automobile with a hammer and a hunting knife, and then defecated on what remained of the driver's seat. Some component of Joe's conscious and unconscious feelings toward his mother may have derived from his experiences during the year of his infancy that he stayed with another woman. In all likelihood, Joe's affect regulation functions were doubly handicapped by a constitutional predisposition to instability that he inherited from his mother, and a preoedipal period that provided meager opportunity for internalization of healthy affect regulation. The preoccupation with control that Joe demonstrated as an adult could relate to his history of early and apparently unsupportive toilet training, as well as to his fear of being vulnerable and his need to control his rage and inner disorganization. As a child, Joe was quiet and withdrawn. He often felt unhappy; but his primary feeling, which was a continuous undertone that now and then burst into the forefront, was an intense fear that combined elements of both terror and horror.

Joe's relationship with his father provided more stability and caring than did his relationship with his mother, and it may have preserved him from psychosis or sociopathy. However, it was far from ideal. Joe's father was in many ways a failure, both in the world and at home. He was ineffectual in the face of his wife's belittling comments, and he did not provide a desirable model for identification. His failure to protect Joe from his mother's rages led Joe both to hate him and to feel sorry for him, a combination that led Joe to feel a contempt for his father that mirrored his mother's attitude. Joe's developing self-care and self-governance functions suffered as a result of these familial patterns, and he learned that the only way he could protect himself was to withdraw so deeply into himself that nothing could hurt him. Joe did not feel unwanted or despised by his father, as he did by his mother; in fact, he sensed that his father needed him. However, Joe felt as a child that he was responsible for his father having to stay with his mother. He consequently felt a deep guilt, and he sometimes believed that when his mother attacked him and no one came to protect him, he was paying the price for his father's lost freedom to leave. While this guilt was painful, Joe's belief that he was responsible for his father having to stay made him feel powerful, and also helped him to make sense of his mother's mistreatment of him. At other times, he believed that he was sacrificing himself to save his father from being mistreated by his mother, and he then felt like a hero and a martyr. He identified himself with the Jesus Christ of his religious upbringing, and for several years during his childhood he had a compulsion to carve the initials "JC" wherever he could. This identification was determined by other factors besides his sense of himself as a martyr; for example, the letter C was not the first letter of his (and his father's) last name, but it was the first letter of his mother's maiden name.

Joe's mother's psychiatric hospitalization when Joe was 7 years old revived the traumatic feelings from earlier separations, and he began to feel agitated and to experience "electric" feelings over his entire body. He then discovered that by masturbating he could relieve his agitation and disquieting physical sensations, particularly when he masturbated while looking at his father's sexually explicit magazines. This behavior represented an identification with his father, who masturbated in the living room. It also provided him, for the first time in his life, with a reliable source of comfort: a means of comforting himself that he could control.

When he was in junior high school, Joe began to use alcohol and other drugs, partly in an attempt to be less alienated from his peers, and partly as a means of managing his inner states. When he later quit using alcohol and other drugs, the underlying anxieties and buried rage that he had been warding off by using the psychoactive substances began to emerge. Joe responded by increasing his reliance on masturbation to regulate his affects, his drives, and his sense of self. Against his conscious will, he found himself drawn more strongly to masturbation than to interpersonal relationships. Gradually, Joe realized that, in order to achieve the effects that he needed, he had to increase the frequency of his masturbation and then to increase the intensity of the masturbatory experience. Unless he did so, he would feel as though he were going to explode, a feeling that represented an undifferentiated blend of explosive rage and fragmentation anxiety. Increasing the intensity of the masturbatory experience, for Joe, meant increasing the sadistic component of the fantasy or pornography to which he masturbated. Joe's unconscious core fantasy was to tie his mother up and to urinate on her, defecate on her, and rape her until she died. The closer to this unconscious fantasy was the conscious fantasy or pornography to which he masturbated, the more intense and satisfying was Joe's masturbatory experience.

Joe's addictive use of masturbation thus served several interrelated functions, which included: (1) to relieve separation anxiety, fragmentation anxiety, and overwhelming feelings of powerlessness, vulnerability, and humiliation; (2) to defend against murderous rage and sadistic impulses; (3) to be in control of his source of comfort, to be able to provide for himself what he needed without having to depend on anyone else; and (4) to affirm his identification with his father and, in the process, further distance himself from the parts of himself that identified with his mother.

Course of Treatment

Joe initially sought help by calling the 12-step group Sex Addicts Anonymous (SAA), about which he had learned from reading self-help books. He began to regularly attend a weekly meeting, and after a month he added another weekly meeting to his schedule. Joe valued the SAA meetings, and he enjoyed the support that he felt from the other group members. Nonetheless, in the three months since he started attending SAA meetings, he was unable to refrain for more than five days from masturbating to pornography or phone sex. Joe managed to adhere to his contract with his SAA sponsor that he would not go to a shopping mall unless he was accompanied by a fellow SAA member. However, he then began to experience spontaneous fantasies of following and raping women whom he saw walking alone. After Joe caused a minor motor vehicle accident because he was watching a female pedestrian instead of the road ahead of him, his sponsor told him that he needed more help than SAA alone could offer, and he referred Joe to me.

By the end of my initial assessment, I had concluded that Joe could soon present a serious threat of perpetrating a rape, a conclusion with which Joe fearfully agreed. Joe and I discussed various treatment options, including behavior modification, anti-androgen pharmacotherapy, and hospitalization. We decided to begin conservatively with twice-weekly psychotherapy sessions, fluoxetine (Prozac), and attendance at SAA meetings at least five times per week for the first three months. We also formulated a detailed contingency plan for what Joe could do if he began to experience urges to act on his rape fantasies. The first level of the plan was for Joe to connect with a fellow SAA group member, either by telephone or in person, and to talk about his urges to rape, what might have triggered them, and what he could do to keep himself from acting on them. If interventions at the first level did not sufficiently diminish the intensity of his urges, the second level was for Joe to call me. We might then set an appointment for as soon as my schedule allowed, or we might talk on the phone for a while. If Joe then still felt that he was in danger of acting on his urges, the third level of the plan was for Joe to go to the emergency room of a local hospital and request admission to the psychiatric unit. I discussed with Joe the potential benefits and risks of antiandrogen therapy, and I invited Joe to keep it in mind as an option if he began to feel that the initial treatment plan was too difficult or was not sufficiently helpful. The plan was developed by Joe and I in collaboration, and each successive step was framed as a safety net or a self-protection option, not as a punishment or a sign of failure.

The individual psychotherapy component of the treatment initially focused on relapse prevention and on life-style issues, particularly diet and exercise. Joe developed a passion for weight training and body-building, which (1) enhanced his sense of manliness and effectiveness; (2) enabled him to feel more comfortable with and less alienated from his body; and (3) provided him with a constructive channel for his aggressive energies. Later exploration in psychotherapy indicated that Joe's enthusiasm for weight training and body-building had derived also from his inference that I lifted weights. Elements of identification, competition, and wishing for approval contributed to Joe's motivation to go to the gym, as did a homoerotically tinged fantasy that he would run into me at the gym.

Joe also decided to refrain from masturbating and from engaging in any other form of sexual activity for three months. I introduced the idea of abstinence from sexual activity, not as a form of penance, but as an experiment, to see what feelings, fantasies, and memories might emerge when sexual activity was no longer being used to cover them up. Joe found this experiment to be very difficult, primarily because of the intense restlessness and affective discomfort that he experienced when he was not masturbating. Increasing the fluoxetine dose helped to make the restlessness and affective discomfort more manageable, but did not eradicate it. In the course of the experiment, Joe experienced a number of "slips," or episodes of masturbation. As Joe and I explored what was going on with him both externally and internally before each episode, we were able to develop an increasingly coherent understanding of how masturbation functioned in his psychic system, how his masturbation and his masturbatory fantasies were connected with other aspects of his personality, and how both his masturbation and other aspects of his personality related to his personal history. At the end of the three months, in consultation with me, Joe elected to continue his moratorium on masturbation, but to allow himself to engage in consensual sexual activity with another person if he concluded that he was not doing so in order to escape or to medicate distressing inner states. As Joe learned, his conclusions were subject to distortion; but talking about these matters in psychotherapy helped him to become aware of when and how his perceptions and thought processes were distorted. Even when Joe did not yet understand the dynamic origins of the distortions, awareness of their nature enabled him to step back from his immediate reactions and "factor in" the distortions before making a decision or acting.

During the first six months of treatment, Joe frequently experienced strong urges to use alcohol, which he acted on several times. On one occasion when he was under the influence of alcohol, Joe used a telephone sex line for the first time in four months. On the second occasion, a police officer observed that Joe was driving too slowly and issued him a warning. The officer did not notice that Joe had been following a female pedestrian. Joe and I discussed the relationship between Joe's use of alcohol and his addictive use of sexual behavior. On one hand, Joe's use of alcohol was an unconsciously directed attempt to meet some of the same psychodynamic functions that he had been attempting to meet with sexual behavior. On the other, the use of alcohol undermined Joe's judgment and his ability to refrain from engaging in self-injurious sexual behavior. Joe realized that his alcohol use constituted a serious problem, and he committed himself to complete abstinence from alcohol. Joe attending meetings of Alcoholics Anonymous for about one year, and did not use alcohol again. He was able also to transfer to alcohol use the relapse prevention techniques that he had learned in the context of masturbation.

While the individual psychotherapy initially focused on cognitive–behavioral and practical issues, the psychodynamic dimension of psychotherapy also was critical during the first months of Joe's treatment. Joe tended to fight against and to sabotage his treatment, both actively and passively. Sensitive exploration enabled Joe and I to realize that Joe was experiencing my treatment recommendations as attempts by me to control or to dominate him. As Joe recognized the connection with his automatic active or passive resistance to treatment and the relationship expectations that he had developed as a result of his childhood experience of his mother, his resistance diminished. Because of the depth and the intensity of the feelings and fantasies that Joe associated with the experience of being controlled or dominated, these issues needed to be addressed and worked through over and over. On each occasion, however, Joe's range of understanding and mastery was expanded. A psychodynamic approach also helped him to understand how his masturbatory urges and fantasies related to current events in his life, to the rest of his personality, and to his personal history. This understanding fostered Joe's development of self-observatory capacity and of his ability to control his masturbatory urges.

As treatment progressed, the psychotherapy became less cognitive–behavioral and more psychodynamic. Joe discovered that he enjoyed the process of learning about himself, even beyond obtaining relief from disturbing symptoms and affective discomfort. He also enjoyed his relationship with me, to whom he would occasionally refer as his "big brother." During his second year of treatment, Joe decided to return to college. This time around, when he discovered that he was having difficulty with his assignments, he did not automatically blame himself as lazy or label himself as a loser. He obtained a comprehensive assessment for learning disabilities. Joe was found to be of superior intelligence, but to have a moderate to severe degree of dyslexia. Through resources that were available at his school and through the American Learning Disabilities Association, Joe learned ways to compensate for his limitations and to take more complete advantage of his abilities. He graduated with a degree in engineering.

After five years of individual psychotherapy, Joe decided to "take a break." His recognized that significant therapeutic work remained to be done, and he said that he looked forward to resuming psychotherapy in a few years almost as much as he looked forward to discontinuing it now. Joe continued to see me for medication visits every two to three months, which enabled the two of us to remain in contact. Joe's attendance at SAA had diminished during the preceding two years, and he now attended one meeting regularly every week and another meeting more or less regularly.

Although he was now married, and his marital relationship seemed to be healthy and fulfilling, Joe continued to experience urges to masturbate. These urges were, however, less frequent, less intense, and much less compelling than they had been when he first sought treatment. On rare occasions, typically when he felt abandoned both by his wife and by me, Joe allowed himself to act on these urges. More often, he used the urges as opportunities to explore something about himself that his internal system had not yet developed healthier, more adaptive ways of handling. Joe had not used pornography or telephone sex since his second year of treatment. From time to time, Joe still experienced fantasies of raping a woman. He also sometimes experienced fantasies of blowing up someone's house, or of machine-gunning a group of people. He continued to struggle with unresolved rage, to which he was particularly vulnerable when he felt betrayed and helpless; but he was much more aware of his inner life, much more able to verbalize it, and thus much less likely to externalize it through action.

WALTER

History of Present Illness

Walter was a cardiologist in his early forties who first began to use cocaine regularly and to frequent prostitutes when he was in medical school. Since his early teens, he had masturbated nearly every night before going to sleep, and sometimes once or twice during the day as well. He dated little, partly from feelings of inadequacy, and partly from a fear of commitment and of having to respond to another person's demands. Walter found that sex with a prostitute could relieve his loneliness without requiring any commitment. Being with a prostitute also gave him a sense of power and of being in control, which mixed well with the feelings that he got from cocaine. Drugs and prostitutes consumed much of the money that he had intended to use for books and living expenses, and his schoolwork began to suffer from his long nights and weekends of drugs and sex. He tried several times to stop or to cut back, but was unable to do so. Under threat of expulsion from medical school, Walter went through chemical dependency treatment. He remained drug-free for about five months. One night, about four months after leaving treatment, the prostitute for whom he had just bought a drink teasingly asked him if he was scared to have a drink with her, and he ordered one for himself too. When she later offered him a line of cocaine, his resistance had been lowered by the alcohol and the familiar scenario, and he saw no compelling reason to pass it up. Three years later, he was in treatment again. This time, he was instructed to stay away from prostitutes as part of his sobriety plan. For ten years, Walter avoided prostitutes and remained abstinent from alcohol and other drugs of abuse. He married, completed his residency and cardiology fellowship, had a child, and joined an active practice. During this time, he rarely had urges to use alcohol or other drugs, and the urges that arose were easy for him to resist. Urges to get a prostitute, however, were a daily struggle. Occasionally, on his way home from work, he would find himself driving through the sleazy part of town where prostitutes waited on street corners, without knowing how he got there. Sometimes, he was able to resist the urge for a prostitute only by masturbating several times a day, and he was becoming increasingly dependent on sadomasochistic pornography. One night, his wife told him that she was disappointed that he did not have more sexual interest in her. He left the house in a rage, started driving, and wound up in the sleazy part of town. When a prostitute came up to his car, he was about to drive off, but reasoned that he deserved a treat. One "harmless" sip of the prostitute's beer led to a beer for himself, and then another, and then a quest for cocaine. By the time he got to treatment again, he had lost his family and his medical license.

Personal History

Walter's parents got married in their late teens because his mother was pregnant with Walter. Walter described the wedding as "a shotgun wedding in a small southern town." His mother, whose father was the town pharmacist, had been planning to go to pharmacy school. She did not want to be financially dependent on and submissive to a man, as her mother had been. She resented the pregnancy that forced her to marry a man whom she did not really love; and she resented the baby, whose neediness imposed such limitations on her life-style. Walter described his mother as out of touch with her feelings, manipulative, troubled, angry, bitter, and convoluted. He stated that she was not emotionally there for him when he was a child, and that she never showed him affection or tenderness. At the same time, Walter felt that his mother needed him. Moreover, he felt that she needed him to be a certain way or else something bad would happen to her, but he could not understand just how it was that she needed him to be. He recalled that she gave him a lot of confusing messages. Walter noted that his mother was a very efficient person, and that she had potty-trained him at 18 months. He continued that she insisted on a performance that was based largely on duty rather than love, and that she lived her life that way. Walter described his mother also as untrustworthy and mean. She was the kind of person, he said, who would say, "Let bygones be bygones," and then would bring up the subject at the next opportunity. She also often would tease Walter until he would cry or get angry, and then she would criticize him sarcastically for his emotional reaction. One of her favorite phrases, Walter recalled, was "Can't you take a joke?" Walter said that his mother would tease him mostly about his chubbiness and his ineptness in athletics. She also would tease him whenever he indicated an interest in girls.

Walter's father worked at the local dairy and drove the milk truck for morning deliveries. Walter initially referred to his father as a country redneck, but he later described his father as a gifted musician and an intelligent man who had a severe learning disability as a child and who grew up in a primitive and abusive household. Walter recalled that his father was a quiet person who sat by himself and drank, not aggressive or ambitious and not very strong. Walter's mother dominated his father and, according to Walter, treated him like dirt. Meanwhile, she would complain to Walter about his father's inadequacies and his impotence, and she would instruct Walter not to tell anyone what his father did for a living. Walter was angry at his mother for how she treated his father, for putting him down and shaming him. At the same time, Walter said, he used to hate his father for what he let Walter's mother do to him. Walter felt sorry for his father, and at the same time he felt contempt for his father's weakness. Walter recalled his father as a disappointed and frustrated man, who went out of his way not to take out his frustration on Walter. He rarely hit Walter, and did so only when Walter's mother commanded him to spank Walter so that he would not grow up to be undisciplined, like his father. Nonetheless, Walter often felt that his father experienced him as a mistake for which he was unfairly being made to pay and pay. Sometimes, when Walter's father had been drinking, he would cry while telling his young son how wonderful his life could have been if Walter's mother had not become pregnant. Walter recalled these "talks" as the times that he felt closest to his father. He also enjoyed riding with his father on the milk delivery route, though his mother forbade it and would berate Walter and beat him if she found out that he had done so.

Walter had one brother, who died at age 5 months when Walter was 6 years old. He had been born prematurely and did not have adequate pulmonary function. Walter reported that he came home from playing ball one afternoon, and his mother was sitting in a rocking chair in front of the house, rocking the dead baby as though she were waiting for it to come back to life. Soon the whole intersection filled with people, and Walter felt pushed around and in the way. Of all the events in his childhood, this was the one that he recalled most strongly.

Walter's maternal grandfather, who was the patriarch of the family, did not like Walter's father. Walter's mother would complain to her father about living in a rented rowhouse and wearing second-hand clothes, and her father would encourage her to "throw the bum out." When Walter was 11 years old, his father left. Walter and his mother then moved in with his mother's parents for three years, while his grandfather supported his mother through pharmacy school. Walter and his mother shared the bedroom that had been his mother's room when she was growing up, since that was the only room available. Though he slept on the floor, he recalled feeling uncomfortable with such intimate proximity to his mother. Walter said that he did not know what had become of his father; but that when he learns conclusively that his father has died, he will go through a real traumatic period, because his father's death would mean that they could never have a chance to get to know each other.

Discussion

Walter's parents had little in common, but they both agreed that Walter's conception had ruined their lives. In addition to her anger about being married to Walter's father, Walter's mother resented the baby and his neediness. She had no use for an infant, and she could not stand his crying. She cared for Walter's basic infantile needs out of duty rather than love, and she invested about as much libidinal cathexis in infant care activities as she did in washing her husband's work clothes. At the same time, she enjoyed showing Walter off after he began to use words at age 8 months, and she was both relieved and excited that he was "starting to become a real person." In effect, she treated Walter as though he were a miniature adult, while he was still a small child. Walter had the good fortune to be highly intelligent, which enabled him to quickly learn which behaviors evoked positive responses from his mother, and enabled him also to perform the cognitively advanced and precociously mature behaviors to which his mother responded positively. In the process, Walter additionally learned that his needs were unlikely to be met by others; and, moreover, that expressing his needs exposed him to additional dangers. He consequently developed an "as if" characterological core that consisted of pseudo-maturity, intellectual exhibitionism, disavowal of his needs, and a preoccupation with being self-sufficient. Walter sensed unconsciously that he served an important function for his mother, beyond her valuation of his intelligence, but he did not know what she needed from him, and he moreover suspected that he would not be capable of providing it. He consequently felt special, but he feared unconsciously that his specialness was a fraud and that he would be severely punished and humiliated for having perpetrated the fraud, even though he did not know what the fraud was.

When 5-year-old Walter found out that his mother was pregnant, he became afraid that he would lose his position of specialness, and that his mother would then ignore him. He was exceedingly solicitous of his younger brother after his birth, in defense against his unconscious wish to strangle the intruder. After his brother died, Walter felt deeply guilty, as though by his being away from home that day he had not only caused his brother's death but also had betrayed and damaged his mother. This additional layer of guilt, for having betrayed and damaged his mother, pointed to another wish, which was defended against even more strongly than was his wish to kill his younger brother: a wish to hurt, to damage, and to kill his mother.

Walter's mother was a verbally adept woman, and she employed her verbal aptitude in the service of bitter sarcasm and sadistic teasing. Walter's father managed to spend little time at home, so Walter became the receptacle for much of the malice that his mother had originally intended for his father. Her teasing was most often directed toward exposing or mocking Walter's physical inadequacies, particularly humiliating him for attributes that she felt fell short of manliness. When Walter began to develop an interest in girls, his mother would sneer at any indication of his interest, however subtle, and she would make derogatory comments about the girls in which he indicated interest. Walter felt that his mother's sneering conveyed both the sense that his interest in girls was shameful, and the sense that he was not man enough to be interested in girls. This ambivalent combination of shameful feelings, which were associated also with Walter's fantasies about his mother, tormented Walter when he and his mother shared a bedroom at his grandfather's house.

Meanwhile, Walter's mother would tell him about his father's impotence, which not only widened a gulf of contempt and guilt between Walter and his father, but also drew Walter into his mother's sexual confidence. When Walter's father left the family, Walter blamed himself for having allowed his mother to shame, browbeat, and seduce him into turning away from his father. In fact, Walter had for years fantasized that his father would leave his mother—and would take him along. This fantasy was related to why Walter had felt so close to his father during those "talks" in which his father would cry to him about how wonderful his life could have been had Walter's mother not become pregnant, and then he would not have had to marry her. Walter imagined that his father's fantasy accorded with his own: that they both wished to be free of Walter's mother and to be together. Walter disavowed the obvious implication that, had his mother not become pregnant, he would not have been born.

Walter's addictive use of sexual activity with prostitutes thus served several interrelated functions, which included: (1) relief from his loneliness, separation anxiety, and depressive feelings; (2) demonstration of his power and control, and thereby repudiation of his feelings of weakness, vulnerability, and shame; (3) confirmation of his masculinity, which bolstered his disavowal of castration anxiety and covert homosexual wishes; (4) affirmation that he had no needs that he was not able to take care of by himself—in this case, by purchasing the means to take care of them—and that he thus did not have to depend on anyone else; (5) both containment and symbolic expression of his sadistic and murderous impulses toward women; (6) avoidance of commitments and of the obligation to respond to another person's demands (the avoidance of which was motivated both by a claustrophobic residue of his mother's control of him, and by an identification with his mother's intolerance of his demands when he was an infant); and (7) preservation of his freedom from pressures for "performance that is based on duty." Walter's sexual activity with prostitutes served many of the same functions as did his use of cocaine, and each greatly enhanced the psychodynamic effectiveness of the other.

Course of Treatment

Walter was referred to me by a medical colleague whom he met at an Alcoholics Anonymous (AA) meeting. Walter had completed a specialized six-month chemical dependency treatment program for physicians two months earlier, and he was now living in a halfway house and working as an apprentice electrician. Walter sought help for two reasons. First, his counselor at the treatment program had told him that he would need to deal directly with his sexual addiction, or he would be unlikely to remain sober. However, Walter did not feel that his work in the treatment program or since his completion of the program had helped him to deal with his sexual addiction in any significant way. Now that he was back in the world where prostitutes were readily available, he was scared that he would "be drawn into the vortex of repeatable history." Walter's second reason for seeking psychiatric help was that he was sleeping poorly, and he consequently felt worn out and irritable all the time. The history that I elicited indicated that Walter had been suffering since his early teens from a condition of tense, irritable, anhedonic, empty dysphoria. This dysphoria was associated also with difficulty falling asleep, a low tolerance of frustration, difficulty staying focused, a tendency to be easily overwhelmed by emotions, and an abnormal sensitivity to sensory stimuli, particularly sounds. Since his middle teens, Walter had used masturbation as a self-treatment for his initial insomnia. In addition to manifestations of tension, irritability, and dysphoric affect, Walter's mental status was notable for subtle lapses of coherence in his thought processes. I believed that the initial focus of treatment should be to address this condition, which seemed to combine features of dysthymia, atypical manic–depressive disorder, attention deficit disorder, and borderline personality disorder. I summarized the pros and cons of antidepressants and stabilizers, and I suggested that we begin with an antidepressant. Walter, however, would not hear of it. He said that he had just been released from his third chemical dependency treatment program, and he was not interested in now becoming dependent on my drugs. I encouraged Walter to talk about what it would mean to him to be dependent on my drugs, and he revealed three factors that contributed to his resistance to taking medication. First, he believed that needing a drug to cope meant that he was weak and defective. Second, he feared that I wanted to make him dependent on me, through my drugs. This fear, in part, represented a defense against his wish to depend on me totally, to be taken care of by me. Finally, Walter expected to be criticized and rejected in his AA group "for using mood-altering chemicals." I suggested that we look at this expectation, and Walter recalled that other members of his AA group had spoken openly about being on antidepressants, and some had even received positive feedback about taking good care of themselves. Further exploration indicated that Walter's expectation of criticism and rejection for taking antidepressants derived from his deeply held belief that, if he were perceived as needy or dependent, he would be scorned and abandoned. Walter decided to give antidepressants a try. Unfortunately, an initial trial of paroxetine (Paxil) seemed to exacerbate Walter's insomnia and agitation; but he responded positively to a combination of divalproex (Depakote) and nefazodone (Serzone).

Walter initially was even less interested in psychodynamic psychotherapy than he was in psychiatric medication. He just wanted a set of tools that would enable him "to beat this prostitution thing." Walter's prior experience in the context of treatment for his psychoactive substance addiction facilitated his acquisition of relapse prevention techniques and eased his entry into Sex Addicts Anonymous (SAA). However, he had difficulty with the process of looking at his urges as signals of inner states. Walter considered introspection to be a self-indulgent waste of time, at best, and often an attempt to concoct excuses for misbehavior. Moreover, his thought processes seemed to be obdurately concrete, and I was unable at the time to sort out how much of

Walter's concreteness was defensive and how much was constitutional. Walter was skeptical when I suggested that a period of abstinence from sexual activity might be helpful, but he complied when his SAA sponsor told him that he would be unlikely to recover if he did not sign and adhere to an "abstinence contract." Walter carried his copy of the abstinence contract in his pocket, and he believed that it protected him from temptation. Initially, he was almost euphoric with pride in his newfound sense of control. However, he was becoming increasingly tense and irritable, even while he was telling everyone how he found sexual abstinence to be wonderfully freeing.

About one month into his sexual abstinence, Walter called me and requested a session as soon as possible. We met on the following day, and Walter began by reporting, in a distraught state, that he could no longer use his computer. Walter continued that he depended on the computer for everything—including his checkbook, his calendar, his list of phone numbers, and his daily journal—and that he felt that his life had ground to a halt. I got Walter to clarify that the problem was not that the computer was malfunctioning, but that Walter felt so uncomfortable when he approached his computer that he could not organize his thoughts. I inquired when this problem began, and then gently encouraged Walter to review with me the events that led up to the onset of his new symptoms. The story that emerged was that two nights earlier, Walter was fooling around on the Internet and wandered into a chat group in which people were exchanging sexual innuendoes. He became sexually aroused and, in a panic, shut down his computer. On the following day, whenever Walter approached his computer, he would experience symptoms of disorganizing panic. Until I had led Walter to review with me the details about his experiences during the day and night before the onset of his new symptom, he did not recall his panic of the previous night; nor did he recall the chat group. With further encouragement, Walter talked about his fear of losing control. I said that it must be awful for Walter to have such a scary experience with something on which he depended. Walter then alluded to an occasion of having lunch with his mother earlier that month. I commented on the transition from what we had just been talking about, Walter's fear of losing control with something on which he depended, to his thoughts about his mother, and wondered aloud if there might be a connection. With more affect than he had demonstrated at any other time thus far, Walter began to talk about how scared he had been of his mother when he was a child. He added that now, even as an adult, he was still scared of her. I said that now we could begin to see what had led Walter to have such a dramatic reaction to his Internet experience: the fear of losing control of his sexual feelings when he was already struggling with them was hard enough, and then his experience of fear of losing control in the context of something on which he depended triggered unresolved feelings that related to his childhood experiences of his mother. At his next meeting with me, Walter reported that his inability to use his computer had disappeared. In the process, Walter's attitude toward psychodynamic psychotherapy had shifted from cynical to enthusiastic, and an extended period of productive work ensued.

Walter was able to refrain from using prostitutes, but he continued to struggle for a long time with urges to masturbate while participating in sexually oriented chat groups. When Walter began to date women, he and I had an opportunity to more fully explore how his beliefs, feelings, and fantasies about sexuality and control related to his inner experiences of women. Walter's expectation that I would try to humiliate him about his interest in women, an expectation that derived from his earlier experience of his mother, further helped to illuminate the connections in his mind between sexual feelings, humiliation, and rage toward women. Meanwhile, Walter experienced me more often in terms that derived from his childhood experiences of and fantasies about his father: usually as a quiet and impotent but gentle and nurturing man, occasionally as a Moses-type hero who would lead Walter to freedom.

When Walter had been taking divalproex (Depakote) for about one and a half years, he told me that he was ready to try discontinuing it. We discussed what had led him to decide that he was ready, and also what thoughts and feelings he associated with taking divalproex and with discontinuing it. For nearly one year, Walter's affective state, frustration tolerance, and impulse control had been fairly stable. His thoughts were coherent and well organized, though sometimes obsessively stuck on superfluous details, and his sleep was sound. His life, too, was in a relatively stable period, with no major changes looming on the horizon. In short, this was a reasonable time to check and see whether Walter still needed to take the divalproex. I told him about the range of potential consequences of discontinuing divalproex, and I described the changes that would indicate that he would need to resume taking the medication. I encouraged him to consider the discontinuation as an experiment, a bit of research that would provide us with useful information, regardless of its outcome. In other words, our discovery that Walter still needed the divalproex would not constitute evidence that he was a failure. Following his discontinuation of the medication, Walter's emotional states became more intense and labile. He became more irritable and more easily frustrated, and he once again had difficulty falling asleep. However, his impulse control and thought processes remained stable, his functioning at work and in interpersonal relationships was not significantly impaired, and he experienced his symptomatic exacerbation to be uncomfortable and inconvenient, but not intolerable. Walter found that melatonin helped him get to sleep; but after a few weeks, he rarely seemed to need it.

Walter's medical license was eventually reinstated, with a stipulation of five years of random body fluid monitoring and documented attendance at AA meetings. He joined a multispecialty clinic that embraced a laid-back, personal approach to medicine, and he committed himself to working no more than 30 hours per week. Walter had started jogging when he was living at the halfway house, and he enjoyed feeling fit for the first time in his life. When back pain forced him to give up jogging, he started bicycling and walking. At the age of 50, Walter decided to learn to play the fiddle. He was mildly disappointed that he did not turn out to be a gifted fiddler, but he had fun playing the fiddle anyhow.

ANDREA

History of Present Illness

Andrea was a maritime lawyer in her late thirties whose expertise in one area of the law led her to do a lot of traveling. She had been treated for depression and bulimia in her twenties, and she was no longer bingeing or purging. However, she still exercised every day, and she was preoccupied with her body. Her chronic depression had shifted to an irregular alternation between a restless, irritable dysphoria and a driven vivacity that verged on hypomania. After being in a string of abusive relationships from her late teens to her early thirties, Andrea decided to stay single, a decision that was reinforced by her itinerant life-style. When she traveled for business, Andrea's typical pattern was to work intensively during the day and into the evening, and then to go out to a bar and pick up a man. She enjoyed the attention, the feeling of power, and the freedom of never having to see the man again. She had intercourse without any form of contraception, which led to four pregnancies that were terminated by abortion (the first when she was in her teens), and she managed to avoid ever being tested for HIV. After once being robbed by a man whom she had picked up, Andrea resolved to stop taking such chances. For the next four business trips, she did not engage in any sexual adventures, though she felt so tense and restless in the evenings that she thought she would explode. On the fifth trip, she could no longer stand the tension, and she resumed her pattern. Another time she was robbed and then raped. She did not go to the police, expecting that they would just blame her for having invited the man to her room. This time, her resolution to quit lasted for just two trips. Only after the next adverse incident, in which she was beaten so badly that she required several days of hospitalization and consequently was unable to fulfill her work commitments, did Andrea finally seek help.

Personal History

Andrea's parents came from wealthy families. They met and courted in a glittery social whirl, and they found out shortly after their wedding day that they had little in common and that their relationship was empty. They then had a child in order to have something in which to share interest. Andrea commented that it was a hard job to be the glue in her parents' marriage.

Andrea's mother Lorraine was an artist of modest talent whose family was "old money." Raised by nannies and live-in tutors, Lorraine hardly knew her parents until she was in her teens. From ages 4 to 12, she was sexually used by her older brothers. Andrea described her mother as moody and unpredictable, adding that Lorraine was hospitalized for six months after a suicide attempt when Andrea was an infant. Andrea recalled that Lorraine sometimes would be affectionate and clingy, holding Andrea on her lap long after Andrea was ready to go and play. At other times, Andrea said, her mother would "go crazy": her face would get dark and twisted, and she would scream and throw things. In this state, she occasionally would beat Andrea with a belt or an extension cord. What Andrea found most disturbing, though, was when her mother would "space out." She would sit and stare without moving, and she would not respond when Andrea talked to her or touched her. Or if she did move, she would seem to be sleepwalking. Andrea remembered one occasion when she was 4 or 5 years old and her mother was holding her on her lap. Andrea had a full bladder, but she was scared that if she said anything, her mother would become upset. Eventually, she wet her pants. She was terrified that she would now be beaten. Instead, Lorraine just sat where she was for a few minutes staring. She then got up and, in her sleepwalking mode, cleaned the chair, showered, changed her clothes, and washed her soiled clothing. She said nothing to Andrea, and seemed not to notice Andrea's presence. Andrea recalled that her mother was always threatening to take something away, and that she consequently learned not to value things that could be taken away. Lorraine also often threatened to send Andrea to an orphanage, and once, when Andrea was 7 or 8 years old, she actually dropped Andrea off in front of an orphanage and drove away. (Andrea, of course, did not know that her mother was only driving around the block.) Meanwhile, Andrea noted, her mother would get upset if Andrea asked to go to a friend's house. She also had Andrea sleep with her until Andrea was 10 years old. Andrea recalled that her mother would sometimes let her skip school for what her mother called a "mental health day," and the two of them would have lunch delivered and watch soap operas. After Andrea went to her first school dance, her mother accused her of being a whore and made it clear to her that if she "got knocked up" she would no longer be welcome at home.

As a child, Andrea was very close with her father, and preferred being with him to being with her mother. He was a real estate lawyer whose work consisted mostly of running the land development company that his father had started. From the time that Andrea was a little girl, he occasionally would take her to his office, despite the protests of her mother. Although she felt guilty about leaving with her father, she enjoyed the freedom and the sense of being special that she felt in her father's world. Her fondest early memory was of sitting on top of a wooden file cabinet in a room that smelled of books, and looking at the sunset through a window high above the city. As Andrea got older, her father sometimes took her to lunch or dinner business meetings, where he would introduce her as his princess. Before these meetings, Andrea's father would often take her shopping for elegant clothes, and then to a beauty salon to have her hair and nails done. He would tell her how beautiful she was, and she felt beautiful and on top of the world. Andrea initially stated that her father was a good father until she reached puberty, and that he then withdrew from her because "he was afraid to touch me." She later recalled that he used to make inappropriate comments about her mother's lack of interest in sex. Moreover, he did not conceal from Andrea his numerous extramarital affairs, but indicated to her that she should help him to protect her mother from such information, which he said would surely devastate her. Andrea noted also that her father had a well-stocked bar at his office, from which he drank every day, and that he had a collection of pornographic magazines in his private restroom.

Andrea reported that she had been preoccupied with finding "perfect love," which she defined as being held and taken care of and totally loved just for who she was. Meanwhile, she also entertained a fantasy of being extremely desirable to men but untouchable, of being able to drive men to desperation by doing nothing. Andrea said that she knew that her sexual behavior with strangers was dangerous, but that the danger excited her and appealed to her sense of adventure. She added that she felt that she was "playing Russian roulette with God." Andrea then recalled a fantasy with which she would put herself to sleep during her latency years and early teens. In this fantasy, Andrea was with a group that was attacked by a band of murderous people. She then did something heroic that saved the group, but in the process she was mortally wounded. However, she miraculously survived the injury, and a male figure would come and sit beside her bed as she recuperated, being there with her. Andrea stopped conjuring this fantasy when she started to engage in masochistic masturbation, which usually involved hitting herself with a hairbrush or pinching her nipples.

Discussion

Andrea's mother suffered from major psychiatric disturbances that seemed to include an affective disorder, a severe personality disorder, and a dissociative disorder. She may at times have been psychotic. In any case, her moodiness, inconsistency, volatility, self-centeredness, and abusiveness constituted an unsuitable environment for the internalization of healthy self-regulatory functions. Andrea experienced neither a holding environment, nor appropriate responses to her affective behavior. Her mother was too desperately invested in employing Andrea as her selfobject to be able to respond empathically to her daughter's developmental needs. Andrea's mother was highly dependent on Andrea: she had Andrea sleep with her, she encouraged Andrea to regress and to stay home with her rather than going to school, and she felt threatened by Andrea's interests in relationships outside the home and by Andrea's sexuality. Instead of feeling cared for and developing a sense of herself as being worth caring for, Andrea felt that she had to take care of her mother, and that if she did not do so she would be destroyed. In the world of Andrea's early childhood, nothing was secure, nothing could be counted on. Andrea learned to deny her needs and her disappointments, and to experience herself as a selflessly and endlessly generous saint-goddess. In effect, she identified with the omnipotent, all-giving mother of her fantasies, and projected onto her mother—with her mother's encouragement—the needy, greedy infant self that she had split off.

Andrea had no background of safety and did not develop basic trust. She lacked confidence in her ability to discern whom to trust and how much to trust. In her words, in place of a "rheo-stat" for trust, she had an "on-off switch." Andrea consequently tended to oscillate between gullibility and paranoia. In response to her mother's instability and her frequent threats to take things away from her or to send her to an orphanage, Andrea learned to disavow her attachments to anything and to anyone. She also developed an underlying conviction that if she ever really did care about something or someone, it or he or she would be abruptly taken away from her. In addition, Andrea experienced throughout her life a continuous sense of anxiety that suddenly, without any warning, a holocaustlike cataclysm would shatter her world. Although she was not Jewish, Andrea identified with the experience of European Jews during the Holocaust, and she often had nightmares in which Nazis overran her house.

Andrea's experience of her childhood led her to be intensely ambivalent about having children. On one level, she wished to have a daughter, to provide for her daughter the caring that her own mother had failed to provide for her, and then to vicariously experience being cared for, through an identification with her daughter. Meanwhile, she had internalized her mother's threat that if she "got knocked up" she would no longer be welcome at home, which she had psychodynamically experienced to mean that if she had a child, the possibility that she herself could ever be cared for like a child would forever vanish. On another level, Andrea was repulsed by the neediness of infants, as a result of her defensive repudiation of her own neediness and of her hatred for her mother's neediness. She was moreover afraid that, while she could vicariously experience being cared for by identifying with her child, she would also envy and resent her child for receiving the good infant care that Andrea never received from her mother and never would receive. At a level still further from conscious awareness, Andrea feared that she would do to her own child what her mother had done to her. This fear reflected both (1) Andrea's defense against her greedy and sadistic wishes to have a child and to omnipotently use the child as her mother had used her, and (2) Andrea's fear of identifying with her mother, which meant not only being "a horrible person" like her mother but also becoming her mother and losing her self.

When Andrea was in her father's world, she felt herself to be a completely different person from who she was when she was in her mother's world. Her father pampered her and showered her with affection. When she was with her father, Andrea felt special, appreciated, loved, and grown up. She also felt grown up when she was with her mother, but that was a very different experience. Being grown up with her mother meant being responsible for things that were beyond her capacity to handle, and also meant not being cared for. Being grown up with her father meant being free and powerful and listened to. Andrea much preferred to be in her father's world, but she felt terribly guilty when she went with him. Part of her guilt was oedipal, triadic guilt: Andrea's father seemed to prefer her company to that of her mother, and he was often seductive and at times sexually inappropriate. Another part of Andrea's guilt was dyadic: she felt that she was betraying and abandoning her mother, and she was afraid that her mother would die in her absence—a fear that to some extent also reflected her unconscious wish. A third aspect of her guilt was narcissistic: she was afraid that by embracing the role of her father's special princess, she was pretending to be someone whom she was not, and that she eventually would be exposed as an impostor and publicly humiliated. At the same time, Andrea also experienced a subterranean agitated frustration when she was with her father. His caring and affectionate behavior stirred up her unfulfilled oral longings to be held and filled up, which she sexualized in response to his seductiveness and his inappropriate sexual comments. Unconsciously, she longed for him to sexually overwhelm her. Her agitation derived partly from her sexual frustration, and partly from her rage at her father for what she experienced (unconsciously) as sadistic sexual teasing. Andrea's complex guilt and her unconscious wish to be sexually overwhelmed by her father combined to energize her masochistic masturbation. Her later fantasy of being extremely desirable to men but untouchable, of being able to drive men to desperation by doing nothing, represented a wish to do to men (and to her father) what her father had done to her.

Andrea was much more inclined to identify with her father than with her mother, and she received mixed messages from him about who he wanted her to be: a powerful operator like himself, or a pampered princess. Andrea herself had no clear sense of who she was. She felt real only when she was needed or wanted. Her fantasy of "perfect love," in which she would be totally loved just for who she was, represented a condensation of (1) oral merger fantasies and (2) her wish for a self, her wish to discover who she was through being loved.

Andrea's addictive use of impersonal sexual activity with unknown men thus served several interrelated functions, which included: (1) to alleviate overwhelming feelings of depression, loneliness, tension, agitation, and emptiness; (2) to enable her to feel real, because she was wanted, and thereby to counter her feelings of deadness and her dissociative tendencies; (3) to stave off feelings of disintegration and to stabilize her sense of self; (4) to simulate an omnipotent sense of freedom and power, because she could go out and have any man she wanted, and thereby to ward off feelings of vulnerability, inadequacy, and helplessness; (5) to confirm her attractiveness and her femininity; (6) to flesh out her identification with her father (with his multiple extramarital affairs and his sexualization), and thereby to defend against tendencies to identify with her mother; (7) to avoid emotional closeness, which would entail claustrophobic anxieties, paranoid anxieties, and the anxieties that would attend the reemergence of her unmet needs; (8) to set herself up for punishment, which would expiate her oedipal, dyadic, and narcissistic guilt; (9) to provide opportunities for the gratification of her wish to be overwhelmed; (10) to act out her ambivalence about having children (by not using contraception); and (11) to gratify her sadistic impulses, by being in control of which man she selected, by kicking the man out the next morning and never seeing him again, and by identifying with the man's sadistic treatment of her. Andrea's sexual behavior fulfilled many of the same functions that her bulimic behavior had fulfilled. During her bulimic years and for a while after her bulimic behavior had quieted down, Andrea was addictively involved in sexual relationships with men whom she employed as sexual selfobjects. Her use of impersonal sex with unknown men to fulfill selfobject functions emerged as her interest in the last of her sexual relationships was beginning to wane, and it blossomed when this relationship ended.

Course of Treatment

Andrea initially consulted a psychologist whom she knew socially, and the psychologist referred her to me. Andrea arrived for her first appointment about twenty minutes late. Her clothing, hairstyle, and makeup were high-level corporate, and she presented her history in an articulate, polished, and entirely detached manner. She actually showed no affective response at all, until I mentioned that our session would be ending in a few minutes. Andrea then realized that I intended to end the session at the appointed time, even though our late start meant that the session would be significantly shorter than my evaluation sessions usually are. She became irate and accused me of being greedy and dishonest, charging her for a full one-hour evaluation session but meeting with her for only forty minutes. She wrote out a check, threw it on the floor, and left in a flurry of slamming doors. Three days later, Andrea called and, in her corporate polished voice, told me that she had looked at her calendar and had noticed that we had not scheduled another appointment.

Andrea and I met again a few days later, and we began by exploring what had happened in our first meeting. In effect, we jumped right into psychodynamic psychotherapy. My assessment was that the most urgent concern in Andrea's case, unlike in the case of Joe or Walter, was not to bring her sexual behavior under control, but to develop a therapeutic alliance with her. She seemed to be labile, protean, action-oriented, and explosive. I suspected that perhaps only a stable, meaningful connection with another person could keep her from accelerating out of control and crashing; and that, in the absence of such a connection, no avenue of treatment would be successful. Our primary focus during much of the first two years of our work together was to recognize, to understand, and to work through the factors that undermined Andrea's capacity to form a therapeutic alliance. By being a reliable, respectful, caring human presence, and by offering interpretations that helped Andrea to organize and to master her inner experience, I hoped to provide a holding environment that could safely contain Andrea's stormy affects. Andrea could then gradually internalize this holding environment, as a means of fostering the development of her own autonomous affect regulation.

Diagnostically, I saw Andrea to be suffering from a borderline personality disorder of the type that also has been called "emotionally unstable character disorder" (Klein, Gittelman, Quitkin, and Rifkin, 1980). In my experience, individuals who suffer from this type of condition usually derive some benefit from serotonergic antidepressant medication, and often benefit even more when a stabilizing medication, such as divalproex (Depakote), is added to the regimen. Andrea stated that she did not want to take fluoxetine (Prozac), because she had heard that it made people homicidal and suicidal. Although I believed that such claims were highly exaggerated, I decided to respect Andrea's (potentially self-fulfilling) concerns. We successively (but unsuccessfully) tried paroxetine (Paxil), nefazodone (Serzone), and venlafexine (Effexor), all of which seemed to exacerbate Andrea's agitation, her insomnia, or her feelings of dissociation. When we then tried divalproex (Depakote), Andrea's emotional and behavioral states stabilized considerably, and her sleep improved. However, she continued to be troubled by restless dysphoria, and by an increasing frequency and intensity of urges to binge. We decided to add venlafexine to the divalproex, since, of the antidepressants that she had tried, venlafexine was the one about which Andrea felt the most positive. She found the antidepressant to help with her urges to binge, and with her restlessness as well as her dysphoria.

Andrea's symptoms and ability to function at work improved, and she began to work more. Since her work often entailed traveling, our appointment schedule became more erratic. The frequency with which Andrea called to cancel or to reschedule appointments increased, and she occasionally did so on the day of an appointment, even though she knew that she would then be charged for the appointment. She also seemed to me to be less engaged in the psychotherapy, more distant and self-contained. When I commented on the frequency of schedule changes and cancellations, Andrea replied that she was more busy with work because she was responding well to my treatment. She said that I should feel proud of how well she was doing, and she added that maybe I was upset by her cancellations because I had become dependent on her. After we explored what it might be like for her if I were dependent on her, I mentioned my sense that she seemed to me more distant and self-contained than she used to be. She looked surprised, and said that she had thought that I was the one who was more distant from her. I asked her when she thought that I had become more distant, and she responded that it was about three months earlier. When I then commented that we had begun to try antidepressants about three months earlier, Andrea burst into tears. We then explored what her tears were about. Andrea had not realized before how much she was troubled by the medications; or, more accurately, by any recommendation that she take medication. Outside of her awareness, she had interpreted my recommendation as indicating that I was irritated by her demands and repulsed by her neediness. She believed that I was giving her drugs in order to avoid closeness with her, in order "to buy (her) off" as a substitute for a relationship with me, since, she thought, no one would want to be involved with someone as needy and pathetic as she had become. Without being aware that she was doing so, Andrea then withdrew from me, partly to sustain the disavowal of her disappointment, rage, and envy, and partly to protect herself from the rejection that she both felt and anticipated. Further psychotherapeutic work indicated that Andrea had been struggling with an inner conflict between (1) her wish that I would magically relieve her suffering, and (2) her fear that I would see her suffering as an indication that she was defective and that I would then reject her. The ambiguous mixture of desperation and defiance that characterized Andrea's way of interacting with me facilitated her transformation of this inner conflict into an external conflict, between her and me: if I did not make her pain go away, then I was withholding; but if I did something to relieve her pain, such as prescribing medication, then I was exposing her defectiveness. Either option allowed her to avoid confronting her own inner struggle over her needs to be cared for.

The course of my psychotherapy with Andrea was stormy. Relatively early in treatment, Andrea developed an intense erotized transference to me. That her fantasies and urges were directed toward me enhanced the salience and the effectiveness of our psychodynamic psychotherapy, while decreasing the likelihood that Andrea would act out sexually in self-injurious ways. Meanwhile, the energy that was consequently channeled directly into the therapeutic relationship sometimes almost exceeded the holding capacity of the psychotherapy (and the psychotherapist). During the first few months of treatment, Andrea often called me between sessions, sometimes late at night, to tell me that she was agitated and suicidal. Twice she called me on her cellular phone from her car, which was at that time parked in her closed garage with its motor running. We found that some of our most productive sessions were those that followed these calls, in which we reviewed the events and feelings that Andrea had experienced before calling me, her fantasies about how I would respond, and how she felt during and after the call. Gradually, the character of Andrea's calls shifted: from desperate demands that I immediately relieve her distress, to tentative inquiries about whether I was available to her—whether she could reach me when she reached for me.

Later during the first year of treatment, Andrea began overtly to ask me to become sexually involved with her. She brought to bear a variety of arguments and approaches: she knew that a loving relationship would help her more than all this talk; she could tell by how I looked at her that I was attracted to her; our feelings of attraction were natural, healthy, and healing, she said, and to suppress them in favor of a Victorian, authoritarian morality was sick; I was doing this to her, I was making her fall in love with me so I could watch her squirm; and, finally, she hinted that if I did not become sexually involved with her, she would report me to the state board of medicine for sexual improprieties with a patient. Andrea could not experience being cared for in any way other than sexually, and she recognized only two basic possibilities in relationships: either be exploited, narcissistically or sexually, or be abandoned. She consequently interpreted my failure to engage sexually with her as an indication that I would abandon her. Moreover, she felt control to be the most critical dimension of a relationship, and she had become accustomed to using money and sex to make sure that she was in control. A relationship in which she could not control the other person filled her with a terror that threatened to overwhelm her. Four times during these months, Andrea went to bars in seedy parts of town and let herself be picked up by dangerous, degraded men. Exploration in psychotherapy of these incidents revealed Andrea's fantasy that I would rescue her from this danger and degradation by taking her home with me, and also her wish to punish me for rejecting her by hurting and degrading herself.

Toward the end of the first year, Andrea went through a period of about two weeks during which she was frankly paranoid. She became more agitated and anxious, and she developed a delusion that I was videotaping our sessions. At first, she believed that I was doing so defensively, in order to be able to prove my innocence to the board of medicine. Then, she reasoned that I was gathering sensitive information about her in order to deter her from suing me. On several occasions, she parked for hours across the street from my home. Andrea's agitation and anxiety responded to small doses of thiothixene (Navane). We eventually were able to understand that Andrea's paranoid episode had been triggered by an occasion when I forgot about a change in our appointment time for a particular day. At the time that Andrea called to request the change and I gave her another time, the computer on which I keep my appointment schedule was malfunctioning, and the schedule change did not get recorded. Not until fifteen minutes after the newly scheduled start time did I hear sounds in my waiting room and, on investigation, find Andrea sitting there. During the session that followed, Andrea denied having any strong feelings about my tardiness. (I made up the missed time at the end of this session and at the end of the following session.) She apologized for the frequency with which her work-related travel required her to change her appointment time, and she said that she was surprised that I did not "space out" on her more often. For the remainder of the session, Andrea was unusually subdued. Her paranoid episode began that evening. Our exploration indicated that my lapse had stirred up the mixture of terror, horror, and guilt that Andrea experienced as a child when her mother would "space out." The content of her delusion, that I was videotaping our sessions, derived from a variety of sources, including (1) Andrea's fantasy that I would want to hold onto her image between sessions as much as she wanted to hold onto mine, and (2) her discovery during her teens, which she had forgotten until we explored this episode, that her father had set up a concealed videocamera in his office bathroom.

Early in the second year of treatment, Andrea reported that she had started binge eating again, and that she was scared that she would completely lose control of her eating. Actually, she had binged sporadically during the first year, about once per month; but her urges to binge had recently increased in frequency and intensity, and she was now bingeing one or two days a week. She would then try to undo her binges by increasing her daily exercise while starving herself. The techniques of relapse prevention, which thus far did not have much of a role in helping Andrea to manage her sexual urges and behavior, were much more useful in helping her to manage her urges to binge. We now focused on the distressful inner states that, we inferred, were signaled by Andrea's urges to binge. In so doing, we came to understand how Andrea's bulimic behavior represented not only an attempt to fulfill many of the same functions that she had attempted to fulfill through sexual behavior, but also (1) a breakdown product of sexualization that had failed, and (2) a means of protecting her from the dangers to which the behavioral expression of sexualization exposed her. As we then explored how Andrea's binge–undo cycles alternated between self-gratification and self-punishment, neither of which required the participation of another person, we were able to see that Andrea's bulimic behavior simultaneously expressed both a denial of what she referred to as her "needy-greedies," and an attempt to satisfy them by herself, without depending on anyone else.

During the second and third years of treatment, Andrea's emotional and behavioral states became more and more stable.

Many psychodynamically important themes emerged, particularly in her relationship with me, and Andrea was able to work through them and integrate them into her newly developing sense of herself. Three successive dreams, which occurred approximately one year apart, provide a glimpse of Andrea's process during those years. Near the end of the first year of treatment, Andrea reported the following dream:

> Judith and I are running to escape from the Nazis, who have just overrun our house. We run, and we hide, and we run again. We are constantly in a state of extreme danger. Sometimes I feel like Judith is rescuing me, and sometimes I feel like I am rescuing her. Finally, when we are about to collapse from exhaustion, we come to a place that is safe. I start to relax. And then Judith reveals that she is one of them, a Nazi.

Judith was the psychologist who had initially referred Andrea to me. Andrea once mentioned that she felt intimidated by me, and she then described what she found to be intimidating about Judith. I hypothesized that Judith in this dream represented me, and Andrea's associations to the dream were consistent with that hypothesis. Andrea had just recently emerged from her paranoid episode, and she continued to have a great deal of difficulty trusting me. On one level, her dream suggested, Andrea was scared to trust me because she expected that I would turn out to be destructive, exploitative, and cruel, just like the people from whom I was pretending to rescue her. On another level, Andrea feared her own rage, her devouring neediness, and her envy, which she projected in her waking life and, in the dream, represented as the Nazis. She feared that this poison within her not only would destroy her but would destroy me as well, if she let me get close to her.

Toward the end of the second year, Andrea reported the following dream:

> I am traveling with a tour group in Egypt and we are attacked by a group of terrorists. Our guide gets shot, and I pick up his gun and start shooting at the terrorists. The next thing I am aware of

is lying on the ground. My head is in a bandage. I hear that all the terrorists are dead, and that I killed them. I am a hero, but I'm dying. The next thing I know, I am in a bed in a luxurious hotel. My head is still in a bandage, but I am not dying, I am recuperating. Someone is sitting in a chair next to me. I can't see who it is, but I think that it's a man.

This dream resembled a recurrent fantasy that Andrea experienced during her later childhood and early teens. After the dream, Andrea experienced strong urges to masturbate while hitting herself, as she used to masturbate in her teens after she stopped conjuring the recurrent fantasy. Andrea connected the dream with her treatment, and she guessed that the unidentified person in the chair next to her represented me. At that time in her psychotherapy, Andrea was struggling with her rage, her envy, and a core fantasy of being a martyr. This fantasy was associated with an underlying belief that if she sacrificed her life to save the other, then she would be truly loved. If she sacrificed her life, however, then she also would be dead. Andrea's fantasy resolved this paradox by having her be brought back to life through the love of the other. We could now recognize the connection between the Nazis in the first dream and the terrorists in the second dream, both of which represented projective manifestations of Andrea's internal dangers. The second dream reflected Andrea's sense of increasing mastery of her inner demons. It also indicated her split experience of me and of our relationship. On one hand, I was the hapless guide who was killed by Andrea's rage and envy (which were expressed projectively as the terrorists). On the other, I was the idealized unseen other who was sitting beside her and nursing her back to life.

Near the end of the third year of treatment, Andrea reported the following dream:

I am holding a baby. The baby's eyes are closed and she looks blissful. An older man looks pleased with me. He might be my father, or he might be the baby's father.

This dream prompted Andrea and I to explore her wishes and fears around the idea of having a child. We also looked at her childhood fantasy that her father would marry her, have a baby with her, and be pleased with her in a way that he did not seem to be pleased with Andrea's mother. We then considered what might have led Andrea to have the dream now. She recalled our preceding session, in which she had felt a particular sense of connection and comfort with me, and she wondered aloud whether her dream reflected a wish to have a baby with me. Then she laughed and said, "Now I get it. We *are* having a baby together. And I'm the baby!" She then talked about how, through our psychotherapeutic work, she had developed a feeling of being cared for: cared for not only by me but also by herself, since the psychotherapy also had helped her to develop the capacity to care for herself.

Toward the end of the second year of treatment, we were able to decrease Andrea's dosage of divalproex (Depakote). One year later, we tried to discontinue it and found that Andrea then became affectively unstable, impulsive, and unable to get to sleep at night. She stabilized again when she resumed taking divalproex (at the lower dose), in addition to her antidepressant.

At the present time, Andrea and I are in our fourth year of working together. Andrea has not had sex with a stranger for nearly two years. Her last eating binge occurred about six months ago (during the interval when we tried to discontinue the divalproex). She has dated a few men, but has not established a relationship. She now has a close female friend, for the first time that she can recall.

PHIL

History of Present Illness

Phil, a college dropout in his late twenties, had difficulty holding a job, though he was a capable computer programmer and a gifted musician. He had no close friends and spent much of his free time by himself, either working on his computer or playing his electric piano through headphones. Sometimes he would go to a casino, which he said that he did in order to be around other people. Phil had been involved in two brief relationships with women, both of whom he drove away by his demanding possessiveness and paranoid jealousy. He tended to develop obsessive crushes on women whom he hardly knew, and he would then feel driven to watch and to follow them. Complaints of harassment by female coworkers had led to his being fired from three jobs, and he was once arrested for stalking. Phil masturbated several times a day, even at work. At night, he sometimes called random telephone numbers until he found a woman who would answer his questions about her sex life while he masturbated. When he had an urge to masturbate and did not act on it, he experienced a disorganizing panic that would intensify until he felt that he was about to die. He found that he could not resist these urges, even when his job or legal trouble was at stake. The strongest urge that Phil experienced was to expose his penis to a woman and masturbate while she looked on in shock and fear. For this reason, he particularly liked to expose himself in elevators, when he and a woman were the only passengers. Even after two arrests, one conviction, and one occasion on which a woman's boyfriend beat him severely, Phil felt driven to continue riding elevators and hunting for unaccompanied women. One time, Phil targeted a woman who had once been raped, after which she vowed that she would never be victimized like that again. She carried a handgun, and when Phil turned toward her with his penis exposed, she panicked and shot him. He survived, thanks in part to the woman's immediate 911 call. Six months after being discharged from the hospital, he was arrested for exposing his penis to a woman in an elevator.

Personal History

Both of Phil's parents came from chaotic backgrounds and had dropped out of high school. At the time that they met, Phil's father was playing bass in a locally successful rock group, and his mother was a cocktail waitress and a part-time prostitute. They got married in the bar where she worked, divorced a year later, and started living together again after another three months. Phil had three older sisters, and he was the first boy to be born into his family. His mother once told him that she kept having children until she had a son. Phil's parents got married again while his mother was pregnant with him.

Phil spent the first two months of his life in the hospital. He did not know why, exactly, though he had been told that both he and his mother were sick, and that his mother had almost died. When they got home, Phil became the family pet. His sisters (who were six, seven, and nine years older than he) told him that, from the time that he first came home, they would carry him around the house and would take him along in a wagon when they went out to play. Their mother taught the girls to change Phil's diapers, and they enjoyed showing their friends what they had learned and pretending that he was their baby. Phil recalled that one of his sisters once told him how smart their mother was: she managed to avoid not only changing Phil's diapers, but also having to buy dolls for her daughters.

When Phil was 2 years old, his father was convicted of selling marijuana and went to prison for three years. For much of the ensuing year, Phil's mother had Phil sleep with her. Phil said that, although he had no specific recollections, he believed that his mother played with his penis and had him fondle her. When he was 3 years old, Phil contracted tubercular spinal meningitis. He was in a coma for two months and remained in strict isolation during his convalescence. While Phil was in the hospital he was put back in diapers, though he had already been toilet trained. He had very little memory of his time in the hospital, but he remembered that the only time that anyone would come close to him was to change his diapers.

Phil recalled that he longed to be released from the hospital so he could go home, where he had received (according to his memory) a lot of adoring attention. When he got home, however, he found a world that was totally different from the world that he had left. His sisters now avoided him and, he felt, treated him as though he were disgusting and repulsive. His mother, meanwhile, was impatient and harshly punitive with him. After his illness and several months in the hospital, Phil was physically weak and uncoordinated, and his verbal skills were impaired. He also had difficulty reestablishing urinary and fecal continence, and he was enuretic until his middle teens. Phil recalled that his mother would berate and humiliate him for his impairments, would call him "Ricky" (for "Ricky Retardo") instead of using his name, and would often drag, shove, or beat him. Sometimes, after a severe beating, she would take off Phil's clothes and hold him. Phil began to have fantasies of seeing his mother naked and of making her take her clothes off.

Phil reported that he had eagerly looked forward to his father's return home from prison, even though he remembered nothing of his father, because he believed that his mother would not be so mean to him if his father were around. After his release on parole, however, Phil's father rarely spent time at home. He had determined to turn his life around, and while he was in prison he completed his GED and took two years of courses in electronics and business. Once he was free, he set up a shop to design and install custom stereo systems in vehicles and boats, and he spent all of his time working. Phil said that his father never took him to the shop, where his father was the boss and apparently was well respected. Phil saw his father only at home, where he was "a wreck of a man" who would not stand up to Phil's mother. Phil recalled that his father would make his mother stop beating Phil only when he could no longer stand the noise.

When he was 5 years old, Phil began occasionally to change his clothes in places where the girls could see him. Once, when he was 7 or 8, a little girl offered herself to him sexually. However, it was a set-up. They went into her basement and when Phil had his clothes off, she ran away and her brothers threw firecrackers at him. Phil recalled a dream that he had recurrently during his childhood: "A woman in a shopping center freezes the world. She then takes off her clothes, and the world starts up again, after which everyone in the shopping center is running around scared."

Discussion

Phil had two childhoods. In the first, which ended when he was hospitalized for meningitis, he was the idolized but neglected pet of his mother and older sisters. His mother had very much wanted a son, but once he arrived she essentially ignored him and left him in the charge of her daughters. Phil's sisters were not abusive toward him, but neither were they maternal. When they felt like holding Phil, they held him. When he fussed, they gave him a bottle or changed his diaper. If neither of these options quieted him, they moved him far enough away that his crying would not bother them. Phil's sisters told him that he quickly learned to stop crying after getting a bottle and a fresh diaper. Apparently, Phil experienced a location beyond earshot to be significantly more aversive than empathic unresponsiveness and inadequate holding. Phil developed a keen sensitivity to sounds, which represented his only way of maintaining contact with others; and his sisters noticed that he would sometimes calm down and relax when he heard the voice of his middle sister, who was the most attentive to him.

Phil's mother told him that he slept with her when his father was in prison; his oldest sister recalled seeing both her mother and Phil naked in the bed; and his middle sister remembered that during the months before he became ill, Phil would often straddle her leg and try to put his hand in her panties. The hypothesis that Phil's mother sexually abused him during this time thus seems to be reasonable. Since Phil probably had suffered since birth from a dearth of both emotional sustenance and bodily contact, these sexualized interactions with his mother were likely to have had an unusually significant influence on his early development. He may have learned to draw on the sexual mode of relating with his mother to compensate for her relative unavailability and to stimulate her interest in him, identifying with her sexualization in order to preserve a link with her. Sexual feelings may have come to represent his substitute for caring, holding, and empathic connection.

Phil's stay in the hospital when he was 3 years old was probably the most traumatic period in his life. What he experienced as most traumatic was his extreme deprivation of emotional and physical contact, his sense that he was being pushed and poked like an inanimate object, and his powerlessness. The changings of his diapers, twice per shift in day or evening and once at night, were the highlights of his day for many days. Phil's experiences during this hospitalization combined with his experiences in his mother's bed and his earlier experience of his diaper changing being a public event among his sisters and their friends, to provide him with an amorphous sense of boundaries and a belief that his body was not really his own.

Phil's second childhood, like his first, began with his discharge from the hospital. When he returned home, his sisters avoided him and his mother berated, humiliated, and beat him for impairments over which he had no control. He felt overwhelmed by feelings of shame, loathesomeness, powerlessness, vulnerability, terror, rage, and horror. When his mother would hold him after a beating, he would go limp, but he was too afraid to relax. Though he experienced sexual feelings while being held, he did not move for fear that his mother would just beat him again. Guided by his prehospitalization history with his mother, Phil sexualized this fear and then gradually sexualized all of the other feelings that he was intensely experiencing in his relationship with his mother: shame, loathesomeness, powerlessness, vulnerability, terror, rage, and horror. His fantasies of seeing his mother naked and of making her take her clothes off represented his sexually sadistic wish to turn the tables on her and to make her suffer as he had suffered at her hands.

The recurrent dream of Phil's childhood ("A woman in a shopping center freezes the world. She then takes off her clothes, and the world starts up again, after which everyone in the shopping center is running around scared.") portrayed first of all Phil's unconscious fantasy about the omnipotence of his mother and of women in general. Freezing the world, in the dream, seemed to mean freezing Phil's inner world. His emotions were frozen, his representational world was lifeless, and he felt himself to exist in suspended animation. Phil's associations to the woman taking off her clothes in the dream suggested that this image represented a confluence of (1) Phil's sexually sadistic wish to make his mother take her clothes off and suffer as he had suffered, and (2) Phil's memories of the occasions prior to his hospitalization, when he and his mother would lie together naked, which were the only times that he ever felt warmth or interest from her. Phil stated that the world starting up again could not refer to a thawing of the frozen world, because his inner world had been frozen from the beginning, so "again" would not fit. Phil believed that the world starting up again referred to his hospitalization, when he was once again helpless, alone, and deprived of emotional and physical contact, and this time even more so than before. Running around scared afterwards then represented the terror and horror that filled his life after his return from the hospital. The shopping center in the dream stood for both Phil's family of origin and his inner world. The first thing that occurred to Phil's mind about "shopping center" was "a bunch of stores that face a parking lot with no connections between them."

Beginning with his father, Phil's history was replete with occasions of being abandoned by men. He searched desperately for a man who could fill the role of protecting him from his sadistic and horrifying maternal introject. After his father, Phil alienated every man who got close to him (other than those who were just exploiting him) with the same demanding possessiveness that drove away the two women with whom he was briefly involved. Though he did not identify himself as homosexual, he occasionally engaged in sadomasochistic sexual encounters with homosexual men who were female impersonators. In these encounters, he sometimes played the masochistic role, but more often he played the sadistic role.

Phil was a schizoid and paranoid man who often struggled with disorganizing panic, murderous rage, and fantasies of inflicting torture on women. His choice of exhibitionism reflected his wish to shock, to terrify, and to horrify women, thereby simultaneously getting revenge on his mother and acting out his identification with her. In addition, Phil's exhibitionism reflected his wish to avoid actual physical closeness with a living female body, which overwhelmed him with fear. Phil preferred to expose himself in elevators in which he and a woman were the only passengers, because the woman would then be trapped and helpless. In the process of evoking shock, terror, and horror in a woman, he could vicariously reexperience these feelings, which for him were highly sexualized, by identifying with his victim, while remaining in control. Phil's choice of exhibitionism may have been influenced also by his experience, both during his infancy and during his hospitalization, that the changing of his diapers was almost the only occasion when he received any attention or physical contact. When Phil masturbated by himself, he typically employed sadomasochistic fantasies or pornography. He did not require that the imagery be sexual, and sometimes he preferred that it not involve any genital contact. What Phil sought in his masturbatory imagery was domination, humiliation, pain, and horror.

Phil's addictive use of exhibitionism, intrusive sexual telephone harassment, and masturbation to sadomasochistic images thus served several interrelated functions, which included: (1) to alleviate feelings of loneliness, isolation, alienation, and deadness; (2) to relieve disorganizing panic (fragmentation anxiety) and to provide him with a sense of self-organization; (3) to maintain control of his body and his sexual needs, and thereby to counter feelings of powerlessness and fears that his body was being controlled by others; (4) to get revenge on his mother for how she had made him suffer; (5) to evoke fantasies of merger with his mother, both by recreating the range of feelings that he had felt with her and by identifying with her sadism; and at the same time (6) to avoid the paranoid, claustrophobic, and castration (mutilation) anxieties that would accompany close physical contact with a living female body.

Course of Treatment

When Phil was arrested, he was brought to the county jail. During his first night in jail, he tried to hang himself. He was then sent to the forensic unit of the county hospital. The psychiatrist who treated Phil during this hospitalization called me for a telephone consultation. On Phil's discharge from the hospital, the psychiatrist recommended to Phil that he see me for treatment when he was released from prison. After a relatively short stay in prison, Phil was selected for early parole, and he was transferred to a halfway house for sex offenders. His early parole was conditional on his attendance and successful completion of an intensive three-year outpatient treatment program for sex offenders, which was run by the state department of corrections. Another condition of his parole was that he be under the care of a psychiatrist, so he called me.

Establishing a sense of connection with Phil was difficult. His affect was flat and vacant, and he rarely spoke except to answer my questions. His clothing and hair were rumpled and unwashed, he was unshaven, and he smelled of old socks and tobacco. Phil told me that, had the correctional system not required him to obtain psychiatric treatment, he probably would not have called me. He did not care to change anything about himself, and he did not figure that anything I could do would make any difference. He also did not want to be locked up in any hospital. Phil presented himself as not really caring about anything. When I asked him about what had led him to try to hang himself in jail, he answered that he could think of no reason to go on living. I then asked him how he felt about living now, and he replied, "The same." Being with Phil felt oppressive to me. I experienced an overwhelming sense of emptiness and deadness, and I had little confidence that I would be able to help him. Yet, I guessed that he must have chosen to call me for some reason, beyond the requirement that he be in psychiatric treatment. And I suspected that the oppressive emptiness, deadness, and hopelessness that I experienced in Phil's presence represented, at least in part, a resonance with how Phil felt.

Shortly after the beginning of our initial session, Phil handed me a form that was entitled, "Treatment Plan," which he said I was supposed to fill out for his parole officer. I told him that we would fill out the form together. We spent the remainder of the session discussing how to fill out Phil's "Treatment Plan" form: in other words, we spent the rest of the session formulating Phil's treatment plan. The surprise, gratification, and mistrust that Phil experienced when he saw that I really intended the two of us to collaborate on filling out the form helped to distract him from recognizing that, through the partial identification with me that our collaboration fostered, he had imperceptibly shifted toward seeing himself as someone for whom treatment was appropriate.

During our treatment planning conference, I presented myself to Phil as his consultant. I would outline the range of treatment options that were available to us, I would describe the probable benefits and the potential disadvantages of each option, and I would then assist Phil in clarifying (1) his goals, what he personally wanted to result from this process of meeting with me, independent of whatever the parole officer might have wanted; and (2) his limitations. Phil would then be in a position to select the combination of treatment options that was most suitable to his own goals and limitations.

Phil acknowledged that he was lonely, that he was tired of the trouble that his exhibitionism had brought him, and that he wanted to get and to be able to hold onto a job that he liked. He noted also that he was often unable to fall asleep until three or four in the morning. Phil identified his primary limitation as financial, since he was still unemployed. He mentioned also that he was not comfortable with other people and preferred to do things by himself. However, he was open to considering his discomfort with other people not only as a constraint on treatment options, but also as an impairment that treatment would be intended to help him overcome. I encouraged Phil to tell me more about the trouble that his exhibitionism had brought him, partly to obtain more information about the nature and extent of his pathology, and partly also to induce Phil to expand on and to consolidate his dawning awareness that his sexual behavior had consequences that he did not want. After we discussed the various treatment options, Phil decided that he was interested in finding out what psychiatric medication could offer him, and that he would check out the support group Sex Addicts Anonymous (SAA). Although he was already involved in therapeutic groups through the sex offender treatment program, he appreciated that SAA offered some advantages that were not offered by the treatment groups: (1) support and helpful suggestions from others with similar difficulties who had tried various ways of handling their difficulties and had found some that worked for them; (2) an opportunity to develop a social network of peers in the community who would know his history and current struggles, and who would still accept him; and (3) an opportunity to develop an identity other than that of a criminal, and to identify with individuals who had similar difficulties and who defined their difficulties primarily as personally maladaptive, rather than as criminal. Phil's financial limitations prevented him from pursuing individual psychotherapy, and he said that he was not interested in that kind of treatment anyhow. We arranged to meet once per month for medication management.

Diagnostically, Phil seemed to be most accurately described as suffering from an empty dysthymia in the context of a schizotypal personality disorder. We found that he responded best to a combination of nefazodone (Serzone) and perphenazine (Trilafon). The perphenazine was particularly helpful in regulating Phil's sleep patterns, relieving the disorganizing anxiety that he had been experiencing when he did not masturbate, and modulating the intensity of his paranoid thoughts. The structure of the treatment program and the support of SAA enabled Phil to refrain from exposing himself. He did, however, continue to make intrusive sexual telephone calls, which he did not reveal to his case manager or his peers in the treatment program, nor to his peers in SAA, nor to me. During his fourth month of treatment, Phil was arrested for telephone harassment. His parole was not revoked, but he was sentenced to six months in the workhouse, of which four were suspended if he completed the three-year program without another arrest. Phil was humbled by the collapse of his delusion that, unlike his peers in the treatment program and in SAA, he could control his sexual behavior and could avoid harmful consequences. Meanwhile, he was heartened to find that the other members of both groups still accepted him. He had expected confrontation, criticism, and contempt; but his peers welcomed him back and seemed to be genuinely glad to see him again. Some even told him that, had they been the ones to slip, they did not know whether they would have had the courage to come back to the group. Phil did not recall having ever before experienced such a sense of being accepted and valued.

A few months after his release from the workhouse, Phil decided to look for steady work, instead of the temporary jobs that he obtained by showing up at the labor pool. He found a night job as a janitor, and after several months he changed to another night job, in the mailroom of the local public radio station. His assignment was to sort the mail, until one night when the mailroom computer crashed and Phil was able to get it running again. Gradually, other departments began to call on Phil to help with their computer problems, and he developed a reputation as an effective fixer. The management found out about Phil's computer ability, and offered him a job as an assistant programmer, with additional responsibilities as a troubleshooter. His self-esteem and self-confidence increased, as he was not only holding a job but advancing and being appreciated.

During these months, Phil's sexual behavior was in fairly good control. He was masturbating daily, usually two or three times per day, but he was not exposing, making lewd phone calls, or otherwise sexually intruding on anyone. Meanwhile, shortly after he was promoted to assistant programmer, Phil noticed that one of the other assistant programmers was an attractive young woman. From a distance, he became infatuated with her. He did not approach her, since he felt certain that she would reject him; but he watched her, whenever he thought that he could do so without being noticed. When this woman spoke to Phil, he would feel exposed as ugly and pathetic, and he would quickly withdraw. Yet, when another man talked with her, Phil would feel possessively jealous and disgusted with her. Phil began to believe that he and this woman had been destined to meet, and that his unorthodox promotion to the same position that she held was not just a coincidence. He began to leave anonymous love notes on her computer screen, and on Valentine's Day he sent her a dozen roses, anonymously. Phil's infatuation with this woman, however, had not escaped her notice. She was aware that she was being closely watched, and she suspected that Phil had left the notes on her computer. When she received the roses, she complained to their supervisor. The supervisor confronted Phil, and warned him that if he did not leave the woman alone, he would lose his job.

By this time, Phil had been seeing me for medication management for about two years. Although we had been meeting for only twenty minutes once a month, we had gradually developed a comfortable working relationship. Twenty minutes was sufficiently brief that Phil did not feel too threatened by intimacy or intrusion. Meanwhile, it was sufficiently long to enable him to tell me some of what was happening in his life, and also to find out, in bearable increments of risk, how I responded to his emotionally significant material. When his supervisor confronted and warned him, Phil experienced the same mixture of disappointment, disillusionment, desperation, rage, and shame that he had felt in similar situations in the past. This time, however, he was able to step back and to recognize that he had a problem, which, if unaddressed, would leave him marooned on the margins of functionality. Phil had begun to experience the rewards of effective functioning, and he was not ready to give them up. Moreover, he had heard enough from his peers in SAA and in his treatment program to realize that his obsessive infatuations were related to his sexual addiction problem, and that they were moreover unlikely to provide him with the intimacy and companionship that he sought. The day that Phil was confronted and warned by his supervisor, he called me, and we set an appointment for a full fifty-minute session. During this session, we reviewed Phil's treatment plan and considered how to proceed from there. Phil realized that he needed more help than he was getting from the medication and the groups, and he felt that he was now ready to address his inner world. In addition, Phil now had a steady job with a decent income, and he calculated that he could afford weekly psychotherapy by compromising in other areas that he believed to be ultimately less critical to his well-being. We arranged to begin psychotherapy on the following week.

Phil and I are now in our second month of meeting once a week. His situation at work has stabilized, though he feels humiliated, and he believes that others at work avoid him and see him as contemptible. Phil understands that his perception of others' responses to him is influenced by his projection of his own self-loathing, and that it also reflects his experience of his family's responses to him when he returned from the hospital after his bout with meningitis. He does not know, however, whether he can ever again feel comfortable working at the public radio station. In the meantime, he continues to work there. As far as the psychotherapy itself goes, Phil and I are still in a honeymoon phase. He idealizes me as the good father who has time for him, who guides him in his dealings with the external world, and who protects him from dangerous women. He is extraordinarily sensitive to signs that I might not be pleased with him, which lead to panic that I will abandon him. At the same time, Phil is quite guarded with me, and I often feel uncomfortable with his hypervigilance. I feel as though I am being overinterpreted, my responses make too much of a difference, and I cannot risk being spontaneous. Maybe my discomfort reflects a fear of his rage and sadism, which I sense will sooner or later be turned in my direction. Perhaps I am also empathically resonating with the anxiety that underlies Phil's guardedness, or even to some extent identifying with it: anxiety that derives partly from his childhood experience of his mother, and partly from fear about the destructive potential of his own aggressive energy. If I continue this line of thought, I realize that my anxiety might relate to concerns not only about Phil's rage and sadism, but also about my own. Working with individuals whose pathology involves primitive aspects of their characters inevitably brings me in touch with primitive aspects of my own character.

References

Abel, G. (1989), Paraphilias. In: *Comprehensive Textbook of Psychiatry*, 5th ed., ed. H. I. Kaplan & B. J. Sadock. Baltimore: Williams & Wilkins, pp. 1069–1085.

Abel, G. G., Lewis, D. J., & Clancy, J. (1970), Aversion therapy applied to taped sequences of deviant sexual behavior in exhibitionism and other sexual deviations: A preliminary report. *J. Behav. Ther. Exp. Psychiatry*, 1:59–66.

——— Osborn, C. (1992a), The paraphilias: The extent and nature of sexually deviant and criminal behavior. *Psychiatric Clin. N. Amer.*, 15:675–687.

——— ——— (1992b), Stopping sexual violence. *Psychiatric Annals*, 22:301–306.

——— Rouleau, J.-L. (1990), The nature and extent of sexual assault. In: *Handbook of Sexual Assault: Issues, Theories, and Treatment of the Offender*, ed. W. L. Marshall, D. R. Laws, & H. E. Barbaree. New York: Plenum Press, pp. 9–21.

Abraham, K. (1908), The psychological relation between sexuality and alcoholism. In: *Selected Papers of Karl Abraham*. New York: Basic Books, 1960, pp. 80–89.

Abrams, D. B., & Niaura, R. S. (1987), Social learning theory. In: *Psychological Theories of Drinking and Alcoholism*, ed. H. T. Blane & K. E. Leonard. New York: Guilford Press, pp. 131–178.

Adesso, V. J. (1985), Cognitive factors in alcohol and drug use. In: *Determinants of Substance Abuse Treatment: Biological, Psychological, and Environmental Factors,* ed. M. Galizio & S. A. Maisto. New York: Plenum Press, pp. 179–208.

Adson, P. R. (1992), Treatment of paraphilias and related disorders. *Psychiatric Annals,* 22:299–300.

Aghajanian, G. K., & Wang, R. Y. (1978), Physiology and pharmacology of central serotonergic neurons. In: *Psychopharmacology: A Generation of Progress,* ed. M. A. Lipton, A. DiMascio, & K. F. Killam. New York: Raven Press, pp. 171–183.

Agich, G. J. (1983), Disease and value: A rejection of the value-neutrality thesis. *Theor. Med.,* 4:27–41.

Agmo, A., & Berenfeld, R. (1990), Reinforcing properties of ejaculation in the male rat: Role of opioids and dopamine. *Behav. Neurosci.,* 104:177–182.

Akil, H., & Leibeskind, J. C. (1975), Monoaminergic mechanisms of stimulation produced analgesia. *Brain Res.,* 94:279–296.

Alford, G. S., Webster, J. S., & Sanders, S. H. (1980), Covert aversion of two interrelated sexual practices: Obscene phone calling and exhibitionism. A single case analysis. *Behav. Ther.,* 11:15–25.

American Psychiatric Association (1980), *Diagnostic and Statistical Manual of Mental Disorders,* 3rd ed. (DSM-III). Washington, DC: American Psychiatric Press.

———— (1987), Diagnostic and Statistical Manual of Mental Disorders, 3rd ed. rev. (DSM-III-R). Washington, DC: American Psychiatric Press.

———— (1994), *Diagnostic and Statistical Manual of Mental Disorders,* 4th ed. (DSM-IV). Washington, DC: American Psychiatric Press.

Amir, S., Brown, Z. W., & Amit, Z. (1980), The role of endorphins in stress: Evidence and speculations. *Neurosci. Behav. Rev.,* 4:77–86.

Anderson, N., & Coleman, E. (1990), Childhood abuse and family sexual attitudes in sexually compulsive males: A comparison of three clinical groups. *Amer. J. Prevent. Psychiatry Neurol.,* 3:8–15.

Anderson, W. P., Kunce, J. T., & Rich, B. (1979), Sex offenders: Three personality types. *J. Clin. Psychol.,* 35:671–676.

Anthony, D. T., & Hollander, E. (1993), Sexual compulsions. In: *Obsessive–Compulsive Related Disorders,* ed. E. Hollander. Washington, DC: American Psychiatric Association, pp. 139–150.

Armor, D. J., Polich, J. M., & Stambul, H. B. (1978), *Alcoholism and Treatment.* New York: Wiley.

Arnon, D., Kleinman, M. H., & Kissin, B. (1974), Psychological differentiation in heroin addicts. *Internat. J. Addict.,* 9:151–159.

Augustine Fellowship (1986), Suggestions for newcomers [pamphlet]. Boston: The Augustine Fellowship, Sex and Love Addicts Anonymous.

Baile, C. A., McLaughlin, C. L., & Della-Fera, M. A. (1986), Role of cholecystokinin and opioid peptides in control of food intake. *Physiol. Rev.*, 66:172–234.

Bak, R. C. (1953), Fetishism. *J. Amer. Psychoanal. Assn.*, 1:285–298.

––––– (1965), Aggression and perversion. In: *Perversions, Psychodynamics and Therapy*, ed. S. Lorand. London: Orto, pp. 231–240.

Baker, T. B., Morse, E., & Sherman, J. E. (1987), The motivation to use drugs: A psychobiological analysis of urges. In: *Nebraska Symposium on Motivation.* Vol. 34, ed. P. C. Rivers. Alcohol and Addictive Behavior. Lincoln, NE: University of Nebraska Press, pp. 257–323.

Balint, M. (1968), *The Basic Fault.* London: Tavistock Publications.

Ballenger, J. C., Goodwin, F. K., Major, L. F., & Brown, G. L. (1979), Alcohol and central serotonin metabolism in man. *Arch. Gen. Psychiatry*, 36:224–227.

Bancroft, J., Tennent, G., Loucas, K., & Cass, J. (1974), The control of deviant sexual behavior by drugs: Behavioural changes following estrogens and anti-androgens. *Brit. J. Psychiatry*, 125:310–315.

Bandura, A. (1970), *Principles of Behavior Modification.* New York: Holt, Rinehart & Winston.

––––– (1977a), *Social Learning Theory.* Englewood Cliffs, NJ: Prentice-Hall.

––––– (1977b), Self-efficacy: Toward a unifying theory of behavior change. *Psychol. Rev.*, 84:191–215.

––––– (1982), Self-efficacy mechanisms in human agency. *Amer. Psychol.*, 37:122–147.

Barlow, D. H., & Abel, G. G. (1976), Sexual deviation. In: *Behavior Modification: Principles, Issues and Applications,* ed. A. Kazdin, M. Mahoney, & E. Craighead. Boston: Houghton Mifflin, pp. 341–360.

Barnes, G. E. (1983), Clinical and prealcoholic personality characteristics. In: *The Biology of Alcoholism. Vol. 6, The Pathogenesis of Alcoholism: Psychosocial Factors,* ed. B. Kissin & H. Begleiter. New York: Plenum Press, pp. 113–195.

Baron, M., Gruen, R., Asnis, L., & Lord, S. (1985), Familial transmission of schizotypal and borderline personality disorders. *Amer. J. Psychiatry*, 142:927–934.

Barrett, R. J. (1985), Behavioral approaches to individual differences in substance abuse: Drug-taking behavior. In: *Determinants of Substance Abuse Treatment: Biological, Psychological, and Environmental Factors,* ed. M. Galizio & S. A. Maisto. New York: Plenum Press, pp. 125–175.

Barth, R. J., & Kinder, B. N. (1987), The mislabeling of sexual impulsivity. *J. Sex. Marital Ther.*, 13:15–23.

Bartova, D., Nahumek, K., & Svestke, J. (1978), Pharmacological treatment of deviant sexual behavior. *Activ. Nerv. Supp.* (Praha), 20:72–74.

Basch, M. F. (1976), The concept of affect: A re-examination. *J. Amer. Psychoanal. Assn.* 24:759–777.

Bateson, G. (1972), The cybernetics of "self": A theory of alcoholism. In: *Steps to an Ecology of Mind*, ed. G. Bateson. New York: Ballantine, pp. 309–337.

Batki, S. L., Manfredi, L. B., Sorensen, J. L., Jacob, P., Dumontet, R., & Jones, R. T. (1991), Fluoxetine for cocaine abuse in methadone patients: Preliminary findings. *NIDA Res. Monogr. Ser.*, 105:516–517.

Baxter, L. R., Schwartz, J. M., Bergman, K. S., Szuba, M. P., Guze, B. H., Mazziotta, J. C., Alazraki, A., Selin, C. E., Ferng, H. K., & Munford, P. (1992), Caudate glucose metabolic rate changes with both drug and behavior therapy for obsessive-compulsive disorder. *Arch. Gen. Psychiatry*, 49:681–689.

Bear, D. M. (1979), The temporal lobes: An approach to the study of organic behavioral changes. In: *Handbook of Behavioral Neurobiology*, Vol. 2, ed. M. S. Gazzaniga. New York: Plenum Press, pp. 75–95.

Beary, M. D., Lacey, J. H., & Merry, J. (1986), Alcoholism and eating disorders in women of fertile age. *Brit. J. Addict.*, 81:685–689.

Beaudet, A., & Descarries, L. (1976), Quantitative data on serotonin nerve terminals in adult rat neocortex. *Brain Res.*, 111:301–309.

Beck, A. T. (1967), *Depression: Clinical, Experimental and Theoretical Aspects.* New York: Harper & Row.

——— Rush, A. J., Shaw, B. F., & Emery, G. (1979), *Cognitive Therapy of Depression.* New York: Guilford Press.

Beres, D. (1958), Vicissitudes of superego functions and superego precursors in childhood. *The Psychoanalytic Study of the Child*, 13:324–351. New York: International Universities Press.

Bergler, E. (1936), On the psychology of the gambler. *Amer. Imago*, 22:409–441.

——— (1943), The gambler: A misunderstood neurotic. *J. Crim. Psychopath.*, 4:379–393.

——— (1946), Personality traits of alcohol addicts. *Quart. J. Stud. Alc.*, 7:356.

——— (1958), *The Psychology of Gambling.* New York: International Universities Press.

Berlin, F. S. (1983), Sex offenders: A biomedical perspective and a status report on biomedical treatment. In: *The Sexual Aggressor: Current*

Perspectives on Treatment, ed. J. G. Greer & I. R. Stuart. New York: Van Nostrand Reinhold, pp. 83–123.

——— Meinecke, C. F. (1981), Treatment of sex offenders with antiandrogenic medications: Conceptualization, review of treatment modalities, and preliminary findings. *Amer. J. Psychiatry*, 138:601–607.

Berzins, J. I., Ross, W. F., English, G. E., & Haley, J. V. (1974), Subgroups among opiate addicts: A typological investigation. *J. Abnorm. Psychol.*, 83:65–73.

Besnard, F., Kempf, E., Fuhrmann, G., Kempf, J., & Ebel, A. (1986), Influence of mouse genotype on responses of central biogenic amines to alcohol intoxication and aging. *Alcohol,* 3:345–350.

Bianchi, M. D. (1990), Fluoxetine treatment of exhibitionism [letter]. *Amer. J. Psychiatry*, 147:1089–1090.

Bion, W. R. (1962), *Learning from Experience.* London: Heinemann.

Birk, L., Huddleston, W., Miller, E., & Cohler, B. (1971), Avoidance conditioning in homosexuality. *Arch. Gen. Psychiatry*, 25:314–323.

Blair, C. D., & Lanyon, R. I. (1981), Exhibitionism: Etiology and treatment. *Psychol. Bull.*, 89:439–463.

Blanchard, G. (1990), Differential diagnosis of sex offenders: Distinguishing characteristics of the sex addict. *Amer. J. Prevent. Psychiatry Neurol.*, 2:45–47.

Blane, H. T. (1968), *The Personality of the Alcoholic: Guises of Dependency.* New York: Harper & Row.

Blashfield, R. K., & Draguns, J. G. (1976), Evaluative criteria for psychiatric classification. *J. Abnorm. Psychol.*, 85:140–150.

Blaszczynski, A., & McConaghy, N. (1989), Anxiety and / or depression in the pathogenesis of pathological gambling. *Internat. J. Addict.*, 24:337–350.

——— McConaghy, N., & Frankova, A. (1989), Crime, antisocial personality, and pathological gambling. *J. Gambling Behav.*, 5:137–152.

——— Wilson, A., & McConaghy, N. (1986), Sensation seeking and pathological gambling. *Brit. J. Addict.*, 81:113–117.

——— Winter, S. W., & McConaghy, N. (1986), Plasma endorphin levels in pathological gambling. *J. Gambling Behav.*, 2:3–15.

Blatt, S. J., Rounsaville, B., Eyre, S. L., & Wilber, C. (1984), The psychodynamics of opiate addiction. *J. Nerv. Ment. Dis.*, 172:342–352.

Block, J., Block, J. H., & Keyes, S. (1988), Longitudinally foretelling drug usage in adolescence: Early childhood personality and environmental precursors. *Child Dev.*, 59:336–355.

Blume, S. B. (1987), Compulsive gambling and the medical model. *J. Gambling Behav.*, 3:237–247.

Blumer, D. (1970), Changes in sexual behavior related to temporal lobe disorders in man. *J. Sex. Res.*, 6:173–180.

Blundell, J. E. (1984), Serotonin and appetite. *Neuropharmacology*, 23:1537–1552.

—— (1992), Serotonin and the biology of feeding. *Amer. J. Clin. Nutrition*, 55(suppl):1555–1595.

Bolen, D. W., & Boyd, W. H. (1968), Gambling and the gambler: A review and preliminary findings. *Arch. Gen. Psychiatry*, 18:617–630.

Booth, D. A. (1978), Mind-brain puzzle versus mind-physical world-identity. *Behav. Brain Sci.*, 3:348–349.

Bradford, J. M. (1988), Organic treatment for the male sexual offender. *Ann. NY Acad. Sci.*, 528:193–202.

—— (1990), The antiandrogen and hormonal treatment of sexual offenders. In: *Handbook of Sexual Assault: Issues, Theories and Treatment of the Offender*, ed. W. L. Marshall, D. R. Laws, & H. E. Barbaree. New York: Plenum Press, pp. 297–310.

—— Gratzer, T. G. (1995), A treatment for impulse control disorders and paraphilia: A case report. *Can. J. Psychiatry*, 40:4–5.

—— Pawlak, A. (1993a), The effects of cyproterone acetate in the treatment of the paraphilias. *Arch. Sex. Behav.*, 22:383–402.

—— —— (1993b), The effects of cyproterone acetate on the sexual arousal patterns of pedophiles. *Arch. Sex. Behav.*, 22:629–641.

Breitner, I. E. (1973), Psychiatric problems of promiscuity. *South. Med. J.*, 66:334–336.

Brickman, A. S. (1983), Preoedipal development of the superego. *Internat. J. Psycho-Anal.*, 64:83–92.

Brill, A. A. (1922), Tobacco and the individual. *Internat. J. Psycho-Anal.*, 3:430–444.

Brook, J. S., Lukoff, I. F., & Whiteman, M. (1980), Initiation into adolescent marijuana use. *J. Genet. Psychol.*, 137:133–142.

—— Whiteman, M., Gordon, A. S., & Cohen, P. (1986), Dynamics of childhood and adolescent personality traits and adolescent drug use. *Dev. Psychol.*, 22:403–414.

Brown, R., & Williams, R. (1975), Internal and external cues relating to fluid intake in obese and alcoholic persons. *J. Abnorm. Psychol.*, 84:660–665.

Brown, R. I. F. (1987), Gambling addictions, arousal, and an affective/decision-making explanation of behavioral reversions or relapses. *Internat. J. Addict.*, 22:1053–1067.

Brown, S. (1985), *Treating the Alcoholic: A Developmental Model of Recovery*. New York: Wiley.

Brownell, K. D., Hayes, S. C., & Barlow, D. H. (1977), Patterns of appropriate and deviant sexual arousal: The behavioral treatment of multiple sexual deviations. *J. Consult. Clin. Psychol.*, 45:1144–1155.

―――― Marlatt, G. A., Lichtenstein, E., & Wilson, G. T. (1986), Understanding and preventing relapse. *Amer. Psychol.*, 41:765–782.

Bulik, C. M. (1987), Drug and alcohol abuse by bulimic women and their families. *Amer. J. Psychiatry*, 144:1604–1606.

Burke, H. R., & Marcus, R. (1977), MacAndrew MMPI alcoholism scale: Alcoholism and drug addictiveness. *J. Psychol.*, 96:141–148.

Buss, A. H., & Plomin, R. (1984), *Temperament: Early Developing Personality Traits.* Hillsdale, NJ: Erlbaum.

Cadoret, R. J., Cain, C. A., & Crowe, R. R. (1983), Evidence for gene-environment interaction in development of adolescent antisocial behavior. *Behav. Genetics*, 13:301–310.

―――― Troughton, E., Bagford, J., & Woodworth, G. (1990), Genetic and environmental factors in adoptee antisocial personality. *Eur. Arch. Psychiatr. Neurol. Sci.*, 239:231–240.

Callahan, E. J., & Leitenberg, H. (1973), Aversion therapy for sexual deviation: Contingent shock and covert sensitization. *J. Abnorm. Psychol.*, 81:60–73.

Campos, J. J., Campos. R. G., & Barrett K. C. (1989). Emergent themes in the study of emotional development and emotional regulation. *Dev. Psychol.*, 25:394–402.

Camus, A. (1955), The myth of Sisyphus. In: *The Myth of Sisyphus and Other Essays,* tr. J. O'Brien. New York: Vintage International, 1991, pp. 1–138.

Carey, C. H., & McGrath, R. J. (1989), Coping with urges and craving. In: *Relapse Prevention with Sex Offenders,* ed. D. R. Laws. New York: Guilford Press, pp. 188–196.

Carlton, P. L., Manowitz, P., McBride, H., Nora, R., Swartzburg, M., & Goldstein, L. (1987), Attention deficit disorder and pathological gambling. *J. Clin. Psychiatry*, 48:487–488.

Carnes, P. (1983), *Out of the Shadows: Understanding Sexual Addiction.* Minneapolis: CompCare.

―――― (1989), *Contrary to Love: Helping the Sexual Addict.* Minneapolis: CompCare

Casals-Ariet, C., & Cullen, K. (1993), Exhibitionism treated with clomipramine [letter]. *Amer. J. Psychiatry*, 150:1273–1274.

Ceasar, M. A. (1988), Anorexia nervosa and bulimia: An integrated approach to understanding and treatment. In: *Bulimia: Psychoanalytic Treatment and Theory,* ed. H. J. Schwartz. Madison, CT: International Universities Press, pp. 111–125.

Cesnik, J. A., & Coleman, E. (1989), Use of lithium carbonate in the treatment of autoerotic asphyxia. *Amer. J. Psychother.*, 63:277–286.

Chalkley, A. J., & Powell, G. E. (1983), The clinical description of forty-eight cases of sexual fetishism. *Brit. J. Psychiatry*, 142:292–295.

Chan-Palay, V. (1977), *Cerebellar Dentate Nucleus: Organization, Cytology and Transmitters.* Berlin: Springer-Verlag.

Chase, J. L., Salzberg, H. C., & Palotai, A. M. (1984), Controlled drinking revisited: A review. *Prog. Behav. Modif.*, 18:43–84.

Chasseguet-Smirgel, J. (1974), Perversion, idealization and sublimation. *Internat. J. Psycho-Anal.*, 55:349–357.

—— (1981), Loss of reality in perversions—with special reference to fetishism. *J. Amer. Psychoanal. Assn.*, 29:511–534.

Chess, S., & Thomas, A. (1986), *Temperament in Clinical Practice.* New York: Guilford Press.

Chessick, R. D. (1985), Clinical notes toward the understanding and intensive psychotherapy of adult eating disorders. *Ann. Psychoanal.*, 22/23:301–322.

Childress, A. R., Ehrman, R., Rohsenow, D. J., Robbins, S. J., & O'Brien, C. P. (1992), Classically conditioned factors in drug dependence. In: *Substance Abuse: A Comprehensive Textbook*, ed. J. H. Lowinson, P. Ruiz, R. B. Millman, & J. G. Langrod. Baltimore: Williams & Wilkins, pp. 56–69.

—— McLellan, A. T., Natale, M., & O'Brien, C. P. (1987), Mood states can elicit conditioned withdrawal and craving in opiate abuse patients. In: *Problems of Drug Dependence, 1986: Proceedings of the 48th Annual Scientific Meeting, The Committee on Problems of Drug Dependence, Inc., NIDA Research Monograph 76*, ed. L. S. Harris. Rockville, MD: National Institute of Drug Abuse.

—— —— O'Brien, C. P. (1986), Abstinent opiate abusers exhibit conditioned craving, conditioned withdrawal, and reduction in both through extinction. *Brit. J. Addict.*, 81:701–706.

Ciarrocchi, J. W., Kirschner, N. M., & Fallik, F. (1991), Personality dimensions of male pathological gamblers, alcoholics, and dually addicted gamblers. *J. Gambling Stud.*, 7:133–141.

Clayton, A. H. (1993), Fetishism and clomipramine [letter]. *Amer. J. Psychiatry*, 150:4.

Cloninger, C. R. (1987), Neurogenetic adaptive mechanisms in alcoholism. *Science*, 236:410–416.

Coccaro, E. F., Siever, L. J., Klar, H. M., Maurer, G., Cochrane, K., Cooper, T. B., Mohs, R. C., & Davis, K. L. (1989), Serotonergic studies in patients with affective and personality disorders. *Arch. Gen. Psychiatry*, 46:587–599.

Coen, S. J. (1981), Sexualization as a predominant mode of defense. *J. Amer. Psychoanal. Assn.*, 29:893–920.

Coleman, E. (1986), Sexual compulsion vs. sexual addiction: The debate continues. *SIECUS Report* 1986, pp. 7–11.

—— (1987), Sexual compulsivity: Definition, etiology and treatment considerations. In: *Chemical Dependency and Intimacy Dysfunction*, ed. E. Coleman. New York: Haworth Press, pp. 189–204.

—— (1992), Is your patient suffering from compulsive sexual behavior? *Psychiatric Ann.*, 22:320–325.

Conger, J. J. (1956), Reinforcement theory and the dynamics of alcoholism. *Quart. J. Stud. Alcohol,* 17:296–305.

Cooper, A. J. (1981), A placebo-controlled trial of antiandrogen cyproterone acetate in deviant hypersexuality. *Compr. Psychiatry,* 22:458–465.

—— (1986), Progesterones in the treatment of sex offenders: A review. *Can. J. Psychiatry,* 31:73–79.

Cooper, M. L., Russell, M., & George, W. H. (1988), Coping, expectancies, and alcohol abuse: A test of social learning formulations. *J. Abnorm. Psychol.,* 97:218–230.

Cordoba, O. A., & Chapel, J. L. (1983), Medroxyprogesterone acetate antiandrogen treatment of hypersexuality in a paedophilic sex offender. *Amer. J. Psychiatry,* 140:1036–1039.

Cox, M. (1979), Dynamic psychotherapy with sex offenders. In: *Sexual Deviation,* 2nd ed., ed. I. Rosen. London: Oxford University Press, pp. 306–350.

Cox, W. M., & Klinger, E. (1988), A motivational model of alcohol use. *J. Abnorm. Psychol.,* 97:168–180.

Cummings, C., Gordon, J., & Marlatt, G. A. (1980), Relapse: Strategies of prevention and prediction. In: *The Addictive Behaviors,* ed. W. R. Miller. London: Pergamon Press, pp. 291–321.

Daley, D. C. (1989), A psychoeducational approach to relapse prevention. *J. Chem. Dep. Treat.,* 2:105–123.

DeJong, A. J., van den Brink, W., Harteveld, F. M., & van der Wielen, E. G. M. (1993), Personality disorders in alcoholics and drug addicts. *Compr. Psychiatry,* 34:87–94.

Dell, L. J., Ruzicka, M. F., & Palisi, A. T. (1981), Personality and other factors associated with gambling addiction. *Internat. J. Addict.,* 16:149–156.

Dewhurst, K., Oliver, J. E., & McNight, A. L. (1970), Sociopsychiatric consequences of Huntington's disease. *Brit. J. Psychiatry,* 116:255–258.

Di Chiara, G., & Imperato, A. (1988), Drugs abused by humans preferentially increase synaptic dopamine concentrations in the mesolimbic system of freely moving rats. *Proc. Nat. Acad. Sci. USA*, 85:5274–5278.

Docherty, J. P. (1984), Implications of the technological model of psychotherapy. In: *Psychotherapy Research: Where Are We and Where Should We Go?* ed. J. B. W. Williams & R. L. Spitzer. New York: Guilford Press, pp. 139–147.

Dodes, L. M. (1990), Addiction, helplessness, and narcissistic rage. *Psychoanal. Quart.*, 59:398–419.

———— (1995), Psychic helplessness and the psychology of addiction. In: *The Psychology and Treatment of Addictive Behavior*, ed. S. Dowling. Madison, CT: International Universities Press, pp. 133–145.

———— (1996), Compulsion and addiction. *J. Amer. Psychoanal. Assn.*, 44:815–835.

Dum, J., Gramsch, C., & Herz, A. (1983), Activation of hypothalamic b-endorphin pools by reward induced by highly palatable food. *Pharmacol. Biochem. Behav.*, 18:443–447.

Dunwiddie, T. V., & Brodie, M. S. (1993), Cellular mechanisms of cocaine action: Effects of brain slice preparations. In: *Biological Basis of Substance Abuse*, ed. S. G. Korenman & J. D. Barchas. New York: Oxford Press, pp. 153–163.

Dwyer, S. M., & Myers, S. (1990), Sex offender treatment: A six-month to ten-year follow-up study. *Ann. Sex Res.*, 3:305–318.

Earls, C. M., & Castonguay, L. G. (1989), The treatment of a bisexual pedophile using olfactory aversion: A single case experimental design with a multiple baseline across behaviors. *Behav. Ther.*, 20:137–146.

Eber, M. (1981), Don Juanism: A disorder of the self. *Bull. Menninger Clinic*, 45:307–316.

Edelman, G. M. (1987), *Neural Darwinism: The Theory of Neuronal Group Selection.* New York: Basic Books.

Edelstein, C. K., Yager, J., Gitlin, M., & Landsverk, J. (1989), A clinical study of anti-depressant medications in the treatment of bulimia. *Psychiatric Med.*, 7:111–121.

Edwards, G., Arif, A., & Hodgson, R. (1981), Nomenclature and classification of drug- and alcohol-related problems: A WHO memorandum. *Bull. WHO*, 59:225–242.

Eisenstein, V. W. (1956), Sexual problems in marriage. In: *Neurotic Interaction in Marriage.* New York: Basic Books, pp. 101–124.

Elkin, I., Pilkonis, P. A., Docherty, J. P., & Sotsky, S. M. (1988), Conceptual and methodological issues in comparative studies of psychotherapy and pharmacotherapy, I: Active ingredients and mechanisms of change. *Amer. J. Psychiatry*, 145:909–917.

Emde, R. (1983), The prerepresentational self and its affective core. *The Psychoanalytic Study of the Child*, 38:165–192. New Haven, CT: Yale University Press.

———— (1988), Development terminable and interminable: I. Innate and motivational factors from infancy. *Internat. J. Psycho-Anal.*, 69:23–42.

Emmanuel, N. P., Lydiard, R. B., & Ballenger, J. C. (1991), Fluoxetine treatment of voyeurism [letter]. *Amer. J. Psychiatry*, 148:950.

Epstein, A. W. (1960), Fetishism: A study of its psychopathology with particular reference to a proposed disorder in brain mechanism as an etiological factor. *J. Nerv. Ment. Dis.*, 130:107–119.

———— (1961), Relationship of fetishism and transvestism to brain and particularly to temporal lobe dysfunction. *J. Nerv. Ment. Dis.*, 133:247–253.

Erickson, T. R. (1945), Erotomania (nymphomania) as an expression of cortical epileptiform discharge. *Arch. Neurol. Psychiat.*, 53:226–231.

Evans, D. R. (1968), Masturbatory fantasy and sexual deviation. *Behav. Res. Ther.*, 6:17–19.

———— (1970), Subjective variables and treatment effects in aversion therapy. *Behav. Res. Ther.*, 8:147–152.

Eyre, S. L., Rounsaville, B. J., & Kleber, H. D. (1982), History of childhood hyperactivity in a clinic population of opiate addicts. *J. Nerv. Ment. Dis.*, 170:522–529.

Eyres, A. (1960), Transvestism: Employment of somatic therapy with subsequent improvement. *Dis. Nerv. Syst.*, 1:52–53.

Eyzaguirre, C., & Fidone, S. J. (1975), *Physiology of the Nervous System*, 2nd ed. Chicago: Year Book.

Fadda, F., Colombo, G., & Gessa, G. L. (1991), Genetic sensitivity to effect of ethanol on dopaminergic system in alcohol preferring rats. *Alc. Alcoholism* (suppl):439–442.

Fagan, P. J., Wise, T. N., Derogatis, L. R., & Schmidt, C. W. (1988), Distressed transvestites: Psychometric characteristics. *J. Nerv. Ment. Dis.*, 176:626–632.

———— ———— Schmidt, C. W., Ponticas, Y., & Marshall, R. D. (1991), A comparison of five-factor personality dimensions in males with sexual dysfunction and males with paraphilia. *J. Pers. Assess.*, 57:434–448.

Federoff, J. P. (1988), Buspirone hydrochloride in the treatment of transvestic fetishism. *J. Clin. Psychiatry,* 49:408–409.

Feigl, H. (1967), *The "Mental" and the "Physical."* Minneapolis: University of Minnesota, Minneapolis.

——— (1981), *Inquiries and Provocation.* Dordrecht, Holland: D. Reidel.

Feldman, M. P., & MacCulloch, M. J. (1968), The aversion therapy treatment of a heterogeneous group of five cases of sexual deviation. *Acta Psychiatrica Scand.,* 44:113–123.

Fenichel, O. (1945a), *The Psychoanalytic Theory of Neurosis.* New York: W. W. Norton.

——— (1945b), Neurotic acting out. *Psychoanal. Rev.,* 32:197–206.

Fernstrom, J. D., & Wurtman, R. J. (1977), Brain monoamines and reproductive physiology. In: *Reproductive Physiology,* Vol. 2, ed. R. O. Greep. Baltimore: University Park Press, pp. 23–56.

Ferrioli, M., & Ciminero, A. R. (1985), The treatment of pathological gambling as an addictive behavior. In: *Proceedings of the Fifth National Conference on Gambling and Risk Taking,* ed. W. R. Eadington. University of Nevada: Bureau of Business and Economic Research.

Field, L. H. (1973), Benperidol in the treatment of sexual offenders. *Lancet,* 1:1006–1007.

Flor-Henry, P., Koles, Z. L., Reddon, J. R., & Baker, L. (1986), Neuropsychological studies (EEG) of exhibitionism. In: *Brain Electrical Potentials and Psychopathology,* ed. M. C. Shagrasi, R. C. Josiassen, & R. A. Roemer. Amsterdam: Elsevier, pp. 279–306.

——— Lang, R. (1988), Quantitative EEG analysis in genital exhibitionists. *Ann. Sex. Res.,* 1:49–62.

Fluoxetine Bulimia Nervosa Collaborative Study Group (1992), Fluoxetine in the treatment of bulimia nervosa. A multicenter, placebo-controlled, double-blind trial. *Arch. Gen. Psychiatry,* 49:130–147.

Fookes, B. H. (1969), Some experience in the use of aversion therapy in male homosexuality, exhibitionism, and fetishism-transvestism. *Brit. J. Psychiatry,* 115:339–341.

Foy, D. W., Nunn, L. B., & Rychtarik, R. G. (1984), Broad-spectrum behavioral treatment for chronic alcoholics: Effects of training controlled drinking skills. *J. Clin. Consult. Psychol.,* 2:218–230.

Freud, A. (1937), *The Ego and the Mechanisms of Defense.* New York: International Universities Press, 1966.

Freud, S. (1892–1899), Extracts from the Fleiss papers (Letter 79, dated Vienna, December 22, 1897). *Standard Edition,* 1:173–280. London: Hogarth Press, 1950.

——— (1905), Three Essays on the Theory of Sexuality. *Standard Edition,* 7:123–243. London: Hogarth Press, 1953.

———— (1908), On the sexual theories of children. *Standard Edition,* 9:205–226. London: Hogarth Press, 1953.

———— (1920), The psychogenesis of a case of homosexuality in a woman. *Standard Edition,* 18:145–172. London: Hogarth Press, 1955.

———— (1923), The Ego and the Id. *Standard Edition,* 19:1–59. London: Hogarth Press, 1961.

———— (1927), Fetishism. *Standard Edition,* 21:147–157. London: Hogarth Press, 1961.

———— (1928), Dostoevsky and parricide. *Standard Edition,* 21:173–194. London: Hogarth Press, 1961.

———— (1940), Splitting of the ego in the process of defence. *Standard Edition,* 23:271–278. London: Hogarth Press, 1964.

Freund, K. (1980), Therapeutic sex drive reduction. *Acta Psychiatr. Scand.,* 287(suppl.):5–38.

Furer, M. (1967), Some developmental aspects of the superego. *Internat. J. Psycho-Anal.,* 48:277–280.

Gabbard, G. (1994), Paraphilias and sexual dysfunctions. In: *Psychodynamic Psychiatry in Clinical Practice.* Washington, DC: American Psychiatric Press, pp. 327–357.

Gagne, P. (1981), Treatment of sex offenders with medroxyprogesterone acetate. *Amer. J. Psychiatry,* 138:644–646.

Galdston, I. (1951), The psychodynamics of the triad: Alcoholism, gambling, and superstition. *Ment. Hyg.,* 35:589–598.

———— (1960), The gambler and his love. *Amer. J. Psychiatry,* 117:553–555.

Ganzarain, R., & Buchele, B. J. (1990), Incest perpetrators in group therapy: A psychodynamic perspective. *Bull. Menninger Clin.,* 54:295–310.

Gartner, A. F., Marcus, R. N., Halmi, K., & Loranger, A. W. (1987), DSM-III-R personality disorders in patients with eating disorders. *Amer. J. Psychiatry,* 144:1283–1287.

Gawin, F. H., Kleber, H. D., Byck, R., Rounsaville, B. J., Kosten, T. R., Jatlow, P. I., & Morgan, C. (1989), Desipramine facilitation of initial cocaine abstinence. *Arch. Gen. Psychiatry,* 46:117–121.

Geha, R. (1970), Dostoevsky and "The Gambler": A contribution to the psychogenics of gambling. Part II. *Psychoanal. Rev.,* 57:289–302.

Geist, R. A. (1989), Self psychological reflections on the origins of eating disorders. *J. Amer. Acad. Psychoanal.,* 17:5–27.

Gelder, M. (1979), Behavior therapy for sexual deviations. In: *Sexual Deviation,* 2nd ed., ed. I. Rosen. Oxford: Oxford University Press, pp. 351–375.

George, W. H. (1989), Marlatt and Gordon's relapse prevention model: A cognitive–behavioral approach to understanding and preventing relapse. *J. Chem. Dep. Treat.*, 2:125–152.

—— Marlatt, G. A. (1989), Introduction. In: *Relapse Prevention with Sex Offenders.* ed. D. R. Laws. New York: Guilford Press, pp. 1–32.

Gilby, R., Wolf, L., & Goldberg, B. (1989), Mentally retarded adolescent sex offenders: A survey and pilot study. *Can. J. Psychiatry*, 34:452–458.

Gillespie, W. H. (1952), Notes on the analysis of sexual perversions. *Internat. J. Psycho-Anal.*, 33:397–402.

Ginsberg, I. J., & Greenley, J. R. (1978), Competing theories of marijuana use: A longitudinal study. *J. Health Soc. Behav.*, 19:22–34.

Glasser, M. (1978), The role of the superego in exhibitionism. *Internat. J. Psychoanal. Psychother.*, 7:333–353.

—— (1979), Some aspects of the role of aggression in the perversions. In: *Sexual Deviation*, 2nd ed., ed. I. Rosen. Oxford: Oxford University Press, pp. 278–305.

—— (1986), Identification and its vicissitudes as observed in the perversions. *Internat. J. Psycho-Anal.*, 67:9–17.

Glen, A. M. (1979), Personality research on pathological gamblers. Paper presented at the 87th Annual Convention of the American Psychological Association, New York.

Globus, G. G. (1973), Consciousness and brain: I. The identity thesis. *Arch. Gen. Psychiatry*, 29:153–160.

Glover, E. (1932), On the aetiology of drug addiction. *Internat. J. Psycho-Anal.*, 13:298–328.

—— (1940–1959), The problem of male homosexuality. In: *The Roots of Crime.* New York: International Universities Press, 1960, pp. 197–243.

—— (1964), Aggression and sado-masochism. In: *Pathology and Treatment of Sexual Deviation: A Methodological Approach,* ed. I. Rosen. London: Oxford University Press, pp. 146–162.

Gold, P. W., Goodwin, F. K., & Chrousos, G. P. (1988a), Clinical and biochemical manifestations of depression: Relation to the neurobiology of stress (first of two parts). *New Eng. J. Med.*, 319:348–353.

—— —— —— (1988b), Clinical and biochemical manifestations of depression: Relation to the neurobiology of stress (second of two parts). *New Eng. J. Med.*, 319:413–420.

Goldberg, A. (1975), A fresh look at perverse behavior. *Internat. J. Psycho-Anal.*, 56:335–342.

—— (1995), *The Problem of Perversion: The View from Self Psychology.* New Haven, CT: Yale University Press.

Goldsmith, H. H. (1983), Genetic influences on personality from infancy to adulthood. *Child Dev.*, 54:331–355.

Goldstein, A. (1989), Introduction. In: *Molecular and Cellular Aspects of the Drug Addictions*, ed. A. Goldstein. New York: Springer Verlag.

Goldstein, J. W., & Sappington, J. T. (1977), Personality characteristics of students who became heavy drug users: An MMPI study of an avant-garde. *Amer. J. Drug Alc. Abuse*, 4:401–412.

Goldstein, S. G., & Linden, J. D. (1969), Multivariate classification of alcoholics by means of the MMPI. *J. Abnorm. Psychol.*, 79:121–131.

Goodman, A. (1990), Addiction: Definition and implications. *Brit. J. Addict.*, 85:1403–1408.

—— (1991), Organic unity theory: The mind-body problem revisited. *Amer. J. Psychiatry*, 148:553–563.

—— (1992), Sexual addiction: Designation and treatment. *J. Sex. Marital Ther.*, 18:303–314.

—— (1993a), The addictive process: A psychoanalytic understanding. *J. Amer. Acad. Psychoanal.*, 21:89–105.

—— (1993b), Diagnosis and treatment of sexual addiction. *J. Sex. Marital Ther.*, 19:225–251.

—— (1993c), Medication noncompliance and the psychodynamics of pharmacotherapy. *Integr. Psychiatry*, 8:181–190.

—— (1994a), Organic unity theory: A foundation for integrative psychiatry. I. Philosophical theory. *Integr. Psychiatry*, 10:68–84.

—— (1994b), Organic unity theory: A foundation for integrative psychiatry. II. Implications for psychiatry. *Integr. Psychiatry*, 10:133–143.

—— (1995a), Addictive disorders: An integrated approach. I. An integrated understanding. *J. Min. Addict. Recovery*, 2:33–76.

—— (1995b), Dépendence sexuelle (Sexual addiction). *Médicine et Hygiène*, 53:1575–1577.

—— (1995c), Recognition of psychodynamics in pharmacotherapy. *Psychiatric Times*, 12:17–21.

—— (1995d), Psychodynamics in pharmacotherapy: Practical application. *Psychiatric Times*, 12:54–55.

—— (1996a), The addictive process: A neurobiological understanding. (Typescript).

—— (1996b), Addictive disorders: An integrated approach. II. An integrated treatment. *J. Min. Addict. Recovery*, 3:49–77.

—— (in press a), Organic unity theory: An integrative mind-body theory for psychiatry. *Theor. Med.*

—— (in press b), Organic unity theory. A foundation for psychiatry as an integrative science. In: *Principles of Medical Biology*, ed. E. E. Bittar. Greenwich, CT: Jai Press.

—— (1997), Sexual addiction: Diagnosis, etiology, and treatment. In: *Substance Abuse: A Comprehensive Textbook*, 3rd ed. ed. J. H. Lowenstein, R. B. Millman, P. Ruiz, & J. G. Langrod. Baltimore: Williams & Wilkins, pp. 340–354.

Goodsitt, A. (1983), Self regulatory disturbances in eating disorders. *Internat. J. Eat. Disorders*, 3:51–60.

Goodwin, D. W., Schulsinger, F., Hermansen, L., Guze, S. B., & Winokur, G. (1973), Alcohol problems in adoptees raised apart from alcoholic biological parents. *Arch. Gen. Psychiatry*, 28:238–243.

—— —— —— —— —— (1975), Alcoholism and the hyperactive child syndrome. *J. Nerv. Ment. Dis.*, 160:349–353.

Gorelick, D. A. (1989), Serotonin uptake blockers and the treatment of alcoholism. *Rec. Dev. Alcohol*, 7:267–281.

—— Paredes, A. (1992), Effects of fluoxetine on alcohol consumption in male alcoholics. *Alcoholism*, 16:261–265.

Gorenstein, E. E., & Newman, J. P. (1980), Disinhibitory psychopathology: A new perspective and a model for research. *Psychol. Rev.*, 87:301–315.

Gorzalka, B. B., Mendelson, S. D., & Watson, N. V. (1990), Serotonin receptor subtypes and sexual behavior. *Ann. NY Acad. Sci.*, 600:435–444.

Graeff, F. G. (1994), Neuroanatomy and neurotransmitter regulation of defensive behaviors and related emotions in mammals. *Brazil J. Med. Biol. Res.*, 27:811–829.

Greenacre, P. (1953), Certain relationships between fetishism and faulty development of the body image. *The Psychoanalytic Study of the Child*, 8:79–98. New York: International Universities Press.

—— (1955), Further considerations regarding fetishism. *The Psychoanalytic Study of the Child*, 10:187–194. New York: International Universities Press.

—— (1960), Further notes on fetishism. *The Psychoanalytic Study of the Child*, 15:191–207. New York: International Universities Press.

—— (1968), Perversions: General considerations regarding their genetic and dynamic background. *The Psychoanalytic Study of the Child*, 23:47–62. New York: International Universities Press.

—— (1970), The transitional object and the fetish with special refernce to the role of illusion. *Internat. J. Psycho-Anal.*, 51:447–456.

—— (1979), Fetishism. In: *Sexual Deviation*, 2nd ed., ed. I. Rosen. Oxford: Oxford University Press, pp. 79–108.

Greenough, W. T., & Black, J. E. (1992), Induction of brain structure by experience: Substrates for cognitive development. In: *Minnesota Symposium on Child Psychology. V. 24. Developmental Behavioral Neuroscience,* ed. M. R. Gunnar & C. A. Nelson. Hillsdale, NJ: Erlbaum, pp. 155–200.

———— ———— Wallace, C. (1987), Experience and brain development. *Child Dev.,* 58:539–559.

Greenson, R. R. (1947), On gambling. *Amer. Imago,* 4:61–77.

———— (1968), Dis-identifying from mother: Its special importance for the boy. In: *Explorations in Psychoanalysis.* New York: International Universities Press, pp. 305–312.

Greenspan, S. I. (1979), Intelligence and Adaptation: An integration of Psychoanalytic and Piagetian Developmental Psychology. *Psychological Issues,* Monograph 47/48, Vol. 12. New York: International Universities Press.

———— (1989), The development of the ego: Biological and environmental specificity in the psychopathological developmental process and the selection and construction of ego defenses. *J. Amer. Psychoanal. Assn.,* 37:605–638.

Grotstein, J. S. (1980), A proposed revision of the psychoanalytic concept of primitive mental states. I. Introduction to a newer psychoanalytic metapsychology. *Contemp. Psychoanal.,* 16:479–546.

———— (1984), A proposed revision of the psychoanalytic concept of primitive mental states. II. The borderline syndrome—section 2: The phenomenology of the borderline syndrome. *Contemp. Psychoanal.,* 20:77–119.

———— (1987), The borderline as a disorder of self-regulation. In: *The Borderline Patient: Emerging Concepts in Diagnosis, Psychodynamics, and Treatment,* ed. J. S. Grotstein, M. Solomon, & J. Land. Hillsdale, NJ: Analytic Press, pp. 347–383.

Gulas, I., & King, F. W. (1976), On the question of pre-existing personality differences between users and nonusers of drugs. *J. Psychol.,* 92:65–69.

Gysling, K., & Wang, R. Y. (1983), Morphine-induced activation of A10 dopamine neurons in the rat. *Brain Res.,* 277:119–127.

Haberman, P. W. (1969), Drinking and other self-indulgences: Complements or counter-attractions? *Internat. J. Addict.,* 4:157–167.

Hammer, E. F. (1968), Symptoms of sexual deviation: Dynamics and etiology. *Psychoanal. Rev.,* 55:5–27.

Hammerman, S. (1965), Conceptions of superego development. *J. Amer. Psychoanal. Assn.,* 13:320–355.

Hanson, R. K., & Slater, S. (1988), Sexual victimization in the history of sexual abusers: A review. *Ann. Sex Res.*, 1:485–499.

Hartmann, D. (1969), A study of drug-taking adolescents. *The Psychoanalytic Study of the Child*, 24:384–398. New York: International Universities Press.

Hartocollis, P., & Hartocollis, P. C. (1980), Alcoholism, borderline and narcissistic disorders: A psychoanalytic overview. In: *Phenomenology and Treatment of Alcoholism*, ed. W. E. Fann, I. Haracan, A. D. Pokorny, & R. L. Williams. New York: SP Medical & Scientific, pp. 93–110.

Harvey, J. A., & Yunger, L. M. (1973), Relationship between telencephalic content of serotonin and pain sensitivity. In: *Serotonin and Behavior*, ed. J. Barchas & E. Usdin. New York: Academic Press, pp. 179–189.

Hatsukami, D., Owen, P., Pyle, R., & Mitchell, J. E. (1982), Similarities and differences on the MMPI between women with bulimia and women with alcohol or drug abuse problems. *Addict. Behav.*, 7:435–439.

Hayes, S. C., Brownell, K. D., & Barlow, D. H. (1978), The use of self-administered covert sensitization in the treatment of exhibitionism and sadism. *Behav. Ther.*, 9:283–289.

Heather, N., & Robertson, I. (1983), *Controlled Drinking*, 2nd ed. New York: Methuen.

Hecker, L. L., Trepper, T. S., Wetchler, J. L., & Fontaine, L. F. (1995), The influence of therapist values, religiosity and gender in the initial assessment of sexual addiction by family therapists. *Amer. J. Fam. Therapy*, 23:261–272.

Hendricks, S. E., Fitzpatrick, D. F., Hartman, K., Quaife, M. A., Stratbucker, R. A., & Graber, B. (1988), Brain structure and function in sexual molesters of children and adolescents. *J. Clin. Psychiatry*, 49:108–112.

Herman, J. L. (1990), Sexual offenders: A feminist perspective. In: *Handbook of Sexual Assault: Issues, Theories, and Treatment of the Offender*, ed. W. L. Marshall, D. R. Laws, & H. E. Barbaree. New York: Plenum Press, pp. 177–193.

———— Perry, J. C., & van der Kolk, B. A. (1989), Childhood trauma in borderline personality disorder. *Amer. J. Psychiatry*, 146:490–495.

Hermann, W. M., & Beach, R. C. (1980), Pharmacotherapy for sexual offenders: Review of the actions of antiandrogens with special references to their psychic effects. *Mod. Prob. Pharmacopsychiatry*, 15:182–194.

Hernandez, L., & Hoebel, B. G. (1990), Feeding can enhance dopamine turnover in the prefrontal cortex. *Brain Res. Bull.,* 25:975–979.

Hershey, D. W. (1989), On a type of heterosexuality, and the fluidity of object relations. *J. Amer. Psychoanal. Assn.,* 37:147–171.

Herzog, D. B., Keller, M. B., Lavori, P. W., Kenny, G. M., & Sacks, N. A. (1992), The prevalence of personality disorders in 210 women with eating disorders. *J. Clin. Psychiatry,* 53:147–152.

Hesselbrock, M. N., Meyer, R. E., & Keener, J. L. (1985), Psychopathology in hospitalized alcoholics. *Arch. Gen. Psychiatry,* 42:1050–1055.

Hoebel, B. G., Hernandez, L., Schwartz, D. H., Mark, G. P., & Hunter, G. A. (1989), Microdialysis studies of brain norepinephrine, serotonin, and dopamine release during ingestive behavior: Theoretical and clinical implications. *Ann. NY Acad. Sci.,* 575:171–193.

Hoenig, J., & Kenna, J. (1979), EEG abnormalities and transsexualism. *Brit. J. Psychiatry,* 134:293–300.

Hoffman, H., Loper, R., & Kammeier, M. L. (1974), Identifying future alcoholics with MMPI alcoholism scales. *Quart. J. Stud. Alc.,* 35:490–498.

Hoffman, M. (1964), Drug addiction and ''hypersexuality'': Related modes of mastery. *Compr. Psychiatry,* 5:262–270.

Hogan, C. (1983), Technical problems in psychoanalytic treatment. In: *Fear of Being Fat: The Treatment of Anorexia Nervosa and Bulimia,* ed. C. Wilson, C. Hogan, & I. Mintz. New York: Jason Aronson, pp. 197–215.

Hollander, E. (1993), Introduction. In: *Obsessive-Compulsive Related Disorders,* ed. E. Hollander. Washington, DC: American Psychiatric Association, pp. 1–16.

——— Frenkel, M., Decaria, C., Trungold, S., & Stein, D. J. (1992), Treatment of pathological gambling with clomipramine [letter]. *Amer. J. Psychiatry,* 149:710–711.

Hollt, V., & Horn, G. (1989), Nicotine and opioid peptides. *Prog. Brain Res.,* 79:187–193.

Houdi, A. A., Bardo, M. T., & Van Loon, G. R. (1989), Opioid mediation of cocaine-induced hyperactivity and reinforcement. *Brain Res.,* 497:195–198.

Huba, G. J., & Bentler, P. M. (1982), A developmental theory of drug use: Derivation and assessment of a causal modeling approach. In: *Life-Span Development and Behavior,* ed. P. B. Baltes & O. G. Brim. New York: Academic Press.

Hucker, S. J., & Bain, J. (1990), Androgenic hormones and sexual assault. In: *Handbook of Sexual Assault: Issues, Theories, and Treatment of the Offender,* ed. W. L. Marshall, D. R. Laws, & H. E. Barbaree. New York: Plenum Press, pp. 94–102.

———— Ben-Aron, M. H. (1985), Elderly sex offenders. In: *Erotic Preferences, Gender Identity, and Aggression in Men: New Research Studies,* ed. R. L. Langevin. Hillsdale, NJ: Erlbaum.

———— Langevin, R., Wortzman, G., Bain, J., Handy, L., Chambers, J., & Wright, S. (1986), Neuropsychological impairment in pedophiles. *Can. J. Behav. Sci.,* 18:440–448.

———— ———— ———— Dickey, R., Bain, J., Handy, L., Chambers, J., & Wright, S. (1988), Cerebral damage and dysfunction in sexually aggressive men. *Ann. Sex Res.,* 1:33–47.

Hudson, J. I., Laffer, P. S., & Pope, H. G. (1982), Bulimia related to affective disorder by family history and response to dexamethasone suppression test. *Amer. J. Psychiatry,* 139:685–687.

———— Pope, H. G. (1990), Affective spectrum disorder: Does an antidepressant response identify a family of disorders with a common pathophysiology? *Amer. J. Psychiatry,* 147:552–564.

———— ———— Jonas, J. M., & Yurgelun-Todd, D. (1983), Phenomenologic relationship of eating disorders to major affective disorder. *Psychiatry Res.,* 9:345–354.

———— ———— ———— ———— (1987), A controlled family history study of bulimia. *Psychol. Med.,* 17:883–390.

———— ———— Yurgelun-Todd, D., Jonas, J. M., & Frankenburg, F. R. (1987), A controlled study of lifetime prevalence of affective and other psychiatric disorders in bulimic outpatients. *Amer. J. Psychiatry,* 144:1283–1287.

Hull, J. G., & Bond, C. F. (1986), Social and behavioral consequences of alcohol consumption and expectancy: A meta-analysis. *Psychol. Bull.,* 99:347–360.

Hunter, J. A., & Goodwin, D. W. (1992), The clinical utility of satiation therapy with juvenile offenders: Variations and efficacy. *Ann. Sex Res.,* 5:71–80.

Irons, R. R., & Schneider, J. P. (1994), Sexual addiction: Significant factor in sexual exploitation by health care professionals. *Sex. Addic. Compulsiv.,* 1:208–214.

Jacobs, D. F. (1989), Children of problem gamblers. *J. Gambling Behav.,* 5:261–268.

Jaffe, H. (1992), Current concepts of addiction. In: *Addictive States,* ed. C. P. O'Brien & J. H. Jaffe. New York: Raven Press, pp. 1–21.

Jarvik, M. E. (1977), Biological factors underlying the smoking habit. *NIDA Res. Monogr. Ser.,* 17:122–148.

Jessor, R., Chase, J. A., & Donovan, J. E. (1980), Psychosocial correlates of marijuana use and problem drinking in a national sample of adolescents. *Amer. J. Pub. Health,* 70:604–613.

———— Jessor, S. (1977), *Problem Behavior and Psychosocial Development: A Longitudinal Study of Youth.* New York: Academic Press.

———— ———— (1978), Theory testing in longitudinal research on marijuana research. In: *Longitudinal Research on Drug Use: Empirical Findings and Methodological Issues,* ed. D. Kandel. Washington, DC: Hemisphere, pp. 41–71.

Johnson, A. M., & Robinson, D. B. (1957), The sexual deviant (psychopath)—causes, treatment, and prevention. *JAMA,* 164:1559–1565.

Johnson, C., & Connors, M. E. (1987), *The Etiology and Treatment of Bulimia Nervosa: A Biopsychosocial Perspective.* New York: Basic Books.

———— ———— Tobin, D. L. (1987), Symptom management of bulimia. *J. Consult. Clin. Psychol.,* 5:668–676.

Jonas, J., & Gold, M. (1986), Cocaine abuse and eating disorders. *Lancet,* 14:390–391.

———— ———— Sweeney, D., & Pottash, A. L. C. (1987), Eating disorders and cocaine abuse: A survey of 259 cocaine abusers. *J. Clin. Psychiatry,* 48:47–50.

Jones, D. A., Cheshire, N., & Moorhouse, H. (1985), Anorexia nervosa, bulimia, and alcoholism: Association of eating disorder and alcohol. *J. Psychiatry Res.,* 19:377–380.

Jones, M. C. (1968), Personality correlates and antecedents of drinking patterns in adult males. *J. Consult. Clin. Psychol.,* 32:2–12.

———— (1971), Personality correlates and antecedents of drinking patterns in women. *J. Consult. Clin. Psychol.,* 36:61–69.

Jorgensen, V. T. (1990), Cross-dressing successfully treated with fluoxetine [letter]. *NY State J. Med.,* 90:566–567.

Kafka, M. P. (1991), Successful antidepressant treatment of nonparaphilic sexual addictions and paraphilias in men. *J. Clin. Psychiatry,* 52:60–65.

———— (1994), Sertraline pharmacotherapy for paraphilias and paraphilia-related disorders: An open trial. *Ann. Clin. Psychiatry,* 6:189–195.

———— Prentky, R. (1992), Fluoxetine treatment of nonparaphilic sexual addiction and paraphilias in men. *J. Clin. Psychiatry,* 53:351–358.

———— ———— (1994), Preliminary observations of DSM-III-R axis I comorbidity in men with paraphilias and paraphilia-related disorders. *J. Clin. Psychiatry,* 55:481–487.

Kammeier, M. L., Hoffman, H., & Loper, R. G. (1973), Personality characteristics of alcoholics as college freshman and at time of treatment. *Quart. J. Stud. Alc.,* 34:390–399.

Kandel, D. B. (1978), Convergences in prospective longitudinal surveys of drug use in normal populations. In: *Longitudinal Research on Drug Use: Empirical Findings and Methodological Issues,* ed. D. Kandel. Washington, DC: Hemisphere, pp. 3–38.

——— (1980), Drug and drinking behavior among youth. *Ann. Rev. Sociol.,* 6:235–285.

Karasu, T. B. (1986), The specificity versus nonspecificity dilemma: Toward identifying therapeutic change agents. *Amer. J. Psychiatry,* 143:687–695.

Karp, S. A., & Kronstadt, N. L. (1965), Alcoholism and psychological differentiation: Long-range effect of heavy drinking on field dependence. *J. Nerv. Ment. Dis.,* 140:412–416.

——— Pardes, H. (1965), Psychological differentiation (field dependence) in obese women. *Psychosom. Med.,* 27:238–244.

Kassett, J. A., Gershon, E. S., Maxwell, M. E., Guroff, J. J., Kazuba, D. M., Smith, A. L., Brandt, H. A., & Jimerson, D. C. (1989), Psychiatric disorders in the first-degree relatives of probands with bulimia nervosa. *Amer. J. Psychiatry,* 146:1468–1471.

Kavoussi, R. J., Kaplan, M., & Becker, J. V. (1988), Psychiatric diagnoses in adolescent sex offenders. *J. Amer. Acad. Child Adol. Psychiatry,* 27:241–243.

Kaye, W. H., Ebert, M. H., Gwirtsman, H. E., & Weiss, S. R. (1984), Differences in brain serotonergic metabolism between nonbulimic and bulimic patients with anorexia nervosa. *Amer. J. Psychiatry,* 141:1598–1601.

——— Gwirtsman, H. E., Brewerton, T. D., George, D. T., & Wurtman, R. J. (1988), Binging behavior and plasma amino acids: A possible involvement of brain serotonin in bulimia nervosa. *Psychiatr. Res.,* 23:31–43.

——— Weltzin, T. E. (1991), Neurochemistry of bulimia nervosa. *J. Clin. Psychiatry,* 52(suppl):21–28.

Kellam, S. G. (1991), Developmental epidemiological and prevention research on early risk behaviors. In: *Self-Regulatory Behaviors and Risk Taking: Causes and Consequences,* ed. S. P. Lipsitt & L. L. Mitnick. Norwood, NJ: Ablex, pp. 51–70.

——— Brown, C. H., Rubin, B. R., & Ensminger, M. E. (1983a), *Mental Health and Going to School: The Woodlawn Program of Assessment, Early Intervention, and Evaluation.* Chicago: University of Chicago Press.

———— ———— ———— ———— (1983b), Paths leading to teenage psychiatric symptoms and substance abuse: Developmental epidemiological studies in Woodlawn. In: *Child Psychopathology and Development,* ed. S. B. Guze, F. J. Earls, & J. E. Barrett. New York: Raven Press, pp. 17–47.

———— Ensminger, M. E., & Simon, M. B. (1980), Mental health in first grade and teenage drug, alcohol, and cigarette use. *Drug Alcohol Depend,* 5:273–304.

Kendler, K. S. (1990), Toward a scientific psychiatric nosology: Strengths and limitations. *Arch. Gen. Psychiatry,* 47:969–973.

Kernberg, O. F. (1967), Borderline personality organization. *J. Amer. Psychoanal. Assn.,* 15:641–685.

———— (1992), *Aggression in Personality Disorders and Perversions.* New Haven, CT: Yale University Press.

Khan, M. M. R. (1962), The role of polymorph-perverse body-experiences and object relations in ego-integration. *Brit. J. Med. Psychol.,* 35:245–261.

———— (1964), The role of infantile sexuality and early object relations in female homosexuality. In: *Pathology and Treatment of Sexual Deviation: A Methodological Approach,* ed. I. Rosen. London: Oxford University Press, pp. 221–292.

———— (1965), Foreskin fetishism and its relation to ego pathology in a male homosexual. *Internat. J. Psycho-Anal.,* 46:64–80.

———— (1969), Role of the "collated internal object" in perversion-formations. *Internat. J. Psycho-Anal.,* 50:555–565.

———— (1979), *Alienation in Perversions.* New York: International Universities Press.

Khantzian, E. J. (1978), The ego, the self and opiate addiction: Theoretical and treatment considerations. *Internat. J. Psycho-Anal.,* 5:189–198.

———— (1980), An ego/self theory of substance dependence: A contemporary psychoanalytic perspective. In: *Theories on Drug Abuse: Selected Contemporary Perspectives,* ed. D. J. Lettieri, M. Sayres, & H. W. Pearson. Rockville, MD: National Institute on Drug Abuse, pp. 29–33.

———— (1981), Some treatment implications of the ego and self disturbances in alcoholism. In: *Dynamic Approaches to the Understanding and Treatment of Alcoholism,* ed. M. H. Bean & N. E. Zinberg. New York: Free Press, pp. 163–189.

———— (1982), Psychological (structural) vulnerabilities and the specific appeal of narcotics. *Ann. NY Acad. Sci.,* 398:24–32.

—— (1985), The self-medication hypothesis of addictive disorders: Focus on heroin and cocaine addiction. *Amer. J. Psychiatry,* 142:1259–1264.

—— (1987), A clinical perspective of the cause-consequence controversy in alcoholic and addictive suffering. *J. Amer. Acad. Psychoanal.,* 15:521–537.

—— (1990), Self-regulation and self-medication factors in alcoholism and the addictions: Similarities and differences. *Rec. Dev. Alcohol,* 8:255–271.

—— (1995), Self-regulation vulnerabilities in substance abusers: Treatment implications. In: *The Psychology and Treatment of Addictive Behavior,* ed. S. Dowling. Madison, CT: International Universities Press, pp. 17–41.

—— Mack, J. E. (1983), Self-preservation and the care of the self. *The Psychoanalytic Study of the Child,* 38:209–232.

—— Treece, C. (1977), Psychodynamics of drug dependence: An overview. In: *Psychodynamics of Drug Dependence, NIDA Monograph #12.* ed. J. D. Blaine & D. A. Julius. Rockville, MD: National Institute of Drug Abuse, pp. 11–25.

—— —— (1985), DSM-III psychiatric diagnosis of narcotic addicts: Recent findings. *Arch. Gen. Psychiatry,* 42:1067–1071.

Khatib, S. A., Murphy, J. M., & McBride, W. J. (1988), Biochemical evidence for activation of specific monoamine pathways by ethanol. *Alcohol,* 5:295–299.

Kiernan, R. J. (1981), Localization of function: The mind-body problem revisited. *J. Clin. Neuropsychol.,* 3:345–352.

Kiersch, T. A. (1990), Treatment of sex offenders with Depo-Provera. *Bull. Amer. Acad. Psychiatry Law,* 18:179–187.

Kilmann, P. R., Sabalis, R. F., Gearing, M. L., Bukstel, L. H., & Scovern, A. W. (1982), The treatment of sexual paraphilias: A review of outcome research. *J. Sex Res.,* 18:193–252.

King, L. S. (1954), What is disease? *Phil. Sci.,* 21:193–203.

Kirkham, T. C., & Cooper, S. J. (1988), Attenuation of sham feeding by naloxone is stereospecific: Evidence for opioid medication of orosensory reward. *Physiol. Behav.,* 43:845–847.

Klein, D. F., Gittelman, R., Quitkin, F., & Rifkin, A. (1980), *Diagnosis and Drug Treatment of Psychiatric Disorders: Adults and Children,* 2nd ed. Baltimore: Williams & Wilkins.

Klein, M. (1957), *Envy and Gratitude.* New York: Basic Books.

Knight, R. A., Rosenberg, R., & Schneider, B. (1985), Classification of sexual offender: Perspectives, methods, and validation. In: *Rape and*

Sexual Assault: A Research Handbook, ed. A. Burgess. New York: Garland, pp. 222–293.

Koenigsberg, H. W., Kaplan, R. D., Gilmore, M. M., & Cooper, A. M. (1985), The relationship between syndrome and personality in DSM-III: Experience with 2,462 patients. *Amer. J. Psychiatry,* 142:207–212.

Kohut, H. (1959), Introspection, empathy and psychoanalysis. *J. Amer. Psychoanal. Assn.,* 7:459–483.

———— (1966), Forms and transformations of narcissism. *J. Amer. Psychoanal. Assn.,* 14:243–272.

———— (1968), The psychoanalytic treatment of narcissistic personality disorders: Outline of a systematic approach. *The Psychoanalytic Study of the Child,* 23:86–113. New York: International Universities Press.

———— (1971), *The Analysis of the Self: A Systematic Approach to the Psychoanalytic Treatment of Narcissistic Personality Disorders.* New York: International Universities Press.

———— (1972), Thoughts on narcissism and narcissistic rage. *The Psychoanalytic Study of the Child,* 27:360–400. New Haven, CT: Yale University Press.

———— (1977), *The Restoration of the Self.* New York: International Universities Press.

Kolarsky, A., Freund, K., Machek, J., & Polak, O. (1967), Male sexual deviation: Association with early temporal lobe damage. *Arch. Gen. Psychiatry,* 17:735–743.

Koob, G. F. (1993), The reward system and cocaine abuse. In: *Biological Basis of Substance Abuse,* ed. S. G. Korenman & J. D. Barchas. New York: Oxford University Press, pp. 339–354.

———— Bloom, F. E. (1988), Cellular and molecular mechanisms of drug dependence. *Science,* 242:715–723.

Kosten, T. R., Kosten, T. A., & Rounsaville, B. J. (1991), Alcoholism and depressive disorders in opioid addicts and their family members. *Compr. Psychiatry,* 32:521–527.

Kraemer, G. W. (1985), Effects of differences in early social experience on primate neurobiological-behavioral development. In: *The Psychobiology of Attachment and Separation,* ed. M. Reite & T. Field. New York: Academic Press, pp. 135–161.

———— (1986), Causes of changes in brain noradrenaline systems and later effects on responses to social stressors in rhesus monkeys: The cascade hypothesis. In: *Antidepressants and Receptor Function* (CIBA Foundation Symposium 123). New York: Wiley.

———— Ebert, M. H., Lake, C. R., & McKinney, W. T. (1984), Cerebrospinal fluid changes associated with pharmacological alteration of the despair response to social separation in rhesus monkeys. *Psychiatry Res.,* 11:303–315.

————— ————— Schmidt, D. E., & McKinney, W. T. (1989), A longitudinal study of the effects of different rearing environments on cerebrospinal fluid norepinephrine and biogenic amine metabolites in rhesus monkeys. *Neuropsychopharmacol.,* 2:175–189.

————— ————— ————— ————— (1991), Strangers in a strange land: A psychobiological study of infant monkeys before and after separation from real or inanimate mothers. *Child Dev.,* 62:548–566.

Krafft-Ebbing, R. (1886), *Psychopathia Sexualis,* tr. F. J. Rebman. New York: Stein & Day, 1965.

Kranitz, L. (1972), Alcoholics, heroin addicts and nonaddicts. Comparisons on the MacAndrew Alcoholism Scale of the MMPI. *Quart. J. Stud. Alc.,* 33:807–809.

Kravitz, H. M., Haywood, T. W., Kelly, J., Wahlstrom, C., Liles, S., & Cavanaugh, J. L. (1995), Medroxyprogesterone treatment for paraphiliacs. *Bull. Amer. Acad. Psychiatry Law,* 23:19–33.

Kreek, M. J. (1992), Effects of opiates, opioid antagonists and cocaine on the endogenous opioid system: Clinical and laboratory studies. *NIDA Res. Monogr. Ser.,* 119:44–48.

Krueger, D. W. (1988), Body self, psychological self, and bulimia: Developmental and clinical considerations. In: *Bulimia: Psychoanalytic Treatment and Theory,* ed. H. J. Schwartz. Madison, CT: International Universities Press, pp. 55–72.

Kruesi, M. J. P., Fine, S., Valladares, L., Phillips, R. A., & Rapoport, J. L. (1992), Paraphilias: A double-blind crossover comparison of clomipramine versus desipramine. *Arch. Sex Behav.,* 21:587–593.

Krystal, H. (1974), The genetic development of affects and affect regression. *Ann. Psychoanal.,* 2:98–126.

————— (1975), Affect tolerance. *Ann. Psychoanal.,* 3:179–219.

————— (1982), Alexithymia and the effectiveness of psychoanalytic treatment. *Internat. J. Psychoanal. Psychother.,* 9:353–378.

————— (1995), Disorders of emotional development in addictive behavior. In: *The Psychology and Treatment of Addictive Behavior,* ed. S. Dowling. Madison, CT: International Universities Press, pp. 65–100.

————— Raskin, H. A. (1970), *Drug Dependence: Aspects of Ego Function.* Detroit: Wayne State University Press.

Kubie, L. S. (1974), The drive to become both sexes. *Psychoanal. Quart.,* 43:349–426.

Labouvie, E. W., & McGee, C. R. (1986), Relation of personality to alcohol and drug use in adolescence. *J. Consult. Clin. Psychol.,* 54:289–293.

Lacey, J. H. (1993), Self-damaging and addictive behaviour in bulimia nervosa: A catchment area study. *Brit. J. Psychiatry*, 163:190–194.

Lamontagne, Y., & Lesage, A. (1986), Private exposure and covert sensitization in the treatment of exhibitionists. *J. Behav. Ther. Exp. Psychiatry*, 17:197–201.

Langevin, R. (1985), The paraphilias. In: *Clinical Criminology: The Assessment and Treatment of Criminal Behavior*, ed. M. Ben-Aron, S. J. Hucker, & C. D. Webster. Toronto: Clarke Institute of Psychiatry.

——— (1990), Sexual anomalies and the brain. The nature and extent of sexual assault. In: *Handbook of Sexual Assault: Issues, Theories, and Treatment of the Offender*, ed. W. L. Marshall, D. R. Laws, & H. E. Barbaree. New York: Plenum Press, pp. 103–113.

——— Bain, J., Wortzman, S., Hucker, S., Dickey, R., & Wright, P. (1988), Sexual sadism: Brain, blood, and behavior. *Ann. NY Acad. Sci.*, 163–171.

——— Ben-Aron, M. H., Coulthard, R., Heasman, G., Purins, J. E., Handy, L., Hucker, S. J., Russon, A. E., Day, D., Roper, V., Bain, J., Wortzman, G., & Webster, C. D. (1985), Sexual aggression: Constructing a predictive equation: A controlled pilot study. In: *Erotic Preference, Gender Identity, and Aggression in Men: New Research Studies*, ed. R. Langevin. Hillsdale, NJ: Erlbaum, pp. 39–76.

——— Lang, R. A. (1988), *Incest Offenders*. Toronto: Juniper Press.

——— ——— (1990), Substance abuse among sex offenders. *Ann. Sex Res.*, 3:397–424.

Lansky, D., Nathan, P. E., & Lawson, D. M. (1978), Blood alcohol level discrimination by alcoholics: The role of internal and external cues. *J. Consult. Clin. Psychol.*, 46:953–960.

Laplanche, J., & Pontalis, J-B. (1967), *The Language of Psycho-Analysis*, tr. D. Nicholson-Smith. New York: W. W. Norton, 1973.

Laschet, U. (1973), Antiandrogen in the treatment of sex offenders: Mode of action and therapeutic outcome. In: *Contemporary Sexual Behavior: Critical Issues in the 1970s*, ed. J. Zubin & J. Money. Baltimore: Johns Hopkins University Press, pp. 311–319.

——— Laschet, L. (1975), Antiandrogens in the treatment of sexual deviations in men. *J. Steroid Biochem.*, 6:821–826.

Leibowitz, S. F., & Shor-Posner, G. (1986), Brain serotonin and eating behavior. *Appetite*, 7:1–13.

Leon, G., Kolotkin, R., & Korgeski, G. (1979), MacAndrew Addiction Scale and other MMPI characteristics associated with obesity, anorexia, and smoking behavior. *Addict. Behav.*, 4:401–407.

Lesieur, H. R. (1988), Report on pathological gambling in New Jersey. In: *Report and Recommendations of the Governor's Advisory Commission on Gambling.* Trenton, NJ: Governor's Advisory Commission on Gambling.

———— Blume, S. B., & Zoppa, P. M. (1986), Alcoholism, drug abuse, and gambling. *Alc. Clin. Exp. Res.,* 10:33–38.

———— Heineman, M. (1988), Pathological gambling among youthful multiple substance abusers in a therapeutic community. *Brit. J. Addict.,* 83:765–771.

Levenson, R. W., Oyama, O. N., & Meek, P. S. (1987), Greater reinforcement from alcohol for those at risk: Parental risk, personality risk, and sex. *J. Abnorm. Psychol.,* 96:242–253.

Leventhal, H., & Cleary, P. D. (1980), The smoking problem: A review of the research and theory in behavioral risk modification. *Psychol. Bull.,* 88:370–405.

Levine, M. P., & Troiden, R. R. (1988), The myth of sexual compulsivity. *J. Sex Res.,* 25:347–363.

Linden, R. D., Pope, H. G., & Jonas, J. M. (1986), Pathological gambling and major affective disorders: Preliminary findings. *J. Clin. Psychiatry,* 47:201–203.

Links, P. S., & van Reekum, R. (1993), Childhood sexual abuse, parental impairment and the development of borderline personality disorder. *Can. J. Psychiatry,* 38:472–474.

Loper, R., Kammeier, M., & Hoffman, H. (1973), MMPI characteristics of college freshman males who later became alcoholic. *J. Abnorm. Psychol.,* 82:159–162.

Loranger, A. W., Oldham, J. M., & Tulis, E. H. (1982), Familial transmission of DSM-III borderline personality disorder. *Arch. Gen. Psychiatry,* 39:795–799.

Lorefice, L. S. (1991), Fluoxetine treatment of a fetish. *J. Clin. Psychiatry,* 52:41.

Louilot, A., Taghzouti, K., Simon, H., & Le Moal, M. (1989), Limbic system, basal ganglia, and dopaminergic neurons: Executive and regulatory neurons and their role in the organization of behavior. *Brain Behav. Evol.,* 33:157–161.

Lowenfeld, B. H. (1979), Personality dimensions of the pathological gambler. *Diss. Abstr. Int.,* 40(1-B):456.

Luborsky, L., McLellan, A. T., Woody, G. E., O'Brien, C. P., & Auerbach, A. (1985), Therapist success and its determinants. *Arch. Gen. Psychiatry,* 42:602–611.

Ludwig, A. M., & Wikler, A. (1974), Craving and relapse to drink. *Quart. J. Stud. Alcohol,* 35:108–130.

Luria, A. R. (1973), *The Working Brain.* New York: Basic Books.

Lyons, J. C. (1985), Differences in sensation seeking and in depression levels between male social gamblers and male compulsive gamblers. In: *Proceedings of the Fifth National Conference on Gambling and Risk Taking,* ed. W. R. Eadington. University of Nevada: Bureau of Business and Economic Research.

MacCulloch, M. J., Williams, C., & Birtles, C. J. (1971), The successful application of aversion therapy to an adolescent exhibitionist. *J. Behav. Ther. Esp. Psychiatry,* 2:61–66.

Macdonald, C. (1989), *Mind-Body Identity Theories.* London: Routledge & Kegan Paul.

Mackay, P. W., & Marlatt, G. A. (1990–1991), Maintaining sobriety: Stopping is starting. *Internat. J. Addict.,* 25:1257–1276.

Mahler, M. S., & Furer, M. (1968), *On Human Symbiosis and the Vicissitudes of Individuation,* Vol. 1. New York: International Universities Press.

———— Gosliner, B. J. (1955), On symbiotic child psychosis: Genetic, dynamic and restitutive aspects. *The Psychoanalytic Study of the Child,* 10:195–212.

———— Pine, F., & Bergman, A. (1975), *The Psychological Birth of the Human Infant.* New York: Basic Books.

Maletzky, B. M. (1974), "Assisted" covert sensitization in the treatment of exhibitionism. *J. Consult. Clin. Psychol.,* 42:34–40.

———— (1980), Self-referred versus court-referred sexually deviant patients: Success with assisted covert sensitization. *Behav. Ther.,* 11:306–314.

———— (1991), Somatic therapies. In: *Treating the Sexual Offender,* ed. B. M. Maletzky. Newbury Park, CA: Sage.

Mandell, A. J., & Knapp, S. (1979), Asymmetry and mood, emergent properties of serotonin regulation. *Arch. Gen. Psychiatry,* 36:909–916.

Margo, G. M., & McLees, E. M. (1991), Further evidence for the significance of a childhood abuse history in psychiatric inpatients. *Compr. Psychiatry,* 32:362–366.

Marks, I. (1990), Behavioural (non-chemical) addictions [editorial]. *Brit. J. Addict,* 85:1389–1394.

Marks, I. M., Gelder, M. G., & Bancroft, J. H. J. (1970), Sexual deviants two years after electric aversion. *Brit. J. Psychiatry,* 117:173–185.

———— Rachman, S., & Gelder, M. G. (1965), Methods for assessment of aversion treatment in fetishism with masochism. *Behav. Res. Ther.,* 3:253–258.

Marlatt, G. A. (1978), Craving, loss of control, and relapse: A cognitive-behavioral analysis. In: *Alcoholism: New Directions in Behavioral Research and Treatment,* ed. P. E. Nathan, G. A. Marlatt, & T. Loberg. New York: Plenum Press, pp. 271–314.

—————— (1983), The controlled-drinking controversy: A commentary. *Amer. Psychol.,* 38:1097–1110.

—————— (1985), Cognitive factors in the relapse process. In: *Relapse Prevention: Maintenance Strategies in the Treatment of Addictive Behaviors,* ed. G. A. Marlatt & J. R. Gordon. New York: Guilford Press, pp. 128–200.

—————— Baer, J. S., Donovan, D. M., & Kivlahan, D. R. (1988), Addictive behaviors: Etiology and treatment. *Ann. Rev. Psychol.,* 39:223–252.

—————— George, W. H. (1984), Relapse prevention: Introduction and overview of the model. *Brit. J. Addict.,* 79:261–273.

—————— Rohsenow, D. J. (1980), Cognitive processes in alcohol use: Expectancy and the balanced placebo design. In: *Advances in Substance Abuse: Strategies for Clinical Intervention,* Vol. 1, ed. N. K. Mello. Greenwich, CT: JAI Press, pp. 159–199.

Marshall, W. L. (1989), Intimacy, loneliness, and sexual offenders. *Behav. Res. Ther.,* 27:491–503.

—————— Barbaree, H. E. (1990a), An integrated theory of the etiology of sexual offending. In: *Handbook of Sexual Assault: Issues, Theories, and Treatment of the Offender,* ed. W. L. Marshall, D. R. Laws, & H. E. Barbaree. New York: Plenum Press, pp. 209–229.

—————— —————— (1990b), Outcome of comprehensive cognitive-behavioral treatment programs. In: *Handbook of Sexual Assault: Issues, Theories, and Treatment of the Offender,* ed. W. L. Marshall, D. R. Laws, & H. E. Barbaree. New York: Plenum Press, pp. 363–385.

—————— Jones, R., Ward, T., Johnson, P., & Barbaree, H. E. (1991), Treatment outcome with sexual offenders. *Clin. Psychol. Rev.,* 11:465–485.

Mathis, J. L., & Collins, M. (1970), Mandatory group therapy for exhibitionists. *Amer. J. Psychiatry,* 126:1162.

Maxwell, G. (1978), Rigid designators and mind-brain identity. In: *Minnesota Studies in the Philosophy of Science,* Vol. 16, ed. C. W. Savage. Minneapolis: University of Minnesota, pp. 365–403.

Mayer, E. L. (1985), ''Everybody must be just like me'': Observations on female castration anxiety. *Internat. J. Psycho-Anal.,* 66:331–346.

McConaghy, N., Armstrong, M. S., & Blaszczynski, A. (1985), Expectancy, covert sensitization and imaginal desensitization in compulsive sexuality. *Acta Psychiatr. Scand.,* 72:176–187.

McCord, W., & McCord, J. (1960), *Origins of Alcoholism.* Stanford, CA: Stanford University Press.

—— —— (1962), A longitudinal study of the personality of alcoholics. In: *Society, Culture, and Drinking Patterns,* ed. D. J. Pittman & C. R. Snyder. New York: Wiley, pp. 413–430.

McCormick, R. A., & Taber, J. I. (1979), The pathological gambler: Salient personality variables. In: *The Handbook of Pathological Gambling,* ed. T. Galski. Springfield, IL: Charles C Thomas, pp. 9–39.

—— Russo, A. M., Ramirez, L. F., & Taber, J. I. (1984), Affective disorders among pathological gamblers seeking treatment. *Amer. J. Psychiatry,* 141:215–218.

McDougall, J. (1972), Primal scene and sexual perversions. *Internat. J. Psycho-Anal.,* 53:371–384.

—— (1986), Identifications, neoneeds and neosexualities. *Internat. J. Psycho-Anal.,* 67:19–31.

McElroy, S. L., Hudson, J. I., Pope, H. G., Keck, P. E., & Aizley, H. G. (1992), The DSM-III-R impulse control disorders not elsewhere classified: Clinical characteristics and relationship to other psychiatric disorders. *Amer. J. Psychiatry,* 149:318–327.

McGuire, R. J., Carlisle, J. M., & Young, B. G. (1965), Sexual deviations as conditioned behaviour: A hypothesis. *Behav. Res. Ther.,* 2:185–190.

Meissner, W. W. (1980), The problem of internalization and structure formation. *Internat. J. Psycho-Anal.,* 61:237–248.

—— (1980–1981), Addiction and the paranoid process: Psychoanalytic perspectives. *Internat. J. Psychoanal. Psychother.,* 8:273–310.

—— (1985), Theories of personality and psychopathology: Classical psychoanalysis. In: *Comprehensive Textbook of Psychiatry,* 4th ed., ed. H. I. Kaplan & B. J. Sadock. Baltimore: Williams & Wilkins, pp. 337–418.

Meyer, V., & Gelder, M. G. (1963), Behaviour therapy and phobic disorders. *Brit. J. Psychiatry,* 109:19–28.

Mezzich, J. E., Fabrega, H., Coffman, G. A., & Haley, R. (1989), DSM-III disorders in a large sample of psychiatric patients: Frequency and specificity of diagnosis. *Amer. J. Psychiatry,* 146:212–219.

Mifsud, J. C., Hernandez, L., & Hoebel, B. G. (1989), Nicotine infused into the nucleus accumbens increases synaptic dopamine as measured by in vivo microdialysis. *Brain Res.,* 478:365–367.

Milkman, H., & Frosch, W. (1977), The drug of choice. *J. Psychoactive Drugs,* 9:11–24.

—— —— (1980), Theory of drug use. In: *Theories on Drug Abuse: Selected Contemporary Perspectives,* ed. D. Lettieri, M. Sayers, & H.

Pearson. NIDA Research Monograph 30, DHS Publication No. (ADM) 80-967. Washington, DC: US Government Printing Office, pp. 38–45.

Miller, L. (1986), "Narrow localizationism," in psychiatric nosology. *Psychol. Med.*, 16:729–734.

Miller, N. S., Dackis, C. A., & Gold, M. S. (1987), The relationship of addiction, tolerance, and dependence to alcohol and drugs: A neurochemical approach. *J. Subst. Abuse Treat.*, 4:197–207.

Miller, P. M. (1979), Interactions among addictive behaviors. *Brit. J. Addict.*, 74:211–212.

Miller, W. R. (1983), Controlled drinking: A history and critical review. *J. Stud. Alcohol*, 44:68–83.

——— Hedrick, K. E., & Taylor, C. A. (1983), Addictive behaviors and life problems before and after behavioral treatment of problem drinkers. *Addict. Behav.*, 8:403–412.

Mio, J. S., Nanjundappa, G., Verleur, D. E., & Rios, M. D. (1986), Drug abuse and the adolescent sex offender: A preliminary analysis. *J. Psychoactive Drugs*, 18:65–72.

Mitchell, J. E., & Goff, G. (1984), Bulimia in male patients. *Psychosom.*, 25:909–913.

——— Hatsukami, D., Eckert, E. D., & Pyle, R. L. (1985), Characteristics of 275 patients with bulimia. *Amer. J. Psychiatry*, 142:482–485.

Mitchell, S. A. (1988), *Relational Concepts in Psychoanalysis: An Integration*. Cambridge, MA: Harvard University Press.

Modell, A. H. (1978), The conceptualization of the therapeutic action of psychoanalysis: The action of the holding environment. *Bull. Menninger Clin.*, 42:493–504.

Modell, J. G., Mountz, J. M., & Beresford, T. P. (1990), Basal ganglia/limbic striatal and thalamocortical involvement in craving and loss of control in alcoholism. *J. Neuropsychiatry Clin. Neurosci.*, 2:123–144.

Mohan, K. J., Salo, M. W., & Nagaswami, S. (1975), A case of limbic system dysfunction with hypersexuality and fugue state. *Dis. Nerv. Syst.*, 36:621–624.

Mohl, P. C. (1987), Should psychotherapy be considered a biological treatment? *Psychosom.*, 28:320–326.

Money, J. (1968), Discussion of the hormonal inhibition of libido in male sex offenders. In: *Endocrinology and Human Behaviour*, ed. R. Michael. London: Oxford University Press, p. 169.

——— (1970), Use of androgen depleting hormone in the treatment of male sex offenders. *J. Sex Res.*, 6:165–172.

———— (1972), The therapeutic use of androgen depleting hormone. *Internat. Psychiatry Clin.*, 8:165–174.

Moore, B. E., & Fine, B. D. (1968), *A Glossary of Psychoanalytic Terms and Concepts.* New York: American Psychoanalytic Association.

Morley, J. E., & Levine, A. S. (1985), Pharmacology of eating behavior. *Ann. Rev. Pharmacol. Toxicol.*, 25:127–146.

———— ———— Rowland, N. E. (1983), Stress-induced eating. *Life Sci.*, 32:2169–2182.

Morse, R. M., & Flavin, D. K. (1992), The definition of alcoholism (for the Joint Committee of the National Council on Alcoholism and Drug Dependence and the American Society of Addiction Medicine to Study the Definition and Criteria for the Diagnosis of Alcoholism). *JAMA,* 268:1012–1014.

Moskowitz, J. A. (1980), Lithium and lady luck: Use of lithium carbonate in compulsive gambling. *NY State J. Med.*, 80:785–788.

Murray, J. B. (1993), Relationship of childhood sexual abuse to borderline personality disorder, posttraumatic stress disorder, and multiple personality disorder. *J. Psychol.*, 127:657–676.

Murray, M. A. F., Bancroft, J. H., Anderson, D. C., Tennent, T. G., & Carr, P. J. (1975), Endocrine changes in male sexual deviants after treatment with antiandrogens, oestrogens or tranquilizers. *J. Endocrinol.*, 67:179–188.

Myers, R. D., & Tytell, M. (1972), Volitional consumption of flavored ethanol solution by rats: The effects of pCPA, and the absence of tolerance. *Physiol. Behav.*, 8:403–408.

Myers, W. (1995), Sexual addiction. In: *The Psychology and Treatment of Addictive Behavior,* ed. S. Dowling. Madison, CT: International Universities Press, pp. 115–130.

Nace, E. P., Davis, C. W., & Gaspari, J. P. (1991), Axis II comorbidity in substance abusers. *Amer. J. Psychiatry,* 148:118–120.

Naranjo, C. A., & Sellars, E. M. (1989), Serotonin uptake inhibitors attenuate ethanol intake in problem drinkers. *Rec. Dev. Alcohol,* 7:255–266.

———— ———— Lawrin, M. O. (1986), Modulation of ethanol intake by serotonin uptake inhibitors. *J. Clin. Psychiatry,* 47:16–22.

Niaura, R. S., Rohsenow, D. J., Binkoff, J. A., Monti, P. M., Pedraza, M., & Abrams, D. B. (1988), Relevance of cue reactivity to understanding alcohol and smoking relapse. *J. Abnorm. Psychol.*, 97:133–152.

Niederland, W. G. (1967), A contribution to the psychology of gambling. *Psychoanal. Forum,* 2:175–179.

Nisbett, R. E., & Storms, M. D. (1974), Cognitive and social determinants of food intake. In: *Thought and Feeling: Cognitive Alteration of Feeling States,* ed. H. London & R. E. Nisbett. Chicago: Aldine.

Nordstrom, G., & Berglund, M. (1987), A prospective study of successful long-term adjustment in alcohol dependence: Social drinking versus abstinence. *J. Stud. Alcohol,* 48:95–103.

North, R. A. (1993), Cellular basis of opioid action. In: *Biological Basis of Sustance Abuse,* ed. S. G. Korenman & J. D. Barchas. New York: Oxford University Press, pp. 143–152.

Novey, S. (1959), A clinical view of affect theory in psycho-analysis. *Internat. J. Psycho-Anal.,* 40:94–104.

O'Brien, C. (1975), Experimental analysis of conditioning factors in human narcotic addiction. *Pharm. Rev.,* 27:533–543.

Ogata, S. N., Silk, K. R., Goodrich, S., Lohr, N. E., Weston, D., & Hill, E. M. (1990), Childhood sexual and physical abuse in adult patients with borderline personality disorder. *Amer. J. Psychiatry,* 147:1008–1013.

Orford, J. (1978), Hypersexuality: Implications for a theory of dependence. *Brit. J. Addict.,* 73:299–310.

———— (1985), *Excessive Appetites: A Psychobiological View of Addictions.* Chichester, U.K.: Wiley.

Ovesey, L., & Person, E. (1973), Gender identity and sexual psychopathology in men: A psychodynamic analysis of homosexuality, transsexualism, and transvestism. *J. Amer. Acad. Psychoanal.,* 1:53–72.

———— ———— (1976), Transvestism: A disorder of the sense of self. *Internat. J. Psychoanal. Psychother.,* 5:219–236.

Panel (1954), Perversion: Theoretical and therapeutic aspects. Reporter: J. A. Arlow. *J. Amer. Psychoanal. Assn.,* 2:336–345.

Panksepp, J., Herman, B., Conner, R., Bishop, P., & Scott, J. P. (1978), The biology of social attachments: Opiates alleviate separation distress. *Biol. Psychiatry,* 13:607–618.

Panzetta, A. F. (1974), Toward a scientific psychiatric nosology: Conceptual and pragmatic issues. *Arch. Gen. Psychiatry,* 30:154–161.

Paris, J., & Zweig-Frank, H. (1992), A critical review of the role of childhood sexual abuse in the etiology of borderline personality disorder. *Can. J. Psychiatry,* 37:125–128.

Parkin, A. (1963), On fetishism. *Internat. J. Psycho-Anal.,* 44:352–361.

Parsons, T. (1951), *The Social System.* New York: Free Press.

Paton, S., Kessler, R., & Kandel, D. (1977), Depressive mood and adolescent illicit drug use: A longitudinal analysis. *J. Genet. Psychol.,* 131:267–289.

Pattison, E. M. (1979), The selection of treatment modalities for the alcoholic patient. In: *The Diagnosis and Treatment of Alcoholism*, ed. J. H. Mendelson & N. K. Mello. New York: McGraw-Hill, pp. 125–227.

Payne, S. M. (1939), Some observations on the ego development of the fetishist. *Internat. J. Psycho-Anal.*, 20:161–170.

Pearson, D. E., Teicher, M. H., Shaywitz, B. A., Cohen, D. J., Young, J. G., & Anderson, G. M. (1980), Environmental influences on body weight and behavior in developing rats after neonatal 6-hydroxydopamine. *Science*, 209:715–717.

Perilstein, R. D., Lipper, S., & Friedman, L. J. (1991), Three cases of paraphilias responsive to fluoxetine treatment. *J. Clin. Psychiatry*, 52:169–170.

Person, E. (1986), Male sexuality and power. *Psychoanal. Inq.*, 6:3–25.

———— Ovesey, L. (1978), Transvestism: New perspectives. *J. Amer. Acad. Psychoanal.*, 6:301–323.

Peveler, R., & Fairburn, C. (1990), Eating disorders in women who abuse alcohol. *Brit. J. Addict.*, 85:1633–1638.

Pfaus, J. G., Damsma, G., Nomikos, G. G., Wenkstern, D. G., Blaha, C. D., Phillips, A. G., & Fibiger, H. C. (1990), Sexual behavior enhances central dopamine transmission in the male rat. *Brain Res.*, 530:345–348.

———— Gorzalka, B. B. (1987), Opioids and sexual behavior. *Neurosci. Biobehav. Rev.*, 11:1–34.

Pithers, W. D. (1990), Relapse prevention with sexual aggressors: A method for maintaining therapeutic gain and enhancing external supervision. In: *Handbook of Sexual Assault: Issues, Theories, and Treatment of the Offender*, ed. W. L. Marshall, D. R. Laws, & H. E. Barbaree. New York: Plenum Press, pp. 343–361.

Plomin, R. (1986), *Development, Genetics, and Psychology*. Hillsdale, NJ: Erlbaum.

Pollack, M. H., & Rosenbaum, J. F. (1991), Fluoxetine treatment of cocaine abuse in heroin addicts. *J. Clin. Psychiatry*, 52:31–33.

Pope, H. G., & Hudson, J. I. (1986), Antidepressant drug therapy for bulimia: Current status. *J. Clin. Psychiatry*, 47:339–345.

Post, R. M. (1992), Transduction of psychosocial stress into the neurobiology of recurrent affective disorder. *Amer. J. Psychiatry*, 149:999–1010.

———— Rubinow, D. R., & Ballenger, J. C. (1984), Conditioning, sensitization, and kindling: Implications for the course of affective illness. In: *Neurobiology of Mood Disorders*, ed. R. M. Post & J. C. Ballenger. Baltimore: Williams & Wilkins.

――― ――― ――― (1986), Conditioning and sensitization in the longitudinal course of affective illness. *Brit. J. Psychiatry,* 149:191–201.

Powell, B. J., Penick, E. C., Othmer, E., Bingham, S. F., & Rice, A. S. (1982), Prevalence of additional psychiatric syndromes among male alcoholics. *J. Clin. Psychiatry,* 43:404–407.

Prescott, J. W. (1971), Early somatosensory deprivation as an ontogenetic process in the abnormal development of brain and behavior. In: *Medical Primatology, Proceedings of the Second Conference on Experimental Medicine and Surgery in Primates.* Basel: Karger.

Protter, B., & Travin, S. (1987), Sexual fantasies in the treatment of paraphilic disorders: A bimodal approach. *Psychiatric Quart.,* 58:279–297.

Purins, J., & Langevin, R. (1985), Brain correlates of penile erection. In: *Erotic Preference, Gender Identity, and Aggression in Men,* ed. R. Langevin. Hillsdale, NJ: Erlbaum, pp. 113–133.

Pyle, R. L., Mitchell, J. E., Eckert, E. D., Halvorson, P. A., Neuman, P. A., & Goff, G. M. (1983), The incidence of bulimia in freshman college students. *Internat. J. Eating Disord.,* 2:75–85.

Quadland, M. C. (1985), Compulsive sexual behavior: Definition of a problem and an approach to treatment. *J. Sex. Marital Ther.,* 11:121–132.

Quinsey, V. L., Bergersen, S. G., & Steinman, C. M. (1976), Changes in physiological and verbal responses of child molesters during aversion therapy. *Can. J. Behav. Sci.,* 8:202–212.

――― Chaplin, T. C., & Carrigan, W. F. (1980), Biofeedback and signaled punishment in the modification of inappropriate sexual age preferences. *Behav. Ther.,* 11:567–576.

――― Earls, C. M. (1990), The modification of sexual preferences. In: *Handbook of Sexual Assault: Issues, Theories, and Treatment of the Offender,* ed. W. L. Marshall, D. R. Laws, & H. E. Barbaree. New York: Plenum Press, pp. 217–295.

Raboch, J., Cerna, H., & Zemek, P. (1987), Sexual aggressivity and androgens. *Brit. J. Psychiatry,* 151:398–400.

Rachman, S., & Teasdale, J. (1969), *Aversion Therapy and Behaviour Disorders.* London: Oxford University Press.

Rada, R. T. (1975), Alcoholism and forcible rape. *Amer. J. Psychiatry,* 132:444–446.

――― (1978), *Clinical Aspects of the Rapists.* New York: Grune & Stratton.

Rado, S. (1933), The psychoanalysis of pharmacothymia. *Psychoanal. Quart.,* 2:1–23.

——— (1946), Psychodynamics as a basic science. *Amer. J. Orthopsychiatry*, 16:405–409.

——— (1949), Mind, unconscious mind, and brain. *Psychosom. Med.*, 11:165–168.

Ramirez, L. F., McCormick, R. A., Russo, A. M., & Taber, J. I. (1984), Patterns of substance abuse in pathological gamblers seeking treatment. *Addict. Behav.*, 8:425–428.

Ramsey, N. F., & Van Ree, J. M. (1992), Reward and abuse of opiates. *Pharmacol. Toxicol.*, 71:81–94.

Rangell, L. (1968), A point of view on acting out. *Internat. J. Psycho-Anal.*, 49:195–201.

Rasmussen, S. A., & Tsuang, M. T. (1986), Clinical characteristics and family history in DSM-III obsessive-compulsive disorder. *Amer. J. Psychiatry*, 143:317–322.

Rees, H., Bonsall, R., & Michael, R. (1986), Preoptic and hypothalamic neurons accumulate (3H) medroxyprogesterone acetate in male Cynomolgus monkeys. *Life Sci.*, 39:1353–1359.

Regier, D. A., Farmer, M. E., Rae, D. S., Locke, B. Z., Keith, S. J., Judd, L. L., & Goodwin, F. K. (1990), Comorbidity of mental disorders with alcohol and other drug abuse: Results from the epidemiological catchement area (ECA) study. *JAMA*, 264:2511–2518.

Reich, A. (1954), Early identifications as archaic elements in the super-ego. *J. Amer. Psychoanal. Assn.*, 2:218–238.

Reich, J. H. (1989), Familiality of DSM-III dramatic and anxious personality clusters. *J. Nerv. Ment. Dis.*, 177:96–200.

Reid, W. H. (1989), Sexual disorders. In: *The Treatment of Psychiatric Disorders: Revised for the DSM-III-R*. New York: Brunner/Mazel, pp. 273–295.

Reis, D. J., Ross, R. A., Gilad, G., & Joh, T. (1978), Reaction of central catecholaminergic neurons to injury: Model systems for studying the neurobiology of central regeneration and sprouting. In: *Neuronal Plasticity*, ed. C. Cotman. New York: Raven Press, pp. 197–226.

Reiser, M. F. (1984), *Mind, Brain, Body*. New York: Basic Books.

Ritvo, S. (1971), Late adolescence: Developmental and clinical considerations. *The Psychoanalytic Study of the Child*, 26:241–263. Chicago: Quadrangle.

——— (1984), The image and use of the body in psychic conflict. *The Psychoanalytic Study of the Child*, 39:449–469. New Haven, CT: Yale University Press.

Ritz, M. C., Lamb, R. J., Goldberg, S. R., & Kuhar, M. J. (1987), Cocaine receptors on dopamine transporters are related to self-administration of cocaine. *Science*, 237:1219–1223.

———— ———— ———— ———— (1988), Cocaine self-administration appears to be mediated by dopamine reuptake inhibition. *Prog. Neuropsychopharmacol. Biol. Psychiatry,* 12:233–239.

Rizzuto, A. M. (1985), Eating and monsters: A psychodynamic view of bulimarexia. In: *Theory and Treatment of Anorexia Nervosa and Bulimia: Biomedical, Sociocultural, and Psychological Perspectives,* ed. S. W. Emmett. New York: Brunner/Mazel, pp. 194–210.

Robins, L. N. (1966), *Deviant Children Grown Up: A Sociological and Psychiatric Study of Sociopathic Personality.* Baltimore: Williams & Wilkins.

———— Bates, W. M., & O'Neal, P. (1962), Adult drinking patterns of former problem children. In: *Society, Culture, and Drinking Patterns,* ed. D. J. Pittman & C. R. Snyder. New York: Wiley, pp. 395–412.

Robinson, P. H., & Holden, N. L. (1986), Bulimia nervosa in the male: A report of nine cases. *Psychol. Med.,* 16:795–803.

Rockman, G. E., Amit, Z., Brown, Z. W., Bourque, C., & Ogren, S. O. (1982), An investigation of the mechanisms of action of 5-hydroxytryptamine in the suppression of ethanol intake. *Neuropharmacol.,* 21:341–347.

Roizen, R. (1987), The great controlled-drinking controversy. *Recent Dev. Alcohol,* 5:245–279.

Rooth, F. G. (1973), Exhibitionism, sexual violence and paedophilia. *Brit. J. Psychiatry,* 122:705–710.

Rosen, I. (1964), Exhibitionism, scopophilia and voyeurism. In: *Pathology and Treatment of Sexual Deviation: A Methodological Approach,* ed. I. Rosen. London: Oxford University Press, pp. 293–350.

———— (1979a), The general psychoanalytic theory of perversion: A critical review. In: *Sexual Deviation,* 2nd ed., ed. I. Rosen. Oxford: Oxford University Press, pp. 29–64.

———— (1979b), Perversion as a regulator of self-esteem. In: *Sexual Deviation,* 2nd ed. ed. I. Rosen. Oxford: Oxford University Press, pp. 65–78.

———— (1979c), Exhibitionism, scopophilia, and voyeurism. In: *Sexual Deviation,* 2nd ed., ed. I. Rosen. Oxford: Oxford University Press, pp. 139–194.

Rosenfeld, H. A. (1965), *Psychotic States: A Psych-Analytical Approach.* London: Hogarth Press.

Rosenthal, R. J. (1985), The pathological gambler's system for self-deception. In: *Proceedings of the Fifth National Conference on Gambling and Risk Taking,* ed. W. R. Eadington. University of Nevada: Bureau of Business and Economic Research.

——— (1987), The psychodynamics of pathological gambling: A review of the literature. In: *The Handbook of Pathological Gambling*, ed. T. Galski. Springfield, IL: Charles C Thomas, pp. 41–70.

Ross, H. E., Glaser, F. B., & Germanson, T. (1988), The prevalence of psychiatric disorders in patients with alcohol and other drug problems. *Arch. Gen. Psychiatry*, 45:1023–1031.

Roy, A., Adinoff, B., Roerich, L., Lamparski, D., Custer, R., Lorenz, V., Barbaccia, M., Guidotti, A., Costa, E., & Linnoila, M. (1988), Pathological gambling: A psychobiological study. *Arch. Gen. Psychiatry*, 45:369–373.

Rubenstein, E. B., & Engel, N. L. (1996), Successful treatment of transvestic fetishism with sertraline and lithium [letter]. *J. Clin. Psychiatry*, 57:92.

Russell, M. A. (1977), Smoking problems: An overview. *NIDA Res. Monogr. Ser.*, 17:13–33.

Rychtarik, R. G., Foy, D. W., Scott, T., Lokey, L., & Prue, D. M. (1987), Five–six-year follow-up of broad-spectrum behavioral treatment for alcoholism: Effects of training controlled drinking skills. *J. Consult. Clin. Psychol.*, 55:106–108.

Sadava, S. W. (1973), Initiation to cannabis use: A longitudinal social psychological study of college freshmen. *Can. J. Behav. Sci.*, 5:371–384.

——— Forsyth, R. (1977), Person-environment interaction and college student drug use: A multivariate longitudinal study. *Genet. Psychol. Monogr.*, 96:211–245.

Salzman, J. P., Salzman, C., Wolfson, A. N., Albanese, M., Looper, J., Ostacher, M., Schwartz, J., Chinman, G., Land, W., & Miyawaki, E. (1993), Association between borderline personality structure and history of childhood abuse in adult volunteers. *Compr. Psychiatry*, 34:254–257.

Sanchez-Craig, M., Annis, H. M., Bornet, A. R., & MacDonald, K. R. (1984), Random assignment to abstinence and controlled drinking: Evaluation of a cognitive-behavioral program for problem drinkers. *J. Consult. Clin. Psychol.*, 52:390–403.

Sandler, J. (1960), On the concept of the superego. *The Psychoanalytic Study of the Child*, 15:128–162. New York: International Universities Press.

——— Kawenoka, M., Neurath, L., Rosenblatt, B., Schnurmann, A., & Sigal, J. (1962), The classification of superego material in the Hampstead Index. *The Psychoanalytic Study of the Child*, 17:107–127. New York: International Universities Press.

Satel, S. L. (1993), The diagnostic limits of "addiction" [letter]. *J. Clin. Psychiatry*, 54:237.

Scarr, S., & Kidd, K. K. (1983), Developmental behavior genetics. In: *Handbook of Child Psychology*, Vol. 4, 4th ed., ed. E. M. Hetherington. New York: Wiley.

Schachter, S. (1978), Pharmacological and psychological determinants of smoking. *Ann. Internat. Med.*, 88:104–114.

Schmidt, C. W. (1992), Changes in terminology for sexual disorders in DSM-IV. *Psychiatric Med.*, 10:247–255.

—— Meyer, J. K., & Lucas, J. (1981), Paraphilias and personality disorders. In: *Personality Disorders: Diagnosis and Management*, 2nd ed., ed. J. R. Lion. Baltimore: Williams & Wilkins, pp. 269–295.

Schneider, J. A., & Agras, W. S. (1987), Bulimia in males: A matched comparison with females. *Internat. J. Eating Disord.*, 6:235–242.

Schneider, J. P., & Schneider, B. (1991), *Sex, Lies, and Forgiveness: Couples Speaking Out on Healing from Sexual Addiction*. Center City, MN: Hazelden Educational Materials.

Schore, A. N. (1994), *Affect Regulation and the Origin of the Self: The Neurobiology of Emotional Development*. Hillsdale, NJ: Erlbaum.

Schuckit, M. (1985), Genetics and the risk for alcoholism. *JAMA*, 18:2614–2617.

—— Li, T.-K., Cloninger, C. R., & Deitrich, R. A. (1985), Genetics of alcoholism. *Alcoholism: Clin. Exp. Res.*, 9:475–492.

Schulz, R., Wuster, M., Duka, T., & Herz, A. (1980), Acute and chronic ethanol treatment changes endorphin levels in brain and pituitary. *Psychopharmacology*, 68:221–227.

Schwartz, H. J. (1986), Bulimia: Psychoanalytic perspectives. *J. Amer. Psychoanal. Assn.*, 34:439–462.

—— (1988a), Introduction. In: *Bulimia: Psychoanalytic Treatment and Theory*, ed. J. Schwartz. Madison, CT: International Universities Press, pp. 1–29.

—— (1988b), Bulimia and the mouth-vagina equation: The phallic compromise. In: *Bulimia: Psychoanalytic Treatment and Theory*, ed. H. J. Schwartz. Madison, CT: International Universities Press, pp. 255–297.

Schwartz, J. M., Stoessel, P. W., Baxter, L. R., Martin, K. M., & Phelps, M. E. (1996), Systematic changes in cerebral glucose metabolic rate after successful behavior modification treatment of obsessive-compulsive disorder. *Arch. Gen. Psychiatry*, 53:109–113.

Schwartz, M. F. (1992), Effective treatment for sex offenders. *Psychiatric Annals*, 22:315–319.

——— Brasted, W. S. (1985), Sexual addiction. *Med. Asp. Hum. Sex.*, 19:103–107.

Scott, M. L., Cole, J. K., McKay, S. E., Golden, C. J., & Liggett, K. R. (1984), Neuropsychological performance of sexual assaulters and pedophiles. *J. Forensic Sci.*, 29:1114–1118.

Segal, H. (1957), Notes on symbol formation. *Internat. J. Psycho-Anal.*, 38:391–397.

——— (1978), On symbolism. *Internat. J. Psycho-Anal.*, 59:315–319.

Seim, H. C. (1988), Evaluation of serum testosterone and luteinizing hormone levels in sex offenders. *Fam. Pract. Res. J.*, 7:175–180.

Seizinger, B. R., Bovermann, K., Maysinger, D., Hollt, V., & Herz, A. (1983), Differential effects of acute and chronic ethanol treatment on particular opioid peptide systems in discrete regions of rat brain and pituitary. *Pharmacol. Biochem. Behav.*, 18(suppl):361–369.

Sex Addicts Anonymous (1986), Abstinence and boundaries in S.A.A. [booklet]. Minneapolis: Sex Addicts Anonymous.

Sexaholics Anonymous (1989), *Sexaholics Anonymous.* Simi Valley, CA: SA Lit.

Sexual Compulsives Anonymous (1989), SCA—a program of recovery [booklet]. New York: SCA.

Shainess, N. (1983), Nymphomania, hostile sex, and superego development. In: *Sexual Dynamics of Antisocial Behavior*, ed. L. B. Schlesinger & E. Revitch. Springfield, IL: Charles C Thomas, pp. 51–74.

Sheard, M. H., & Aghajanian, G. K. (1968), Stimulation of midbrain raphe neurons: Behavioral effects of serotonin release. *Life Sci.*, 7:19–25.

Shedler, J., & Block, J. (1990), Adolescent drug use and psychological health: A longitudinal inquiry. *Amer. Psychol.*, 45:612–630.

Sherman, J. E., Jorenby, D. E., & Baker, T. B. (1988), Classical conditioning with alcohol: Acquired preferences and aversions, tolerance, and urges/craving. In: *Theories on Alcoholism*, ed. C. D. Chaudron & D. A. Wilkinson. Toronto: Addiction Research Foundation, pp. 173–237.

Sideroff, S., & Jarvik, M. E. (1980), Conditioned responses to a videotape showing heroin-related stimuli. *Internat. J. Addict.*, 15:529–536.

Sifneos, P. E. (1967), Clinical observations on some patients suffering from a variety of psychosomatic diseases. *Proceedings of the Seventh European Conference on Psychosomatic Research, Rome. Acta. Med. Psychosom.* Basel: S. Karger, pp. 452–458.

Simmel, E. (1920), Psychoanalysis of the gambler. *Internat. J. Psycho-Anal.*, 1:352–353.

Slywka, S., & Hart, L. L. (1993), Fluoxetine in alcoholism. *Ann. Pharmacother.*, 27:1066–1067.

Smith, B. H., & Sweet, W. H. (1978), Monoaminergic regulation of central nervous system function: I. Noradrenergic systems. *Neurosurgery*, 3:109–119.

Smith, G. M. (1977), *Correlates of Personality and Drug Use—I. RAUS Cluster Review No. 3.* Rockville, MD: National Institute of Drug Abuse.

——— Fogg, C. P. (1978), Psychological predictors of early use, late use, and nonuse of marijuana among teenage students. In: *Longitudinal Research on Drug Use: Empirical Findings and Methodological Issues*, ed. D. Kandel. Washington, DC: Hemisphere, pp. 101–113.

Snaith, P. (1983), Exhibitionism: A clinical conundrum. *Brit. J. Psychiatry*, 143:231–235.

Snaith, R. P., & Collins, S. A. (1981), Five exhibitionists and a method of treatment. *Brit. J. Psychiatry*, 138:126–130.

Sobell, M. B., & Sobell, L. C. (1973), Alcoholics treated by individualized behavior therapy: One year treatment outcome. *Behav. Res. Ther.*, 4:449–472.

——— ——— (1976), Second year treatment outcome of alcoholics treated by individualized behavior therapy: Results. *Behav. Res. Ther.*, 14:195–215.

——— ——— (1984), The aftermath of heresy: A response to Pendery et al.'s (1982) critique of "Individualized behavior therapy for alcoholics." *Behav. Res. Ther.*, 22:413–440.

Socarides, C. W. (1973), Sexual perversion and the fear of engulfment. *Internat. J. Psychoanal. Psychother.*, 2:432–448.

——— (1988), *The Preoedipal Origin and Psychoanalytic Therapy of Sexual Perversions.* Madison, CT: International Universities Press.

Sours, J. (1974), The anorexia nervosa syndrome. *Internat. J. Psycho-Anal.*, 55:567–576.

Sperling, M. (1949), The role of the mother in psychosomatic disorders in children. *Psychosom. Med.*, 11:377–385.

——— (1983), A reevaluation of classification, concepts, and treatment. In: *Fear of Being Fat: The Treatment of Anorexia Nervosa and Bulimia*, ed. C. Wilson, C. Hogan, & I. Mintz. New York: Jason Aronson, pp. 51–82.

Spitz, R. A. (1958), On the genesis of superego components. *The Psychoanalytic Study of the Child*, 13:375–404. New York: International Universities Press.

Stein, D. J., Hollander, E., Anthony, D. T., Schneier, F. R., Fallon, B. A., Liebowitz, M. R., & Klein, D. F. (1992), Serotonergic medications for sexual obsessions, sexual addictions, and paraphilias. *J. Clin. Psychiatry*, 53:267–271.

——— ——— Liebowitz, M. R. (1993), Neurobiology of impulsivity and the impulse control disorders. *J. Neuropsychiatry Clin. Neurosci.*, 5:9–17.

Steinberg, M. A. (1990), Sexual addiction and compulsive gambling. *Amer. J. Prevent. Psychiatry Neurol.*, 2:39–41.

——— Kosten, T. A., & Rounsaville, B. J. (1992), Cocaine abuse and pathological gambling. *Amer. J. Addictions*, 1:121–132.

Sterkmans, P., & Geerts, F. (1966), Is benperidol (RF 504) the specific drug for the treament of excessive and disinhibited sexual behaviour? *Acta Neurol. Psychiatrica* (Belg), 66:1030–1040.

Stermac, L. E., Segal, Z. V., & Gillis, R. (1990), Social and cultural factors in sexual assault. In: *Handbook of Sexual Assault: Issues, Theories, and Treatment of the Offender,* ed. W. L. Marshall, D. R. Laws, & H. E. Barbaree. New York: Plenum Press, pp. 143–159.

Stoller, R. J. (1970), Pornography and perversion. *Arch. Gen. Psychiatry*, 22:490–499.

——— (1975), *Perversion: The Erotic Form of Hatred.* New York: Pantheon.

Stolorow, R. D. (1975a), Addendum to a partial analysis of a perversion involving bugs: An illustration of the narcissistic function of a perverse activity. *Internat. J. Psycho-Anal.*, 56:361–364.

——— (1975b), The narcissistic function of masochism (and sadism). *Internat. J. Psycho-Anal.*, 56:441–448.

——— (1979), Psychosexuality and the representational world. *Internat. J. Psycho-Anal.*, 60:39–45.

Strenger, C. (1991), *Between Hermeneutics and Science: An Essay on the Epistemology of Psychoanalysis.* Madison, CT: International Universities Press.

Strupp, H. H., & Hadley, S. W. (1979), Specific vs. nonspecific factors in psychotherapy. *Arch. Gen. Psychiatry*, 36:1125–1136.

Sugarman, A., & Kurash, C. (1982), The body as a transitional object in bulimia. *Internat. J. Eating Disord.*, 1:57–67.

Sutker, P. B., & Archer, R. P. (1979), MMPI characteristics of opiate addicts, alcoholics, and other drug abusers. In: *MMPI: Clinical and Research Trends,* ed. C. S. Newmark. New York: Praeger, pp. 105–148.

Swett, C., Surrey, J., & Cohen, C. (1990), Sexual and physical abuse histories and psychiatric symptoms among male psychiatric outpatients. *Amer. J. Psychiatry*, 147:632–636.

Swift, W., & Letven, R. (1984), Bulimia and the basic fault. *J. Amer. Acad. Child Psychiatry*, 23:489–497.

Symmers, W. S. C. (1968), Carcinoma of the breast in transsexual individuals after surgical and hormonal interference with primary and secondary sexual characteristics. *Brit. Med. J.*, 2:3–85.

Szasz, T. (1974), *Ceremonial Chemistry.* Garden City, NY: Anchor Press/Doubleday.

Szechtman, H., Hershkowitz, M., & Simantov, R. (1981), Sexual behavior decreases pain sensitivity and stimulates endogenous opioids in male rats. *Eur. J. Pharmacol.*, 70:279–285.

Tarter, R. E., Alterman, A. I., & Edwards, K. L. (1985), Vulnerability to alcoholism in males: A behavior-genetic perspective. *J. Stud. Alcohol,* 4:329–356.

Teasdale, J. D. (1973), Conditioned abstinence in narcotics addicts. *Internat. J. Addict.*, 8:273–292.

Templeman, T. L., & Stinnet, R. D. (1991), Patterns of sexual arousal and history in a "normal" sample of young men. *Arch. Sex. Behav.*, 20:137–150.

Thomas, A., & Chess, S. (1980), *The Dynamics of Psychological Development.* New York: Brunner/Mazel.

Timmerman, M. G., Wells, L. A., & Chen, S. (1990), Bulimia nervosa and associated alcohol abuse among secondary school students. *J. Amer. Child Adol. Psychiatry,* 29:118–122.

Tolpin, M. (1971), On the beginnings of a cohesive self: An application of the concept of transmuting internalization to the study of the transitional object and signal anxiety. *The Psychoanalytic Study of the Child,* 26:316–352. Chicago: Quadrangle.

——— Kohut, H. (1985), The disorders of the self: The psychopathology of the first years of life. In: *The Course of Life,* Vol. 2, ed. S. I. Greenspan & G. H. Pollock. New York: International Universities Press, pp. 229–253.

Torgerson, S. (1980), The oral, obsessive and hysterical personality syndrome: A study of hereditary and environmental factors by means of the twin method. *Arch. Gen. Psychiatry,* 37:1272–1277.

——— (1984), Genetic and nosologic aspects of schizotypal and borderline personality disorders: A twin study. *Arch. Gen. Psychiatry,* 41:546–554.

Torres, A. R., & de Abreu Cerquiera, A. T. (1993), Exhibitionism treated with clomipramine [letter]. *Amer. J. Psychiatry,* 150:1274.

Travin, S. (1995), Compulsive sexual behaviors. *Psychiatric Clin. N. Amer.*, 18:155–169.

——— Bluestone, H., Coleman, E., Cullen, K., & Melella, J. (1985), Pedophilia: An update on theory and practice. *Psychiat. Quart.*, 57:89–103.

———— Protter, B. (1993), *Sexual Perversion: Integrative Treatment Approaches for the Clinician.* New York: Plenum Press.

Trop, J. L., & Alexander, R. (1992), The concept of promiscuity: A self psychological perspective. In: *Psychotherapy and the Promiscuous Patient,* ed. E. M. Stern. New York: Haworth Press, pp. 39–49.

Truax, R. A. (1970), Discussion of Mathis and Collins (above). *Amer. J. Psychiatry,* 126:1166.

Trunnel, E. E., & Holt, W. E. (1974), The concept of denial or disavowal. *J. Amer. Psychoanal. Assn.,* 22:769–784.

Tucker, D. M. (1992), Developing emotions and cortical networks. In: *Minnesota Symposium on Child Psychology,* Vol. 24, ed. M. R. Gunnar & C. A. Nelson. Hillsdale, NJ: Erlbaum, pp. 75–128.

Tyndel, M. (1963), Gambling: An addiction. *Addictions,* 10:40–48.

Vaillant, G. E. (1975), Sociopathy as a human process: A viewpoint. *Arch. Gen. Psychiatry,* 32:178–183.

———— (1983), *The Natural History of Alcoholism.* Cambridge, MA: Harvard University Press.

———— Milofsky, E. S. (1982), The etiology of alcoholism: A prospective viewpoint. *Amer. Psychol.,* 5:494–503.

van Praag, H. M., Kahn, R. S., Asnis, G. M., Wetzler, S., Brown, S. L., Belich, A., & Korn, M. L. (1987), Denosologization of biological psychiatry or the specificity of 5-HT disturbances in psychiatric disorders. *J. Affect. Disorders,* 13:1–8.

Vicary, J. R., & Lerner, J. V. (1983), Longitudinal perspectives on drug use: Analyses from the New York Longitudinal Study. *J. Drug Ed.,* 13:275–285.

Vogel-Sprott, M. (1972), Alcoholism and learning. In: *The Biology of Alcoholism,* Vol. 2, ed. B. Kissin & H. Begleiter. New York: Plenum Press, pp. 485–507.

Vuchinich, R. E., & Tucker, J. A. (1988), Contributions from behavioral theories of choice to an analysis of alcohol abuse. *J. Abnorm. Psychol.,* 97:181–195.

Wachtel, P. L. (1977), *Psychoanalysis and Behavior Therapy: Toward an Integration.* New York: Basic Books.

Waelder, R. (1936), The principle of multiple function: Observations on over-determination. *Psychoanal. Quart.,* 5:45–62.

Wakefield, J. C. (1992), The concept of mental disorder: On the boundary between biological facts and social values. *Amer. Psychol.,* 47:373–388.

Wakeling, A. (1979), A general psychiatric approach to sexual deviation. In: *Sexual Deviation,* 2nd ed., ed. I. Rosen. Oxford: Oxford University Press, pp. 1–28.

Walker, P. A., & Meyer, W. J. (1981), Medroxyprogesterone acetate treatment for paraphilic sex offenders. In: *Violence and the Violent Offender: 12th Annual Symposium, Texas Research Institute of Mental Sciences, Nov. 1–3, 1979,* ed. J. R. Hayes, T. K. Roberts, & K. S. Soloway. New York: Spectrum Publications, pp. 353–373.

Walsh, B. T., Hadigan, C. M., Devlin, M. J., Gladis, M., & Roose, S. P. (1991), Long-term outcome of antidepressant treatment for bulimia nervosa. *Amer. J. Psychiatry,* 148:1206–1212.

Ward, N. G. (1975), Successful lithium treatment of transvestism associated with manic-depression. *J. Nerv. Ment. Dis.,* 161:204–206.

Warwick, H. M. C., & Salkovskis, P. M. (1990), Unwanted erections in obsessive-compulsive disorder. *Brit. J. Psychiatry,* 157:919–921.

Washton, A. M. (1989), Cocaine may trigger sexual compulsivity. *US J. Drug Alcohol Depend.,* 13:8.

Watson, C. G. (1987), Recidivism in "controlled drinker" alcoholics: A longitudinal study. *J. Clin. Psychol.,* 43:404–412.

Watson, S. J., Trujillo, K. A., Herman, J. P., & Akil, H. (1989), Neuroanatomical and neurochemical substrates of drug-seeking behavior: Overview and future directions. In: *Molecular and Cellular Aspects of the Drug Addictions,* ed. A. Goldstein. New York: Springer Verlag, pp. 29–91.

Wawrose, F. E., & Sisto, T. M. (1992), Clomipramine and a case of exhibitionism [letter]. *Amer. J. Psychiatry,* 149:843.

Weaver, T. L., & Clum, G. A. (1993), Early family environments and traumatic experiences associated with borderline personality disorder. *J. Consult. Clin. Psychol.,* 61:1068–1075.

Weiss, K. J., & Rosenberg, D. J. (1985), Prevalence of anxiety disorders among alcoholics. *J. Clin. Psychiatry,* 46:3–5.

Weissberg, J. H., & Levay, A. N. (1986), Compulsive sexual behavior. *Med. Asp. Hum. Sex.,* 20:127–128.

Westen, D. (1986), The superego: A revised developmental model. *J. Amer. Acad. Psychoanal.,* 14:181–202.

Whittaker, L. H. (1959), Oestrogens and psychosexual disorders. *Med. J. Austral.,* 22:547–549.

Wieder, H., & Kaplan, E. H. (1969), Drug use in adolescents: Psychodynamic meaning and pharmacogenic effect. *The Psychoanalytic Study of the Child,* 24:399–431. New York: International Universities Press.

Wijesinghe, B. (1977), Massed aversion treatment of sexual deviance. *J. Behav. Ther. Exp. Psychiatry,* 8:135–137.

Wikler, A. (1971), Some implications of conditioning theory for problems of drug abuse. *Behav. Sci.,* 16:92–97.

———— (1973), Dynamics of drug dependence: Implications of a conditioning theory for research and treatment. In: *Opiate Addictions: Origins and Treatment,* ed. S. Fisher & A. Freedman. Washington, DC: L. Winston, pp. 7–21.

———— (1980a), *Opioid Dependence: Mechanisms and Treatment.* New York: Plenum Press.

———— (1980b), A theory of opioid dependence. In: *Theories on Drug Abuse: Selected Contemporary Perspectives,* ed. D. Lettieri, M. Sayers, & H. Pearson. NIDA Research Monograph 30, DHS Publication No. (ADM) 80-967. Washington, DC: US Government Printing Office, pp. 174–178.

Wilson, G. D., & Gosselin, C. (1980), Personality characteristics of fetishists, transvestites, and sadomasochists. *Person. Ind. Diff.,* 1:289–295.

Wilson, G. T. (1988), Alcohol use and abuse: A social learning analysis. In: *Theories on Alcoholism,* ed. C. D. Chaudron & D. A. Wilkinson. Toronto: Addiction Research Foundation, pp. 239–287.

Wincze, J. T., Bansal, S., & Malamud, M. (1986), Effects of medroxyprogesterone acetate on subjective arousal, arousal through erotic stimulation, and nocturnal penile tumescence in male sexual offenders. *Arch. Sex. Behav.,* 15:293–305.

Wingard, J. A., Huba, G. J., & Bentler, P. M. (1979), The relationship of personality structure to patterns of adolescent substance use. *Multivariate Behav. Res.,* 14:121–143.

———— ———— ———— (1980), A longitudinal analysis of personality structure and adolescent substance use. *Person. Ind. Diff.,* 1:259–272.

Winnicott, D. W. (1952), Psychosis and child care. In: *Collected Papers.* New York: Basic Books, 1958, pp. 219–228.

———— (1953), Transitional objects and transitional phenomena. *Internat. J. Psycho-Anal.,* 34:89–97.

———— (1965), *The Maturational Processes and the Facilitating Environment.* New York: International Universities Press.

Winokur, G. (1972), Depression spectrum disease: Description and family study. *Compr. Psychiatry,* 13:3–8.

Wise, R. A. (1987), The role of reward pathways in the development of drug dependence. *Pharmacol. Ther.,* 35:227–262.

Wise, T. N. (1979), Psychotherapy of an aging transvestite. *J. Sex. Marital Ther.,* 5:368–373.

———— (1989), Fetishism and transvestism. In: *Treatment of Psychiatric Disorders: A Task Force of the American Psychiatric Association,* ed. T. B. Karasu. Washington, DC: American Psychiatric Press, pp. 633–646.

———— Meyer, J. K. (1980), The border area between transvestism and gender dysphoria: Transvestic applicants for sex reassignment. *Arch. Sex. Behav.*, 9:327–342.

Witkin, H., Karp, S., & Goodenough, D. (1959), Dependence in alcoholics. *Quart. J. Stud. Alcohol*, 20:493–504.

Witzig, J. S. (1968), The group treatment of male exhibitionists. *Amer. J. Psychiatry*, 125:179–185.

Wood, D., Wender, P. H., & Reimherr, F. W. (1983), The prevalence of attention deficit disorder, residual type, or minimal brain dysfunction, in a population of male alcoholic patients. *Amer. J. Psychiatry*, 140:95–98.

Woollcott, P. (1981), Addiction: Clinical and theoretical considerations. *Ann. Psychoanal.*, 9:189–204.

Wurmser, L. (1977), Mr. Pecksniff's horse? (psychodynamics in compulsive drug use). In: *Psychodynamics of Drug Dependence*, ed. J. D. Blaine & D. A. Julius. Rockville, MD: National Institute of Drug Abuse, pp. 36–72.

———— (1978), *The Hidden Dimension: Psychodynamics in Compulsive Drug Use.* New York: Jason Aronson.

———— (1980a), Drug use as a protective system. In: *Theories on Drug Abuse: Selected Contemporary Perspectives*, ed. D. J. Lettieri, M. Sayers, & H. W. Pearson. Rockville, MD: National Institute on Drug Abuse, pp. 71–74.

———— (1980b), Phobic core in addictions and the paranoid process. *Internat. J. Psychoanal. Psychother.*, 8:311–337.

———— (1981), Addictive personalities. In: *Personality Disorders: Diagnosis and Management*, ed. R. Lion. Baltimore: Williams & Wilkins, pp. 221–269.

———— (1982), Psychodynamics of substance abuse. In: *Substance Abuse—Clinical Problems and Perspectives*, ed. J. H. Lowinson, & P. Ruiz. Baltimore: Williams & Wilkins.

———— (1984), The role of superego conflicts in substance abuse and their treatment. *Internat. J. Psychoanal. Psychother.*, 10:227–258.

———— (1987), Flight from conscience: Experiences with the psychoanalytic treatment of compulsive drug abusers—part two: Dynamic and therapeutic conclusions from the experiences with psychoanalysis of drug users. *J. Subst. Abuse Treat.*, 4:169–179.

———— (1988), "The sleeping giant": A dissenting comment about "borderline pathology." *Psychoanal. Inq.*, 8:373–397.

———— (1995), Compulsiveness and conflict: The distinction between description and explanation in the treatment of addictive behavior.

In: *The Psychology and Treatment of Addictive Behavior*, ed. S. Dowling. Madison, CT: International Universities Press, pp. 3–64.

————— Zients, A. (1982), The return of the denied superego. *Psychoanal. Inq.*, 2:539–580.

Wurtman, J., & Wurtman, R. J. (1979), Drugs that enhance central serotonergic transmission diminish elective carbohydrate consumption by rats. *Life Sci.*, 24:895–904.

Yalom, I. D. (1975), *The Theory and Practice of Group Psychotherapy*, 2nd ed. New York: Basic Books.

Yoshida, M., Yokoo, H., Mizoguchi, K., Tsuda, A., Nishikawa, T., & Tanaka, M. (1992), Eating and drinking cause increased dopamine release in the nucleus accumbens and ventral tegmental area in the rat: Measurement by in vivo microdialysis. *Neurosci. Letters*, 139:73–76.

Yoshimoto, K., McBride, W. J., Lumeng, L., & Li, T.-K. (1991), Alcohol stimulates the release of dopamine and serotonin in the nucleus accumbens. *Alcohol*, 9:17–22.

Zanarini, M. C., Gunderson, J. G., Marino, M. F., Schwartz, E. O., & Frankenburg, F. R. (1989), Childhood experiences of borderline patients. *Compr. Psychiatry*, 30:18–25.

Zavitzianos, G. (1971), Fetishism and exhibitionism in the female and their relationship to psychopathy and kleptomania. *Internat. J. Psycho-Anal.*, 52:297–305.

Zohar, J., Kaplan, Z., & Benjamin, J. (1994), Compulsive exhibitionism successfully treated with fluvoxamine: A controlled case study. *J. Clin. Psychiatry*, 55:86–88.

Zucker, R. A. (1979), Developmental aspects of drinking through the young adult years. In: *Youth, Alcohol, and Social Policy*, ed. H. T. Blane & M. E. Chafetz. New York: Plenum Press, pp. 91–146.

————— Noll, R. B. (1982), Precursors and developmental influences on drinking and alcoholism: Etiology from a longitudinal perspective. In: *Alcohol and Health Monograph 1: Alcohol Consumption and Related Problems*. DHHS Publication No. (ADM) 82-1190. Rockville, MD: National Institute on Alcohol Abuse and Alcoholism.

Name Index

435

Subject Index